M000204568

BREAKER MORANT

BREAKER MORANT

THE FINAL ROUNDUP

JOE WEST &
ROGER ROPER

AMBERLEY

First published 2016

Amberley Publishing
The Hill, Stroud
Gloucestershire, GL5 4EP

www.amberley-books.com

Copyright © Joe West and Roger Roper 2016

The right of Joe West and Roger Roper to be identified as the Authors of this work has been asserted in accordance with the Copyrights, Designs and Patents Act 1988.

All rights reserved. No part of this book may be reprinted or reproduced or utilised in any form or by any electronic, mechanical or other means, now known or hereafter invented, including photocopying and recording, or in any information storage or retrieval system, without the permission in writing from the Publishers.

British Library Cataloguing in Publication Data.
A catalogue record for this book is available from the British Library.

ISBN 978 1 4456 5965 7 (hardback)
ISBN 978 1 4456 5966 4 (ebook)

Typeset in 10pt on 13.5pt Sabon.
Typesetting and Origination by Amberley Publishing.
Printed in the UK.

Contents

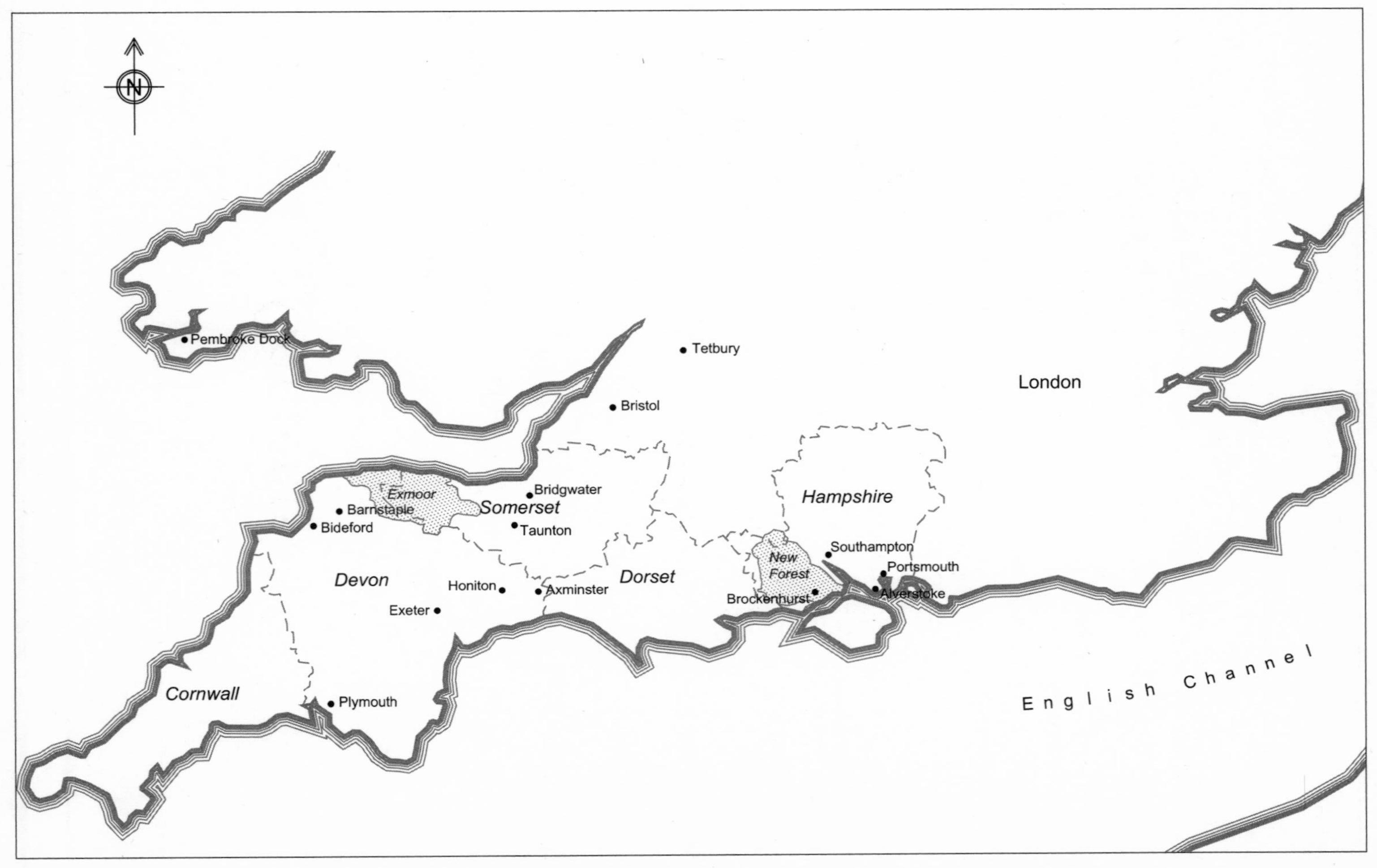
N
Pembroke Dock
Tetbury
Bristol
London
Exmoor
Bridgwater
Barnstaple
Somerset
Bideford
Taunton
Hampshire
Southampton
New Forest
Portsmouth
Devon
Honiton
Axminster
Dorset
Alverstoke
Brockenhurst
Exeter
Cornwall
Plymouth
English Channel

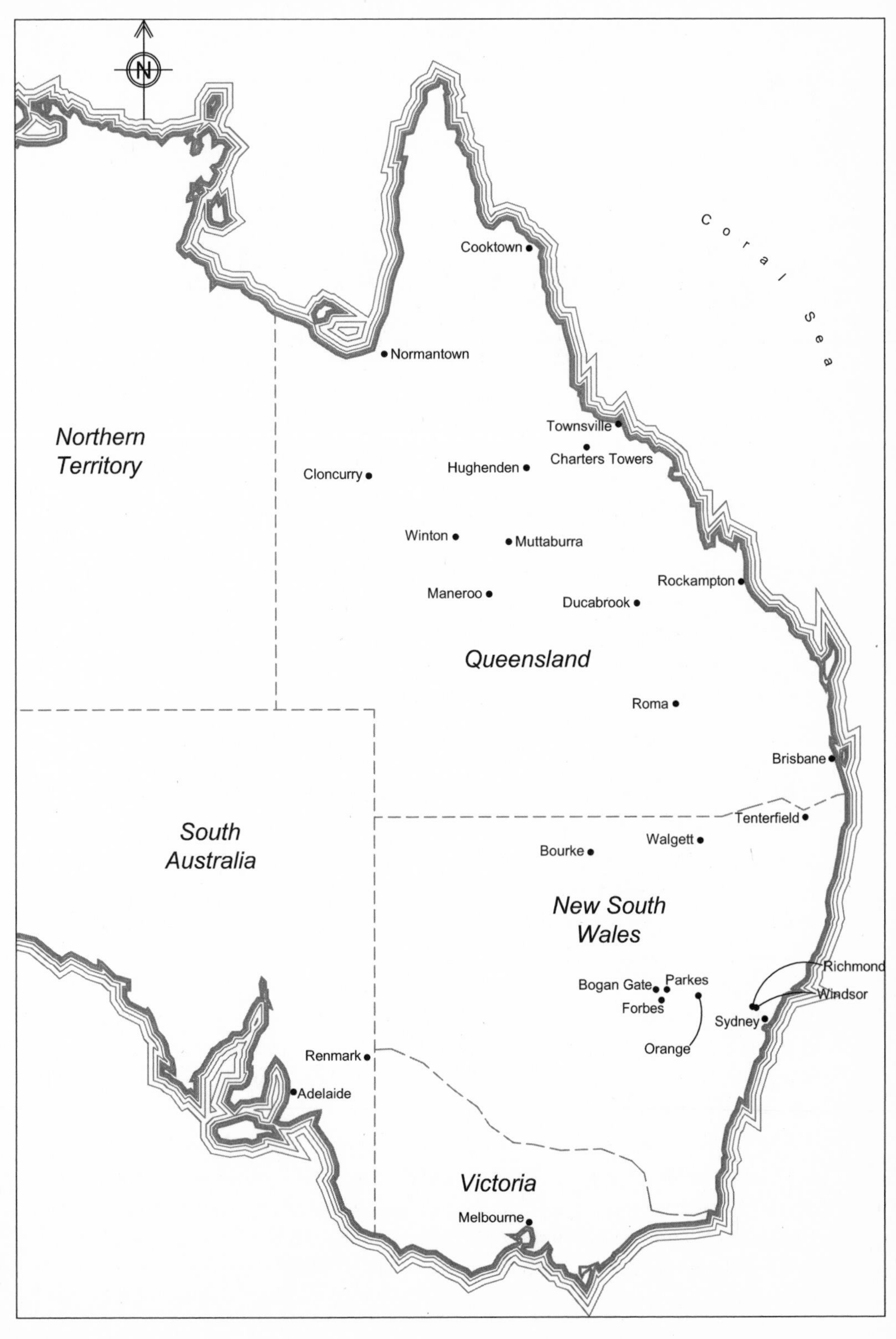
N
Coral Sea
Cooktown
Normantown
Northern Territory
Townsville
Charters Towers
Cloncurry
Hughenden
Winton
Muttaburra
Rockampton
Maneroo
Ducabrook
Queensland
Roma
Brisbane
Tenterfield
South Australia
Walgett
Bourke
New South Wales
Richmond
Bogan Gate
Parkes
Windsor
Forbes
Sydney
Orange
Renmark
Adelaide
Victoria
Melbourne

Foreword by Charles Goodson-Wickes

It is an extraordinary thing that nearly 115 years after his death by firing squad, Breaker Morant's life and fate continue to excite controversy.

The seminal work about him was written by Frank Fox (under a pseudonym) in *Breaker Morant – Bushman and Buccaneer* published in 1902. This was the only contemporary account of Morant's exploits. The book has recently been republished and is available on www.sirfrankfox.com and Amazon.

Fox was on the staff of the *Sydney Bulletin*, and presumably came to know of Morant through their mutual friendship with 'Banjo' Paterson, the composer of *Waltzing Matilda*.

Something of a buccaneer himself in print, on a horse (the artist Norman Lindsay described him as 'an equine exhibitionist') and in battle, Fox's portraits of the time reflect a curious affinity with that of Morant, and of their mutual interests. Fox's book was the basis of the play by Kenneth Ross, and later the highly successful film made by the Australian producer Bruce Beresford in 1979.

Morant's story is essentially a romantic one. Who would not love the account of a roistering horseman, drinker and womaniser in the Australian Outback? This alone would be enough for a drama, let alone his obscure past, his compulsive versifying, and his unorthodox military exploits in a war of the British Empire.

The myth persists, and only now have researchers in England and Australia uncovered some of the truth in this brilliantly researched book. His declared origins have been debunked, as have accusations that his trial by Court Martial was conducted unfairly. The latter cause is still being pursued in Australia by those pressing for a posthumous pardon.

Not only was Morant of humbler stock than he maintained, but his outlandish conduct in South Africa during the Boer War seems to have been judged in proper and orthodox fashion.

Australian attempts to justify his actions apparently no longer stand the test.

Despite this, nothing can take away the daredevil image of the charming, reckless and brave man whose ventures and verses have kept his memory alive for over a century.

Dr Charles Goodson-Wickes (great-grandson of Sir Frank Fox)

Foreword by Frank Shields

When the authors invited me for input into their book, I did so with a little trepidation as I had spent more than enough years on the Breaker Morant story after stumbling across his and Peter Handcock's grave in Pretoria cemetery around 1970. This innocent find resulted in a documentary film called *The Breaker.*

After my film aired on Australian television in 1975, little did I know then I had spawned an industry as few people really knew the story or the character. Historian Margaret Carnegie contacted me to collaborate with her on a book and feature film, as she was part of a syndicate that had just made the feature *Mad Dog Morgan* based on one of her books. She thought the Breaker Morant story would make a great film.

We didn't make the film but we did publish a book, *In Search of Breaker Morant.* Margaret, who was nearly 70, had unrelenting energy and enthusiasm for Oz history. She was also a great researcher and one of the gems she unearthed was that Morant had married another Australian legend, Daisy Bates. A real coup. The book also challenged the 'Breaker' myth.

Prior to this, I guess I became intoxicated by the myth of the daring horse-breaker, poet, soldier-cum-cavalier. So much so, I left out of my film the most important piece of research I had uncovered, this being a letter of 1929 between George Witton and J. F. Thomas. My only excuse was being blinded by the myth, which I owned up to when adding a Director's postscript to my documentary on it being released on DVD.

Over the years, the story grew as new research was unearthed. The authors here have taken that research a whole lot farther, revealing his early years in England, which had eluded other scribes; also new revelations about his life in Australia. Here, a study of Morant's true character is laid bare and leaves the reader with the conclusion that Morant was a victim of his own instability. What emerges is that Morant was one of the most colourful and controversial characters in Australian history. The authors' research throughout has been thorough and methodical.

Love him or loathe him, the 'Breaker' myth is hard to quash entirely. The Morant saga in South Africa itself reads like a Greek tragedy, taking its place alongside the likes of *Mutiny on the Bounty* and *Ned Kelly*. With a pedigree like that, is this the 'Final Roundup'?

Frank Shields, writer/producer/director of the documentary *The Breaker* (1973), co-author (with Margaret Carnegie) of *In Search of Breaker Morant – Balladist and Bushveldt Carbineer* (1979)

Acknowledgements

We cannot thank Jim McJannett in Cooktown, Queensland, enough. He has over the years provided us with the benefit of his decades of research, intimate knowledge of horses, experience as a rodeo rider and as a historian. Jim discovered that Edwin Murrant attended the Royal Masonic School the hard way by wading through miles of microfilmed newspapers long before we discovered the same through digitisation and optical character recognition. He has always been generous in his sharing of research, knowledgeable in most areas and direct in his criticism. It is testament to his courage, commitment and generosity that he has continued to do this in the face of illness.

We would also like to thank Frank Shields, for providing us access to his research and original draft of his book, *Breaker Morant, Balladist and Bushveldt Carbineer*.

Bill Woolmore of Blackburn, Victoria for support and sharing his knowledge of the history of the BVC over the years and for his hospitality in Melbourne.

Charles Leach of Louis Trichardt for his enthusiastic support and hospitality and sharing his deep knowledge of the history of Northern Transvaal. Everyone interested in these events should join him on one of his tours of the Zoutpansberg to get a South African perspective.

Charles Goodson-Wickes, great grandson of Frank Renar, for writing a foreword and for his interest over several years.

Andrew Bermingham of Bermuda who is one of the leading collectors of BVC medals. His provision of the photo of Major Bolton and family is much appreciated.

Edward Morant of Brockenhurst, Hampshire and John Murrant of Waterlooville, Hampshire for providing the family trees of their respective families. There is no Henry Harbord Morant in either tree.

Louise Pichel at The Library and Museum of Freemasonry for her help with records relating to the Royal Masonic Institution for Boys.

Veronique Tison who very generously travelled around Paris conducting research into the family of Captain Percy Hunt, not all of which, unfortunately, could be used in this book.

David Blackburn, at Villa Hutton, Pau in the Pyrenees for obtaining Percy Hunt's birth certificate and providing background information on his mother's family.

Megan Griffiths at Bromsgrove School for access to records relating to Percy Hunt's education. Vilhjalmur (Bill) Finsen for sharing his knowledge of the Hunt Family.

Tessa King and Adrienne Kelsey for conducting searches in the archives in South Africa.

John Dalton (snr) of the Ellis Park Rugby Museum, Johannesburg for finding the picture of General Beyers and the 1896 Transvaal team.

Deborah Mason, Collections Officer, RFU Museum, Twickenham for pictures and details of Major Bolton's international rugby career.

Hampshire County Cricket Club Archive for details on Robert Poore's cricket career and for photographs.

Brian Jenkins, Chatham Naval Museum, for a picture of Admiral Digby Morant.

Royal Watercolour Society Archive (Secretary Hannah Hawkesworth) for information about Reginald Hunt, Capt. Hunt's brother.

Bernie Deasy, Provincial Archivist, Archives of the Order of the Sacred Heart in Dublin for information on Daisy Bates' school days in Roscrea.

Several at the National Archives of Zimbabwe, Harare for their knowledgeable and friendly assistance.

Library and Museum of Freemasonry, London (Diane Clements, Director) for help in exploring Morant's Masonic connection.

Members of the Masonic Lodge, Virtue and Honor no 494, Axminster, Devon for hunting through their records to find the initiation of Morant's father into Freemasonry.

Martin de Bertodano for information about his grandfather.

Members of Stevenstone Hunt, Devon (Secretary Miss H Cole) confirming they have never heard of Henry Harbord Morant hunting with them.

Anthony D'Arcy Irvine for assistance with photographs and for his skill in improving several old Victorian photographs.

Lenore Frost of Melbourne, Victoria for genealogy and historical assistance and advising on Australia and for general support over 16 years.

Angus Douglas Hamilton, the late 15th Duke of Hamilton for permission to access Poore's Boer War diary in the Scottish Archives and to Miss Alison Lindsay, Assistant Registrar for her assistance.

Mike and Tony at the Blake Museum, Bridgwater for allowing us to use photos of the Maltshovel and the Workhouse.

Dr Gillian Gear and the staff at Barnet Museum.

Neil Burrows (Burrows Norman Design Services Ltd) for producing the maps.

Sue West, for her excellent proofreading.

Frances Watt, Membership Secretary, Cavalry and Guards Club, London for searching records for Percy Hunt's membership.

Judith Knox and Patsy Graham for sharing their knowledge of their ancestor Arthur Henry Knox/Archibald Hamilton Keith; and Raymond Roberts for his research into Keith.

Jeremy Lonsdale, author of a book on Poore's cricketing exploits *The Army's Grace* for his advice.

Members of Wimborne Cricket Club, Dorset and the late Jack Douch for providing the photo of Poore in the 1899 Gentlemen v Players match.

Preface

We recognise that much has been written on this subject. Written history is inevitably influenced by the biases of the author and historians should always attempt to resist their own prejudices. As will become apparent to the reader, we consider that in some of what has been written before, no attempt to counter this bias has been made. In fact, we believe that in some works there has been deliberate omission of certain facts and evidence, and considerable 'artistic licence' has been applied in order to present a picture coloured more by recent politics than pure historic curiosity. We have attempted to counter this. In so doing there is a danger that, to a reader new to the Morant story, this account may appear biased in the opposite direction. We have tried to provide as much of the original evidence as possible.

In so doing this book uses extensive quotes by members of the Bushveldt Carbineers. Many of these quotes use language and terminology which is demonstrative of the endemic racism of the time, which would be considered deeply offensive today. We apologise if this does indeed offend the reader and the views and language expressed in these quotes are clearly not those of the authors.

Besides Edwin Henry Murrant himself there are a surprising number of characters in the story who re-invented themselves. This seems to have been a considerably more common phenomenon in the days of Empire when one could move to another country and lie about one's past with little risk of getting caught out. It also seems particularly prevalent in Charters Towers. We realise this may appear like lazy or inadequate research. We wish to assure you it is not.

I

The Early Days

Breaker Morant was born at Bridgwater Workhouse in Somerset, in the south west of England on 9 December 1864 and was christened the following year as Edwin Henry Murrant. [1] This son of the workhouse master, over the years, became Henry Harbord Morant, the son of an admiral. The legend transforms him from thief, fraudster, liar and war criminal into a national hero. It even transforms his nationality. The forces behind the apparent immorality of making a criminal into a hero are complex and have now culminated in a drive to gain a pardon for his crimes. For over 100 years researchers have been trying to discover who Morant was and where he came from. Some Australians claim him as one of theirs and some will say they are welcome to him: but what was an Australian in those days and how did you qualify?

The reader will find that many of the people in his story reinvented themselves and their pasts. This story is about an Englishman named Henry Harbord Morant, but no one of that name was ever listed in the birth records of England or Australia. We now recognize that this identity was the invention of the fertile imagination of Edwin Henry Murrant. This man was in reality totally unconnected with a wealthy Hampshire family named Morant he claimed as his own, who lived in the small town of Brockenhurst in the beautiful New Forest, not far from the old capital of England at Winchester.

Luckily for researchers, the names of Murrant and Morant are relatively rare in Britain. Anyone looking for ancestors in the British Isles is fortunate that superb census and other genealogy information is now available on-line. In the 1881 census there were fewer than 500 people named Morant, Morrant or Murrant in England. Of these, about 115 were named Murrant, the greater number of whom came from Hampshire and adjoining counties.

The name Morant appears to have arrived in England after the Norman Conquest, long before spellings became standardised, and it is quite likely that Murrant and Morant do have the same origin.

Edwin Murrant's family can easily be traced back to the seventeenth century using internet resources. They are to be found in the east of Hampshire and appear to have been of yeoman stock. This line continued in Hampshire until a George Murrant was christened in Alverstoke near Portsmouth in 1807 and we then find George marrying Ann Hunt at St Mary's church at Portsea (Portsmouth) on the 6 April 1829.

George and Ann continued to live for some time in the Alverstoke area, and their four sons were christened in pairs in the local church between 1830 and 1837. On 5 October 1834, Henry and William were christened and younger brothers Edwin and George were christened together on 5 March 1837. They were not twins, Edwin probably being born in 1835 and George two years later, but double ceremonies were convenient and probably cheaper. The 1841 census shows George as a schoolmaster living in Alverstoke with his family, but by 1851 he appears as the master of a workhouse in Mere, Wiltshire, with Ann as the matron. It is probable that for two of them to run a workhouse was more lucrative than teaching. Accommodation would have been provided in the workhouse by the authorities.

Ten years later we find them in the 1861 census in Lincolnshire. Their son Edwin had been married the previous year in the Church of England parish church in the nearby town of Fleet to a school mistress called Catherine Riely. She was described as being of full age and the daughter of John Riely, an Irish farmer. On the marriage certificate Edwin is described as being 25 years old and the Master of a Union Workhouse. The same profession is given for his father. Nothing is known of the Rielys and John Riely was not a witness to the marriage. There is no evidence her parents were in England and it is quite possible that Catherine had come to England by herself seeking a better life. In later censuses Catherine gives her age as 38 in 1871 and 48 in 1881 suggesting a birth year of 1833. She is consistent in every census until her death in 1899. She always gives her place of birth as Ireland. It is possible that Catherine was christened in Killarney, Kerry, on 28 June 1834, the daughter of John Riely and Catherine Hassett.

George and his son Edwin had found their way to Lincolnshire in eastern England to work in one of the union workhouses that had been developed to try and deal with the perennial Victorian problem of the poor. George and son were in charge of the workhouse at Holbeach near Boston. Shortly after their marriage, Edwin and Catherine applied for their own positions as a master and matron and were successful in being appointed to the union workhouse in Honiton, Devon. [2] There obviously were problems at Honiton because the married couple who had previously been master and matron were required to resign in May 1860 after 14 years in office and advertisements for the positions went out. Shortly afterward Holbeach workhouse wrote assuring Honiton that E Murrant and C Murrant discharged their duties as master and schoolmistress to the satisfaction of the Guardians. After attending for an interview, when both said they were 30 years old, they were appointed to the posts of master and matron. They remained there until a vacancy came up in the Bridgwater workhouse a year later. This was larger than Honiton and undoubtedly paid more.

The workhouses were British institutions in which paupers, vagrants and the mentally ill (within limits) were maintained. The term 'union' refers to the fact that a number of parishes united to operate workhouses (following the Poor Law Amendment Act of 1834) and elect those who administered the establishment as a Board of Guardians under regulations prescribed by a central authority. Destitute persons were admitted to the workhouse by a written order of the Board or the relieving officer or, in exceptional circumstances, by the master or matron without an order. All inmates were subject to strict discipline whilst remaining in the workhouse and were not allowed to leave without giving reasonable notice. The mentally ill who were accepted were defined as lunatics, imbeciles and idiots in official documents.

Primitive workhouses were first established in the 18th century, but the Poor Law Act of 1834 produced a more regular and generally accepted system. This act set up about 600 Poor Law unions in England and Wales by combining groups of parishes into one authority or union. The unions came under the Poor Law Commissioners until 1847 and the Poor Law Board until 1871. The administration then became known as the Local Government Board (LGB) until the Ministry of Health was formed in 1919. The Poor Law Commissioners established a centralised national system for assisting the poor and destitute. The Board of Guardians was the elected body in each union whose duty was the relief of destitution. Guardians had to be ratepayers occupying property worth at least £25 a year. They were elected annually, usually at the start of April, by the ratepayers of each parish that made up the union. The Board acted like other local authorities, through committees dealing with separate departments of its work and through its permanent officials. The most important of these were the clerk (often legally qualified), the master and matron of the workhouse, the relieving officers and the medical officers. Under their control was other staff such as schoolteachers, nurses, vaccination officers, industrial training officers, porters, cooks and domestics.

The workhouse costs were mainly met from the local rates but also from considerable grants-in-aid provided by the national exchequer. The Local Government Board in Whitehall eventually administered all the workhouses.

The Bridgwater Union workhouse was situated near the north end of the town. Most of the fifty elected Guardians were recruited from the worthy middle class who had the time to meet once a week. The minutes of their meetings, which were normally well attended, still exist and are in the Somerset County Archives in Taunton [3].

The two key figures in any workhouse were the master and matron. The master was responsible to the Guardians and to the Poor Law Commissioners for the proper running and administration of the workhouse. He was also required to be 'the friend and protector of the inmates'. He had to be at least twenty-one years old, literate and numerate, and possessed of a 'strength of will and firmness of purpose'. Another qualification was that he should 'never exhibit (or allow others to) a violence of temper or use profane language'.

A master held office for life, unless he resigned or was dismissed. Where, as often happened, master and matron were married, and the wife died, resigned or was dismissed, then the master had to vacate his post unless the Guardians and Commissioners agreed to re-appoint him. The same applied if the master died. The matron acted as deputy to the master in his absence, and also had specific responsibilities of her own, mostly relating to the supervision of the female occupants and the workhouse's domestic arrangements.

Vacant positions were advertised in the Press and often indicated a preference for a pair who were man and wife, ideally without children and under fifty years old. The posts paid at least £40 per annum for the master and £20 for the matron (larger unions paid more) plus rations, coals, candles, washing and unfurnished accommodation. It is not clear if any children (if those with progeny were grudgingly appointed) also received free rations officially. In April 1861 Edwin and Catherine applied for the position as master and matron of the workhouse at Clifton, Bristol. Although they made the short list of two couples, they were unsuccessful by seventeen votes to ten. [4] Another opportunity soon arrived, however.

At the Bridgwater Workhouse Guardian's meeting on 14 August 1861 the then master and matron tendered their resignations with effect from 29 September. The Guardians immediately ordered the clerk to advertise for replacements and by the meeting on 11 September there were five viable applications, all married couples. In addition, it was proposed at the meeting that a Mr William H. Inman should also be considered. The Guardians took a vote on the last proposal and turned down the application. Inman prepared a specially printed paper with several testimonials to his character, including one from a former Mayor, which he included with his application; but he had no relevant experience. The five couples were invited to the next meeting. The efficiency of the Victorian mail and transport systems can only be admired when it is appreciated that the applicants only had one week to receive the mail, make arrangements and then travel to Bridgwater. Candidates were required to appear in person on the day of election and pay their own travelling expenses.

On 18 September only Mr and Mrs Murrant and another couple appeared and were examined by the board. The Murrants were elected by twenty-five votes to ten and offered the posts of master and matron of the Bridgwater Union Workhouse at a salary of £55 and £35 per annum respectively. On 30 September Mr Inman made a representation to the board that he had been unfairly excluded, but the Guardians refused to change their decision. This controversy rumbled on and in the end the Local Government Board (LGB) supported the decision of the Guardians. A civil servant at the LGB wrote in the margin of the letter, 'Mr Inman is a most unfit person for master of a workhouse.' [5]

The Murrants filled in forms giving their details and Edwin wrote that he was aged 31 (really 26) and had been the Master of Holbeach (not so) and Honiton Workhouses and his religion was Church of England. Catherine stated she was also 31, Church of England (though probably Roman Catholic) and had been the Matron of Honiton Workhouse. Why both Murrants overstated their ages is a mystery. Whenever a master or matron was appointed there was a paragraph on their details form which stated: 'If it is proposed that any of the children shall reside in the workhouse, the ages and sex of the children and what sum per week is to be paid for the maintenance of each child [is to be established]'. They did not fill in this paragraph because they had no children at the time, but the reason for the Guardians' displeasure with Catherine in later years will become apparent.

For conspiracy theorists the Breaker Morant story is a more fertile area than the rich pastures of Somerset. When the word 'conspiracy' appears on a page the word 'Masonic' is often lurking in the shadows nearby. The arch Masonic mastermind of the alleged Morant conspiracy, according to some of those theorists, is Lord Kitchener, a well-known Freemason who will enter the story later. The masons do indeed play a major role in the Morant story but the truth is more straightforward. Whilst master at Honiton, Edwin Murrant (senior) applied to join the Freemasons and was proposed on 13 November 1860 for the Virtue and Honor Lodge at Axminster, a small town on the Devon and Dorset border eleven miles from Honiton. [6] At that time Honiton did not have a lodge and Edwin probably took advantage of the newly constructed railway to attend meetings. The lodge minute book records, 'Proposed by brother Heath and seconded by

Bros Helier and Webber that Edwin Henry Murrant, master of the Honiton Union Workhouse and John Murch, ironmonger, be initiated into Masonry in this lodge.' They were both unanimously elected and initiated into the first degree on 11 December 1860. Murrant was passed into the second Degree on 8 January 1861 and raised to the third Degree on 12 February 1861. On the opening of the Honiton Lodge shortly afterwards he moved his allegiance closer to home. Later, on taking up his post at Bridgwater, he moved to the Rural Philanthropic Lodge at Burnham on Sea. [7] He remained a member of this lodge until his death and was there for nearly three years.

The Murrants took up their posts and the first time that they appear in the Guardian's minutes was on 8 January 1862 when Edwin Murrant reported the schoolteacher, Mr Berridge, for 'exciting the boys to acts of insubordination'. The Guardians called upon Mr Berridge to resign his office (worth £30 per annum) and instructed the clerk to advertise for a new schoolteacher.

A schoolteacher was duly selected, but at the meeting of 4 June 1862 Edwin Murrant reported the new schoolteacher for 'having destroyed and appropriated property to his own use and otherwise misconducted himself'. The teacher had in fact relieved the school of two of the pupils' desks, and used his own woodworking skills to convert these into frames for cloches for his cucumbers. He had persuaded workmen at the workhouse to glaze these frames with glass also purloined from the workhouse. This report led to a reprimand for the teacher. [8]

On 8 February 1863 Catherine Murrant gave birth in the workhouse hospital to a daughter who was christened Annie Kate Murrant. [9] Compared to her younger brother who would leave a trail broader than a cattle drive across three continents, Annie Kate would leave a faint glimmer that is very difficult for researchers to follow. Edwin and Catherine's personal joy was soon absorbed into more nationwide celebrations when the Board of Guardians ordered the master to give the inmates a dinner of roast beef and plum pudding on 10 March 1863 to celebrate the wedding of the Prince of Wales (later King Edward VII) to Princess Alexandra of Denmark. [10]

Edwin and Catherine had moved to Bridgwater in search of higher income and with an extra mouth to feed it was time to ask for more. In October 1863 they wrote to the Guardians pointing out that they had now been in their posts for two years and requesting an increase in their salaries. The clerk was instructed to seek information about salary scales from other unions and his findings obviously influenced the Guardians offer of a £5 per annum increase to both their salaries, this being ratified by the Poor Law Board in Whitehall on 31 October 1863. [11]

In March 1864 the schoolmaster Cornelius Penrose along with the schoolmistress Mary Penrose resigned and Mr Shearer and Miss Berrisford were appointed in their stead. Shearer only lasted a couple of months and when he requested a testimonial on his departure, the Guardians decided he was a drunkard and refused. Mr Robert Gulliford was then appointed and remained in the post for several years. [12]

By this time, Catherine was pregnant with her second child and she and Edwin must have been fairly content with their position in life. Not for long. Edwin contracted rheumatic fever and, after a two-week period, died on 21 August 1864 of 'inflammation of the heart and brain'. He had been well enough to play cricket for Bridgwater only a couple of weeks before. [13] He was buried in the Bridgwater Wembdon Road cemetery, and a headstone was erected, which is still there, with the Masonic emblem carved upon it and probably paid for by the Freemasons. Until 2012 this head stone had escaped the attentions of historians and only a perceptive few appreciated the Masonic connection, which was to play an enormous part in the story of 'the Breaker'. Wild conspiracy stories to do with the Freemasons still circulate – but even Col Sanders (of KFC fame) has the masonic square and compasses on his grave.

The Board of Guardians met on 24 August and passed a vote of sympathy for Catherine. They stated that they had lost a very efficient officer and excellent master of the Union. In the previous April the workhouse had been visited by a Mr Ponsford of Axbridge Union who had reported that it was extremely clean and in excellent order. The Guardians observed that this report was highly creditable to Mr and Mrs Murrant. Consequently, they resolved that Mrs Murrant be elected matron in her own right. [14] Edwin Murrant's Masonic lodge also expressed their sympathy and assisted in a more practical manner. The records of the Royal Philanthropic Lodge at Burnham show they sent Catherine a cheque for £16, an impressive sum of money. [15] Shortly afterwards Catherine wrote to the board thanking them for their kind sympathy in the time of her sad affliction. The appointment of Catherine as matron as a single woman was unusual and might have owed something to the Masonic connection; but reports of her conduct were in any case exemplary.

On 31 August, the Clerk, Paul Reed, wrote to the LGB informing them that the Guardians had appointed Catherine as matron in her own right and explaining that this was due to the death of the Master. The LGB immediately responded saying they knew nothing about this and requested details. Reed wrote saying that Edwin Murrant had died after a short illness starting with rheumatic gout and ending with congestion of the brain. By 16 September the Board approved the appointment of Catherine as matron and a minute stated, 'Mrs Murrant is one of the most efficient matrons in my district and the Guardians have done wisely in reselecting her.' Though it meant that the

Guardians had to find a master without appointing his wife, which would lead to problems later.

Among others, William Murrant, Edwin's brother, applied for the position, but Thomas Baker was appointed master soon afterwards and he was to remain at the Union for many years, eventually becoming a chairman of the Guardians.

On 9 December Catherine gave birth to a son in the workhouse and he was christened Edwin Henry Murrant in memory of his father. Later in life he chose to call himself Henry Harbord Morant and became known as 'the Breaker'. Even with a newborn and a one-year-old, Catherine's duties at the workhouse had to be fulfilled. It was almost Christmas and Catherine and Thomas Baker made arrangements for the workhouse to be decorated. The walls, which were normally cold and cheerless, wore quite a genial aspect with mottos, wreaths and evergreens. The inmates were treated to roast beef, plum pudding, apples, nuts and oranges. [16]

Christmas, however, comes but once a year and the walls of the workhouse soon returned to their normal dreary blankness. Much has been made of the fact that Edwin Henry Murrant was born in a 'grim workhouse' and Victorian workhouses were undoubtedly grim. Edwin certainly could not be classed as being privileged, though neither was he destitute, and emphasis placed on the ugly industrial nature of the Breaker's birth place is misleading. Bridgwater is possibly the only town in Somerset which could then be classed as industrial. In recent years the county has become almost synonymous with quaint rurality and rosy faced rustics half stupefied by the cider brewed on almost every farm from the apples grown in the numerous orchards of the county. This image is not accurate either, though for the county as a whole it is closer than the red brick industrial landscape painted by some Morant biographers. In late Victorian England, rural poverty kept the workhouses in business. Locally born destitute farm labourers and their families formed the majority of the population of Somerset's workhouses; and the locally brewed cider was as much the fuel of domestic violence as it was of happy torpor.

Bridgwater sits near the mouth of the River Parret that meanders its way across the central levels of Somerset, an area of reclaimed salt marsh at or just above sea level and prone to flooding in winter. It is not large. Bridgwater's population in 1881 was 14,727, only 341 higher than it had been in 1871. Young Edwin could be walking in the flat green fields or fishing in the rhynes and rivers of the Somerset levels within minutes of his home. If he turned south westward and travelled for a few hours he would gently rise into the stunning landscape of Exmoor.

It was these areas which formed the catchment area for the market town of Bridgwater. Cheese and dairy products came from the verdant levels, baskets were manufactured from the withies of the same areas, sheep from the Quantock hills and eels and elvers from the numerous watercourses would be traded in the town. In addition to these commodities, wild Exmoor ponies would be driven down once a year from the moors to be sold at St Matthew's fair, established in 1200. In 1881 almost 700 horses were on display; cart colts selling for £45 whilst unbroken Quantock and Exmoor ponies sold for £6 to £8. [17]

Besides being a market town Bridgwater was a thriving port for coastal and to some extent international trade. It was the type of small river port that no longer exists in Britain, the roads and rail lines having pushed them into obsolescence. The workhouse in which Edwin Murrant was born was close enough to the docks to hear the slap of sheets, and in the 1870s and later Edwin Murrant could have met the crews of small ships from Wales Ireland, France and other ports of Britain around the chandleries and pubs. The port brought wines and spirits from France, Italy, Spain and Barbados. Timber and furs came from Scandinavia and hides, cider, livestock, bricks and tiles were exported. Bridgwater even had its own shipbuilding industry producing 88 ships between 1850 and 1900, mostly sloops and schooners, all of timber construction, mainly oak from the Quantock hills. [18] In 1881 the Medical Officer of Health for the port sanitary authority reported that 59 ships had arrived from foreign ports and 3603 from home waters; and that 143 vessels and 591 sailors were registered at the port.

Amidst such trade and industry the unskilled agricultural labourer suffered – from the Enclosure Acts, technological advances and the requirement for skilled labour. Emigration soared; but the workhouse was never likely to be empty. Catherine, Thomas Baker and the Poor Law Union were never short of work.

In November 1865 the minutes of the Guardian's meeting noted that Stephen Channon had been appointed to the post of porter. This position paid £15 per annum with a gratuity of £5 for cutting the hair and shaving the inmates. Channon stayed in this position for several years but he maintained contact with Catherine after he left the workhouse and set up as a cab proprietor. Catherine continued to work in her post of matron whilst bringing up two children.

It appears that Catherine and Thomas Baker, the new master, got along well, though some of the inmates harboured some resentment. In September 1866 thirty inmates made a complaint in relation to the master and matron to the surgeon, Hervey Spencer, who passed the complaint on to the Poor Law Board. The letter set out a number of complaints:

> Certain vegetable productions produced in the workhouse were carried away and consumed elsewhere by the master and matron whilst the inmates did not get the class of food they were entitled to.

> The sick in the hospital did not receive the succulent ale and wine that had been prescribed by the medical officer and that these were consumed by the master matron and their friends.
>
> The paupers were not properly clothed and some women in the hospital had not changed clothes in a month.
>
> That certain friends of the master and matron are often in the house eating and drinking the best of everything and playing music and dancing till 12 o'clock at night. Certain friends of the master and matron are in the house five days a week. Some friends have stayed for a fortnight.
>
> The master often stays out till 11 or 12 o'clock.
>
> The meat was unfit for human consumption.
>
> The master and matron are hardly ever at the service in the chapel.
>
> The master and matron rarely went to bed without being worse for wear. [19]

An enquiry was held by Mr Gulson, the Poor Law Inspector and other Poor Law Guardians at which Thomas Baker denied all the charges, arguing that the matron had sometimes made Mr Gulson and Mr Ling, a Guardian, a cup of tea and this was the extent of the use of workhouse resources. Mr Ling submitted that the allegations were particularly cruel on Mrs Murrant since she had provided particularly good service to the Guardians and provided exceptional value for the tax payers' money.

If some of the inmates were dissatisfied with their lot, some of the younger ones were not – at least for one day – on Monday 22 April 1867. Catherine and Thomas Baker accompanied 70 children from the workhouse to an event at the Town Hall, having been treated by the two parliamentary representatives of the area. The event was designed to raise money for the Fifth Somerset Rifle Corps Band and included gymnastic displays, singing and band performances. The children were treated to an orange and bun each.

On 18 March 1869 a fire was discovered in Catherine's sleeping quarters at the workhouse. The fire had started in the kitchen chimney, which passed through Catherine's room. Somehow, timbers in Catherine's floor in contact with the chimney caught fire. On discovery, the floor boards were ripped up to isolate the fire, which was prevented from spreading. [20] It is not documented where the six-year-old Annie and four-year-old Edwin were at this point.

Other than the workhouse records, nothing is known of the life of the family, although she and the children were present at the 1871 census. The census gives her age as 38 and her birthplace, as usual, Ireland. The next event of note occurred on 1 September 1874 when Catherine wrote a letter to the board pointing out that she had managed the union for eight weeks in the absence of the master 'and I have had great responsibility in keeping the stores and accounts which have since been certified and found correct.' She respectfully requested additional remuneration for this responsibility. [21] The Guardians thought this was in order and awarded her £4.

In later years in Australia it would be noted that Edwin Murrant was an intelligent, well spoken, well read and well educated young man. Indeed, he would not have been able to pass himself off as a prodigal remittance man if he were not. So how did the son of a workhouse master and matron gain his education and refinement? The answer according to some researchers is to believe that Morant's oft told yarn about him being the son of Admiral George Digby Morant was true. This cannot be, since no one called Harry Harbord Morant exists in the birth records and the Admiral denied it. The conspiracy theorists' counter is that Edwin Henry Murrant was the illegitimate son of Admiral Morant and therefore the Admiral would say that, wouldn't he? It must be stressed that the Breaker never made any claim to be the *illegitimate* son of the Admiral, merely the son disowned for some social transgression in his youth. Catherine Murrant happened to have an affair, we are asked to believe, with a naval officer with a name homophonic to her own. These same authors ask us to believe that there was a conspiracy orchestrated by Lord Kitchener. The real story is much better.

In October 1871 young Edwin was put up as a candidate for schooling at The Royal Masonic Institute for Boys (RMIB) [22] in Wood Green, London. This was a boarding school which gave a good boarding education to sons of 'deceased or indigent' Freemasons. The procedure was for candidates to apply for education at the school and lodges voted, their voting power being related to their contributions to the charity. It appears that votes were in some sense bartered and traded within the lodges as the minute books of the Lodge of Perpetual Friendship, Bridgwater, records that it was 'proposed by the Worshipful Master and seconded by Brother R. J. Hodges, Past Master, that the three votes belonging to this lodge and the two votes presented by Bro M. Beale to this lodge for the boys school be given in favour of Edwin Henry Murrant and handed to Bro Bridges.' [23] The voting system was cumulative and the votes for unsuccessful candidates were carried over to his next application. Edwin was eventually elected after his fourth application in April 1873. [24] He entered the school on 19 September 1873 although his entry was deferred 'owing to ill health' [25] and remained there until 9 December 1880 at the not inconsiderable cost to the Freemasons of £318 5s 6d. [26] The breakdown of this figure is that in his first year it cost £15 to keep him and in subsequent years it cost about £42. In the first year boys were given clothes to the value of over £6 and about £5 in subsequent years.

There are few existing records of the school of his time there, but he does appear in the general committee minutes in 1879. Murrant, along with two other pupils, Peter Heaviside and Harry Pinsen, was reported to the committee for theft and being in possession of a key 'to gain access to prohibited places', The following are the extracts from the headmaster's report:

> 7 September. – punished Heaviside and others for coming downstairs after all were in bed and taking bread and cheese. Heaviside was also connected with the boy who robbed the Donation Box three years ago. [27]
> 17 September. – Heaviside again came down stairs after all were in bed and stole butter, plums, currants, matches. Two forged keys were found upon him, of his own make, to enable him to gain access to prohibited places. The example of such a boy as Heaviside is most injurious to the younger boys after they come to school. Heaviside is one of the boys remaining at the school during the holidays, during which time much dishonesty generally occurs with constant trouble. [28]

Heaviside, the older boy who expressed no remorse, was expelled; Murrant, who had expressed regret, was severely punished and his mother informed and he was told that he narrowly escaped expulsion. Pinsen was punished by the headmaster.

Details of the education offered are sketchy, but boys were entered in public exams and seem to have had grounding in subjects similar to that of a grammar school. Shortly after Murrant started at the RMIB, the Revd Dr Richard Morris took over as headmaster. An academically focussed man, he had been trained as a teacher at St John's College, Battersea and in 1869 he had been appointed Winchester Lecturer in English Language at Kings College School. He had been awarded the Lambeth Diploma of LLD the following year and his own study and research had gained him a reputation as a scholar and philologist with an expert knowledge of English and Pali (a language akin to Sanskrit).

Some students remember him, however, as a man of short temper with little sympathy for, or understanding of, less academic pupils. His affection for the brighter boys or those likely to enhance the reputation of the school was however noteworthy. It appears that he was unjust to those he disliked, but kind and generous to his academic favourites. [29]

Morris introduced changes designed to relate to the needs of modern scholars more closely than the previous classics-biased curriculum. The new, challenging curriculum included physics, hydrostatics, advanced maths, history, geography and even gymnastics. [30]

The young Murrant was expected to be at lessons at nine in the morning and would attend three forty-five minute lessons and one hour-long lesson. This included Saturdays though on that day the final hour would be devoted to 'preparation'. In the afternoons there would be two hour-long lessons except Saturdays which were 'half-holidays'. There would also be 'preparation' during the evening until past eight.

The school also employed a Drill Sergeant and during Murrant's time this was Sergeant Major Waterman, a Middlesex Volunteer Engineer, formerly of the 67th Regiment. [31]. He had served through the China War and had taken part in the storming of the Taku Forts, a battle for which seven Victoria Crosses were awarded, and the subsequent occupation of Beijing. He was appointed in August 1866, having just returned from China via South Africa and appears to have been in post until 1890 and was considered by the boys to be a kind, considerate and capable man.

A number of boys from Murrant's year took the Cambridge Local Examinations Paper although Murrant does not appear among them. We gain some indication of Edwin's aptitudes from a printed programme inserted into the Minute books in June 1880 describing the annual distribution of prizes, on 26 June 1880, under the presidency of the Right Hon, The Earl of Lathom, Grand Master of West Lancashire. Murrant received prizes for Classics, French and German. [32]

After being commended on his linguistic skills, the young Murrant was afforded the opportunity to hone another talent for which he would become notorious; impersonation. The young men of his year gave a performance of an 'English Play, Jacks Delight, a farce in one act by Thomas J Williams' in which Edwin donned a dress to play Peggy (a lady's maid).

Subsequently, in the programme under the 'Special Prizes presented by the House Committee', and presumably having divested himself of Peggy's dress, Edwin was presented with first prize for dictation. 'Furthermore among prizes "Presented by Private Donors" in this case, Bro. the Revd Dr Morris, the prize for elocution went to: E. H. Murrant and G. Sparkes.' Clearly 'the Breaker' had been blessed with the gift of the gab. Not surprising then that Edwin Murrant was chosen to play the lead role of Dick in 'English Play, "Turned Head", A Farce in one Act by Gilbert A. A. Beckett' in which Dick opens with the words 'This is a queer place I've got into – I never was among such a rum set in all my life'. Strangely prophetic.

There was no school magazine at the time, but about ten years later there is an article in the new magazine suggesting that the school trained boys to be clerks capable of earning £25 a year. Murrant does not appear to have joined the old boys' club founded some time later. He left school on 9 December 1880 (his sixteenth birthday) and was presented with a Book of Common

Prayer, a bible and a gratuity of ten shillings. He returned to Bridgwater that night according to the Guardians' minutes. For those who have concocted a history of nascent horsemanship in the Barnet area back to 1876 for the Breaker there is one other disappointment contained in the Masonic minute book. This notes that he was to be employed as an assistant master at Silesia College, Higher Barnet from 2 March 1881, which is exactly where the census enumerator found him a month later. He was given £5 by the Masons as an outfit allowance to buy a suit for his new job.

2

The Teenage Murrant

Whilst Edwin was away at school in London, brushing up the accent and charm which would later provide him with respectability in some quarters, his mother struggled with the administration of the workhouse. The routine can be traced through the minutes of the Guardians' meetings. In September 1875 the Guardians resolved that the matron be called upon to pay £5-5/- in the discharge of past maintenance of her daughter and that she pay 5/- per week so long as her daughter continued to reside with her. The master was directed to keep an account of such maintenance and to show times of absence of the daughter. Following this resolution is another one, crossed out but readable, which says that 'with regard to Mrs Murrant's child Edwin's visits to his mother during his holidays, no payment at present be asked for such holidays'. On 29 December 1876, there is a minute in the book which states that 'matron be not called upon to pay anything for her son while residing with her during his Christmas holidays'. Resolved: 'that the Matron's little boy is welcomed home for his holidays'. [1]

In May 1878, events were about to take a turn for the worse. Mr Baker having retired, James Winterson became the master and on his application form he gave his details as 38 years old and single but with two children. He also mentioned that he had previous military service. [2]

The problem with her children seems to have been the only blot on Catherine's career at this stage, which surely came about because she was drawing free rations from the Union and thereby causing concern about costs among the Guardians. There were further comments in the minutes about this on 29 January and 30 July 1879. The Poor Law Union had advertised for a single man to take up the role of workhouse master. James Winterson, however, was not single and this was about to cause friction.

In February 1881 the whole matter came to a head and there is an entry in the minute book to the effect that 'the Guardians are much dissatisfied that matron's children have been living with their mother in the house – son from 9 December 1880 [the day he left the RMIB] and daughter from 15 September 1880'. Catherine wrote to the board on 23 February a letter which is in the minutes:

> I am sorry I should have given offence by having had my children with me during the Christmas holidays and the late inclement weather, but considering that you have had the best twenty years of my life, as well as that my children were born here and having lost their father here, I hope you will exercise a kindly feeling towards me in this matter. During these many years I have in addition to my own duties performed those of every officer in the house for weeks when their respective offices have been vacated and one time did the master for six months as well as during shorter periods. I would also add that I draw no rations nor in fact could I, as I have no keys to the stores, whatever was necessary for my children I purchased for them. They have both now left me. I am Gentlemen,
> Yours respectfully, C. Murrant [3]

The census for 1881 occurred on the night of the 3/4 April and Catherine aged 48 and born in Ireland is shown in the workhouse, but the enumerator gave her surname as 'Newvrant'. This error probably dates from the transcription into the computerised format at a later date, but her daughter is noted as 'Murrand'. Annie Kate is shown as being at the house of Stephen and Mary Channon (the ex-workhouse porter) in Bridgwater with Professor of Music as her occupation. Enquiries have been made at the two major Colleges of Music in London to see if Annie ever studied at either of them but there is no trace. The Royal College of Music did suggest that it was not unusual for piano teachers at that time to describe themselves as professors.

Edwin Henry is shown in 1881 as being a tutor at Silesia College in Chipping Barnet in Hertfordshire. He was living in the house of Mr James Russell, the headmaster, who was born at Othery near Bridgwater. Mr Russell seems to have packed his house with people from the West Country. Fellow tutors were Edward Tilcombe (17) from Honiton and George Baker (19) from Bridgwater. Kate Denner (17) from Bridgwater was visiting and Margaret Govier (18) from Dulverton and Lucy Richards (20) from Taunton were domestics. [4] Kate's father was from Bridgwater but was working in London as a wine and spirits merchant who can be found in the Royal Philanthropic Lodge Masonic records. It seems likely that Kate Denner was a friend of Edwin or George Baker, or both.

At some time before 1869 James Russell and his wife, Annie, had set up a 'Gentlemen's' School' in Bridgwater known as Lonsdale House School in Dampiet Street. During this time James and Annie resided at a prestigious address at King's Square in the town where the 1871 census shows them living with eleven teenage boarders and two assistant school masters. In June 1876 [5] the Russells sold the school to Revd Dr Thomas Nichols and William Parkes, moved to Barnet and established a new school in Silesia House on Belles Hill. This house had previously been established by the Royal Patriotic Fund as an orphanage, originally for orphans of soldiers killed in the Crimean War.

James Russell must have been planning to move to London prior to selling his school in Bridgwater since it is recorded that he joined the Phoenix Lodge, London (173) of the Freemasons on 13 November 1875. He was 'Passed' on 11 December the same year and 'Raised' on 11 March 1876. [6] The Masonic records later reveal that James Russell, of Silesia College High, Barnet, moved to the Wood Green Lodge on 18 October 1884. [7]

It seems too much of a coincidence if, when Edwin Murrant left the Masonic School at Wood Green in 1881 to take up his first job as Tutor at Silesia College along with another Bridgwater boy, George Baker, the position was not gained through either the Masonic or Bridgwater connections, or both. Whether Murrant had ever attended James Russell's Lonsdale House School in Bridgwater prior to 1873, when he left Bridgwater for the Masonic School, is not known.

Silesia College at High Barnet was quite a substantial establishment with Mr J. Russell as Principal and Head Master assisted by fourteen masters. It advertised itself as being 'situated on a sheltered eminence on the northern heights near London, encompassed by its own grounds, nearly fifteen acres in extent, surrounded by extensive picturesque scenery, and the air is pure and invigorating'. It took boys under twelve in the Junior School and they moved to the Senior School from twelve to eighteen. The object of the school was 'to afford complete education to boys destined for the Professions, Mercantile, or Agricultural pursuits, combined with home comforts, at a moderate expense'. Fees were 25–35 Guineas per annum for boarders and 5–10 Guineas for day pupils inclusive of books and extras. An invoice for the term ending in April 1883 exists, sent to a Mrs Keane. This showed that board and tuition for her son came to £10 but with extras, including violin lessons, she paid a total of £14 7s 2d. The following term, ending on 26 June, she paid £15.3.0 but this included 'getting the lad's violin bow rehaired and various repairs to the violin'. No doubt he also received a clip round the ear because she was charged four shillings for him wilfully breaking a window. [8]

The school was a reputable college and received favourable mentions in the local papers. A former pupil, Dai H. Lewis, who played rugby for Wales in 1886, wrote in his memoirs *America Bid me Welcome* how all the pupils enjoyed the facilities of the large recreation ground. Indeed, the school had a very good soccer team and even beat Tottenham Hotspur, four goals to three away and two to one at home! On one day Mr Russell took 160 pupils to Crystal Palace to commemorate the event of having registered 53 new pupils in one term. This party, 'accompanied by staff and friends had a very enjoyable day and returned to High Barnet by the 9.30 p.m. train, the boys cheering lustily as they passed through the streets again on their way to college'.

Unfortunately, further records no longer exist and although the school flourished until the 1890s it has been impossible to dig deeper into young Edwin's career as a teacher prior to his departure for Australia on 1 April 1883. We do know that the school had some notable pupils including Jose Marie Rivas Groot, a Columbian writer and later a professor at Bogota University and a Government minister. [9] Another pupil, Gerald van Casteel, practised at the bar in Washington DC. [10] One distinguished English pupil was Charles Henry Mabey junior who followed in his father's footsteps as a sculptor; some of his notable work can be seen at County Hall, Westminster Bridge in London, where he was responsible for the heraldic shield on the Crescent Friezes, the caskets, torches and other details around the ceremonial entrances. [11] The post of pupil teacher was a common one at late Victorian schools and Edwin, even at seventeen, would probably have been able to cope with simple teaching in the junior school.

Also in the 1881 census are George and Ann Murrant, Edwin's grandparents, who are shown to be living at Pitminster, a parish of Taunton, and running a general shop. Living with them was 11-year-old Cecilia Mary Stuart from High Barnet and described as a granddaughter. [12] It is possible that they had moved into the area to assist with the children although there is no evidence of this.

At the workhouse James Winterson was still making his presence felt. On 11 May 1881 Miss Mary Walsh, the nurse, was dismissed as a result of a report from the master James Winterson: 'I have to report that Nurse Mary Walsh left the house with my permission and was brought back drunk by PC Goodrich at 10 50 p.m.' [13]

In early November 1881 problems arose at the workhouse, and although not minuted, it is apparent that Catherine was rude and abusive to the Guardians at a meeting. On 10 November the master complained to the Guardians that the matron was in the habit of taking tea with the industrial trainer, Miss Everleigh, in the master and matron's sitting room.

He said that in the past it was the practice of the head officers to take their meals together, but for a long time such practice had been discontinued. He asked the Guardians to state if the practice should continue. In response, the matron accused the master of obtaining his present appointment by misrepresentation and falsehood and of not treating her and other officers of the house with proper respect and consideration. [14] It seems fairly clear that Winterson ultimately wanted his wife to act as matron, which meant pushing out the widow Catherine. He had indeed lied about being single on the application for the post of master and there is no doubt that there was bad blood between Catherine and him.

The Guardians organised a committee to look into the allegations. Sure enough, Winterson was married when he became master, with a wife and two children. A third child was born in November 1878, who died a year later. In 1881 another child was born. Matron alleged that the master went home to tea every day and often to dinner. The matron attributed the master's conduct to his wish to get rid of her and other officers so that his falsehoods and deceits would not be discovered and to make room for his wife. The master admitted he was married and the Board recommended that a Government Inspector should be sent to examine the whole matter. The master alleged that the matron had entered the house drunk on 5 November 1880 on Bridgwater Carnival night. [15] In a recent TV documentary on Morant, an interviewee alleges that Catherine Murrant was an alcoholic. There is scant evidence of this, and if being drunk on carnival night is a condition for such an affliction, a fair proportion of the folk of Bridgwater would have qualified both then and now.

Reading the Guardians' minutes it is apparent that some were for the master and some for the matron. Catherine took the step of employing a local solicitor, James Chapman, and he wrote on her behalf on 9 December an eloquent letter suggesting, or rather complaining, that some Guardians were indeed supporting the master. He pointed out that Catherine's forthright expressions were warranted. It would seem that the violent conduct was entirely verbal. It must be assumed that the Freemasons appointed and paid for Mr Chapman's services because then as now, recourse to the law was not cheap. The Guardians, acting on further information from Catherine, discovered that Winterson had lied that he was single when he had been appointed assistant master at Stepney Workhouse. As a result of this misrepresentation and his later one he was required to resign [16] and did so before the end of 1881.

The Guardians decided that there should be an enquiry, which was organised by the Local Government Board in Whitehall. This enquiry was run by Mr H. B. Courtney of Exeter and took place on 9 January1882.

Courtney's enquiry was quite high-powered since Catherine was again represented by Mr Chapman whilst Paul Reed, the Clerk, himself a solicitor, appeared for the Guardians. There were two charges drawn up against Catherine:

> Matron was drunk on Nov 5 1880 (Guy Fawkes night)
> She behaved in an improper manner on 2 November 1881 in the boardroom in front of the Guardians.

The witnesses against her were Mr Little, the instructor in shoemaking, Miss Edavean (later Mrs Little), Miss Deacon and Mr Edwin Heard the porter. Witnesses for Catherine were Miss Everleigh, the industrial trainer and three inmates, Charlotte Willis, Annie Payne and Elizabeth Hurly. Catherine stated that she was in fear of the master and that was the reason she was excitable before the Guardians. She thought the master was to blame for the report on her son and daughter staying in the house. [17] It is interesting that several of those witnesses, including the Littles and the porter and his assistant, left the workhouse shortly afterwards.

Both sides gave conflicting evidence about the drunkenness and some said they saw Catherine blowing on a tin whistle whilst others failed to notice it. Catherine produced some impressive testimonials including one from R. A. Burck, a former master, who wrote from Devonport Workhouse and others from R. J. Moss, another former master, and Henrietta Baker, the matron of Hereford Hospital. The most interesting is from Colonel F. B. Ward, a Poor Law Inspector who said at the end of his testimonial, 'I trust you will be successful in your application for the appointment of matron at the schools at Leavesden.' Whether Catherine was successful in this has not yet been found. Another ex-Poor Law Inspector, Edward Grilson, wrote, 'I consider Mrs Murrant to be of exemplary character. She is kind in disposition, energetic and careful in her management and firm in carrying out the orders of her superiors.' He mentioned that he had known her both at Honiton and Bridgwater.

Courtney determined that there were problems with the administration of the workhouse in addition to the accusations that caused the enquiry and that the master and matron should resign their posts. In his findings he noted that matron was 'violent and disrespectful towards the Board in November'. Catherine left the workhouse in February 1882, Winterson having already resigned.

It is not known when young Edwin Murrant gave up his position at Silesia College. A report on the Bridgwater amateur athletic meeting in the *Bridgewater Mercury* on 2 August 1882 mentions Edwin Murrant as a competitor. This meeting was a major attraction and brought spectators and competitors from far and wide. Though the Great Western Railway Company declined to run excursion trains to the event, as they had done in previous years. There was a good attendance nevertheless and gate receipts were considerable. Edwin ran in the 100 yards handicap and was given a six yard start and also appeared in the mile handicap and was given 100 yards. Also appearing in the 100 yards and representing Taunton (with a 5 yard start) was young Ernest E. Hammett, a 19-year-old land surveyor. Nineteen years later he would join an irregular mounted infantry unit in South Africa called the Bushveldt Carbineers and would be arrested in Pietersburg with Edwin. Neither competitor won, but no doubt they enjoyed the refreshments provided by Edwin's local, 'The Malt Shovel'. Edwin's presence at the athletics meeting in August may not necessarily suggest that he was living back in Bridgwater at this time, since Silesia College were also taking part in an athletics meeting in the area the previous week.

Late that year however, Edwin is shown in *The Mercury* playing rugby in the Bridgwater Alliance second team versus the Independent College XV on 8 November and despite being three short, Bridgwater won. A week later Murrant scored in a game against Weston Super Mare Rangers. On 17 November 1882 the *Western Gazette*, a local newspaper, shows that E. Murrant played rugby as a forward against Street and he is found a month later in the *Gazette* appearing for the Alliance against Weston-Super-Mare Crusaders. Thus it is probable that by late 1882 Edwin had given up his job at Barnet and returned home. Maybe he took on a job in town working with horses.

In the same edition of the *Gazette* there are reports of a man called George Randall giving talks in two villages about emigrating to Queensland. Randall, an English emigrant and wealthy confectionary manufacturer, was appointed by the Governor of Queensland to boost emigration to the colony. He confounded the government by not requesting a salary. With untiring energy he toured England and encouraged agricultural labourers and others experiencing depressed conditions to emigrate. He is the subject of a book. [18] In his publicity material he mentioned the government gave assisted passages and that it only took 42 days to get to Queensland by ship, now that the Suez Canal had opened.

The 1883 *Kelly's Directory* shows that Catherine was living at 2 Bradford Villas, Wembdon, which nowadays is a suburb of Bridgwater. Nothing is known of her subsequent life until her death in 1899 aged 66, except the 1891 census records her as being the retired matron of a county asylum. Edwin's grandparents, George and Ann Murrant, died in 1889 and 1886 in the Barton registry district in Gloucestershire and a Cecilia Mary Murrant (probably formerly Stuart) was married there in 1891.

Catherine died at 4 Crown Hill Terrace, Torquay on 25 July 1899. On her death certificate she is described as Catherine Murrant, widow of Edwin Murrant. She died of Bright's disease, a kidney complaint. T. Newcombe of 3 Crown Hill Terrace, evidently her next-door neighbour, reported her death and she was buried in the Torbay Extra-Mural cemetery on 29 July 1899 with the vicar of St Johns officiating. The location of her resting place has been identified from cemetery records (which show that two others lie in the same grave) but there is no standing memorial on the spot.

We know that in later life Harry Morant had a flair for poetry and a certain facility with the English language and it must be assumed that his love of literature was nurtured during his time at the RMIB. His mother was, however, described as a schoolteacher on her marriage certificate and she may have inspired his love for books and poetry.

Morant always suggested that he was at the 'Naval College' and one assumes that he meant Dartmouth, but again, very good records exist that show no trace of him there or anywhere else in the navy. Indeed, the only sign of anything remotely to do with the sea comes from Witton (*Scapegoats of the Empire*) where he mentions that Morant called the escorting officers, when they were under arrest, 'tug boats'. There is also a piece in a letter to Lt Hannam: 'Should the Lord allow that I ever see the Ushant Light four points on the starboard bow once more and steam safely into Southampton Water or Plymouth Sound...' These snippets are hardly indicative of time in the navy. The workhouse was very close to the thriving port of Bridgwater and it must be expected that the young Murrant played in the dock area and was familiar with the seafarers and ships.

An Australian friend of Morant's suggested that at some time he was sponsored by George John Whyte-Melville (1821–1878) who was a soldier, novelist, poet and huntsman and who lived the latter part of his life in Tetbury, Gloucestershire. The Breaker certainly knew of him and owned a copy of his novel *Katerfelto*. [20] In the *Windsor and Richmond Gazette* on 24 September 1898 he had mentioned Whyte-Melville in a letter to the newspaper on the subject of hunting declaring the author knew the difference between riding to the hounds and hunting.

Whyte-Melville was born in Scotland in Fifeshire, near St Andrews, the home of golf, the son of John Whyte-Melville and his wife, Lady Catherine, the youngest daughter of the fifth Duke of Leeds. After an education at Eton he purchased a commission in the 93rd Highlanders in 1839 and exchanged into the Coldstream Guards in 1846, before retiring by sale of his commission as a captain in 1849. He was a golfer and was elected to the Royal and Ancient golf club in 1839 and captain in 1851. When he left the Guards he settled down with his wife Charlotte and daughter Florence into the life of a moderately wealthy gentleman of leisure, firstly in Northamptonshire, then London and eventually in Tetbury. He started to write and by the time of his death had produced twenty-four novels, three anthologies and numerous poems.

In 1854, at the start of the Crimean War, he joined the Turkish Irregular Cavalry and served throughout the conflict. Afterwards he settled down again to writing and the pleasures of a sporting gentleman. He continued to live a very full life. Apart from the social whirl and writing novels, he spent much of the summer playing golf in Scotland, and his winters hunting. In about 1875 he and his wife moved to Tetbury, about 70 miles from Bridgwater, so that they could follow the Beaufort Hunt.

It is unlikely that he visited Bridgwater because there was no hunt based in the area but he certainly hunted on Exmoor. On these occasions he took a train to Taunton and then rode to some convenient hunting hotel. He is known to have stayed at the Luttrell Arms in Dunster and to have known Dulverton well and probably stayed in one of the three hotels there on the fringes of the moor. Exmoor is a large area of open moorland in Somerset and North Devon. It used to be great hunting country and even today there are nine hunts in the area. Both foxes and stags were hunted before the law was recently changed to ban hunting with dogs.

All the royalties from his writing were devoted to charitable purposes, and he assisted young lads to become grooms and hunt servants and he also provided reading rooms in hunt stables for the benefit of the stable boys. It is entirely possible that young Edwin Murrant might have been fortunate enough to be assisted in this way, though since almost nothing of his own account of his youth told in Australia has turned out to be true, the idea must be treated with caution. Whyte-Melville was renowned for turning young horses into efficient hunters and seems to have spent much of his time on horseback. He was killed hunting, four days before the Breaker's fourteenth birthday, near Malmesbury, Wiltshire, in December 1878, breaking his neck when his horse fell heavily whilst crossing a ploughed field. He was buried at Tetbury.

There is a memorial to Whyte-Melville in the centre of St Andrews in the form of a drinking fountain and there was another in the Guards Chapel (destroyed by a flying bomb in 1944) in London. His books, which all featured hunting or racing scenes, remained in print and were very popular up until the start of the First World War.

Young Edwin Murrant could have known Whyte-Melville but this is considered unlikely. The only realistic window of opportunity would have been the years 1875–1878, at which time Whyte-Melville lived in Tetbury and the young Murrant was at school in London. They could only have become acquainted in school holidays. Evenings spent with a copy of Whyte-Melville's latest book on Murrant's knee are much more likely than with the old horseman bouncing the young Breaker on *his* knee. It is known that Murrant read Whyte-Melville's novels and it is probable that he then concocted a connection with the great man. He seems to have acquired the nickname in South Africa 'Tony' (Lumpkin) probably after a character in the *Memoirs of an Irish RM* which was a best seller just prior to the Boer War. (The name Tony Lumpkin is found originally in Oliver Goldsmith's 1773 play *She Stoops to Conquer* – in which Lumpkin is a trickster and playboy.) There is no doubt that the Breaker was a voracious reader and probably not above incorporating passages from popular novels into his own life.

One of the early Australian bush poets was Adam Lindsay Gordon (1833–1870), who wrote many poems which are still well regarded today. His style is similar to Morant's and he also published in the *Bulletin*. In 1876 an anthology of his poems was published in Australia and it remained in print for many years. Gordon dedicated one of his poems to Whyte-Melville and obviously was familiar with his history and his writings. An example, perhaps, of the colonial cultural cringe: Gordon's validity as a poet required British confirmation and the admiration between the two was apparently mutual. Gordon was a similar figure to Morant and had attended Woolwich Military Academy before emigrating to Australia, becoming a leading stockman and horsebreaker. His poetic style in such poems as *The Sick Stock Rider* and *How We Beat the Favourite* certainly inspired later bush poets such as Lawson, Banjo Paterson and probably Breaker Morant. Gordon took up horse breaking in Australia and is commemorated by an obelisk, erected 1887, at the Blue pool near Mount Gambier for a daring leap he made on a horse. He is also commemorated by a bust in Poet's Corner, Westminster Abbey. Morant may have possibly taken aspects of Gordon's lifestyle and writing and incorporated them into his own – thus helping to obscure the trail to his own past.

3

The Morants

Most biographies cover the early life and often the parentage of their subject, though it might seem odd to delve deep into the ancestry of the main character. It may appear even odder to delve into the history of a family which in reality had nothing to do with him or her – but Breaker Morant was a man who invented himself and it is therefore necessary to explore the origins of his deceits. Over his years in Australia the Breaker's identity metamorphosed from Edwin Murrant, son of the workhouse, through Edwin Morant, son of a clergyman, to Harry Harbord Morant, son of an admiral. If Edwin Murrant was the caterpillar, the son of Admiral George Digby Morant has become the butterfly pinned in the display case of history. Even 90 years after his death, a further transformation has occurred: that he was the *illegitimate* son of the Admiral. This is a claim the Breaker himself never made. So who were the Morants of Hampshire?

A family called Morant were among the early settlers in Jamaica in 1655 when the British captured the island from the Spanish. The Morants were apparently from yeoman or artisanal stock and combined with a family called Gale to develop land in Clarendon parish in the south of the island, where they had plantations worked by many slaves, mainly producing sugar. In 1770 Edward Morant, using some of the vast wealth that flowed from the family estates, purchased Brockenhurst House, a late Stuart farmhouse in the New Forest. He rebuilt it as a large Georgian mansion and laid out the land around it to his plan and the estate became Brockenhurst Park. His son, John, continued to run the family business. He married Lady Catherine Hay in 1823 and ensured the continuation of the dynasty. The major event that occurred in John's time was the emancipation of the slaves in 1838. The British Government bought out all the slave owners and paid about £22,300 for the 1,115 slaves owned by the Morants, roughly £20 per slave. John settled in England and left the enormous sum of £250,000 on his death in 1857.

The New Forest is bounded by Southampton, Ringwood and Winchester and the sea to the south and includes one of the largest tracts of unenclosed pasture, heath and forest in the south of England. It is a beautiful place to visit and take a stroll. It is now an extremely popular National Park. It was an agreeable location for a family of gentry with its facilities for country sports and good communications to Southampton and London.

Edward Morant sat as a Member of Parliament from 1761 until 1787 and is remembered as a strongly independent member who never held office, nor solicited any office or favour. After him no other Morant took up politics and the family were content to live off their Jamaican income, becoming part of the Hampshire rural gentry and no member of this branch of the family ever came to prominence.

By the time of the construction of the railway in the next century the family were a force to be reckoned with in the village and they arranged for their personal level crossing to allow them to pass unhindered over the line to their magnificent entrance gate.

Later in the century the income from the Jamaican estates declined considerably. This did not stop the family enlarging but they had to make their way in the world. One branch of the family, known as the Shirley Morants, settled in Northern Ireland and another branch became known as the Hay Morants and moved to Ringwood on the western edge of the New Forest.

The Shirley Morants were so called because they lived in Shirley House, Carrickmacross, Monaghan. The estate was owned by the Shirley family who were absentee landlords and Capt Morant acted as agent. He and his wife Lydia, who came from Tipperary, had four sons and seven daughters. The eldest was George Digby Morant who was born in Dublin in 1837.

George passed into the Royal Navy in 1850 after an education at Dr Burney's naval academy and was destined for much active service in his early days. He served as a midshipman on HMS *Fox* in a campaign in Burma and then went off to fight in the Crimean War for three years, after which he received a Turkish decoration, the Order of Medjidieh, fifth class and was promoted lieutenant. In June 1858 he went off to the China Station aboard HMS *Cormorant* and served in the war against China until returning to Europe to serve in the Mediterranean from 1862 until March 1864.

It is part of the legend of Breaker Morant, widely credited in Australia, that he was the son of Admiral Sir George Digby Morant. Breaker Morant was born on 9 December 1864 in Bridgwater workhouse; George Digby Morant was posted to Pembroke Dock in Wales having returned from the

Mediterranean with effect from 8 March 1864. He was struck off strength of HMS *Formidable* on 1 March and is recorded in the ship's log of HMS *Blenheim* as arriving on board at Pembroke Dock on the morning of 12 March.

One writer who propounds the theory that the Breaker was truly the illegitimate son of the Admiral presents no more evidence for this than the Breaker's claims that the Admiral was his father and that Catherine and George Digby Morant were both in southern Britain at the same time. Pembroke Dock is near the western extremity of South Wales whilst Bridgwater is in south west England. It's quite a distance for a tryst. Recognising this fact the proponent of the theory suggests that they may have both visited the Brockenhurst area of Hampshire at the same time. Brockenhurst was, however, not the home of George Digby Morant. That was Shirley at Carrickmacross, Ireland and that is exactly where George Digby Morant was on 8 March 1864: at a ploughing match at his home, probably on leave between postings, and not sowing any wild oats in Somerset or Hampshire. The *Dublin Express* for 8 March 1864 shows he arrived on the 7th aboard the Royal Mail steamer from Holyhead, North Wales. By 12 March he was on board the *Blenheim* at Pembroke Docks. Travelling from Pembroke Dock to Bridgwater in 1864 would involve a long and difficult journey around the River Severn. The railway line did not reach Pembroke Dock until August 1864 although there was a line to Bridgwater from 1841. Catherine Murrant and George Digby Morant moved in widely differing social circles and it was highly unlikely they would arrange a dangerous liaison in a workhouse. The workhouse records show several instances of Catherine requesting leave of absence and whether it was granted. No such request was made around March 1864.

Digby Morant was then given command of the gunboat *Grasshopper* on the China Station and was involved in several successful operations against pirates. On one occasion he was specially thanked by the Admiralty and Foreign Office for destroying a large pirate ship and capturing two others, after a battle lasting six hours, thereby liberating five cargo junks.

This gallant affair brought him early promotion to commander and his subsequent career was very successful. Promoted captain in 1873 he spent five years as 'Captain of the Irish Lights', which was the equivalent of Trinity House and involved the administration of all the lighthouses, beacons and buoys and other aids to marine navigation around the Irish coast. When he retired from this post to take command of HMS *Valorous* the British Board of Trade expressed regret at the loss of such a zealous and efficient officer from the employment of the Commissioners. He advanced to rear admiral in 1887 and full admiral in 1901 and shortly afterwards, in May, retired from the service. In November he was awarded the KCB. Breaker Morant obviously followed the Admiral's career assiduously because in December 1901, whilst under close arrest, he wrote to Major Lenehan, his commanding officer, 'My governor got a KCB in November.' In retirement the Admiral, who died at his London house in 1921, was chairman of the Royal Humane Society and was actively associated with various undertakings connected with the navy, including the Fairfield Shipbuilding Company of which he was a director. His obituary in *The Times* indicates he had a genial, cheery nature and his talents as a raconteur made him very popular among a wide circle of friends and acquaintances – which suggests that he and the Breaker would have got on well together.

The Admiral probably did not know he allegedly had a prodigal son living in Australia. In May 1902 when the news of the executions was widely publicised in the Australian and British papers, it was reported that 'Admiral Sir George Digby Morant writes to the papers indignantly denying the offensive statement that he is the father of the man Morant executed for shooting unarmed Boers.' It was further noted that 'he is a gallant old officer, who was fighting as long ago as the Burmese war, and nearly 30 years ago won fame as a pirate exterminator in Chinese waters. He wears a gallery of medals, including the Burmese, the Baltic, the Crimea and the China tokens, and it is hard that in his old age he should be falsely accused of the paternity of one who, from such evidence as we yet possess, seems to have been a peculiarly bad sort of scoundrel.' [1]

Back in Brockenhurst, the Morant family had discovered that there was a cuckoo in the nest. A letter addressed to G. D. Morant Esq., New Forest, Hampshire, with a South African stamp was delivered in early February 1901 to Brockenhurst Park. Flora Morant, the widow of John Morant who had died in 1899, asked the butler to open it. The letter, dated 23 January 1901, came from the newly constructed Mount Nelson Hotel, Cape Town:

> We shall be obliged if you will give us particulars as to the whereabouts of Mr H. H. Morant. This gentleman, whom we understand is your son, stayed at this hotel in November last, representing himself to be a correspondent attached to the staff of the *Daily Telegraph*. As he left without discharging his liability amounting to £16.13.00 we shall esteem it a favour if you will let us know what course we had better adopt. We are averse to taking the matter to court till we have heard from you.

This letter shows that the spurious Morant had a slight knowledge of the family but probably did not realise that the Admiral lived in London at this time. The Breaker had adopted a policy in Australia of 'shooting the moon', scooting from hotels without paying and this is a classic example.

Flora Morant convened a meeting which included the Admiral, who came down from London, and other senior members of the family plus her solicitor and in the end responded to the hotel that she knew nothing of the spurious guest and suggested the *Daily Telegraph* should be invited to pay and nothing more was heard.

In 1915 a book was published by Maurice Harbord in London called *Froth and Bubble.* [2] Harbord was a South African police reservist and also a captain in the Imperial Light Horse. He describes a night in the Mount Nelson Hotel when he sat up with Bennet Burleigh and 'Tony Morant' and comments that he had never laughed so much in his life listening to the other two telling stories. He records that Morant was one of the most amusing fellows he ever met and a gifted raconteur. Harbord wrote quite a bit about Morant in his book, most of it wrong, but the incident in the Mount Nelson hotel he describes obviously led to the letter to Brockenhurst. The naming of Morant as 'Tony' seems to have started in 1901 and he signed letters in some cases as Tony or Tony Lumpkin. As mentioned, the name probably comes from the book *The Experiences of an Irish Resident Magistrate* which was much in vogue at the time and first published in 1899. Tony Lumpkin was an amiable rogue always up to tricks, especially in the matter of horse stealing.

The story does not end here because Flora Morant's second son was serving in the Imperial Yeomanry in South Africa. [3] Francis George Morant enlisted in Barnstaple, Devon, on the 4 January 1900 describing himself as aged 30 with previous service in the Cape Mounted Rifles and the British South African Police. He declared he had a tattoo of a snake on his right arm, a lady and dagger on his left arm and the royal coat of arms on his chest. He was discharged on 23 September 1901 and presumably returned to England. The Breaker wrote a will the night before he died and bequeathed his Mauser rifle to Francis Morant of Brockenhurst Park, Hampshire, England. Thus he must have met Francis during his time in South Africa and discovered the address of the Morant family. It is not known if Francis received the rifle and there is no record of it. Francis, the second son, would not inherit anything of the estate so he went off to Canada and made a new life there. His son, Nicholas, became a very successful and much published photographer with the Canadian Pacific Railway.

The Morant family sold Brockenhurst Park mansion half a century later and the main building has been demolished, although the park still exists. Edward Morant and his family now live in Roydon Manor nearby.

4
Mrs Morant

The year 1881 saw Catherine Murrant and her son Edwin in seemingly secure positions. In early April the census taker found Edwin employed in his first job as a tutor at Silesia House School in Barnet, now north London, and Catherine at her post in Bridgwater. Tensions had grown, however, between Catherine and the master, Mr Winterson, which led to both leaving under a cloud in early 1882. Catherine took lodgings in Wembdon, near her husband's grave, just outside Bridgwater. Reports in the local papers, the *Western Gazette* and *Bridgwater Mercury* of him playing in four matches for the local rugby club, Bridgwater Alliance, in late 1882 suggest that Edwin was no longer working in Barnet. There are accounts in the same papers of the Australian recruiting agent George Randall lecturing in the local area trying to encourage more emigrants to go to Queensland and Australia. There is no trace of any compelling reason for young Edwin to have left his school post. There is no hint in the newspapers of criminal behaviour or evidence of card debts, expulsion from Dartmouth Naval College, of his running off with a ward of court, or being involved in racing scandals – as suggested by some authors – to cause him to leave his mother and sister and disappear off to Australia.

On 1 April 1883 Edwin Murrant stood on the dockside at Plymouth possibly wondering if 'All Fools Day' was an auspicious time to be embarking on such a journey. He was probably near the spot where a man of different character and integrity, Robert Mitchell Cochrane, had boarded a ship for Australia eight months previously; a man who would ultimately play a part in the Breaker's demise,

Edwin climbed the gangway and boarded the 2500-ton steamship, *SS Waroonga*. This gleaming vessel was owned by Gray, Dawes and Co, Glasgow and operated on their behalf by British India Associated Steamers Company taking emigrants to Australia through the Suez Canal, which had been opened thirteen years before. She had recently been launched and fitted out in Scotland and was on her maiden voyage. She had space for 53 saloon passengers and 1361 emigrants but for this voyage she was only carrying about 600 emigrants. Murrant is shown on the manifest under the category 'free', which meant a passage was granted by the colony of Queensland for someone who was in a category particularly required there, in his case this probably meant agricultural worker. Being eligible but unable to afford the full fare, he paid one pound for his passage and had to agree to reside in Queensland as contracted. It is not known if Catherine travelled to Plymouth to see him off, but he carried aboard a bible, probably given to her at her wedding and inscribed on the flysheet 'Catherine Murrant 1860'. A Charters Tower resident and friend of Daisy Bates, Helen Veal, took this to the editor of the *Northern Miner* in April 1902 after the news of the executions was published in Australia and enabled the newspaper staff to start to solve the puzzle of the Breaker's identity.

The maiden voyage was beset by problems. The *Queensland Times* on 7 June 1883 reported that between Aden and Colombo the *Waroonga* lost two propeller blades and had to put into Ceylon for repairs. Two days out of Colombo the high pressure piston rods were damaged and she had to sail for twenty-four hours under canvas before docking at Batavia in the Dutch East Indies for further repairs, which took fourteen days. En route for Australia she lost a further propeller blade two days out of Booby Island off the tip of Cape York. This island, named by Captain Cook and visited by Captain Bligh, is a small desolate isle which had a lighthouse to help seafarers navigate the treacherous Torres Strait and also served as a mailbox where crews could pick up and leave letters. A few miles further on was Thursday Island which served as a quarantine port and where the Breaker would have seen a small tropical paradise with reefs and palm trees. Chinese, South Sea Island and Japanese sailors manned the 200 pearling luggers operating out of there. When he stood on deck he would have felt the intensity of the sun burning his face. This small port was a regular stop for vessels trading between the east Coast of Australia and South East Asia. During the course of the prolonged voyage one woman and two men died and two children were born before the ship docked initially at Cooktown. Edwin finally disembarked at Townsville on 5 June 1883.

We don't know what happened when Edwin disembarked and his initial movements are unknown but shortly afterwards he appeared in the town of Charters Towers. This was about 80 miles to the west of Townsville and connected by a newly built railway. The town was at this time the second largest in Queensland with a population of about thirty thousand. It was stuck in the middle of nowhere, but the discovery of gold there a few years before definitely made it somewhere.

All that glisters is not gold but the attractions of the gold fields had made Charters Towers a vibrant, rollicking town full of prospectors and gold miners keen to find their fortunes and bar owners, con men and hangers-on eager to get a share of the new-found wealth. You can't eat gold and agricultural workers were in great demand in the area.

Although not yet 20 years old, Edwin had probably grown to his full height and we know from the prison record book at Pretoria prison in 1902 that he was just short of 5 feet 7 inches with grey eyes, brown hair and a prominent nose. Other descriptions suggest he was stocky and strong and this ties in with existing photographs. Apparently within a short time Edwin found a job at a large farm, Fanning Downs about fifteen miles outside town. There he met an Irish girl called Daisy O'Dwyer who later became better known as Daisy Bates. Daisy's part in the story is small but important because briefly she was his wife and technically remained so until his death. There was no divorce. Referred to by the more charitable as a romantic, Daisy was a fantasist and inveterate liar. Like Edwin Henry Murrant, she has managed to pull the wool over the eyes of many researchers and biographers. The *Australian Dictionary of Biography* falls down in its article on Bates and unfortunately many seekers of the truth have copied parts of the piece. The author gets the date of her birth wrong by four years, and her name at birth wrong. Her father, who ran a small leather goods and boot repairing business in Roscrea in Tipperary, probably does not fit the description of 'gentleman'. One sentence deserves special attention: 'Though applauded for the self-sacrifice of her welfare work, Daisy Bates had no illusion about her own motives which she privately identified with those that had previously impelled her to enjoy such sports as hockey, tennis and fox hunting.' Daisy was from an Irish family of modest means and probably never saw a hockey stick or rode to the hounds in her life and in her youth tennis did not exist. [1] She had reinvented her early days to give a hint of an upper class Protestant background that was a myth.

The marriage of Edwin Henry Murrant and Daisy May O'Dwyer in Charters Towers, was a rare transaction indeed, for it is one in which Murrant was the more honest party. Daisy's own story has her born Daisy May O'Dwyer in the village of Ballichrine, north of Tipperary in either 1861 or 1863. The certificate for her marriage on 13 March 1884 gives her birthplace as Glenacurra, Tipperary, and her age as 21. On this document her father is named as James Edward O'Dwyer, gentleman, and her mother as Marguerite Hunt. The woman Edwin Murrant married was actually born Margaret Dwyer at Roscrea, Tipperary on 16 October 1859. Her twin brother Francis died shortly after birth. She was baptised on 21 October 1859 at St Cronans Church in Roscrea. [2] Her father was James Dwyer, a shopkeeper who carried on business as a boot and shoemaker at No 2 Main

Street, and her mother was Bridget, the daughter of Michael and Catherine Hunt. Her parents were married in Roscrea in January 1856. She had two older sisters, Catherine, baptised on 3 August 1858 and Mary Ann, who was born on 25 November 1856, a younger brother, James, baptised 5 February 1861 and younger twin siblings, Anne and Joe. Mary Ann entered St Paul's convent at Selly Park, Birmingham in May 1874 under the surname of O'Dwyer and took her final vows as a nun in April 1879 becoming Sister Flavia. She worked as a school teacher in various parts of England and returned to die at the convent in March 1917. When she entered the convent she said she had been born in Roscrea and that her father, James, was a cattle dealer. He was indeed a cattle dealer in a small way and his son, also James, followed in this line of business. The Dwyers were not dirt poor and were a middling farmer family with a cottage, a few acres as well as thirty acres of leasehold land.

Her mother Bridget died of TB in February 1862 and is buried in the Protestant side of the cemetery of St Cronan's church Roscrea. James had to look after a young family and run his business. Luckily he had the support of Catherine Hunt, his mother-in-law and also employed a local girl, Mary Dillon, to help with the children. He married her in September 1864. James is described by some as an alcoholic. He might have turned to the bottle as a result of the death of his young wife. The pair set off for the USA, the raging civil war being no deterrent, the following year but James seems to have died en route and nothing more is known of him. Some say that Mary returned to Roscrea, but if that was the case there would be no mystery about where they went and what happened to James. The Hunt family farmed 77 acres at Ballycrine (three miles from Roscrea) and were comfortably off, but not rich.

The Dwyer children were brought up by various relatives and the girls were educated by the Sisters of the Sacred Heart at the Air Hill National School in Roscrea. The faded records for the school from 1871 list the Dwyer girls as pupils describing them as orphans residing in Main St and their religion as Roman Catholic. Margaret is first shown on the register in 1871. Given her age it is possible she was there earlier, but the register only runs from that year. In the growing panoply of religious villains none is more chillingly depicted than this order of nuns in the film *Philomena*. Girls were encouraged to follow self-denial and mortification of the flesh to get closer to God and were expected to do menial tasks to expiate their sins. In Daisy's time, however, it was probably a pretty normal school. The nuns, French and Belgian, were part of a teaching order founded in 1840 in France. The boys were educated elsewhere. Margaret is shown as missing a year at the school when she was 14 and when she was 18 and 19 she is shown as a monitor. Margaret was struck off the school records on 23 December 1879, by which time she would have been 20 years old and possibly employed by then as a pupil teacher. [3] Margaret might have been sent off to a family for a year when she was 14 to help look after children.

The Dwyer girls were lucky to receive a reasonable education and although the school concentrated on the usual three Rs, Daisy showed signs later in life of understanding French and also a familiarity with the classics of English Literature. She had a retentive memory and until the end of her life could recite English poetry at length including all twenty-eight verses of James Buchanan's *The Ballad of Judas Iscariot*. She could also dance an Irish jig to her own singing until well into her seventies. The nuns were probably preparing her to work as a governess.

How did it become known that Daisy Bates was in fact Margaret Dwyer? Firstly, she gave the names of her parents accurately at her marriage in March 1884 and also the county and country of her birth. She made an entry in a birthday book in 1948 at Streaky Bay, South Australia, where she was staying on 16 October 1948 'Daisy Bates aged 88, 1948' the day and month is correct even if the year is one out. Most revealingly, her niece, the daughter of her brother James, was able in later years to confirm the connection. Daisy's tombstone in Adelaide gives her age as 91 in April 1951 and this would make 1859 the year of her birth.

After leaving school both middle Dwyer girls subtly changed their names, possibly to rise above their station and marry well. The two girls had a reasonable education, good manners, beauty and spirit but they had been trained for a life of service, probably as governesses. Margaret reinvented herself as Daisy May O'Dwyer and became a voracious reader and romanticiser. She created an idyll of her childhood spent with her brother Jim where they lived in a large residence called Ashbury House, which actually exists but was not inhabited by the Dwyers. She wrote an unpublished poem about this fantasy, the second verse of which reads:

> Oh Ashbury House on the back of the hill where I was born and bred,
> And in childhood traced the thirty odd springs that made the wide river bed,
> And the little banks with their fairy flowers and fairy tenants too
> We saw them always, my brother and I, as we made ourselves fairies too...

Later in life Daisy told stories about meeting Queen Victoria, riding to the hounds, of a doting father who introduced her to the works of Dickens and took her to Dublin to meet his wealthy Protestant friends. She described accompanying the rich family of Sir Francis Outram on a grand tour of Europe (including meeting the Pope) as governess. This was all nonsense but over the years was believed by several biographers. By various means she had picked up and then communicated the subtle clues that indicated status in the society of rural Ireland.

Catherine was more successful and it was as Kathleen O' Dwyer that she wed Robert Brownrigg from Co Wicklow in 1882 in London. He was in the British Army, but died young leaving her with two daughters. She later married Capt Graves Chapman Swan and went to live in Jersey before embarking on a messy divorce case.

There is a gap in Daisy's life from 1879 when she left school. The daughter of her brother James later suggested that she went into service and a young man killed himself because of his unrequited love for her. She appears on the manifest of the SS *Almora* bound for Australia as a free emigrant leaving Plymouth on 22 November 1882 (she missed her sister's wedding) landing at Townsville on 15 January 1883. The *Almora* was a 2608-ton, 350-foot British India Steam Navigation (BISN) steamer that plied the Australian route after the opening of the Suez Canal. She paid £1 and promised to reside in Queensland. The minimum legal time was for three months and Daisy fulfilled her obligation in this respect. The terms for these passages were well advertised in British regional newspapers and there was an enormous recruitment drive to encourage young women to go to Australia. In steerage Daisy was under the orders of Matron Jane Chase, who strictly supervised the young unmarried female passengers.

The State Library of Queensland holds a shipboard diary [4] written by an unknown saloon passenger on this trip, in which Daisy is mentioned. The pages reveal an irrepressible spirit who came into conflict with the dour matron. The voyage on *Almora* started from Plymouth on 22 November 1882, thence through the Suez Canal on 6 December, departing Batavia 2 January and on to Townsville, where the single girls disembarked on 15 January. Daisy later wrote about this voyage suggesting she travelled first class and had a front row seat at the eruption of Krakatoa, which in fact occurred on 26 August 1883. [5]

At the end of 1882 the *Almora* put into Batavia in the Dutch island of Java, possibly to undertake the filthy task of coaling and take on additional stores. Six saloon passengers boarded for the final part of the journey through the glittering seas of the Dutch East Indies to Queensland. [6] Among them were two people of particular interest. The first was a gentleman, Mr J. C. Hann, scion of a well-known Queensland pastoralist family who farmed Maryvale Station about 100 kilometres from Charters Towers. Apparently he had earlier boarded a ship in Queensland to go south down the coast but woke up to find his ship heading north and had to continue on until the next stop at Batavia.

The other passenger of note boarding here was a merchant navy officer called Ernest Clark Baglehole. He was a young Englishman, born in April 1854 and christened shortly afterwards in a Church of England church in Deptford, south east London. Baglehole was apprenticed as a deck officer at a time when the British Board of Trade was trying to raise the standard of ships' officers and all British ships of a certain size had to have a quota of apprenticed deck officers. He received his second mate's certificate in March 1876 [7] and took up a career as a ships officer, initially coasting around Britain. Baglehole found time away from his nautical duties to get married, in 1881, to Jessie Rose in St Marks Church, Lewisham, Kent, now part of London's suburbia. Jessie was related to Ernest through his mother.

It is obvious that Hann and Baglehole enjoyed their trip and both became friendly with the single girls. Baglehole, who was employed by the British India Steam Navigation company (BISN) had no duties and was probably going to join a ship in Brisbane. James Hann had such charm that he was wined and dined by society in Batavia whilst waiting for a ship to take him south. Aboard the *Almora* his charisma extended to all the females, even breaking the ice with the fierce matron, Jane Chase. He remembered the ship with such fondness that he named his grand home in Victoria after the ship. Hann left the ship on arrival in Australia and went on to Victoria whilst Baglehole went on to Brisbane.

Daisy suggested, later in life, that she disembarked (as a saloon class passenger) and went to stay with the Bishop of Northern Queensland, the Right Revd Dr Henry Stanton, to whom she allegedly had an introduction. The *Australian Dictionary of Biography* also mentions that she went south to Berry, NSW, to take up an appointment as a governess, which would mean leaving Queensland and thus being liable for her passage costs. The local Australian papers often commented on the arrival of emigrant ships and usually made the point that most of the emigrants got employed quickly. In Daisy's case most of the single girls were indentured emigrants and were claimed on arrival by their new employers. It is possible that J. C. Hann was impressed by the feisty Irish girl and suggested she look for some form of employment at Maryvale, owned by the Hann family, 120 kilometres North West of Charters Towers, or at the neighbouring spread of Niall where his niece, Louisa Keppel and her husband lived. She may have been employed as a 'jillaroo', and would have learnt to look after horses and ride. In fact she was an accomplished horse woman already and as an affectation sometimes rode side saddle. Conditions at Maryvale were fairly sparse, and some time later Daisy managed to get employment at Fanning Downs Station, 20km from Charters Towers, [8] owned by Frederick Hamilton. Hamilton was assisted by his farm manager, an Irishman named Bernard Naughton. Hamilton, born in England, was a successful and enthusiastic breeder of horses and worked hard to improve the blood line of his horses whilst running a large station. Daisy was employed as a governess or something similar as the Hamiltons had ten children. She attracted interest amongst the young men of nearby Charters Towers and one in particular set his sights on her.

Charters Towers was a gold rush town, where the miner was king, money was abundant and the consumption of strong beverages was enormous. The town's newspaper was *The Northern Miner,* which is still published. The proprietor and editor was an Irishman who called himself Thaddeus O'Kane, who at some time in his career defamed most of the great and the good in Northern Queensland including Frederick Hamilton of Fanning Downs, who sued him for £100 for libel in 1881. Working for the newspaper as a journalist or possibly an accounts clerk was a young American named Arnold Knight Colquhoun. Needless to say, as is often the case with Daisy, neither of these men were who they seemed. Timothy O'Kane had left England fifteen years previously after he had accused the 79-year-old Lord Palmerston of adultery. He claimed the peer had seduced Margaret O'Kane, his wife, an erstwhile actress and demanded £20,000 in damages. The case was thrown out of court and declared to be an attempt at extortion. Timothy left swiftly for Australia on board the fast clipper *Norfolk* on 29 January 1864 before the case was finished, arriving in Melbourne. He adopted the bogus name of Thaddeus and eventually reached Charters Towers in about 1873, where he purchased *The Northern Miner.* This story gave rise to the quip in London: 'She may be Kane but is Palmerston Able?'

Colquhoun, who was madly in love with Daisy, was a drug addict. It is likely that his real name was Jeremiah Coffey and that he had worked for the Chinese Imperial Customs in 1874 as a third class tidewaiter (a customs officer who boarded ships on their arrival). If he was in China at all, he left quickly and there is no information on the Imperial Customs staff list about where this man worked or when he left. He could have picked up an opium habit there. He surfaced in Australia and ended up in Northern Queensland where his sister and brother-in-law lived. There is no trace in immigration records of his arrival under either name. There was a large Chinese community in the area and he possibly spoke a dialect of Chinese. His sister Helen Coffey had married an 'American adventurer' called James Hopwood Veal who certainly had worked in China.

Veal, like so many people in the story of Daisy and the Breaker, was bogus. He made out that he had been born in Portsmouth, New Hampshire in about 1853 and had sailed with the US Navy and ended up in China after jumping ship. In fact he had been born in Alverstoke, near Portsmouth, Hampshire, England, where the Breaker's father and uncles had also been born and it is highly likely that they knew, or knew of, each other. Veal was really James Long Veal, born in 1850. His elder brother was Robert Hopwood Veal who served in the Royal Navy. Veal did serve in the Chinese Imperial Customs, probably in Canton or Hong Kong and spoke Cantonese. He worked for a time in the Palmer gold field, where there were many Chinese, and was an interpreter.

Arnold Colquhoun had a falling out with his employer, left town and went to Townsville where he found employment as a clerk. This fell through so he returned to Charters Towers in late October 1883 to see Daisy and plead for his job back with O'Kane. He was certainly rejected by the latter and probably by the former. He went off to the local chemist and bought a large amount of morphine, which was easily available in those days, swallowed it and died. (Drugs such as morphine were treated casually then; the obituary for the well-known author Wilkie Collins, published in 1889, noted that he took on a daily basis more laudanum than would have sufficed to kill a ship's crew or company of soldiers.) *The Northern Miner* on 1 November 1883 published an account of his death. He left a note to John O'Kane (Thaddeus' son) and another to Daisy. At the inquest it was found that his death was due to a drugs overdose. The letter to Daisy was not published. The newspaper mentioned that drink excited him in an extraordinary manner and he suffered from pecuniary embarrassment: a rehearsal for the arrival of Daisy's next beau. There is evidence that she worked for some time as a domestic for the 63-year-old O'Kane and his wife Margaret.

The following year, 1884, Edwin Murrant, a well-spoken, well-educated young Englishman with a reckless streak and a sense of humour arrived in town. Eventually he arrived at Frederick Hamilton's Fanning Down station and was taken on as a horse boy at fifteen shillings a week. Hamilton had some very expensive horseflesh on his station and would not have employed unskilled labour to look after it. A horse boy had to ensure that his charges were put on good feed and water at night and be available for work in the morning. The station had a mixed bunch of horses including working horses, children's pet hacks, buggy horses and race horses. The station horses were grass fed and would have to be watched as there was little fencing in those days. After carrying out these duties there was also grooming, mucking out and saddling to be done. A horse boy was at the bottom of the food chain but there was no reason why he should not learn to be a skilled horseman.

Murrant and Daisy must have met whilst both worked at Fanning Downs. He would have come over as sophisticated, well read and educated and a good conversationalist and she would have spun her stories of high life in Dublin and London and fantastical European tours. The two frauds obviously fed off each other and agreed to marry perhaps with the blessing of the Hamilton family.

As the union was apparently of mixed faiths, the story goes that no clergyman would marry them; but Daisy was at this stage sometimes passing as a Protestant and Edwin was Church of England, so theoretically there was no problem. The two lovers took up the offer of James and Helen Veal to have the ceremony at their house in Plant Street, Charters Towers and the Veals signed as the witnesses on the marriage certificate. [9] Daisy probably knew them after her brief encounter with Arnold Colquhoun, who was probably Helen's brother. The local newspaper [10] suggests that the Roman Catholic priest, Father Peter Bucas, declined the invitation to officiate because it would have been a mixed marriage. Allegedly, Daisy was so hurt by this refusal that after the wedding she had nothing further to do with the Roman Catholic faith and became a critic of its influence in Australia and Ireland. In her old age she became ardently anti-Catholic and also an imperial patriot. From this date she was an Anglican; but a cynic might say it was because this gave more social opportunities.

The local Church of England curate, the Reverend Christopher George Barlow, later Bishop of North Queensland, took on the job, apparently for a fee of £5, to be paid when Murrant's remittance came through from England; an unusual example of the never-never. The marriage took place on 13 March 1885 with Murrant declaring himself to be twenty-one, though he was actually nineteen, and a gentleman. Daisy did not declare her position but *The Northern Miner* says that she had been a governess and at one time was the 'youthful housekeeper of a journalist in town'. The marriage was not legal because Murrant was under age whilst Daisy, possibly unknown to Murrant, knocked four years off her age and declared herself to be twenty-one. With all this deceit, what could possibly go wrong? She wore a cap and collar of Limerick lace and her bouquet and corsage were of white roses. *The Northern Miner* carried a report and a picture of Daisy in her wedding finery.

It is possible that Murrant had already lost his job at Fanning Downs because his occupation, 'gentleman', was a term suggesting that the person did not need an occupation – or was unemployed. Daisy gave no occupation. Some reports say that Hamilton allowed them to live in a cottage on the station, but if that is so, it was not for long. Prior to the wedding, Murrant had conned a Mr Lathbury, the owner of the Burdekin Brewery, to support him before his remittance from England arrived. Murrant was thus chronically short of money and on 16 April a warrant was issued against him, along with a mate George Palmer, for stealing over thirty pigs belonging to a Mr Reardon and also a saddle belonging to a

Mrs Brooks. Interestingly, he is described as E. H. Morant on the court documents although *The Northern Miner* calls him Murrant. This is probably an error by the court clerk because he had not used this name before. After a couple of remands, the cases came up and among those who deposed in the pig rustling case was Bernard Naughton, the manager at Fanning Downs Station and his son John. It must be assumed that Morant was no longer in employment or living on the station because Mr Hamilton, a pillar of the community, would not have supported a petty criminal living on his spread. This is borne out by Mary Jane Brooks, the aggrieved saddle owner, who mentioned that Morant had been living with her for a fortnight. [11] The magistrate dismissed both charges because no prima facie crime had been proved.

Murrant probably did not appreciate that in colonial Australia it was no easy matter to outreach the law. In Queensland in general, and Charters Towers in particular, the government had quickly established the rule of law. After the explorers, hard on the heels of the settlers came policemen and magistrates. The police force was ethnically uniform: if you were Irish and Catholic it was the career path for you.

A meeting was called at the Veal's Plant Street house to discuss the way forward. It had become apparent to Daisy and the Veals that Murrant was shameless. These discussions were aired in *The Northern Miner* in 1902 after news of the executions was published in Australia. Helen Veal went to the newspaper office carrying the bible with the inscription 'Catherine Murrant 1860' and with lots of other information to prove that Breaker Morant was in reality Edwin Henry Murrant. [12] Daisy apparently had said that if he continued along the path of lying and deceit then he could go his own way and she would go hers. Mrs Murrant acted throughout with considerable spirit and returned some jewellery to a Mr Deitz (presumably the ring) which had been purchased for her on the strength of the remittances which were always allegedly coming. The final decision at the meeting was that Daisy would leave her new husband, but if he came back to her, wherever she may be, within thirty months having changed his ways, she would have him back. Edwin H Murrant left Charters Towers to metamorphose, slowly but surely, into Henry Harbord Morant. Apparently, the last Daisy heard of him was that he had gone south with a mob of cattle.

Those who criticise Daisy for not getting a divorce before remarrying should remember that in England it was virtually impossible to divorce prior to the Matrimonial Causes Act of 1857; that increased the numbers from three cases prior to the Act to 300 the following year. Australian law was the same. This time was a period of energetic marital non conformity and marriage was treated flexibly. It is interesting there is no evidence in the

Charters Towers newspapers of 1902 of any sympathy for Morant in the town, despite his desperate end.

Daisy thus moved out of any part in the life of Breaker Morant. She drifted down to New South Wales and on 17 February 1885 she married stockman Hugh John (Jack) Bates at Nowra New South Wales in a bigamous marriage (though it can be argued the first one was not legal). It has been suggested that Daisy Bates had been employed as the governess to the Bates children, but that is unlikely as they were older than she was.

On 10 June 1885 she married, for the third time, Ernest Clark Baglehole (from the *Almora* at Batavia) in a Sydney suburban church. Ernest had gone back to sea and is shown on existing crew lists as second mate on the British India Steam Navigation (BISN) ship *Burwah* which was sailing around the East Australian coast in 1883. Strangely, on one voyage his birthplace is given on the crew list as Ireland. Later he appears on the list as fourth mate on a larger ship, the *SS Zealandia*, in 1884 and 1885, on the Sydney to San Francisco run. On the first journey he is described as Irish but subsequently English. Daisy produced a son on 26 August 1886 who was named Arnold Hamilton Bates. She effectively had little to do with him for the rest of his life and he ignored her [13]. The father of the child was probably Jack Bates but Ernest could have been. The fate of Ernest is obscure; he returned briefly to England and his wife produced a son in London in March 1887. [14] Sadly, the son, William Hillyard Baglehole, died in September 1887. In the 1891 census his wife is described as a widow and presumably she must have been told of her husband's death to describe herself as such, but there is no trace of his death in maritime or other records. He seems to have been working out of India as a second mate with BISN in 1887 and deserted his ship in 1889, either there or possibly Honolulu.

Although Daisy plays no further part in the story of Henry Harbord Morant, she became a famous figure in Australia. For the first fifty years of the twentieth century she became one of the best known and most controversial ethnologists and she undoubtedly put Aboriginal culture on the map. She lived at a small railway station on the Trans-Australia line in the middle of the Nullabor Plain effectively cutting herself off from 'normal' civilisation. She was awarded a CBE (Commander of the British Empire) in 1934 [15] for service to the welfare of Aborigines and was sufficiently interesting for the great Australian artist Sydney Nolan to paint her portrait in 1950. 'Daisy Bates Ooldea 1950' was shown in an exhibition at London's National Portrait Gallery in 2000 called 'Painting the Century 1900–2000, 101 Portraits'. Thus the old fraud had arrived and she would have been proud to be included in the greats of the twentieth century. She died in Adelaide in 1951 and is buried in the North Road cemetery there.

5

The Wilderness Years

Edwin Murrant departed from Charters Towers following his court appearance where he was acquitted of stealing pigs and the larceny of a saddle. [1] The magistrate, M. E. Atkins JP found there was no *prima facie* case established. Murrant was also up before the bench for disobeying a summons, but this was dismissed, and he was free to go on 24 April 1884. The summons had been served at his last known place of residence, which was given as Fanning Downs station, where he no longer lived. He was charged not as Murrant but as E. H. Morant and this was the first recorded time that he dropped the Murrant and become a Morant. He also quickly dropped Edwin, which probably did not sound sufficiently 'outback' for a bushman. After the case, he went back to Plant Street and following discussions with his wife and the Veals swiftly left town and probably never saw Daisy again.

It is not proposed, in this chapter, to give every station or small town where he might have spent a few days but to give the general flavour of his existence over the next sixteen years, particularly where primary sources exist. Some events are set in tablets of stone but many are written in sand. The advent of Trove, the digitization of early Australian newspapers has helped in the search but his travels over vast areas are mostly poorly documented. He seems to have moved slowly through Queensland and thence south. After leaving his new bride, it is said he ventured beyond the extent of the railway in 1882, to the town of Hughenden 200 miles to the north west. The residents of Charters Towers were not sorry to see the broad back of the petty criminal riding away, trailing a second horse behind and were uninterested in his destination so long as he was gone.

In the wake of Morant's execution *The Northern Miner* investigated and established some facts, publishing them in several editions in April and May

1902. Indicating he had already clocked up a few debts, *The Bulletin* on 17 May 1902 claimed that:

> Shortly after the marriage broke up, Morant went to Hughenden where it was alleged that he expectantly cabled a titled person in England for funds. The money, however, was not forthcoming. Fleeing from his creditors, he went on to Esmeralda Station, and after working there in a menial capacity on to Winton. [2]

Before rubber stamp technology had arrived in the bush, Pelican Waterholes, a town in the middle of nowhere had just changed its name when the part-time post master, Robert Allen, decided it was easier to write 'Winton', a suburb of Bournemouth, England and his birthplace, when cancelling stamps.

Eventually, Morant arrived in Cloncurry, doing odd jobs as a station hand. Having two horses enabled Morant to cover the great distances involved and he must have found intermittent work to fund his basic lifestyle. When financial conditions were dire, a man could survive by humping his swag and taking to the track. It was called 'going on the wallaby'. No wallabies necessarily wound up on a spit over the camp fire but it was a convention in the bush that swagmen calling on a station must be given some basic rations such as flour, meat, sugar and tea. In theory this was because they had come to work, but a true member of the wallaby brigade such as the Breaker often timed his arrival for sundown and disappeared at dawn. There were always men travelling around and in Queensland the distances are so vast that they sometimes would help themselves without asking.

Banjo Paterson published an anonymous poem about the itinerant swagmen in his 1905 book *Old Bush Songs*, of which the first verse reads:

The Wallaby Brigade

> You often have been told of regiments brave and bold,
> But we are the bravest in the land;
> We're called the Tag-rag Band and we rally in Queensland,
> We are members of the Wallaby Brigade.

Where Morant developed his riding skills has proved difficult to determine though it is believed that he had some skill before he came to Australia. The porter at Bridgwater workhouse left when he was still a boy and is shown as a cab proprietor in the 1881 census. He may have shown the lad the basics of working with horses, which of course would have been a much more common workplace skill than it is today. He also apparently had a connection with the veterinary officer in the West Somerset Yeomanry Cavalry and he could have had an input. Wild Exmoor ponies were often sold at St Matthew's Horse Fair at Bridgwater where members of the Hawkins family broke horses but no connection to Edwin Murrant has been found. There is no doubt however that whatever skill Morant had with horses was hugely enhanced in Australia. A fine horseman called Jim Keenan, president of the Australian Drovers and Overlanders Association for many years, claimed he schooled Morant in the finer skills of riding in Australia. He wrote before his death in 1935 to a friend, Bill Bowyang, of having tutored Morant over forty years before and that the Breaker 'was as game as they make them ... he was never a good horseman, and was a failure in scrub or mountain, but he was a wild reckless rider on a rough horse.' The truth of the matter is probably that his bravery allowed him to develop his basic skills on the job in the outback.

The Northern Miner on 25 April 1902 reported that in 1885 Morant had stayed at the Corella River police camp, having arrived from Cloncurry, a town which bears the name of the lovely Lady Cloncurry of Co Galway. Her friend Robert Burke, leader of the Transcontinental Expedition, had named the river after her. Burke apparently lodged with Frederic Charles Urquhart, a sub inspector in the Queensland Native Mounted Police. The Mounted Police was an aboriginal force from the south, led by white sub inspectors which, armed to the teeth, showed no great reticence in slaughtering their northern cousins. Urquhart was English, a former Royal Navy midshipman, a fearless rider who would throw his leg over the wildest brumby and show his men jumpers. He was also a published minor bush balladeer. He was a dark character who had come from the Overland Telegraph Department where he claimed to have worked with aboriginal people and knew some of their languages. He averred that in cases of outrage committed by blacks they must be dealt with promptly and firmly. This was a time when there was serious trouble in the area between settlers and the Kalkadoon people. Urquhart led a detachment of armed settlers and the Mounted Police against the Kalkadoon and the campaign culminated in a pitched battle in which many natives were slaughtered. The depravity of Urquhart's actions was rigorously concealed and is still a matter of embarrassment in Australia today. He went on to become the police commissioner for Queensland.

About this time the Breaker is said to have been at Grenada Station, where he broke in a few colts, jumping one of them, Hooper, 'over the paddock gate'. He then went to Quarmby before returning to the police camp and eventually found his way to Maneroo West of Longreach.

In 1887, he was admitted to Muttaburra Hospital on 25 May with sciatica and discharged four days later. In the details he gave, still existing in the hospital admissions register in the Queensland Archives, he said he was Harry Morant employed as a horse breaker at Maneroo Station. Claiming his birthplace as the picturesque little port of Lynemouth, Devon, he gave his mother's name as Catherine nee Hunt. This document also provides the first incarnation of his father as Edwin Morant, occupation, clergyman. This is probably the first time Morant is described as a horse breaker. William McMillan, the boss of the station, was on the admittance slip under 'on whose application'. The ride from Maneroo Station to the hospital was about 100 miles, which must have been a painful experience with sciatica. The admission slip perhaps provides some insight into the Breaker's mind in that he claims he had been in the colony for five years and he arrived on the SS *Potosi*. It is hard to understand why he should lie about the ship though it may have been somewhat prophetic in that 26 May 1887 was the last day this ship set off on the Australia run. Perhaps there lay some metaphorical severing of his links with his past in his untruth.

In April of the following year, 1888, Morant gave his address as Harding's Hotel, Muttaburra in regard to a matter in the Police Magistrates Court where he was a witness. On 16 June a poem signed by 'The Horse Breaker' appeared on page 925 in *The Queenslander*'s section of original poetry. This poem predates any known submissions to *The Bulletin* by a year.

Old Harlequin

Oh do you remember the first time I rode you,
The same day I roped you in Dufferem's yard?
One foot in the stirrup, I'd hardly bestrode you,
When down went your head bucking uncommon hard.

Old fashioned buckjumping, 'no pig jump' nor 'rooting';
Your tail was jammed tight 'tween your muscular thighs;
Your back is an arch. Lord how you went shooting,
Snorting and squealing up to the skies!

The day that we had you run in to be broken,
The stockmen all dubbed you 'as handsome as paint,'
You laid your ears back, and your eye was the token
The temper you owned was not that of a saint.

Five years ago since all hands on the station
Swore roundly they never had seen such a fall
As you gave me that day, when, without hesitation,
You got clear of your rider, your saddle, and all.

Hard and often you bucked, before you grew steady,
Or suffered your rider his stockwhip to crack;
And now after a spell you're uncommon ready
To shift any new chum who gets on your back.

There easy old man! Let me slip on your bridle
And stroke your slim neck, so glossy and brown,
Three whole month's spell, it's too long to be idle,
You may carry me quietly into the town.

Muttaburra
The Horsebreaker

This is almost certainly the work of the Breaker who had a horse called Harlequin and the name crops up in a poem 'The Nights at Rocky Bar' that was published by *The Bulletin* on the 28 May 1892. He wrote 'Who's Riding Old Harlequin Now?', published in 1897. Whether he got paid for this work or how much he received for his contributions to *The Bulletin* is not known. In 1897, Will Ogilvie received £2 6s for four poems he had sent to Sydney. At the time he was earning £3 per week as a supervisor, so writing was not particularly highly paid but that wasn't an entirely nominal sum.

In 1888, a warrant was put out for the arrest of the Breaker. He is described as 'being about 26, 5 feet 8 inches tall, stout build, brown hair and moustache, slight stammer in speech and boasts of aristocratic friends in England'. The description must have been accurate, down to the stammer, for on 24 December he was arrested at the small town of Dingo, put on a train and one week later appeared before the police court in Rockhampton as a bailee, charged with larceny of £10. Rockhampton at this time was the main port for the developing Central Queensland hinterland exporting wool and also gold from nearby goldfields. The case went to court and was reported in *The Rockhampton Morning Bulletin* on 5 January:

> The bench had before them this week a man named Harry Morant, to all appearances a well-educated, refined young fellow, who was charged with obtaining money by false pretences from Mr Samuels of Muttaburra. The accused complained 'it was a trumped up case brought against him by Samuels for the purpose of paying off a spite'.
>
> The magistrate, Mr Lukin: 'It does not say where the offence was committed. I shall have to remand you to Muttaburra'.
>
> Morant, defendant: 'I suppose it is no use my giving you any particulars of the case?'

> Mr Lukin: 'Not the slightest. All I have to do is remand you to Muttaburra.'
> Defendant: 'Very well, I was in Muttaburra with Samuels for a long time, and we had a disturbance. I suppose this is the outcome of it.'
> Mr Lukin: 'I cannot help it. You are remanded to Muttaburra.'
> The case was remanded to Muttaburra.
> Morant noted that this was where Samuels was and said that he would make it hot for that gentleman.

Whether Morant had made it 'hot' for him or not, on 19 January 1889, Harry Morant was brought up under arrest for obtaining money by false pretences having sold a horse to Mr Samuels of Forest Grove, 'for which he had already sold and given receipt for same to Mr J. H. Grimshaw'. Morant was found guilty and given three months with hard labour in Rockhampton Gaol.

In early 1889, the Australian press widely published news of the death of Lt Gen. Horatio Harbord Morant in late December 1888. In one Queensland paper there is a report both of the General's death and of Morant's court case. Soon after this, Morant started using the middle name Harbord, though he started writing seriously for *The Bulletin* in 1889 merely signing his rhymes with a'B'. Certainly by 1891 he was using the pen name 'The Breaker' and continued to do so from this time onwards. For the next ten years the Breaker submitted verse to *The Bulletin* and also to other newspapers but never became rich on the proceeds. Nor was he as highly regarded as some of his contemporaries such as Paterson, Ogilvie and Lawson. In 1894 he submitted a poem entitled 'Much a Little While', which was one of his best. However, he was accused of plagiarizing Robert Herrick, the great English poet.

Love me little, love me long:
Laggard lover sung such a song;
Rather, Peg, in other style,
Love me much – a little while.

If of old that minstrel knew
Maid so kissable as you
(Like you? There was never such!)
He'd have warbled, 'love me much.'

Since creation, never yet
Aught arose, but it must set;
Wayward Love at Time may flout,
But Father Time shall rub him out.

Brown-eyed, bright-faced Margaret,
Kiss me, whilst you're able yet!
Sweetheart, with the sunny smile,
Love me much – a little while.

It runs contrary to his normal style, but shows him as having some emotional depth. One South Australian reader complained it could not be by Morant because it was perfect!

Sometime after his release from gaol, he started to work for Morris Hawkins on the Ducabrook Station in the Brigalow country, west of Rockhampton. Hawkins was a Yorkshire man who bred horses for Cobb and Co and ran stagecoaches through Queensland and New South Wales. Known as 'Yorky', he and Morant became friends. Yorky's son, also Morris, wrote a 65-page memoir and described Morant's time on the station. He apparently lived away from the other stockmen and slept in a tent rigged up between a hayshed and the roundhouse. The round house was a custom-built building for breaking horses. In the hayshed Morant kept his weights, punch bags and other fitness equipment in order to keep in trim. Young Hawkins and his brother were frightened of the Breaker and kept out of his way, although occasionally he used to come into their school room to flirt with their governess. Young Morris Hawkins' description of Morant describes the darker side to his character. The way he attacked the black fellows in the round house and the fear that he inspired in the Hawkins boys show a sadistic side to him. Morris wrote that one of his favourite acts was to entice an unsuspecting 'blackfellow' into the round house where he trained the horses and put the gloves on him. When things got too hot for the aboriginal, he could not find the door until Morant had finished with him. He never got the same man in twice.

Whether in sadistic and violent mood or not, the love of literature Edwin Murrant had developed at the Royal Masonic Institution did not fall by the wayside in his transition into Harry Morant. In 2011, the librarian at the Royal Victoria Historical Society in Melbourne discovered a book, *Explorations in Australia* by John Forrest, published 1875, on a shelf in the library. The fly leaf inscription is 'Harry H. Morant Ducabrook Station'. It was said that the Breaker always had books in his saddle bags and this must have been one of them.

About this time The Breaker received an introduction to A. B. (Banjo) Paterson. He had obviously met Paterson's uncle, Andrew Barton, a Queensland grazier, and had made an impression on him, as he wrote to Banjo:

> There is a man going down from here to Sydney and he says he is going to call on you. His name is Morant. He says he is the son of an English

> admiral and he has good manners and education. He can do anything better than most people, can break horses, trap dingoes, yard scrub cattle, dance, run, fight, drink and borrow money, anything except work. I don't know what the matter with the chap is. He seems brimming with flashness. He will do any dare devil things as long as there is a crowd to watch him. He jumped a horse over a stiff three-rail fence one night by the light of two matches which he placed on the posts. [3]

This introduction served the Breaker well because in time he met many of Paterson's friends, particularly those writing for *The Sydney Bulletin* and also the hunting and horse racing set in Sydney.

The Bulletin, in which the lore of the bush was a recurring theme, became known as the bushman's bible. It was a weekly magazine and in its early years from 1880 onwards played a significant role in the encouragement of nationalistic sentiments. It was owned by J. F. Archibald who was born John Feltham Archibald but, like so many in this story, he adopted another name and became a faux Frenchman called Jean Francois Archibald. The Englishman as the foreigner, ever ready to undermine the Australian way of life, became one of his targets. *The Bulletin* fostered violently anti-British attitudes in the sheep shearers' hut, the gold miners' tent, beside the billabong and under the coolibah tree. Its pink cover was seen as far afield as New Zealand and it spread the derogatory new term, 'Pommy', almost certainly a word play on pomegranate/immigrant. By 1886, its masthead slogan was 'Australia for the White Man', and it had a brash right wing and republican flavour. It evolved, becoming a platform for young and aspiring writers and by 1890 it was the focal point of an emerging literary nationalism. Whilst hostile towards the old country, Archibald was an admirer and promoter of French culture, which made sense in his scheme: French culture was remote, did not threaten Australian ways and could be promoted as a counter to English influence. Reassuringly he went barking mad and was put in an asylum, although he later made a full recovery. A number of its contributors, later known as bush poets, have become greats of Australian literature. The Breaker became a regular contributor to *The Bulletin* and to other newspapers and journals.

The early 1890s was a time of considerable labour unrest in Queensland that led to the shearers' strike, but there is no newspaper report of Morant becoming involved. Surprisingly, temporarily overcoming his aversion to hard work, the Breaker turned to sheep shearing for a time and had a great friend called Samuel Foreman Nicker (Sam Nicker) who later described Morant's contribution to the labour unrest. A recent book, *The Bushman of the Red Heart,* by Judy Robinson, which is mainly about the Nicker family, mentions the Breaker peripherally. Though it can be assumed the Breaker knew he had a good berth with Yorky Hawkins and did not become deeply involved.

Although Harry Harbord Morant may have divorced himself from Edwin Murrant, others had not. *The Queensland Police Gazette* of 16 April 1892 carried an appeal requesting information as to the whereabouts of Edwin Henry Murrant. The description was correct, as were the details of his passage on the SS *Waroonga*. It suggested that he resided with Mr Hamilton of Townsville on landing, and that he was last heard of from Winton in June 1884, when he left with a mob of bullocks for Sydney. This appeal was instituted by The Revd Montague Stone-Wigg of St John's, Brisbane. Stone-Wigg later became the inaugural Bishop of New Guinea and it is assumed that Catherine Murrant had written to him. It is said that the Breaker wrote to his mother to say that he was working for Mr Hamilton, which he did at Fanning Downs, although not for long. Just as there is no trace of him ever mentioning his education at the Masonic School, there is no trace of the Breaker ever communicating with his family or even talking about his mother and sister except perhaps in oblique terms. He wrote a poem for *The Bulletin,* published on 10 December 1898 that was almost certainly referring to his mother, who was to die within the year. The Breaker had no Kitty (Catherine) to brush away the cobwebs.

Kitty's Broom

When Kitty glides into the room
There I contrive to stay.
And watch her while she with her broom
Sweeps all the dust away.

For bright-faced, slender Kitty's such
A comely sight to see,
She grasps the broom with magic touch
And waves it witchingly.

And with her white and shapely arms,
Where dimples love to play
She wields that magic wand and charms
Dull care – and dust – away.

All this life's care and sad concerns,
No longer darkly looms,
And shadow into sunlight turns
When Kitty 'does' the room

Along life's thorny path of gloom
I'd mend a cheerful way
Did heaven send Kitty with her broom
To brush the briers away.

The darker side of Morant's character, mentioned by Morris Hawkins, reappears in an amazing article in the *Sunday Times of Sydney* on 27 April 1902. The article is entitled 'Golden Hours with The Breaker'. It was written by Mina Rawson, a sort of Australian Mrs Beeton who was a very well-known writer and novelist. She told of an occasion when living in the Rockhampton area with her family in the 1890s when she hosted a large house party, one of the guests being Morant. She was very complimentary about him, but described how some months after the party she received a parcel of curios from him. Amongst them was a human skull fashioned roughly into a receptacle. Morant wrote that the skull was for her to use as a sugar bowl or tobacco jar. He claimed he had killed an aboriginal man for the purpose, taking care to select a man with a large skull. In the letter he also suggested that he and his friends had eaten the man at a bush camp. He wrote 'Don't give us away, he died easy and life is still sweet so, yours sincerely The Breaker'. Mina Rawson was well respected throughout Australia and it would have been completely out of character for her to have made up such a story. What is truly shocking to modern sensibilities is not only the fact that this story was published at all but the matter of fact way in which the story is related. Later Mina Rawson went to live in Wiltshire, England, with her new husband, Colonel Ravenhill and the same story, but with greater detail, was published in the *Warminster and Westbury Journal* in October 1904. Shortly afterwards she returned to Australia to resume her writing career.

After working at Ducabrook for some time, Morant went south (possibly with cattle) to New South Wales, probably to the cattle yards at Bourke. He had spent several years in what can be called *Waltzing Matilda* country, it being the area that his newfound friend Banjo Paterson knew well and immortalised in the song. The Breaker worked around Bourke, Walgett and Parkes (at Nelungaloo station). At this time, in the early 1890s, he cultivated Banjo Paterson and visited Sydney more than once. He wrote a letter to Paterson:

> Had an English letter the other day from an old schoolfellow who is presently yachting in the Hebrides to put in time ere stag-hunting commences in Devon. Stag-hunting starts this week there. How I hate this Brigalow desert sometimes! Thirty years next Christmas, but feel

> fifty! Would like a whole open season, well carried in Leicestershire, and wouldn't growl at a broken neck at the finish. A better lot than dreary years in the bush with periodic drunks!

So the Breaker would be in the pink in hunting pink back in the old country? It's clever and quite convincing posturing. In between trips to Sydney, after driving cattle to Southern markets and sojourns to the Hawkesbury and Richmond districts, he went back to the bush and most of this time is chronicled in letters he wrote around 1895 to 1897, now in the Mitchell Library in Sydney.

In the mid-1890s the Breaker met and socialised with the young Scot Will Ogilvie, who, like him, was a contributor to *The Bulletin*. Ogilvie, five years younger than the Breaker, wrote under the name of Glenrowan and is considered on a par with Banjo Paterson and Henry Lawson as a poet. Like the other two, he received the accolade of having a volume of his work published by *The Bulletin*. The Breaker's work lacked the emotional depth of the other three and never achieved the same distinction.

Ogilvie and Morant were great mates for a time despite their widely differing personalities and worked together on several locations near Parkes and Nelungaloo. Ogilvie realised that many people were repelled by Morant at times and when drunk he could be a filthy, loathsome animal but when sober he presented a polished cultured manner and could mix in any society. There was always the dark side ready to come to the fore, which would ultimately lead to his downfall. He described the Breaker as 'a man who would do anything for a friend and generous to a fault. If he had any money it was yours as well as his, and as he seldom had any, yours was his if he could get it.'

Whilst at Nelungaloo they were joined by another *Bulletin* poet, Gordon Tidy, who wrote under the pen name 'Mousquetaire' and like the Breaker was accomplished but limited. Tidy got a job as a tutor on a station and when that came to an end he became editor of *The Western Champion* at Parkes. The three of them often drank together causing high spirited mayhem and more than once ended up in the newspaper offices, late at night, helping Tidy produce the Monday edition of the paper.

In 1897, whilst living in Parkes, he met Sam Cohen, a cattle buyer from Bathurst for whom he would work for a short period. According to a Bushveldt Carbineer (BVC) Trooper Hameline Glasson, who lived on a property called Godolphin, Morant worked on the adjacent property, Willow Cottage at Byng near Orange. When he joined the BVC, Glasson was a prolific letter writer and one wonders why he never mentioned the famous poet when he wrote home. However, Glasson would later write that some of his letters must have been confiscated by the BVC officers, particularly those which mentioned what was going on around Fort Edward in South Africa.

The life of a rolling stone and escaping creditors began to pall and in the late 1890s the Breaker adopted a more sedentary existence in the Hawkesbury area. During this time he wrote for *The Richmond and Windsor Gazette*. Besides producing verses for *The Bulletin,* Morant had already contributed to other publications including *The Pastoralist's Review, The Orange Leader, Coonamble Independent* and *Walgett Spectator.* He is often to be found in the town gossip column, several times for falling off his horse, and was also acknowledged as a contributor. On 30 April 1898 there was a short piece: 'Mr A W Janker, composer of the song *I was dreaming* is now hard at work at an opera for which Mr Breaker Morant is writing the lyrics. Mr Janker has already set one of Mr Morant's old *Bulletin* songs to music entitled *When the moon rose round and white.*' Whether this venture ever came to fruition is not known.

In late 1896, he and Will Ogilvie cleared an open space at Bogan Gate near Parkes, NSW, and created a polo pitch. The Breaker had taught Will and a few others to play polo and the ground adjacent to the Bogan Gate Hotel (officially the Selectors Arms) became the scene of the first unofficial polo international between Great Britain and Australia. This was sponsored by Victor Foy whose family ran a large Sydney Department store and he put up a liberal purse for the winners in the pub. The captains were Foy and Morant and the match was seriously contested with Great Britain ending up the winners. Ogilvie wrote a piece for *The Windsor and Richmond Gazette* published in 6 February 1897 that described how 'The Breaker bathed in gore went sailing through the scrimmages more fiercely than before.' Banjo Paterson wrote a poem entitled *The Geebung Polo Club* that undoubtedly describes the same event.

Shortly after the match Ogilvie wrote a poem, now in the Mitchell Library, Sydney for the *Bulletin*: [4]

When the Breaker is Booked for the South
He will leave when his ticket is tendered
A bundle of debts I'm afraid –
Accounts that were many times rendered
And bills that will never be paid;
Whilst the tailor and riding boot maker
Will stand with their thumbs in their mouth
With a three-cornered curse at the Breaker
When the Breaker is booked for the South.

This poem does not refer to South Africa, as many believe, because it is far too early but possibly to an occasion when Victor Foy took a horse to the Melbourne races along with Will and the Breaker. *The Bulletin* did not publish the poem for the good reason that it was libellous and having just been bitten by two costly suits it did not want another one.

During this time Morant was mixing periodically with the Sydney hunting set, but lacking the financial resources, he was always on the fringe. Nevertheless he was educated, spoke well and could dress properly for the occasion, so was accepted at the hunts, gymkhanas and other events in Sydney.

There are several reports in the Sydney and local papers at this time of the activities of the hunting crowd of which the Breaker was part. *The Windsor and Richmond Gazette* reported on 16 July 1898 a jolly day enjoyed by the hunt in the local area. This involved coming in by train from Sydney, a good lunch and then loading the hounds and horses on the train and back to town. The names of those taking part would become familiar later: Lieutenant Colonel Airey who was to command the New South Wales Bushmen; the Dangar family, whose son Henry Phelps Dangar was a 13th Hussar and proposed Captain Percy Hunt for membership of the Cavalry Club in London; Major Thomas, another Bushman and later defence counsel for Morant in South Africa; Major Lenehan, a prominent Sydney solicitor who would become commander of the Bushveldt Carbineers in the Boer War – and of course Mr Harry Morant.

By 1897 Morant was still drinking heavily and the days of racing horses, driving cattle, scamming and dodging creditors were taking their toll. He told Paterson that he tried to go 'home to the land of my forefathers and feed on fatted calf', but was unsuccessful in getting passage as a deckhand on the SS *Oronsay* and could not afford the cheapest single fare of £25, an impossible sum for a man with his dissolute lifestyle to accumulate. He probably never knew that his wife had made it back to England, around Cape Horn, four years before on a three-mast barque, the *Macquarie* of 1867 tons; according to her in first class, but in reality as a governess to a Dr Hansen's son.

A well-known Queensland character H J W (Bull) Harrington put his memories of Morant on paper in 1957. Harrington worked with the Breaker casually in 1897/98 and also saw him in South Africa. He started out as a stock dealer in western NSW and ended up a very wealthy man as a Queensland grazier and investor. He said that Morant liked horse work but didn't take to manual work. He was a good horseman, game as anything on young colts. He didn't stop long at anything and would make for the city and blow his cheque. He was well known as a good horseman in all states and he was always on the move, always in demand and as a horseman he stopped at nothing. In camp he would get a bit merry and make up funny rhymes about people and make everyone laugh. He was of medium build, wiry, with brown hair. He was well known and seemed to have plenty of connections, being an English gentleman type when he wanted to be and would be heard of appearing at, say, a hunt club ball. [5]

Although the Breaker's career was generally losing its lustre, 1897 brought Morant's greatest moment. Tales of his riding skills were legion, but at the Hawkesbury Show he rode the outlaw horse Dargin's Grey. This horse, originally named Misty, was bought by Arthur Dargin, who had been searching for an outlaw. Morant backed himself for big money (probably not his) and some even bigger side bets were laid. Dargin specified that no water was to be applied to the saddle (wet saddles offered more grip) and if the horse fell all bets were off. However, if Morant could remount in the event of a fall, that was allowed. This ride was reported in full in *The Windsor and Richmond Gazette* on 15 May 1897 under the heading of 'The Buck Jumper':

> Dargin's Grey, the horse that slung the Danderloo rough riders from the Bogan, and thirty two other crack riders at the various shows in the colony, was brought to the Hawkesbury Show on Friday, to give an exhibition of his bucking powers – with a well merited reputation as an outlaw. The animal is an eighteen-year-old rough looking grey, but very muscular, yet to look at him one would hardly think he had a buck left. However he was successful in sacking one of his riders and another took such a grip of the horse's head that it was impossible for the horse to buck. Then Mr H. H. Morant (otherwise 'The Breaker', a frequent contributor to this Journal) without any ado got astride the grey horse, amidst a chorus of 'him ride, a newspaper johnny – him sit a buck, I hear it'll be an inquest, sure as eggs', and many similar remarks from incredulous onlookers. Evidentially they did not know about The Breaker's riding capabilities, though his pluck was in evidence anyway, the horse was successfully ridden by Mr Morant and he was deservedly awarded the Society's prize for the best exhibition of horsemanship. The ovation he received from the occupants of the grandstands and the throng of people about the grounds showed how popular was his victory over the hitherto unbeaten Dargin's Grey. Mr Morant lost both his stirrups after the first few bucks but seemed to sit very comfortably in the saddle whilst the horse gyrated and whizzed around like a bunch of rockets. Many people hereabouts who only know the rider as a rhymer expected to see a heavy

> and precipitous fall but one or two of the Breaker's Queensland mates who were present knew it would take something to shift him from the saddle. An old drover's remark 'he'll ride him alright', was well justified. The grey horse was a bad one and the sudden tumble he gave to the rider who preceded the Breaker encouraged him to do his utmost to dislodge our contributor who gave the outlaw his head and allowed him to buck hard and fast.

It should be remembered that Dargin's Grey was, and still is, a legend amongst the buck jumping community. Morant did not just ride him for eight seconds as they do in contests nowadays, but rode him to a standstill. The horse had been ridden before by at least four riders including Arthur Dargin, but the Hawkesbury ride marks Morant out as one of the great Australian buck jumpers. The Breaker probably made a lot of money – some say the committee put up £50 – from his ride and also through side bets, but no doubt it was soon frittered away. A later report, which appeared after his death in *The Narromine News and Trangie Advocate* of 17 October 1902 stated 'The Breaker was carried shoulder high all over the ground. A collection was taken up and a good sum realised but when offered to Morant he smilingly said "give it to the hospital".'

Hero or not, there were comments about his horsemanship in the press. One notable one [6] appeared in the local paper:

> As announced last week Mr Harry Morant (The Breaker) met with an accident and suffered the dislocation of his right shoulder. This is not the first occasion on which Mr Morant has met with a similar mishap, for the unlucky shoulder of his has been broken or dislocated twice before whilst the escapes he has had from total annihilation in consequence of frequent falls from his horse have been legion. The only wonder is that he lives to tell the tale.

His doings were always good to fill a few lines in the local paper and on 15 October 1898 this was published, possibly in the expectation that he was going for good: 'Mr Harry Morant (The Breaker) left Windsor last week for the back blocks. The Breaker possesses a great gift of song and during his stay in this district he wrote much that was in excellent taste. Eccentric to a marked degree he is what his circumstances and nature made him and he carries away with him, amongst others, many kindly thoughts.'

Much of the story about the Breaker depends on daring exploits on horseback and other than Dargin's Grey there are only a few printed references. However, one of the most famous was reported in the loyal *Windsor and Richmond Gazette* of 18 June 1898:

> Harry Morant, The Breaker, was last week jumping his horse Cavalier over a four foot rail filling a gap in the fence at the rear of the old Racecourse Hotel, Clarendon (Windsor NSW district). The horse swerved and going too fast to stop, cleared the 7 foot palings. The horse is a five-year-old gelding bred by Freedom out of Clara, an imported trotting mare owned by the late Andrew Town of Hobartville. The jump was done in the presence of Mr Kelly of Clarendon and some half dozen others and the measurement was well authenticated. The fence is a ti-stake one such as Chinamen usually erect to protect their gardens.

The Breaker's name was remembered by old timers for many years after his death, and as late as 1920 *The Grenfell Record and Lachlan District Advertiser* carried a story of his exploits:

> A reminiscence of 'The Breaker' has disappeared with the removal of an old 4ft 3ins gate from the Royal Hotel, Coonamble. Long before the Boer War, Morant with a number of companions was enjoying himself in bush fashion in the bar room of the hotel when the ability of his horse as a hurdler was questioned. Morant offered to take the horse over the gate of the hotel yard at night – it was as dark as pitch. The wager was accepted and, placing a candle on each of the posts, Morant added another incident to his long list of dare devil escapades by clearing the top bar with inches to spare.

Around 4 November Morant was charged at Penrith with being drunk and disorderly at Springwood but the summons was not served. The Breaker decided to depart. The local paper in Windsor maintained an interest in his activities. Just before Christmas 1898 it announced he had got as far as Gunnedah and had written sending his Windsor friends the compliments of the season.

The paper mentioned he had written a song *In the Sighing of the Pines* that was in a Christmas annual that could be obtained from the *Gazette's* office. On 7 January 1899 it retransmitted from the *Merriwa Standard* the news that 'Mr. H. H. Morant, better known as "The Breaker," was in Merriwa on Saturday last, enjoying life out in the open on a droving trip. This talented individual has travelled all over the inland parts in his time and lately had a long spell at Windsor.'

Some suspicion has fallen on Harry Morant in relation to a horrific incident of rape and murder that occurred during this trip. John Meredith, author of *The Breaker's Mate,* has suggested that the perpetrator of this crime may have been going under the name of Thomas Day, a mysterious character who appeared in the area shortly before the crime and left shortly afterwards. Meredith suggests that Thomas Day was in fact Harry Morant, as no records seem to exist for Thomas Day. Day was also known to carry books around with him and to read at night, as the Breaker did. Morant's movements were hazier at the time Meredith wrote his book; but the advent of digitised newspapers on the Trove website have made it easier to piece together both Morant's and Day's movements.

The Gatton police had questioned Day in relation to the murders and he was detained by them until the morning of 30 December 1898, presumably near Gatton. The newspaper recorded: 'A man named Thomas Day was interrogated by the police on Thursday night, and detained until yesterday morning, when the account given of his doings on Monday was found to be satisfactory.'

So Thomas Day was near Gatton on the morning of 30 December 1898 and Morant was in Merriwa on 31 December 1898. The distance between Gatton and Merriwa is about 500km. It would have been impossible for Morant to cover 500km in one day and therefore he and Day could not be the same person. In any case it appears that the police did not consider Thomas Day to be responsible.

The Australian mentioned a week later he was on the road home to Windsor. Morant arrived back in Windsor on 16 March 1899. After around three months back in Hawkesbury Morant seems to have bitten the bullet and left town since the *Windsor and Richmond Gazette* announced on 8 July that 'The Breaker is at present in Melbourne on his way to the Old Country.' If Morant was seriously intent on returning to England, he failed.

On 13 April 1900 the *Windsor and Richmond Gazette* announced 'the existing doubt as to whether Harry Morant has really gone to South Africa, we can now set at rest on the best evidence, a postcard from 'The fighting Lines'. The few hurriedly scrawled words are characteristic of the Breaker. He mentions casually that over here one has the consolation of a speedy exit to paradise. Later on September 1901 it published a piece on Admiral Morant announcing that ' Admiral G M Morant, father of Mr H Morant, who has been superintendent at Pembroke yard and from 1892–1895 was Admiral Superintendent of Chatham Dockyard, England, has retired after 64 years of meritorious service.'

In 1899 The Breaker was thirty-five and moving towards forty, and feeling it. Pining for his native West Country and perhaps aware that his mother was near death, the years of dreary drunken time in the bush were grinding him down. In his sober moments he was no longer the-devil-may-care horseman, for he now needed a stiff drink before tackling a hard ride. Essentially, by mid-1899 Morant was destitute; his clothes shabbier than before, his drinks longer, his morale lower and his debts higher. Since he had little or no intention of paying them, the latter may have been of small concern unless his creditors were hard on his tail. The previous year, his best, he had had ten verses published. He writes a last verse to *The Bulletin*, 'Departing Dirge' bidding sad farewell to all his friends and to the one he treasures most of all – his horse. This appeared in the *Bulletin* on the 5 August 1899 and in the *Windsor and Richmond Gazette* a week later.

Girls in town and boys out back,
I've rolled up my little pack,
And on June's chilly wintry gales
Sail from pleasant New South Wales,
Ere I go-a doggerel song
To bid the whole caboose 'so long!'

Saddle gear and horses sold
Fetched but scanty stock of gold –
Scanty!! Yet the whole d-----d lot
Publicans and Flossies got.
Since I in this country landed
Ne'er before was I so 'stranded'

Now I'm leaving Sydney's shore
Harder up than e'er before
A keen appetite I feel
To taste a bit o' British veal;
And let's trust, across the foam
They have the fatted calf at home.

From Duns and debts (once safe aboard)
Pray deliver me, Oh Lord!
Here's the burden of my song.
'Good bye, old girl! Old chap, so-long'
Hardest loss of all I find.
To leave the good old horse behind.
So-long 'Cavalier!'

After eighteen years perhaps the eastern states had grown tired of the Breaker too. His stories of having just been robbed or waiting for a cheque were wearing a little thin. In any case the Breaker set out to South Australia, probably by train, and made acquaintance with some English settlers in the Renmark district, about 200 miles north of Adelaide up the Murray River. Legend has it that he found employment with the Cutlack family who were tenant farmers on Paringa station. This is probably not correct. F. W. Cutlack emigrated from England in 1891 and ended up in Renmark. He apparently tried his hand at manual labour and then became an agent for a steamship company and also did the books for various companies in the area. In 1893 the Chaffey Brothers, Canadian irrigation engineers who founded Renmark's fortunes, went bankrupt and the future looked bleak. Frederick William Cutlack called a meeting of local inhabitants and proposed that the local fruit farmers should found a co-operative and continue trading. Cutlack was voted secretary, a post he held for over 20 years. In 1907 the Renmark Fruit Packers Association became the Australian Dried Fruit Association and shortly afterwards appointed Frank McDougall to oversee it. In 1915 he married Cutlack's daughter Joyce and over the years grew the business impressively. Cutlack became a JP and was a man of substance in the town until he died in 1952. He also started a lending library in the co-op building and employed his young thirteen-year-old son, F. M. Cutlack, as the library assistant.

Young Cutlack published the book *Breaker Morant – A Horseman Who Made History* in 1962 when he would have been 76. Perhaps his memory was fading since some of his assertions are contradicted by newspaper accounts of the time. He obviously met Morant in town, possibly in the library, the Breaker being a voracious reader. The Breaker was introduced to an old settler who ran an orange orchard, Colonel Morant. Colonel May Allen Morant had served many years in India and was renowned in the region for his great kindness and courtesy. He was hospitable to the Breaker. Never one to miss an opportunity the wily Breaker suggested to the Colonel that they were relatives. The Colonel was probably a distant relative of the English Morants, but he was certainly not a brother to the Admiral and, of course, he was not a relative to the Breaker. Like many others, Colonel Morant was conned by the fantasist, liar and socially adept stranger he had befriended and whose familial connections were totally contrived.

Just before Christmas 1899 the Breaker published a brief poem in *The Critic* on 16 December 1899 and this was probably his last published Australian work.

Wattle v Mistletoe

At Christmas time, with Cousin Kate,
He helped the hall to decorate,
'What shall we use, sweetheart, d'ye know
In place of good old mistletoe?

That roguish berry doesn't grow
Upon these Austral shores, you know,
And in its place say what'll do?'
And Kitty echoes 'Wattle do'
'Will wattle do'? She whispered 'Yes,
Since there is no mistletoe, I guess
On Austral shores a lot'll do,
As we – and make the wattle do'

The Breaker

At the start of the Boer War, the requirement for soldiers was widely advertised and publicised. Morant rode his horse into the upstairs bar of the Renmark hotel (now called The Breaker Bar) and then set off excitedly on Boxing Day 1899 with some friends to Morgan, the railhead for Adelaide, to join up. *The South Australian Register* reported that: 'Harry Morant and five of his Renmark Defence Rifle club mates set out towards Adelaide by special coach via Morgan to volunteer for the second contingent bound for Transvaal.' Not surprisingly they all passed the medical examinations, shooting trials and finally a riding examination. It was at this stage that the Breaker gained the nickname 'Buller', having more than a passing resemblance to Sir Redvers Buller, one of the senior generals at the front.

The five Renmark boys were Henry Balfour Ogilvy, William Cuttle, Herbert Fetch, who had served in India in the Indian Defence Rifle Corps, Frederick Solly-Flood, who had served as an officer for over ten years and Ramsay Nutthull, another who had been in India. Ogilvy had four brothers who all served in the war. Their family farmed 2,500 hectares at Paringa where Morant seems to have worked as a stockman and apparently asked if he could accompany the party to Adelaide. Morant had appeared in Renmark in 1899 looking for work. Meeting Henry Balfour Ogilvie [7] and his brother, Walter, both Irishmen, Morant was soon taken on by the brothers. Shortly afterwards Walter left and went to manage a station in

Victoria. Hard times had fallen on the area due to drought in 1898–99 and the brothers had lost £20,000 on their cattle venture.

It could have been that the Breaker's motive for enlistment was patriotism, but more probably the war seemed to him to be some sort of a miracle. At a time when his fortunes and his spirits were at their lowest, here was a chance of glory – and a free passage to England. On 13 January he was enlisted into the second South Australia contingent as number 37 along with Victor Newland, number 58 and number 73, John Morrow. Newland was later to witness his execution in Pretoria, and Morrow was the warder for his last night.

The month of January was spent in preparation. There was still time for fun and the Adelaide Polo Club challenged the contingent to a game. A team was raised and dubbed the Geebung boys and *The Adelaide Evening Journal* of 22 January 1901 reported a win for the Geebungs and included a couplet:

> But their style of playing polo was irregular and rash –
> They had mighty little science but a mighty lot of dash

Whilst in Adelaide, the contingent was entertained by the Governor and his wife. In March 1902 Lady Audrey Tennyson wrote to her mother expressing the shock of the people at the events in South Africa. [8] She mentioned a young Mr Morant, cousin of the Brockenhurst Morants, their friends: 'I remember very well talking to him up here, a very jolly wild sort of fellow, immensely popular and very amusing – but regular dare-devil sort of nature.' Maybe she checked the silver after he left.

The South Australian Register on 27 January 1900 published the names of all those with the contingent and a pocket biography of each one. According to the Register the Breaker was 'the son of Vice Admiral Morant of the United Services Club in London, who had served in the West Somerset Yeomanry and Cavalry and who was born in Devon on 9 December 1870'. He was 'a member of the Sydney Hunt Club and single'. All wrong of course except his birthdate is correct, although he knocks six years off his age. 9 December does connect him to Edwin Murrant. After two weeks, he sailed, as a lance corporal, aboard the transport *Surrey* for South Africa. The New South Wales boys were already on board quartered aft, the South Australians were accommodated on the portside leaving space for the West Australians, who would be loaded at Perth in the forward 'tween' decks with the horses stabled aft, a combined muster of men of 341.

Shipboard rivalry among the groups manifested itself in literary contributions to two on-board publications commented on by the *Adelaide Observer* on 7 April 1900. *The Vedette* was produced by the South Australians, to which the Breaker contributed, whilst its rival *The Reveille* was published by the West Australians. The final complete *Vedette* was purchased by the skipper, Captain McGibbon, for £3 7s with all the signatures of the South Australian contingent within. Before disembarkation the light-hearted insults between the two publications ended with *The Reveille* being subject to a libel action by the publishers of *The Vedette* for comments made about Corporal Morant.

As Morant sailed away Australia seemed to be defining itself in both politics and literature. The self-image was of individuals facing great odds with swagger. This image of the self-reliant bushman was fostered most of all by the literature of the 1890s, in particular that of Henry Lawson, Banjo Paterson, Will Ogilvie and Breaker Morant. In due course Breaker Morant would generate a further national myth, that of the sacrifice of Australian soldiers in the name of the Empire, a charge which was to be repeated at Gallipoli. His faults were freely admitted, but the Breaker, like Ned Kelly, would become a hero.

The South Australians landed at Cape Town on 23 February 1900, all on board being awestruck by the beauty of Table Mountain and the might of the Royal Navy anchored beneath. Before leaving Australia Morant had jokingly claimed, 'Ladysmith will not be relieved till we get to South Africa.' The Second Contingent had been in Cape Town two days when news of the relief of Ladysmith came through. By 6 March the contingent had reached the inland town of De Aar. Then, having trained and collected additional horses, they became part of General Roberts' drive to Pretoria. In his written statement to the Courts Martial, the Breaker mentioned that he was in the South Australian second contingent for nine months. In March 1900 he carried despatches for the flying column to Prieska under Colonel Lowe. This episode occurred when there was a rebellion amongst Boers in a North Cape area and troops had to be diverted to quell it. By all accounts some hard riding was done but the squadron managed to bring their horses back in fair condition to De Aar. After returning to the main advance on Bloemfontein, the contingent took part in the engagements at Karee Siding and Kroonstad and other events with Lord Roberts until entry into Pretoria. He said he was at Diamond Hill and then was attached to General French's staff, Cavalry Brigade, as war correspondent with Bennet Burleigh for the *London Daily Telegraph*. He accompanied that column through Belfast and Middleburg to the occupation of Barberton, after which he went home to England. Morant's statement concurs generally with what happened to the contingent.

At the latter end of the campaign, the South Australians held posts around the east of Pretoria and by mid-June their time was up. They were fully paid on 31 July and most went south and returned to Australia in October. Morant's luck at this time is described by a colourful character named Colonel Joseph Maria Gordon [9] who at the time was in charge of South Australian Forces in South Africa. He details in his book how he was having lunch in the Pretoria Club with Bennet Burleigh, the *London Daily Telegraph* war correspondent, who remarked that he needed a despatch rider. Gordon, seeing Morant coming across the square, whom he also knew as 'Corporal Buller' and who had sailed over to South Africa on the same ship, recommended him for the post. His period of enlistment having expired, Morant was able to accept the offer.

Burleigh, like many associated with the Breaker, was not quite what he seemed. Having left Glasgow, he changed his name from Burley. He had served in the Confederate Forces in the American Civil War and had a brief career as a pirate, but he was a good journalist. The avuncular Burleigh and Morant hit it off at once and stayed together until the notorious night in the Mount Nelson Hotel, after which they went separately to England.

Morant had had a good war and his South Australian commanding officer, Lieutenant Colonel C. J. Reade, wrote him a fine farewell letter and recommendation:

> My Dear Morant,
> There seems to be an immediate probability of the S.A. regiment returning either to Australia or going to England, so I hasten to send you a line wishing you *Au Revoir.* I desire to wish you most heartily every success in your future career, and to express my entire satisfaction with your conduct while with the South Australians. Your soldierly behaviour and your continual alertness as an irregular carried high commendation – and deservedly – from the whole of the officers of the regiment. I trust that in future we may have an opportunity of renewing our pleasant acquaintanceship. [10]

On 10 July [11] L/Cpl H Balfour-Ogilvy, one of Morant's Renmark mates and his employer, wrote:

> Morant has just returned from a spell in Pretoria looking very fit, smart and well. He has secured a commission in Baden-Powell's Force, to be raised at the end of the war and is trying to get into the police till then. The pay is 25/- a day. It sounds good but it only means really between 5/- and 10/- a day to yourself, as living is so expensive. However he is lucky to get it. Any force raised in Natal would be good as living is so cheap.

The Breaker would write of his old comrades to the *Renmark Pioneer* on 14 June 1901:

A dedication to the Cosmo Mess of the 2nd S.A.M.R.

Old comrades of the 4th M.I, Australia's loyalest and best,
I'll think of you, when, by and bye, we're scattered to the east and west
Of days we skirmished far and wide, and gathered unconsidered trifles,
When we the honour had to ride
With South Australia's Mounted rifles

Our deeds of 'derring do' I guess, in years to come we'll well recall
The merry members of our mess,
Good comrades and – moss-troopers all
'Husky' this rhyme I dedicate to you, in memory of the time
You were a willing worthy mate, in deeds of craftiness and crime.

The Dutchman's ducks on which we dined you scored them by some
process risky,
And some red letter nights, I mind,
We drank 'The Queen' in borrowed whisky
Those times, old man, yourself you showed a bold unbashful buccaneer,
When past Pretoria side we rode
And proved our right ---- to commandeer

'The Breaker'

Husky is almost certainly Trooper Arthur Frederick Huskinsson. It would appear from this paean to plunder that Morant had not yet become the paragon of virtue and discipline which some would have us believe he became as an officer of the BVC.

Ironically, Balfour-Ogilvy would take up the role of Sergeant-Major in Baden-Powell's Police whilst Morant's fate was to ride in a different direction. Balfour-Ogilvy later became a district officer in New Guinea having returned to Renmark some time after the war.

Morant received his final pay with a month's bonus from the 2 South Australian Contingent on 31 July 1900. [12] There appears no direct evidence for the Breaker's movements over the next few months, but probably they mirror those of Bannett Burleigh, who reported from VanWyks Vlei (21 August) Galuk Farm (25 August) and General French's HQ (26 and 27 August). Gordon wrote of this period:

> Occasionally during the advance to Koomatipoort, Morant would turn up and pay me a visit. He usually arrived with a bundle of any old newspapers he could get, which he gravely and without a smile handed over to me, hoping they would be very welcome. But there was a look in his eye that I knew well. 'Have a whisky and soda Morant?' I'd say. 'Well sir I don't think it would be so bad. I would like one very much.' He would then settle himself down comfortably, light his pipe and start to tell me all sorts of bits of news that had come his way. I often had but a few minutes to give him and I had to leave him in possession, telling him to look after himself and be happy. Which he did. [13]

Burleigh interviewed Paul Kruger and ventured to Delagoa Bay and Lorenco Marques (now Maputo) in Portuguese Territory (now Mozambique) and subsequently made his way back, via Pretoria, to Cape Town on 16 October 1900.

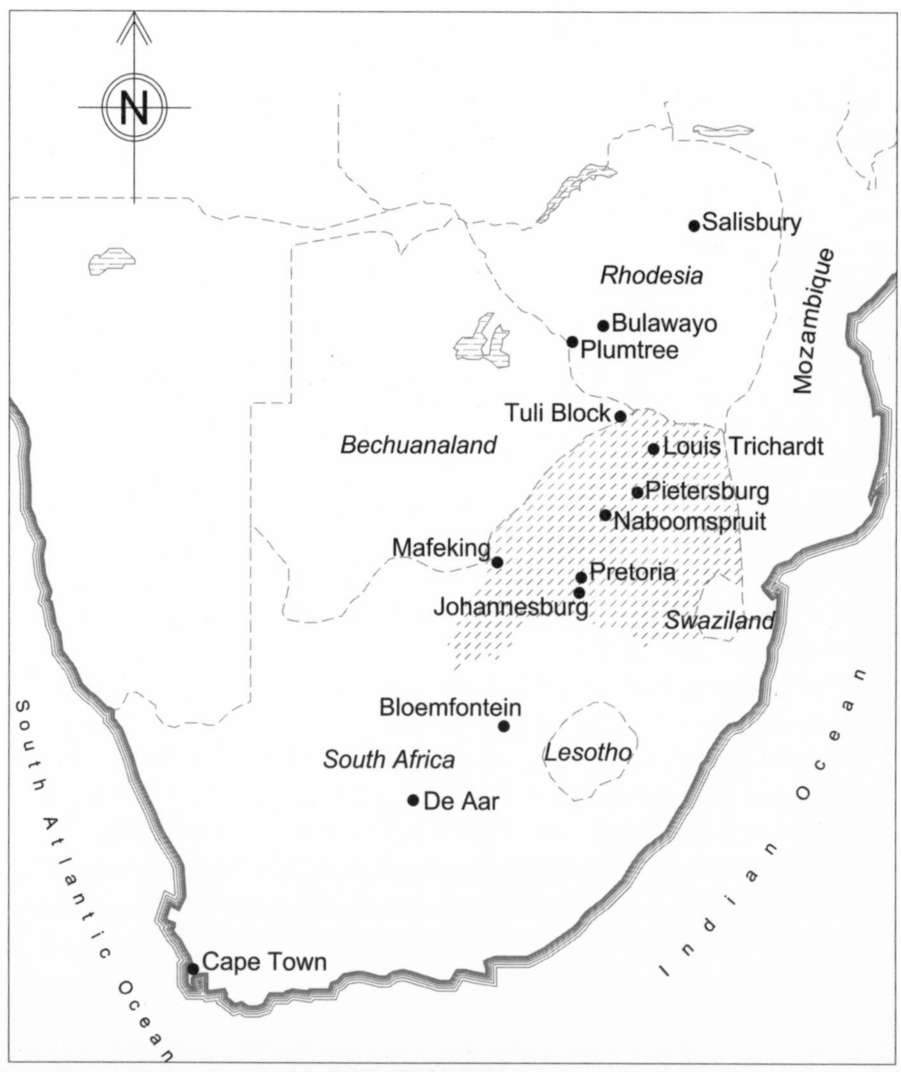

6

The Bushveldt Carbineers (BVC)

After 11 August 1900 Bennett Burleigh was writing his despatches from Belfast and towns east of Pretoria that were not at this stage in British hands, the main columns having halted at Middelburg on 27 July. It appears that Burleigh was passing freely between areas held by the Boers and those by the British and these reports were published significantly before the British columns closed in on these areas. These reports must have been of significant value to the British commanders and it seems surprising to later sensibilities that Burleigh was not shot as a spy! An example is given from the *Western Gazette*, Friday 17 August:

> Middelburg, Sunday, August 12. Yesterday I shook hands with Generals Botha and Belfast. Railway thither through to Delagoa Bay is intact. About 300 Boers are at Belfast, with guns. The country open and undulating, The enemy's main position is upon Bothasburg, north of Belfast, where there are probably about 8,000 Boers, with number of cannon. The Boers at Belfast are chiefly Zarps and Irishmen.

Whilst the main bodies of the columns of Lord Roberts force were waiting at Middelburg with patrols edging eastward, Sir Redvers Buller's column was pushing northward from Ermelo towards Carolina and Belfast, where ultimately it was planned the columns would converge.

At this time Sir Redvers Buller was instructed to halt his advance in order to allow British troops and Lord Roberts to reach Belfast. However, Buller was impatient with the slow advance of his troops and, in a private letter to his wife on 18 August, he grumbled about the missed chances of capturing the ZAR Government. Only on 21 August could Buller order his troops to march to the farm, van Wyksvlei, 24km south-east of Belfast. The offensive against the

Boers could then start in earnest. The Battle of Bergendal (Belfast), in which the South Australian Contingent took part, occurred between 21 and 27 August.

In a description of the fight at Belfast a South Australian correspondent wrote 'At last our orders come, and we leave our sheltering hollow, riding "sections open order" to our work upon the veldt, as our poet, "Breaker" Morant, puts it in a remarkably spirited set of lines. We soon find out that the Boer 100-pounder is still in position. A common shell bursts just beyond our first two sections.' Since Morant had already left the contingent by this time it is likely that he played no part in this confrontation, though he may have been in the area with Bennett Burleigh. The 'remarkably spirited set of lines' is:

Drawing fire

(Dedicated to J. Botting R.H.A., in loving memory of the many times they opportunely turned up.)

In the cool fresh, fragrant morning come the troopers riding by,
With their profiles silhouetted 'gainst the Dawn's faint orange sky,
As silently and slowly Night's sombre shadows drift and melt.
And 'tis 'Sections !' 'Open order !' to our work upon the veldt.
But the loveliness of Morning there's small leisure to admire
When the Mounted Rifles' mission is to find and 'Draw the fire!'

Drawing fire! Drawing fire!
The enemy's position to definitely enquire.
Drawing fire—but alack,
When the Mauser rifles crack
There'll be men who won't ride back.
Or turn their horses 'files about' to order of 'Retire!'

Oh, we rouse the hare and hartebeest, and the springbock stands alert;
We flush the startled partridge that may whirr away unhurt;
But the enemy is 'round us in positions safe and strong,
So it's 'Ride in open order!' and it's 'Pass the word along—
There is something seems suspicious on the flat long kopjes crest,'
And the Mounted Rifles' presence will soon put it to the test.

For they're out to draw the fire,
The enemy's position to definitely enquire.
Drawing fire. But, alack,

When the Mauser rifles crack
There'll be men who won't ride back.
Or turn their horses 'files about' to order of 'Retire!'

Though you've been in many a tight place, you've not realised your luck
Till you've seen the horse that's next you by a bit of shrapnel struck.
The wide world may be wide enough, yet there seems but scanty space
When three bullets in succession pass— three inches from your face.
Of the enemy's position there is very little doubt
When the bullets from the Mausers come a-sputtering about.

Their location has been found
When the bullets 'ping' around,
And the Mounted Rifles in the game no longer need to stay,
For when Boers are shooting straight
They just cooey for a mate,
Who is very up-to-date,

And they swing up at a gallop do the R.H.A.
When you see the spitting bullets toss the dust up from the ground,
When you hear the screaming shrapnel exploding all around;
When the bullets 'ping' around you, then your little work is done,
For you've found and drawn the firing, and may make way for the gun
That shall swing up at a gallop, and the Rifles ride away.
And can trust the Horse Artillery to finish out the play.

For the enemy's been found
When their bullets 'ping' around,
And the Mounted Rifles in the game no longer need to stay.
For when Boers are shooting straight
They've a handy sort of mate,
Who is very up-to-date,

And he's carried in a carriage of the R.H.A.
All your luck you may require
When you're sent to draw the fire;
But there's one thing when you've drawn it your anxiety allays.
And that is just to hear
At a gallop in your rear

The music in the rattle of the R.H.A.

HARRY HABBORD MORANT
South Australian Mounted Rifles,
Johannesburg.

The Battle of Bergendal (Belfast) marked the end of the first phase of the Anglo Boer War. Buller's troops broke through the Boer lines and advanced to Machadorp. A few days later on 1 September Lord Roberts declared the entire South African Republic to be British Territory. Sir Redvers Buller would head back to England on the same ship as Bennett Burleigh on 24 October 1900. Lord Roberts also left in December, leaving Lord Kitchener, formerly his chief of staff, as the new Commander in Chief. The main body of the Boer General Botha's forces remained intact however and they now dispersed to Lydenburg and Barberton and broke up to commence what would become known as the Guerrilla phase of the war. This would last longer than the first phase.

It had been recognised that the cumbersome British Army was not suited to combatting the guerrilla tactics which had already been used by the Boers. The Boers, who were used to living off the land they knew intimately, could strike at the British Army and disappear back into the bush to be supported by the civilian population on the thousands of dispersed farms. The long, slow and vulnerable supply columns and trains of the British Army could do little in retaliation. New tactics were required.

The new tactics developed included a number of controversial elements. One of the aims was to separate the Boer combatants from the support they were receiving from the civilian population. The people were therefore moved to camps where they could provide no support for the Boer Commandos. The concentration of the civilian population in this way led to the dread term 'concentration camps'. Whilst the purpose of the British camps in South Africa was not to annihilate their inhabitants, from the start they were badly conceived with little or no sanitation and totally inadequate arrangements for food and clean water supply, compounded by the parallel policy of the destruction of the farms and crops from which the population was removed. The result was painfully predictable and around 42,000 people died in these camps, mainly from disease and malnutrition. Children suffered disproportionately. Conditions only improved after campaigners like the famous Emily Hobhouse had brought the truth about them home to the British public and government.

The second part of the new British tactics was the formation of Irregular Army Units. The aim of these units was to operate in the same way as the Boer Commandos, being highly mobile and living off the land, requiring the minimum of logistical support. These units attracted many time-expired men from the colonies used to living in such a way. One of these units would become known as the Bushveldt Carbineers.

The Bushveldt Carbineers (BVC) was a mounted infantry regiment raised in Pretoria to operate in Northern Transvaal after the invasion of the area led by Colonel Plumer in April 1901. The invading troops, many of them Australians, captured the region along the railway towards Pietersburg and then the land adjacent to the borders with Rhodesia and Bechuanaland, which consisted of the unoccupied part of Northern Transvaal. The BVC was an imperial unit and part of the British Army order of battle and had no affiliation administratively or operationally with Australia. It has been assumed by some that the regiment was a sort of special force designed for strategic mounted operations in the Zoutspanberg, Spelonken and Waterberg areas of Northern Transvaal and mainly Australian in composition. The truth, however, may be found in the diary of the man who formed it, Robert Montague Poore, the Provost Martial [1] in Pretoria under Lord Kitchener. Poore wrote up his diary every day.

Poore is one of the most remarkable men is this whole story. He was born in Dublin in 1866 of a wealthy military family. One of the sources of their wealth were shares in the well-known Turkish baths in Jermyn Street in central London. His father thought he should go into the army, but Poore consistently failed the entrance exam for Sandhurst. He was sent off to a crammer but to no avail. Eventually, Poore managed to join the militia battalion of the Wiltshire Regiment, which was a back door route to a commission. True to form, he failed the militia exams. By some miracle he eventually passed his army exams and received a commission in the regular army in the Wiltshire Regiment then stationed in Jersey. In 1886 his father used his influence to get a transfer for him into the Seventh Hussars, a very well regarded cavalry regiment full of wealthy young officers, and he served with them in Rhodesia and South Africa. He was also *aide de camp* to Lord Harris, a notable cricketer and the governor of Bombay.

What he lacked academically Poore made up for with his sporting achievements. He was a good tennis player, West of India champion, and beat the Wimbledon champion. He played cricket for South Africa, where he was serving, against England and then for Hampshire. In 1899, as a serving army officer, he seems to have played the whole season for Hampshire and ended with a batting average of over 91 and in an innings against Somerset he scored 304. Whilst scoring this triple century, he and his partner set the highest sixth wicket partnership in English cricket of 411 runs, a record which still stands in county cricket. He was selected as a Wisden's cricketer of the year for 1900 and until recently was the only Irish-born player with this distinction.

The end of the 1899 cricket season coincided with the start of the Boer War and Poore, after a brief period buying remounts in the USA, became, as a major, the Provost Martial of the South African Field Force under Lord Roberts and later Kitchener. This position was effectively the Army's chief of police.

On 8 February 1901 he wrote in his diary: 'At Lord Kitchener's instigation I am forming a Boer Commando of those who have surrendered, their object is to loot cattle from the enemy'. Later, on 19 February, he had a visitor: 'a man came to see me today called Levy, he had been sent by Lord Kitchener to raise a corps called the Bushveldt Mounted Rifles, the corps to be composed of men who had been turned adrift by the Boers and I am to organise the corps.'

Joseph Ruben Levy, a 50-year-old Manchester-born trader and latterly a storekeeper at Pienaar's River had gained the attention of Kitchener with an idea to form a unit around a nucleus of men who had been expelled by the Boers from the Pietersburg area.

Poore chaired a meeting at a local hotel on 20 February and noted: 'I set forth the object of the corps and its proposed composition. A fund is being formed in the corps which is to be invested and the interest is to go to help any of its members who may be damaged.'

Early attestation papers have the name Bushveldt Mounted Rifles but the name shortly afterwards became the Bushveldt Carbineers (BVC).

Poore commenced enrolling men on 21 February and two days later he wrote that the fund stood at £810 10s but men were not rolling in as quickly as they might. The diary makes it plain that the fund was a form of insurance and the money was not to finance the regiment, as has often been suggested. This is corroborated by a letter written by an ex-BVC orderly in the *Register* of 9 April 1902. After the first day of recruiting only eight officers and nine men had been recruited, but by the latter part of March the numbers stood at nine officers and 110 men. Levy had overstated the numbers of men waiting to join in the north and few disaffected Boers were tempted. Although the aim was to recruit 500 men, the numbers never exceeded 350, despite the high rates of pay offered.

The regiment took shape and Poore wrote on 23 March that two days earlier just outside Pretoria a trooper of the BVC was caught by the Boers who shot his horse and took all his clothes and equipment but let him go. He wrote four days later that he had arranged for the BVC to operate with Plumer's expedition to the north. He went to see them entrain at the station and found them all singing. At this stage the regiment was probably at about squadron strength. By 8 April Poore wrote that they had done very well and had captured several prisoners, among them men who had been blowing up the railway lines. A couple of days later he noted the BVC were still doing well and Lord Kitchener was pleased with them. By late April Pietersburg was taken and Poore recounted that the town had been shamefully looted, principally by the Australian Bushmen. The BVC became part of the garrison of the town and recruitment continued to try to bring the regiment up to its planned strength. By the end of April he commented in his diary:

> The beginning of the BVC was a certain number of British subjects who were turned out of Pietersburg and these made the beginning of the corps. They have been augmented by Australians who were due to return to their country but elected to remain, so the corps is a pretty good one and there are lots of men who know the country to the north.

Levy was made up to Captain and became the paymaster. Several of his friends became officers including Lt Michael Kelly, a Pietersburg businessman, and Lt Fred Neel, who called himself a doctor but seemed to have no qualification. These three made good contributions to the fund with Levy chipping in £500 and Kelly £100. Levy advertised throughout Natal and Cape Province by notices and flyers suggesting that recruits were wanted who 'can ride and shoot' and stating special inducements were available for those wishing to join. The reason for Levy's enthusiasm for recruiting men and for the push north soon became apparent: he applied for the licence to run all the bars and restaurants of the newly captured stations up to Petersburg. He was somewhat surprised and indignant when his request was refused. The captain was recognised by some of the soldiers who had been served drinks by him two weeks previously.

The advertisements announcing the formation of the regiment were displayed around South Africa, especially in local newspapers. *The Natal Mercury* had such an advertisement on 10 March 1901. The only skill required was to be able to ride and shoot. Special inducements for men joining the Corps were hinted at but not explained and 'every facility given to those desirous of leaving before the termination of the war'. This advertisement was signed by J. D. Gill, a forty-nine-year-old South African who enlisted on the first day of recruiting and manned the Durban recruiting office for a short time, before being discharged in mid-March 1901.

Despite the qualifications mentioned in the advertisements, little effort was made to ensure the recruits were competent. Trooper Silke recorded in his diary: 'I happened to ride by the side of Jones who had never ridden a horse before, it was highly amusing.' This was probably Trooper Herbert Jones, a twenty-six-year-old clerk from New South Wales who had no previous service. Silke was hardly a skilled soldier himself, having been employed on horse boats taking remounts to South Africa. He and several of his friends enlisted in Durban after bringing a boatload of horses from Italy.

Trooper James Christie was impressed with neither the horsemanship nor the horses of the BVC, writing in late 1901:

> Got a few tents and pitched a camp, and went to inspect the horses. They were a sorry crowd, and we all felt sick and used powerful language at the idea of being served out with such a mangy lot of crocks. Put in one night in discomfort and growling, and next day picked the horses, and adjusted saddlery, etc, Spent another night in discomfort—it is a bleak and barren looking spot, and left at daylight for a ten days' patrol to Strayjspoort, 25 miles distant—no kit to be taken.
>
> A sicker or sorrier crowd of men who arrived at (I can't say rode into) camp would be hard to picture; some had left their horses on the road and put their saddles on the waggon, others towed wearily at their horses—no horse in this country has been trained to lead—some had been thrown and lamed through their being bad riders, and the horses unbroken. Some had never ridden a horse before, and you know what a 25-mile ride is on a novice.

Another recruit from the horse boats was Trooper Hameline Glasson who came from Orange, New South Wales. At some time Morant lived in a cottage next door to his parent's farm. Glasson wrote regularly to his sister and mother and in 1970 twenty of these letters were found in an outhouse and are now in the Mitchell library, Sydney. He comments that 'some officers are such asses'. He was also sure that officers at Fort Edward were opening letters and destroying those which criticised them. Other new recruits were found to be deserters from the New Zealand Mounted Rifles, and although they played a part in the terrible events later, they were eventually sent back to their own national units. Several of the South African recruits from Northern Transvaal were probably more interested in looting Boer cattle than anything else. Squadron Sergeant Major Kenneth Morrison, who had been living at Pienaar's River, was possibly in the forefront of this enterprise, though Alfred Taylor of the Intelligence Department was certainly a major beneficiary. Sergeant Major George Clarke was also suspected of being involved in cattle theft. Several men enlisted in the BVC but then failed to appear.

George Witton brought about a dozen soldiers into to the unit, mostly Victorians who had served with the Fourth Imperial Victorian Bushmen, Witton was rewarded with a commission. The idea was that some of these men would form an artillery or special gunnery section but this never came about. It was common for some mounted infantry units to have a section with a pair of pom-poms (small cannon firing one pound shells) or two Colt machine guns. The BVC probably reflected the experience level of other units in South Africa. It certainly did not attract a large pool of experienced and committed soldiers.

Going through the attestation papers [2] of those who enlisted before September 1901 it is apparent that approximately 35% had no previous service, so the overall experience level was low, but probably compared reasonably well with similar units. Part of the Australian take on things is that this unit was mainly composed of Australians, many of whom were still in South Africa having completed their original enlistment period. The numbers of British and Australians were in fact similar at about 40% each, but many who came from Australian units were British men who had emigrated. Similarly, those who declared South African addresses were also probably British or Irish. Recruits with obviously Afrikaner names come to about 6% of the enlistments. It can be said that the unit was mainly of British extraction, but with the majority of the officers from Australia.

One of the problems is how to define an Australian. Technically, there was no country called Australia prior to federation on 1 January 1901, when the six colonies joined together. Many of the Australians who enlisted in the BVC had arrived in South Africa before the federation, so were from the British colonies. Australians were also technically British until 1949 when legislation finally determined who was an Australian.

One of the first tasks was to recruit officers, but many of those who joined with a commission were inexperienced. The man picked to command the regiment was Captain Robert Lenehan, a wealthy, well-connected and successful Sydney solicitor. He had been a major in the Volunteer Artillery but opted to take a drop in rank to captain to command a squadron in the 1st New South Wales Mounted Rifles under Sydney socialite Lt Col Airey. Both of them were Sydney Hunt Club members, knew Morant at home and came across him at equestrian events. Morant had written a poem entitled 'Hunt Club at Windsor' to commemorate the visit of the Sydney Hunt Club, including Lenehan and Airey, to the small town where Morant was living in 1898. Lenehan was an experienced mounted rifleman and seemed to be an ideal candidate. In reality he seemed content to stay back at base in Pietersburg or even Pretoria and really never had a strong control of the unit. The other people who were commissioned were less equipped to command mounted soldiers. Fred Neel lived in the Pietersberg area and had served as an assistant surgeon in the Malaboch campaign of 1894 under General Joubert. He was well thought of in his medical role but seems to have been totally unqualified. He was commissioned as a lieutenant after a few months service in the BVC. Michael Kelly was another Petersberg resident and had accompanied Warren's force in an expedition in Bechuanaland in 1884. Since then he had been a store keeper but had been thrown out by the Boers and attested in the BVC early on being rewarded with a commission as a lieutenant. Several of the new officers such as Picton, Edwards, Hannam, Baudinet and Morant came recommended as good non-commissioned officers. One excellent NCO who should have been commissioned was Sergeant Frank Eland and if this course of action had taken place there probably would not have been a BVC story. Eland was born in Ireland and along with his mother and another woman, Sarah Heckford, purchased a farm near Duivelskloof in 1893. Eland knew all the settlers, missionaries and Africans in the area. He served in the Imperial Light Horse before joining the BVC, to be killed within 10 miles of his farm.

Captain Percy Hunt had previous service in the militia in England in the 3rd Battalion York and Lancaster Regiment, which he joined as a 2nd Lieutenant on 14 February 1893. He held this rank for 16 months before being promoted to Lieutenant in July 1894. The York and Lancasters during this period were stationed in Ireland. Hunt served with this militia unit until December 1896 when he transferred to the 13th Hussars. After having served some 17 months with the Hussars, Hunt resigned his commission in May 1898. In the period between leaving the Hussars and going to South Africa Hunt was breeding and showing horses. During this time he became a member of the prestigious and exclusive Cavalry Club in London having been proposed by the Commanding Officer of the 13th Hussars and seconded by Australian Lieutenant Henry Phelps Dangar. Hunt and Dangar's names appear at a number of society functions around this time. Both Hunt and Dangar relinquished their membership of the Cavalry Club at the end of 1899.

After the outbreak of the Anglo Boer War Hunt enlisted in the Imperial Yeomanry early in 1900 and was made up to sergeant on the day he signed on. He later served with French's scouts. The extent of his experience in mounted infantry operations must have been limited as he was on the staff in the Military Government in Pretoria. He was the registrar of antenuptial contracts and police appointments. He left this position on 15 June 1901 and was made Captain in the BVC the following day. Most of his short regular service was in Ireland where he seemed to have spent his time at horse shows and attending levees at Dublin Castle.

Peter Joseph Handcock was originally a blacksmith and served as shoeing smith with the New South Wales Mounted Rifles. He came recommended as 'a really good man' and somehow obtained a commission as a Veterinary and Transport Officer, though he never seemed to devote time to these functions. He described himself as poorly educated.

An officer with some military experience, including the relief of Mafeking, was Lt Lewis, an American who had served with the Southern Rhodesia Volunteers and Rand Rifles. Later, in 1904, he organised 'The Great Boer War Spectacle' at the St Louis Exposition and in 1911 fought in the Battle of Juarez in the Mexican revolution alongside Boer General Barend Viljoen.

Stephen Midgley was a BVC officer who went on to distinguish himself. He had previously served in the Queensland Forces 1889–1899. He then served in South Africa as a sergeant with the Queensland Mounted Infantry and as a Lieutenant with the BVC from 1 April 1901. Ending the war as a captain with a Mention in Despatches (MID) he returned eventually to Australia and engaged in mining. He re-enlisted into the Australian Army for the First World War and ended up as a Lieutenant-Colonel DSO, CMG, with further mentions in despatches.

One of the difficulties of recruiting a unit of this nature was attracting middle-ranking officers of senior Lieutenant or Captain status. In fact, there was an enormous gap between Lenehan, the Major in command, and the other officers. There was no one with real experience of commanding a squadron. This is likely to have been a contributing factor in the inordinate influence of 'Captain' Alfred Taylor, the only person the junior officers could really look up to. Taylor, the acting native commissioner and intelligence officer, was an Irishman who had been involved in wars in Africa for ten years. Taylor's influence on the junior officers of the BVC proved to be a real problem.

The squadron commanders, with the rank of captain, of A and B squadrons respectively were James Huntley Robertson and Percy Hunt. Robertson was a twenty-seven-year-old Scot who had been born in Miraflores, Mexico, where his father ran a spinning mill and organised the Methodist community there. Robertson can be found as an apprentice spinning engineer in Accrington in 1891. It is believed that he arrived in Perth as a ships engineer and enlisted in the Second West Australian Mounted infantry as a corporal. Later in life he enlisted in the Royal Flying Corps in the First World War, having returned to the UK from Mexico and was commissioned and awarded the Military Cross. [3] The BVC initially took Huntley Robertson on as a Lieutenant and made him the unit Adjutant before he became Captain commanding A squadron.

There is evidence that the Intelligence branch at Pretoria was involved with the forming of this regiment, but the recruitment and early administration seemed to have been left to the Provost Marshal and his staff. There were already two regiments of Kitchener's Fighting Scouts (KFS) operating with Plumer's forces in Northern Transvaal and the obvious solution for recruitment would have been to form a third regiment of this unit and cross-post experienced officers and NCOs into the BVC. The KFS regiments each contained about 400 men and many had come from the Rhodesian Regiment when it had been disbanded. The two commanding officers were Lt Col J. W. Colenbrander and Lt Col A. E. Wilson, veterans of local wars, and both extremely experienced in mounted infantry style warfare in Africa. The aim would probably have been for the BVC to be of a similar size, consisting of a headquarters and up to four companies, but the BVC only ever consisted of two companies. The KFS had a reputation for no nonsense, and at times outright brutality. Poore wrote on 17 June 1901: 'Capt Bolton the Assistant Provost Martial at Pietersburg gave me fearful accounts of the way of the KFS with Cols Colenbrander and Wilson at their head; nothing is safe with them anywhere near.' It is possible that some in the BVC sought to emulate this reputation.

Capt. Bolton came under Poore in the performance of his duties. He was commissioned into the Wiltshire Regiment from Sandhurst in 1883 and played rugby for England between 1882 and 1887. He was at one time instructor in fortifications at Sandhurst and head of physical training. Bolton went to South Africa with the Wiltshire Regiment and was in action from the early days until he received a wound to the shoulder in August 1900. He was mentioned in despatches, awarded the DSO and made up to Brevet Major for his work. He was given the Assistant Provost Marshal position in Pietersburg.

The BVC had no cap badge, shoulder titles or other accoutrements and was essentially just a name. The administrative facilities were poorly structured and whilst there was an orderly room in Pretoria where Levy, as paymaster, worked alongside a sergeant clerk and a storeman, no one obviously filled any of the other positions that would normally be found in a regiment of this nature. Lenehan commanded the regiment from the base at Pietersburg and was assisted by Lt Edwards, who operated as the adjutant. Several of the early recruits were sent out to places such as Durban, Green Point at Cape Town, East London, Maitland, Pietersburg and Pretoria to act as recruiting officers. Among these was Trooper Ernest Berry, who had been wounded on the Jameson raid in 1895, served in the Matabele Rebellion in 1896 and was given the role of recruiting officer until discharged three months later. Most of those who were from the Afrikaner community joined at Pretoria or Pietersburg.

It is clear from reading the enlistment papers that some of the recruits should never have been signed up. Trooper Adams was blind in his right eye and severely wounded but gamely saw out his enlistment. Trooper William Chapman was suffering from 'remittent fever' and was much debilitated as a result of poisoning through working in lead mines and was eventually discharged as medically unfit. Trooper William Browe, who served 112 days with the BVC, had to be discharged with rheumatism 'not caused by war service'. Another stoic member was Trooper Telfer Anderson (aged 54) who enlisted with bullet wounds in the head but saw out his enlistment of six months. Forty-one-year-old Corporal John Baker was minus his right thumb but enthusiastically served his time, later reenlisted in the Pietersburg Light Horse and was mentioned in despatches by Lord Kitchener at the end of the war. Robert Leeds was missing a big toe but this did not stop him serving resolutely for nine months. Trooper Frank Carter had served six months imprisonment with hard labour after deserting from First Brabant's Horse. After serving six months with the BVC he joined the Second Brabant's Horse and was sentenced to two years' hard labour after committing a variety of other offences. A trooper with the wonderful name of Hyacinth Daly served for a short time but on the roll his name is marked as 'undesirable' after being discharged for drunkenness.

Several seemed somewhat elderly for the challenging role envisaged for the unit, some of whom, despite their age, had no military experience. Included in this group are Michael Madden (53), Johannes Vorster (52), Edward Beviss (45), Thomas Elsey (54) and the probable grand daddy of them all, Thomas Hackett, who was left with seven children when his 59-year-old wife died in 1898. Others were hardly more suitable: George Cordey was dismissed from Roberts' Horse as 'useless and undesirable and not up to standard for Roberts' Horse' but he served for six months with the BVC; Thomas Snowden had been sentenced to one year's hard labour for theft in his previous unit and subsequently received 56 days hard labour for stealing boots from a comrade.

This was not a unit at the cutting edge of military usefulness. That said, it was similar to many other irregular units recruited from men who were wandering around South Africa having completed their enlistments or been thrown out of other units. Nevertheless, there were some good men attracted to the regiment by the terms of service and the money, which was much higher than the pay of most other colonial units. The men that George Witton recruited from time-expired Fourth Victoria Imperial Bushmen in early July 1901 all gave good service. One or two others had interesting previous military experience: Sergeant Major Edward Smith had served in the New South Wales Artillery in the Sudan and Trooper Threlfall had served with a New South Wales ambulance unit there in 1885. All the men who ultimately signed Trooper Cochrane's complaint about events in the BVC proved to be good soldiers, though some were inexperienced. Robert Mitchell Cochrane was a Justice of the Peace in Western Australia, a journalist and man of substance in the communities there and in Queensland.

In 1892 he edited a short-lived left wing newspaper in Charters Towers called *The Eagle*. He also held several patents for improving extraction in the gold industry, as did Lt Baudinet. Two of his fellow signatories quite possibly worked with him at Coolgardie. Trooper George Lucas pegged out a gold claim at Red Hill in 1897 and Cochrane was later the manager of the Red Hill Gold Mines. Trooper Thompson worked for a company in Coolgardie and went with Lucas on the same ship to South Africa in 1901. They enlisted together in the BVC. One trooper's full handle was the Honourable Aubrey Bruce Cooper Cecil (his father had played cricket for Hampshire) and another, Sgt Wrangham, had a comprehensive entry in Debrett's Peerage. Trooper Foulis was the son of a baronet and he eventually became the eleventh baronet himself.

About twenty of the soldiers would go on to serve with the Australian Army in the First World War, when at least one, Tpr Beavan, was killed. Two others served with the South African Forces. At least four were decorated other than Midgley. Sergeant Stevens serving with the South African Army received a Distinguished Conduct Medal (DCM) as did Tpr John Nagle, wounded in the Middle East. Captain Robertson won a Military Cross on the Somme. Trooper Thompson won an MC with the Tenth Light Horse as a lieutenant.

One of the most interesting stories is that of Sergeant Potts, who was commissioned into the 2nd Light Horse Regiment, served in Gallipoli and was cashiered for 'fraudulently misapplying Regimental money'. In 1917 he rejoined the army as a private and by the end of the war was promoted to Battery Quartermaster Sergeant. Major Robert Lenehan served in a training role in Australia, reaching the rank of acting brigadier. His involvement as co-respondent in a high profile divorce case in Sydney in 1917 brought his military career to an ignominious end. It is not known how many British soldiers went on to serve in the First World War owing to the destruction of records by the Luftwaffe during the second.

After the Morant affair, the BVC was reorganised and became the Pietersburg Light Horse from the beginning of December 1901. A new regular commanding officer, Major Henry Vallancey, was appointed. He was an extremely experienced officer from the Argyll and Sutherland Highlanders and saw the regiment through to the end of the war.

The Bushveldt Carbineers probably reflected the recruiting pattern of other irregular units in the war, but it has to be remembered that the Australian Government had no input in the formation and later operations of this unit. Simply, a good proportion of its members were Australians.

7
The Old Country

If the hotel manager at the newly opened Mount Nelson Hotel in Cape Town had known that there might be difficulties with one of his clients, he might not have kept the drinks flowing so freely, but perhaps captivated by the wit and charm of his guests, he ensured their glasses were rarely empty. Breaker Morant enjoyed his stay at the opulent hotel in late 1900, as did Lt Maurice Harbord. The pair spent the evening with Bennett Burleigh, the *Daily Telegraph* war correspondent and Morant's erstwhile employer. The evening was so good that Harbord suggested that he had never laughed so much in all his life. [1] Later, no doubt thinking that the whole episode was an oversight, the general manager, Mr Oggier, sent the Breaker's share of the bill, £16 13s 0d, to the man he claimed to be his father, Admiral George Digby Morant, in the New Forest. The fact that the Admiral did not live in Hampshire was not known to him – nor to Breaker Morant.

Soon after this this shindig Bennet Burleigh would return to England on 24 October aboard the luxury liner *Dunvegan Castle*, along with Sir Redvers Buller [2] and other senior officers, many of whom believed the war was, to all intents and purposes, over. After a brief coaling stop at Madeira, they arrived in Southampton on 10 November. There was speculation that Burleigh had been recalled by *The Daily Telegraph* because his writing was too sympathetic to the Boers. He returned to South Africa at the end of December.

The Breaker had lost his employer and consequently his source of income. He possibly had the last of his army pay and whatever Burleigh had paid him, but why waste that on hotel bills? The South Australian contingent had gone back to Australia and we must assume that he had a passage booked to England, through the army on board a troopship, in lieu of a trip back to Australia. It is not known how the Breaker returned to England. If he went on a civilian ship, his name would be on the passenger lists, which still exist, but there is no trace. If he went on an army troopship, his name would not be on any published list as he had been a non-commissioned officer and only the names of commissioned officers are normally shown.

We know that Morant had arrived in London by 23 November (as reported in *The Adelaide Observer* on 29 December) when he called upon the Agent General for South Australia, Sir John Cockburn, [3] introducing himself as the son of Colonel Morant of Renmark. So Morant was able to pass himself off as the son of an Australian farming colonel whilst in England, and of a British admiral, soon to be knighted, when in Australia. The crafty bushman probably knew the Admiral was living in London and transferred his paternity to the fruit farming colonel. He mentioned to Sir John that his stated intention was to return to South Africa and take up a commission in Baden-Powell's South African Constabulary.

A major underpinning of the Morant myth is that whilst in England, Morant went back to Devon with Percy Hunt and the two of them enjoyed a life of hunting, drinking and chasing girls. They then became engaged to sisters. The picture is an attractive one. Hunt was a rich, young ex-Hussar officer whose family lived in Pau in the Pyrenees. He was described as one the handsomest men in the army and spent a significant amount on clothes. After his death Hunt's estate of £193 6s 7d [4] was administered by a tailor, John Henry White [5] who worked for Gieves and Hawkes, the prestigious Savile Row military tailor. Morant was the charmer, witty, intelligent and able to reel off poetry at the drop of a hat. They would have made an impressive double act. Hunt's father was wealthy and declared himself a rentier (one who lives off the income from investments or property, a man of independent means) on Percy's birth certificate in 1873. [6] His mother Anna Benkard was even wealthier, coming from an American family who were endlessly embroiled in law suits in Britain and the US with those eager to relieve her of her riches. As mentioned earlier, Hunt did not shine academically at school, though he made the 1st XV rugby team. [7] He gained a commission in the militia battalion of the York and Lancaster Regiment in 1892 as a second lieutenant, a way to gain a commission in the regular army for those without the brains to pass the Sandhurst exams. In 1896 he transferred into the 13th Hussars, then serving in Ireland. He resigned his commission eighteen months later, having seen no active service but having performed valiantly at Irish horse shows. [8]

Hunt enlisted in the Imperial Yeomanry at Canterbury on 31 January 1900. By lunchtime he had been promoted to the rank of sergeant, probably because he declared service in the 13th Hussars as a second lieutenant. He gave his next of kin as his mother with her forwarding address as a bank in Charing Cross Road, London. In fact, by then his family lived on the Bois de Boulogne in Paris, in a house later bought by the French composer Debussy. This accounts for his enlistment in Kent, probably at the nearest recruiting office to the Dover ferry terminal. He sailed for South Africa on 28 February. It would be expected that he serve in the Imperial Yeomanry for at least six months, that being the normal period of enlistment at the time but records of the South African Mounted Irregular Forces (SAMIF) show he was appointed with them as Lieutenant on 17 April 1900. [9]

He appears to have served with SAMIF for the standard six months since on 13 November 1900 he was taken on strength in French's Scouts [10]. [11]

After Roberts had arrived in Pretoria in early June the army had to take over all the functions of a normal government. Hunt worked in the Transvaal Administration as a registrar of Ante-nuptial contracts and Police Appointments. [12] Hunt was made redundant from this position on 15 June 1901. The correspondence relating to his redundancy notes 'he would rejoin his corps'. [13] Presumably he was either still a member of French's Scouts or already a member of the BVC at that point. On 16 June, Lieutenant Percy Hunt was made a Captain in the Bushveldt Carbineers. [14] Hunt signed on with French's Scouts on 13 November. We know that Morant was back in England by 23 November. Unless Hunt was immediately allowed to go on leave on joining French's Scouts, it is very unlikely that he would have been in England at the same time as Morant, and if he served the standard service of six months, without leave, in French's Scouts, he could not have returned to England in 1900/1901 at the same time as Morant.

We know that the Breaker was in London and there was a further sighting reported. On Saturday 23 March 1901 *The Chronicle of Adelaide* published a description of Queen Victoria's funeral on Saturday 6 February. It described the role played by the many colonial troops in attendance and names some. An adjacent panel reads: 'Lt Morant of the Baden-Powell Police (BPP) who went out with the second contingent as a corporal is now in England and is visiting friends in Devon.' In the usual Morant way there are one or two discrepancies: he was not a lieutenant as he was no longer in the army and had no rank, nor had he been an officer at this point, having only risen to corporal. The BPP had started recruiting in September 1900 and eventually became the South African Constabulary. Although Morant suggested he had been recruited into this organisation, he never appears to have joined. This story is backed up by a piece in *The South Australia Review* of 23 August 1900 in another little gossip entry about the doings of the second contingent: 'Corporal Morant, "The Breaker" of *The Bulletin* and *Critic* fame, has left us, having obtained a commission in a military police corps started by Baden-Powell.' This was an opportunity to join a well-paying organisation and it looks as if the Breaker was tempted. Apparently, he told friends later, he had been offered a commission but the offer was only open for six months and he reapplied too late.

In the Commons on 10 June 1901, Mr Dillon MP, the member for Mayo, asked the Secretary of State for the Colonies 'whether any, and if any, evidence to character has been required for candidates for Baden-Powell's South African police'. Joe Chamberlain responded: 'All candidates have been required to furnish at least two testimonials to character and to give names of two references to respectability of character and fitness for service.' This would have caused the Breaker some difficulty.

That the Breaker was in Bideford, a small town on the north Devon coast, probably in late 1900 or early 1901, is evidenced by the finest photo ever taken of him from that time. He is pictured in hunting clothing in Mr W. H. Puddicombe's Electric Studio on the Strand in Bideford. In fact, the picture is so perfect it looks like Morant has put his head through a hole with the body immaculately dressed in hunting clothes painted on a board. This picture was recently discovered in the National Archives, amongst copyrighted material from Stationer's Hall. [15] In those days anyone who wanted to copyright something could send a picture or document along with a form and a small sum of money to Stationer's Hall and they would retain the material and register the copyright. Mr Puddicombe sent the picture in late April 1902, along with another one of a Major with the inauspicious surname of Pine-Coffin, to the Hall. The Pine-Coffin family were local and had lived in Port Ledge Manor for eight centuries. *The Times* published a report on the Courts-Martial and executions on 17 April 1902 and Mr Puddicombe, probably realising he had a unique picture of the late Lt Morant, wasted no time sending his form off to Stationer's Hall. At the time the photo was taken, Mr Puddicombe was the Freemason's Worshipful Master for Lodge Benevolence 489 in Bideford. The Breaker, never one to miss a financial opportunity, probably got a discount as an old boy of the Royal Masonic School. Why was it taken? It is unlikely to be for Morant's bedside table, but it could have been an engagement picture, a keepsake for his sister, or to be used, as was often the case, as a visiting card.

Having not seen her since his departure in 1883, Morant probably travelled to Bideford because his sister Annie Kate was living near there. Annie is found in the 1901 census living in a small village called Lee in North Devon, 12 miles from Bideford. She also appears as a visitor in a household where the head of the family, Willie McMichael, is described as a Clerk in Holy Orders and it is possible that Annie was the church organist who played for board and lodging. Annie was described as a professor of music in one census and later in life was the organist at a church near Axminster on the Dorset and Devon border. In later life Annie Kate lived in Treviglas, St Columb Minor in Cornwall at least between 1822 and 1832 [16] after which she moved to St Teath, Cornwall, where in 1939 [17] she working as the organist and lived in the Vicarage.

Although it is one of the major elements in the story of the Bushveldt Carbineers, no evidence has been found of Captain Percy Hunt ever being in Devon, or even leaving South Africa for that matter, and the carousing and hunting by the Breaker and Hunt may be a fabrication. It is said that the pair hunted in the North Devon area with the local hunt. At that time a seriously wealthy landowner Mark Rolle ran the local pack of hounds and seems to have spent most of his time hunting. This later became the Stevenstone Hunt and still exists. It hunted a large area of North Devon on two or three days a week. Hunting was expensive. You joined the hunt and became a subscriber. Visitors could pay a fee, known as a cap, to hunt for the day and this was allowed for a few days a year. However, if you exceeded a certain number of caps, you would have to become a subscriber. The other expense would be that you had to be properly clothed and bring your own horse. The secretary of the Stevenstone Hunt has searched her records but found no sign of Morant or Hunt being subscribers or taking a cap. In those days the local newspaper published the doings of the hunt at tedious length but there is no report of either man riding with them. Hiring a horse for the day would not be cheap and possibly quite difficult to organise unless you had a circle of horsey friends with spare mounts.

Another of the stories that comes out of the interlude in North Devon which was repeated at the courts martial is that Hunt and Morant became engaged to sisters. Based on known connections the obvious candidates for this would be the Murray girls of Westward Ho! In Morant's will, written the night before he was shot, he left all the money in his possession and in the Standard Chartered Bank of South Africa to Mary Ella Wickett (formerly Murray), the wife of George Augustus Wickett, residing at Holmwood House, Bideford, North Devon, and he left his gold signet ring to Maud Murray of Rowena, Westward Ho!, N Devon. He also left a ring with a turquoise stone and a gold chain to Lilian Hunt of 64 Avenue de Bois de Boulogne, Paris.

Mary Evalina Murray, born 1868, married a local vet called George Augustus Wickett and gave birth to a son in 1899. Another sister, Maud, born in 1878, lived at the family business, Rowena Guest House at Westward Ho! Her father, an old army man, was a lodging house and carriage proprietor with a licence to let post horses. He died some time in the 1880s and his wife ran the family guest house until she died in 1899. Maud and another sister, Helen Lucy then took over the business until Helen herself married in March 1902. It is unlikely that Hunt and Morant became engaged to these two sisters since Mary was already a wife and mother and the twenty-two-year-old Maud never married. Maud continued to run the guest house until the late 1930s. Other than Maud, the only unmarried sister at the time was Helen Lucy, but she was engaged to, and soon married, a local man. However, Morant knew a lot about the family and gets the names correct, so undoubtedly he had some connection with them. Similarly, he gets Lilian Hunt's name and address right. If Morant had married Maud he could have ended up running a Devon guest house. There is no doubt that the Murray sisters were not in Hunt's league, financially or socially.

It is difficult to work out when Hunt and Morant might have actually met. It was probably in Pretoria sometime between July and November 1900. Since Percy Hunt was a registrar of Police Appointments and Morant had sought a police position in South Africa it is possible this is how their paths crossed. We know from the visitors' book of the Transvaal Hotel in Pretoria that Corporal Morant of the South Australian Mounted Rifles stayed at the hotel on 7, 9 and 15 July 1900. At that time staying at this hotel was the thing for the well-to-do visitors to the town. It shows that Morant was clearly not deterred from mixing with commissioned officers of the army. He might have met Hunt at this period, but there is no convincing evidence that they went to Devon together and they certainly did not go to school together, as some sources have claimed.

In Ireland Hunt traded in horses before and after leaving his regiment. Some say he sold Kitchener a pair of polo ponies in Pretoria. A mutual friend could have been Major Henry P. Dangar, who had served with Hunt in Ireland in the 13th Hussars and who was from a rich Australian farming family. He was the second-in-command of the NSW Bushmen in South Africa and members of his family had been active in the Sydney Hunt club prior to the war, at a time when Morant, when he was in funds, was mixing with the hunting set. In 1897 he seconded Hunt's application for membership of the Cavalry Club in London. [18] Dangar was invalided to London with malaria in July 1900 and died there suddenly in July 1901. Morant and Hunt might have stayed with him in his palatial Pall Mall house in early 1901. Living with him there was his twenty-one-year-old Canadian girlfriend, Violet Gertrude Twining. She inherited a fortune on his death and immediately went on to marry the bankrupt eighty-year-old Marquess of Donegal and happily ensured the succession to his title in very quick time. He died within eighteen months a happy man because he had a son and heir. Violet, having done her duty, later became a pillar of London Society.

It is also possible that the Breaker was invited to Paris and there came across Lilian, Percy Hunt's sister. There is no sign that they actually met.

Lilian had been born in Pau in 1875 and therefore would have been a bit young for Morant, but she never married and died in 1959. She is, however, to be found in the 1946 French census living in Paris with Marie Louise Dupont, twenty-five years her junior and described as 'amie', which can mean 'girlfriend'; this might indicate the reason for Lilian's spinsterhood.

Thus, unless some convincing primary evidence appears, it is hard to make a case for Hunt and Morant hunting in North Devon and when not in the field finding the time to woo and pop the question to some Devonian sisters in early 1901.

8

Alfred 'Bulala' Taylor – The Rhodesian Soldier

In order to understand the events that led to the downfall of Morant, Handcock and the other officers, it is useful to have some understanding of the other characters who played their part in the events in Northern Transvaal. Foremost amongst these is 'Captain' Taylor.

The role of 'Captain' Alfred Taylor in the troubles in Northern Transvaal in 1901 has never been in doubt. Ramon de Bertodano, the intelligence officer for the area, in his memorandum on the Bushveldt Carbineers (written very late in life) suggested that he was the instigator of many of the events that occurred (*fons et origo* of the troubles) in Spelonken and Zoutpansberg. This is almost certainly true. De Bertodano, despite his Spanish name, was an Australian lawyer who served in Rhodesia and then the South African War. He met Taylor in Rhodesia. Initially in awe of Taylor, this soon gave way to a deep loathing, which was probably mutual. While de Bertodano was appalled by Taylor's arbitrary cruelty, Taylor saw through de Bertadano's pomposity. Whilst Taylor was out in the field walking the walk, de Bertadano was riding a desk, talking the talk. Later in 1901, there would be an impenetrability about Taylor who, although not a member of the Bushveldt Carbineers, exercised a pernicious influence on the officers of the regiment.

Taylor was born in Dublin in November 1861 and christened in early 1862 at Eustace Street Presbyterian Church, Dublin. In his death notice, for Probate purposes, it is written that he was 78 years old on 24 October 1941 which would indicate a birth date of 1862, but this is not the case. His parents were William Taylor and Charlotte Bennet. It was confirmed in his death notice that Taylor's father was called William, but the name of his mother had been forgotten. They were married in Dublin in October 1851. William Taylor was the only son of Alfred Taylor, a Dublin solicitor and he went on to become a solicitor himself. Charlotte's father was a Dublin land agent and auctioneer and both families were Protestant. The firm of Bennetts still exists in Dublin as auctioneers and house agents. They had a large family of at least four girls and five boys from 1856 until 1869, one of whom was Alfred. One of the boys became a solicitor. In the 1881 census two of the boys, Adrian (1866) and James (1864) were at boarding school in England. Adrian later emigrated to the USA. Charlotte died in Dublin in February 1879 and is buried in Mount Jerome cemetery.

William Taylor went off to Texas in 1877, where he died. There is a notice in *The Irish Times* on 18 May 1877 which records his demise: 'At Gonzales County, Texas, USA, William Taylor, Esq, Solicitor, late 14 Lower Ormond Quay, Dublin and only son of the late Alfred Taylor, Esq, of 185 Great Brunswick Street, Dublin aged 45 years'.

Gonzales County at this time was one of the most violent places in America and is where the gunfighter John Wesley Hardin became involved in the vicious Taylor–Sutton range war. William possibly went there because the Taylors involved in the fighting were related. The feud, which went on for over a decade, was the longest and bloodiest in Texas history and only ended when the Texas Rangers entered the conflict. It is hard to imagine why and how a Dublin solicitor ended his life there.

Alfred Taylor served an apprenticeship as an engineer on the Dublin, Wicklow and Wexford Railway. Shortly after completing his articles, his father died and unhappy after the death, he signed on a coal ship bound for Bombay, due to return with jute from Calcutta. In Calcutta, fed up with starvation rations, he found that he could get tea and cakes four times a week by getting 'saved' by Evangelists.

Taylor jumped ship and found employment in a jute mill setting up machinery. He later returned as a fourth engineer on another jute ship, arriving in Dundee shortly after the Tay Bridge disaster in December 1879 to find he was an orphan. He worked in the Dundee jute mills for a time, having an uncommonly good time of it – large mills staffed with high spirited female labourers – about a dozen to one man! He used to quote a poem written by F. E. Weatherly, *They all love Jack in Dundee*, as an example of his time there:

When he's sailed the world all over,
And again he steps ashore,
There are scores of lasses waiting,
To love him all the more,
He may love his golden guineas,
But a wife he'll never lack,
If he'd wed them all they'd take him,
For they all love Jack.

Taylor eventually returned to Dublin in order to see relatives, although it is not known when. In about 1881 he signed on for a voyage, Cardiff – Cape Town – California, but on arrival in Cape Town he left the ship and took a job at the Vulcan Iron Works. Sometime later he was summoned to appear for assault having 'decorated a young Dutchman'. He hastily took the train to Beaufort West, then the railhead, and looked around for employment. The Kimberley diamond fields were in full production, but Taylor had no money to get there. Eventually he got a job as a wagon conductor and arrived in Kimberley with half a crown in his pocket.

He initially found it difficult to get a job, as those already there had cornered the market. Taylor claimed he was a painter and was given a job by a Charlie Olsen. He transferred to operating a winding engine for Dan Francis (hence Francistown) and then found his way to the Blue Jacket mine at Tati in what was then Bechuanaland, now Botswana. This gold mine was part of a gold rush in the area. The main street in Francistown is still Blue Jacket Street. This chronology is possibly muddled, for Taylor suggests in a handwritten and undated document [1] that he did not go to Tati until 1886. What is certain is that he went to Transvaal in about 1884 and at Klerksdorp he was 'commandeered'. He found himself as part of a commando under Hendrik Cronje fighting the Taaibosch Koranas, who were stealing cattle, led by Daniel Massouw (Mashow) near the present-day Schweizer-Reneke on the Harts River. The Koranas were a mixed race people. Warfare decimated their numbers and destroyed their tribal organisation.

This commando saw plenty of action and the town is named after Captain C. H. Schweizer and Field Cornet C. M. Reneke, who were killed in the campaign, which ended with the battle of Mamusa Hill and the death of Massouw in December 1885. This hard-fought battle in which Generals Joubert, Cronje and De la Rey earned their spurs resulted in the deaths of ten Boers. One of those wounded was Taylor's friend, Donald Campbell, for whom Taylor extracted the bullet and cleaned up the wound. Campbell wore the bullet on his watch chain and many years later, Taylor met an old Boer in Plumtree who had lent him the knife he used for the surgery.

Taylor suggests that he returned to Tati in January 1886 and erected machinery. At about this time he met Frederick Selous, 'Elephant' Phillips and other old Africa hands from Matabeleland who invited him to go hunting with them. Selous was a very famous white hunter who played a significant part in the early development of Rhodesia. It seems that Taylor had just put money into a hotel business and initially declined the offer. Apparently he was in partnership with a Jewish man until the hotel clerk tipped him off that he was being 'done down' by his partner. Taylor said that it was Ireland versus Jerusalem and after a short time, Ireland won!

Eventually Taylor re-joined Selous and his friends at Jacobsdahl. Another member of the party was named Collinson who was an Old Oxonian remittance man with an allowance of £800 per year, much of which went on drink. Others in the group were Alf and George Musson, Charlie Austin, Tom Fry and Steve Thomas, all legendary Rhodesian pioneers, typical hard cases of the time whose uncompromising character was reflected in the Rhodesian forces which would later enter into the Anglo Boer War from the north. Taylor also met Chief Khama who was the local Paramount chief. During this period he was making contacts with future leaders in the area.

On 12 September 1887 Taylor married Phoebe Clark at Shoshong in Bechuanaland, which is about fifty miles North West of Northern Transvaal. Phoebe was still married to Taylor when he died in 1941 and they had eight surviving children.

Phoebe's mother was the daughter of Hasiboni, King of the Battaping tribe of the Bechuanas. She was born at Kuruman which now just lies within South Africa in the North West Cape. Her English father died when she was aged about three. Her mother then married another Englishman called Robert Roxby. [2] Phoebe originally married a man called Wolfenden, who by all accounts knew Lobengula, the legendary chief of the Matabele people, and who was interested in his exploits in the Zulu War.

Phoebe first met Taylor at Tati when he was foreman for the Tati Concession Company. When Taylor's job finished there, the Wolfendens persuaded him to go to Bulawayo with them to witness 'the Inxwala' (harvest dance) held every year about February. After the ceremony was over, Taylor received a letter from Sam Edwards at Tati asking him to return as soon as possible to assemble more machinery that had just arrived. Meanwhile, Wolfenden became seriously ill and called Phoebe to him and said 'Phoebe, I am going ... you are young and know nothing about the world, God bless you. If you are in trouble send for Mr Taylor.' Three months later Taylor rode into her life again and they married shortly afterwards.

Phoebe said Taylor came by his name of 'Bulala' because having roughed it in his early days he was a pretty tough character and could use his fists and a stick with such good effect that he surprised Lobengula's young warriors. They called him 'Bulala Abantu', which was shortened to 'Bulala', which means 'killer'.

There is little record of Taylor's life over the next few years. It is possible that he started farming at this stage. At his death he owned Avoca Farm at Mangwe, which is adjacent to Botswana near the border crossing point of

Plumtree. Avoca is the name of a small town and river south of Dublin on the railway where he had been apprenticed.

The period from 1890–97 was one of great instability in Rhodesia and Taylor played an active part in the fighting against the major tribes. In the hand-written account in the Zimbabwe archives, he mentions that he rode despatches from Bulawayo to Frank Selous, who was with the 1890 column at Tuli.

Taylor was undoubtedly involved in the events that resulted in the takeover of Rhodesia by Rhodes. He apparently knew Lobengula well and was in his capital when the Rudd concession, which gave Rhodes mining rights throughout the Matabele Kingdom, was made in October 1888.

Taylor was involved in the uprisings in 1893, 1896 and 1897. He received the medal for the campaign in 1893 and this is comparatively rare, only 1,596 having been issued. In 1896/7 he commanded a unit called Plumer's Scouts and was shot in the leg in the Matopo Hills in the South of Rhodesia in Matabeleland. There is an 1896 photo of the Salisbury Field Force, with Cecil Rhodes in the centre and Taylor proudly standing near him. Colonel Plumer, after whom the Scouts were named, was the spitting image of Colonel Blimp, but in Rhodesia and later in South Africa and France as a general, he was a very effective commander.

There is an interesting account of Taylor's activities during the 1896/97 uprisings that comes from a transcript in the national archives of a 1969 interview with eighty-three-year-old Johanna Quested [4]. As a ten-year-old girl she was present in the Mangwe Fort during the rebellion. This fort was constructed near Plumtree in 1893 by Lt Col Goold-Adams and was made from timber and earth. It was then abandoned, but when the Matabele Rebellion broke out in 1896, farmers, traders and miners with their families from the surrounding districts took refuge in the dilapidated fort. During this time 150 Europeans including 42 children lived in the fort for three months.

Mrs Quested remembered the time that Taylor shot the 'Mlimo', an ancient Karanga God revered by both the Matabele and Mashona, who was believed to be orchestrating the uprising. It would seem that during the troubles that there were several live manifestations of this deity. A man called Dallamon, a large native, was brought into the fort and was apparently the incarnation of the 'Mlimo'. 'Dallamon' is the name for the cattle lung sickness that was rife at the time of his birth. Mrs Quested watched Taylor take Dallamon to a large granite rock and shoot him in the back with a revolver. He got up and 'cheeked' Taylor, who shot him in the back again, with the same result. Eventually, the prisoner expired after seven shots and left a pool of fat on the rock. He was apparently so fat that he didn't bleed.

Mrs Quested referred to Taylor as 'Bulala', which means killer in Zulu, Ndbele and other local languages and he used this name throughout his life. On the 40th anniversary of Bulawayo in 1933, he signed his name on an illuminated list of pioneers as 'Alf Bulala Taylor'.

Mrs Quested also referred to Taylor's family. Mrs Taylor was described as a very respectable woman, Taylor as an Irishman, a proper Irishman, and the two children, both fluent in African dialects, were a son, not named but still alive in 1969, and a daughter called Georgina. They may have been from Phoebe Taylor's first marriage.

Taylor, by his own account, was entitled to the British South Africa Company medal with clasps 'Matabeleland 1893', 'Rhodesia1896' and 'Mashonaland 1897'. He probably returned after the troubles to his farm near the present-day town of Plumtree. This town was founded in 1897 when the railway to Bulawayo was constructed. It lies in the Bulalima-Mangwe district (Bulalima, the area where the Bulalima people dwelt and Mangwe, after a chief of that name). It now boasts one of the best schools in Zimbabwe, which was founded by the railway mission in 1902 to cater for the children of employees of the old Cape Government railway. Taylor probably sent his children there and certainly worked as a handyman in the early days. He was mentioned in the *Bulawayo Chronicle* of Saturday 23 September. He is described as being known as 'Bulala Taylor' and described as pioneer, hunter, prospector, miner, transport rider and farmer. It goes on to mention that he had two farms, Vale of Avoca, fifteen miles from Plumtree Siding, and Glenmore. Both were spreads of 3000 morgen, this being the size of the grant from the British South African Company for those who fought in the various uprisings. Glenmore still exists.

In 1898, The Southern Rhodesian Volunteers (SRV) were formed, divided into an Eastern Division and a Western Division with headquarters in Bulawayo. Taylor was an early volunteer and was probably based at Plumtree. By 1905 he was the commanding officer of M Troop of the SRV, based at the drill hall at Plumtree. The SRV were raised as a force for internal security and in the Boer War they faced an enemy and a style of warfare for which they were not trained. The authorities understood this and formed the Rhodesia Regiment to take over their role. The SRV then served in small detachments or as individuals in an intelligence role. In the first three months of the war, the SRV guarded the drifts along the Limpopo and Crocodile Rivers. By December 1899 the rivers were in flood and the 1500 Boers from Northern Transvaal who were threatening Rhodesia returned home.

Taylor was mobilised in the SRV at the start of the Boer War as a Lieutenant in the force under Colonel Plumer that operated on the Rhodesian/Bechuanaland border against the Boer Commandos who came up from Northern Transvaal. He appears in a book published in 1932 by T. G. Trevor, who served as a lieutenant and was appointed to the intelligence section by Plumer. F*orty Years in Africa* describes how the author and Taylor were sent on a reconnaissance into Northern Transvaal. On Christmas day 1899, as they were working their way back hungry and tired, they met a runner coming from Plumer carrying a bottle of whisky and a Christmas pudding, as well as despatches. (Trevor met Plumer at a London reception 24 years later.)

In another book by Robert Burrett (*Plumer's Men, The Rhodesian Regt 1899–1900*) published in 1908 it is mentioned that Taylor and Lt Trevor were employed to make deep patrols into the heart of Northern Transvaal. The soldiers were all natives, Venda refugees from Transvaal. On 27 December, presumably replete with whisky and Christmas pudding, Trevor, Taylor and their native scouts were reconnoitring towards the Makato (which is also called Zoutpansberg) Mountains when they clashed with a large party of native scouts working for the Boers. In the encounter the Rhodesians lost three men. Taylor continued with Plumer's forces and took part in the relief of Mafeking. He was in hospital after this, having picked up dysentery during the operations.

Once he regained his fitness, he was sent along with six men to find a way into Fort Botha, a prefabricated bullet-proof portable steel fort situated in the Makato Mountains. On arrival they found two Boers in the fort and after capturing them destroyed the telephone system. They were then confronted by a Boer Commando and retired into the mountains north of Louis Trichardt and remained there until they met up with a column of Kitchener's Fighting Scouts (KFS) led by Colonels Grenfell and Colenbrander, both experienced, hard-bitten fighters. The KFS occupied Louis Trichardt and it was burnt to the ground, allegedly on Lord Kitchener's orders. Taylor is said to have enthusiastically torched the town, much to the annoyance of one of his intelligence agents, Leonard Ledeboer, who owned a substantial timber and iron house there and who had been promised his house would not be burnt.

Shortly afterwards, Taylor negotiated the surrender of Commandant van Rensburg and his 150 burghers after tracking them through the low veldt. He was summoned personally by Lord Kitchener and sent back to Makato as an Intelligence Officer and acting Native Commissioner. It should be noted that the post of Native Commissioner was an appointment by the

Civil Government, and not a military position. Colonel David Henderson, Director of Military Intelligence, wrote about this in his final report after the war and this is probably the reason why Taylor was described as holding a civilian appointment and was tried by military court rather than Court-Martial.

His African experience and his familiarity with the local native languages made him ideal for these posts. He established his headquarters at Bristow's House on Sweetwaters Farm near Elim. He swiftly set up a network of native informers who reported to the junior intelligence officers. There were several units working in the vicinity, including the BVC, the KFS and the Highland Mounted Infantry (HMI). Two infantry battalions, the Wiltshires and the Gordon Highlanders, were based at Pietersburg. The actions of the KFS and the HMI in the area are usually neglected by historians of the Morant episode.

Taylor was very successful at producing intelligence, but there was concern about the insensitive, often brutal, way he went about his duties as a native commissioner. There were also grave suspicions that many of the cattle captured from Boer farms were being driven north towards Avoca farm at Plumtree in Rhodesia. There was a tale of 5000 cattle taken from Beyers, the Boer commandant. There were also reports of considerable thefts of cattle from friendly Kaffirs. In September, Mr Enraght-Mooney of the Transvaal department of Native affairs referred to information that Taylor had misappropriated cattle owned by blacks. Trooper Cochrane, who assisted the preparation of evidence against Morant and his friends suggested that Taylor employed his own Kaffirs in the work and that Squadron Sergeant Major Morrison was an interested party in the business. Apparently the cattle were driven up to Taylor's farm or into Portuguese East Africa. Taylor was also implicated in taking gold dust and nuggets from the wagons after the first murders on 2 July 1901. So there was a coterie whose motive was to accumulate land, cattle and gold, to be distributed after the war.

Taylor was deeply involved with the events that led to the trial of Breaker Morant and his friends and he was also a major participant in other questionable incidents where he acted with the KFS. One was the execution of Corporal Jacob. An intelligence agent and mine owner, Malcolm Clark, was ambushed at Buffels Hill on 18 May 1901 as his party was bringing some surrendered burghers into Pietersberg. Three were killed (all members of the Intelligence Department) and after scattering live ammunition over the bodies the Boers made off. Taylor, acting on information from natives, took a party of KFS and apprehended Corporal Jacob who had led the ambush party. General Beyers, the Boer commander, thought Jacob's behaviour was unsporting and did not protect him. He was brought before a drum head court-martial and sentenced to death. Barney Williams, [5] the old Rhodesian hangman, was given £1 to execute him. This he did in the sawmill outside Pietersburg.

After the war Taylor received a King's South Africa medal with both bars (1901 and 1902). The requirement for this was to have been serving in South Africa for 18 months prior to June 1902 and to have served in the forces after 1 January 1902. Taylor is on the Southern Rhodesia Volunteers roll and by his name is written 'for special services under Lord Kitchener June 1901–April 1902'. His South Africa medal had the clasps 'Rhodesia, Relief of Mafeking and Transvaal'.

There appeared an advertisement in *The Bulawayo Chronicle* on Saturday 22 March 1902, barely three weeks after the execution of Morant: 'Captain Alf Taylor has received permission to raise a troop of Scouts under Volunteer conditions, the troop to be called Taylor's Scouts. Men wishing to join are requested to apply to Captain Taylor at Plumtree or the Orderly Room of the SRV.'

After the Anglo Boer War, Taylor returned to his farm at Plumtree and played his part in the small community there including continuing to serve with the Southern Rhodesian Volunteers. During the First World War, he served in France receiving the British War and Victory medals. He made his own way to England, arriving on the *Comrie Castle* on 31 March 1917 to join the South African Native Labour Corps. At the end of the war he went to Ireland at the invitation of Louise Butler Eyre of Eyrecourt, Galway. She was the sister of a British officer, Lewes Hart Stewart, whom Taylor had buried when he died on a shooting trip in Western Matabeleland in 1894. Taylor was given an engraved rifle.

There is a small piece in *The Rhodesia Herald* of Friday 25 April 1919 which mentions that 'the many friends of Capt Bulala Taylor will be pleased to hear that he is returning to Rhodesia at last. He is one of Rhodesia's early pioneers and he has been over two years in France. For the last couple of months he has been at the aero engine works at F. C. Berwicks and was one of the few that remained at his post and refused to go on strike. He has been appointed as officer commanding and organising officer of the Legion of Frontiersmen in Rhodesia.' The Legion was founded in 1904 and one of its aims was to be 'the eyes and ears of the Empire'. It became quite popular in several parts of the Empire, particularly Canada, but never amounted to much.

Taylor continued to live at Plumtree and some accounts suggest that he became a Member of Parliament, but the existing records of elections to the Rhodesian Parliament show no trace of of this.

Alfred 'Bulala' Taylor died at the Memorial Hospital at Bulawayo on 24 October 1941 after an illness of three days, reportedly aged 78. In his will his estate was valued at £1,531 17s 4d, most of it being 2990 morgens of land valued at 8/- per morgen. He was survived by his wife Phoebe and eight children. In about 1960 the farm became part of the tribal territories in the area.

Taylor had many detractors and was a rough man of the pioneering era and was undoubtedly indifferent to the fate of some of the natives, but he proved his abilities in combat and had an impressive collection of medals. He was an original Rhodesian and typical of the hard cases who were at the forefront in Africa in the late nineteenth century.

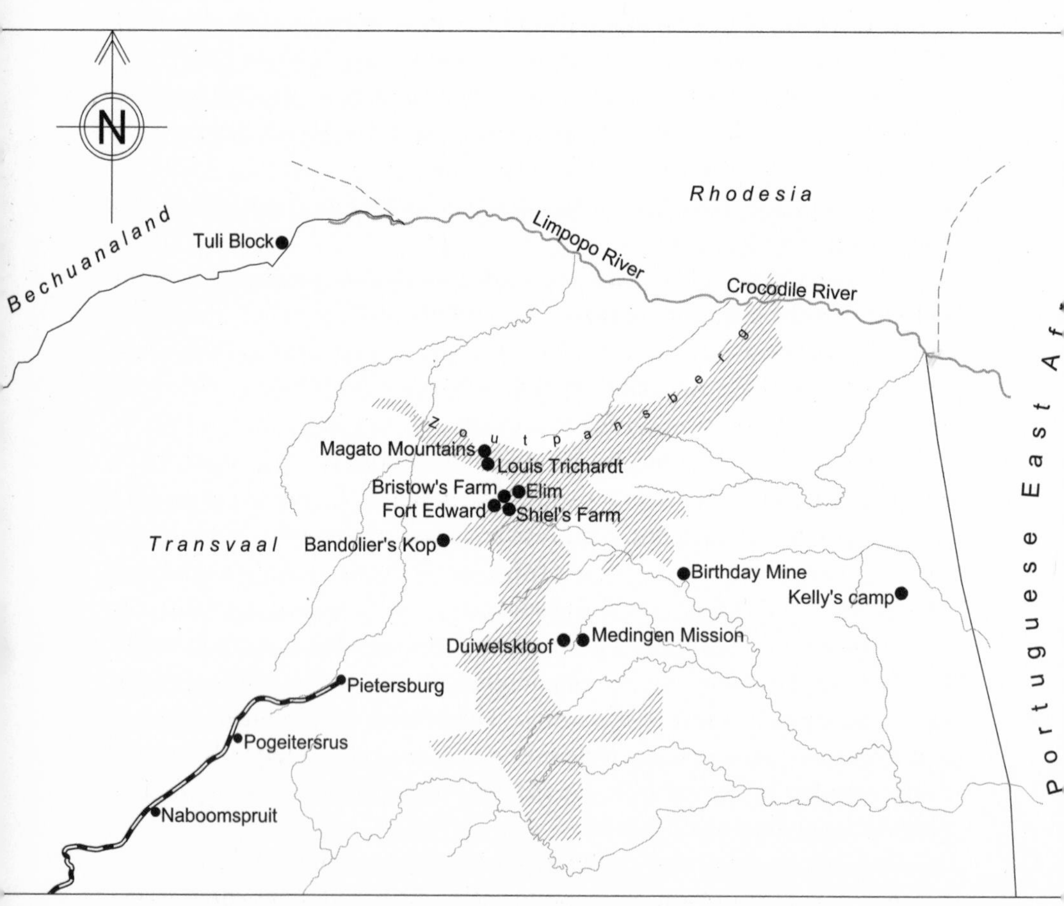

9
Events in Northern Transvaal

The Northern Transvaal was a remote and rugged area where British forces did not arrive in any numbers until early 1901. Even then, the vastness of the area and relatively small numbers of soldiers meant that they had little hope of controlling it. The soldiers soon realised that the isolation and relatively poor communication systems also meant that the army command structure had a fairly tenuous hold over them too. In less than a year, this would result in a Court of Inquiry into multiple murders and ensuing Courts-Martial that would remain contentious for the next century.

The first killing known to have received any attention from the Court of Inquiry of October 1901 was the killing of C. J. van den Berg. The most detailed account of the killing is provided by Charles Skeen, a great Grandson of C. J. van den Berg, as related by Charles Leach. [1]

Having contracted a fever, possibly malaria, C. J. van den Berg, a member of the Zoutpansberg Commando, had been sent home to Zwagershoek in the Zoutpansberg Mountains to recover. Around 4 May 1901 about fifteen soldiers of Kitchener's Fighting Scouts and a Mr Devenish, a surveyor from Pietersburg, arrived at the van den Berg farm with orders to remove Mrs van den Berg and her children to the concentration camp in Pietersburg. Van den Berg retired to some nearby rocks with his rifle, leaving instructions with his wife that if she felt threatened or abused to wave her bonnet as a signal.

After finding that van den Berg was not in the house, some of the soldiers started killing chickens and ducks and hanging them on their saddles. Mrs van den Berg felt the troops were getting out of hand and gave the signal. Van den Berg fired and in the ensuing exchange one of the British soldiers was wounded.

Calling a cease fire, Devenish declared that the family would not be harmed on condition that the wounded man, Robert Herbert Summers of the Field Intelligence Department and previously of the Rhodesia Regiment [2] was cared for until a patrol returned to take him to a military hospital in Pietersburg. Confiscating van den Berg's rifle, the soldiers departed. Why they did not take the whole party to Pietersburg is not clear. Despite Mrs van den Berg's best efforts Summers died about a week later with no patrol having returned for him.

A few days later a group of six soldiers including 'Captain' 'Bulala' Taylor and a man named Mickey Henderson returned under the guidance of a local 'joiner' named Vogel. ('Joiner' was the name given to those of Dutch decent who, for whatever reason, decided to fight on the British side.) Van den Berg's wife was forced to bring her bedridden husband to the door, helped by her teenage daughter. He was ordered to walk away from the house and after a few paces he died in a volley of rifle shots. Van den Berg was hastily buried in a gully and the family were given five minutes to collect their things and taken to the concentration camp in Pietersburg. The farm was burned. [3]

A different version appeared in the newspapers:

> There are still very few particulars available concerning the death of R. H. Summers, who was killed on or about May 4th in the Northern Transvaal, but it is stated that he was shot through the back at a distance of 40 yards by Boer of the name of van der [sic] Berg. Summers' two companions, Alf Taylor and Keith, were made prisoners. General Plumer afterwards captured van der Berg, who was sentenced to be shot, he having broken his parole and the sentence was confirmed by Lord Kitchener. Taylor and Keith were released also by General Plumer's force. [4]

The newspaper account appears to be a conflation of different events outlined later and is clearly very different to Charles Skeen's. This is not the only account which claims that one of Taylor's confederates in these activities was a man often referred to simply as 'Keith'. A. H. Keith is a peripheral and shadowy figure in the BVC story. In 1901 he held the same nominal rank as 'Captain' Taylor in the Intelligence Department and appears on the medal roll of the unit alongside Taylor as Arthur Henry Keith. He had formerly been a sergeant of B Squadron of the Rhodesia Regiment. [5] Keith had been operating in the Southern Rhodesia/Northern Transvaal area for years and had taken part in some of Cecil Rhodes' British South Africa Company's shadier exploits since 1891 [6] and was known to be an ex-naval officer. The true identity of Arthur Henry Keith is elusive but it is strongly suspected that he is in fact Arthur Henry Knox, generally known as Archibald Hamilton Keith. [7] His descendants relate family lore that he was a British Naval Officer who had operated as a spy against the Boers during the war of 1899–

1902. [8] If this is our man then he, like Taylor, was born in Ireland but ten years earlier. As far as we know, Keith would play no further role in the BVC's activities. The same cannot be said of Alfred 'Bulala' Taylor'.

To fully understand the Bushveldt Carbineers affair and particularly 'Captain' Alfred Taylor's role in it, we must consider the geography and immediate history of the Zoutpansberg Area of Northern Transvaal before 'Breaker' Morant and B Squadron of the Bushveldt Carbineers arrived. The Zoutpansberg is skirted to the north by the Limpopo (or Crocodile) River beyond which was southern Rhodesia, stronghold of the British South Africa Company (BSAC). East of both Zoutpansberg and southern Rhodesia was the border with Portuguese East Africa, now Mozambique. Both of these borders would play a role in the Morant affair. The area was the ancestral home of the people known as the Venda.

In 1898, a year before the start of the 2nd Anglo-Boer War, a confrontation between the Boer South African Republic and the Western Venda led by Mphefu Alilali Tshilamulela (commonly referred to as Mphefu) had resulted in the expulsion of Mphefu and the overrunning of the part of the Western Venda 'state' south of the Limpopo in Zoutpansberg. The western Venda had been a thorn in the side of the Boer republic for most of its existence and had forced the abandonment of Schoemansdahl in 1867 merely by threat, after growing resentment towards an increased Boer presence, taxes and claims to land and labour. [9] Makhado, Mphefu's father had refused to allow the Boer republic to establish mission stations on his land. During the first British annexation of the republic (1877 –81) Makhado had been marginally friendlier to the British and briefly contributed to a police force in 1880, but paid little more than lip service to British sovereignty. Though according to Braun (2013) 'Makhado and Mphefu both consequently held a higher opinion of the apparently light hand of British colonialism compared to the onerous immediacy of the Boers.'

As a result of the 1st Anglo Boer War, Boer governance of the area was re-established in 1881. Makhado refused to recognise any restriction on his territory, pay taxes, conduct censuses or recognise boundaries that the Boer republic attempted to impose in 1887, 1889 and 1895, seeing these, natrurally enough, as direct threats to his sovereignty. By 1895 the Boer republic was deeply concerned at the threat of an attack from the Venda and according to T. V. Bulpin:

> He [Makhado] seemed doubly menacing at the time, for he had with him half-a-dozen white renegades, led by an ex-naval officer named Keith (or Shangwahlali to the Africans). This character acted as a variety of Commodore to the Venda, and affected an odd costume made of chamois

> leather, with a broad-brimmed hat and jackboots. He had originally been one of the men involved in the celebrated Countess of Carnarvon incident, which almost caused a war between Britain and Portugal. Now his presence in Vendaland gave the Republic an added alarm, from the idea that he was probably running guns and instructing the tribe in the use of modern European weapons. Fortunately for the Republic, at this time of mounting trouble, Makhato was sickened from dropsy and in no condition to lead a war.

In 1895 the Boer republic was not prepared for the expense of war with the Venda but the death of Makhado in September that year, presumably from dropsy (oedema) mentioned by Bulpin, led to internal conflict within the Venda. Makhado had chosen Maemu, a young son of his senior wife as his successor. This was an unusual choice and was not popular with some. Mphefu had been a strong contender but was at this time in exile at the Kimberley Mines. Sinthumule, one of his brothers, was also a potential claimant who was in Rhodesia at Tuli and was probably Makhado's liaison with the British South Africa Company (BSAC). Those opposed to Maemu's appointment retrieved these two, who quickly forced Maemu out. Inevitably, tension between Mphefu and Sinthumule soon arose and the latter sought refuge with the Boer state. Although the Boers provided protection for Sinthumule they did not provide further support and, as needs must, he settled his differences with Maemu, who had been nurturing the notion within the Boer republic that Mphefu had plans to attack white settlers in Zoutpansberg. Mphefu viewed the ZAR's harbouring of Maemu and Sinthumule with equal suspicion fearing that the Boers may arm them to his disadvantage. Mphefu had remained friendly with the BSAC across the Limpopo in Rhodesia, which further irked the ZAR. For a while, Mphefu maintained peace by seeming less opposed to censuses being held on his territory. Later however, he warned Boer representatives to stay away and started demanding taxes be paid, by the Venda, to him alone. [10]

The ZAR sent an armed force to negotiate but these negotiations soon failed. Mphefu had hedged his bets and already sought permission to take refuge north of the Limpopo with the BSAC, should the need arise. By the time the ZAR launched its three-pronged attack and took his capital at Luatame on 16 November 1898, some of his chiefs had already surrendered, one of his white 'friends' Whitfield James, had been arrested and Keith had slipped off into the bush. [11] Mphefu's royal village was torched and Mphefu retreated north-eastward hoping for military assistance from the BSAC. When this was not forthcoming he was forced to move into BSAC territory by crossing the Limpopo. The BSAC refused the requests of the

ZAR for extradition. They allotted him land at Vhuxwa, district of Belingwe, in early 1899. South of the Limpopo the more compliant Sinthumule was recognised as the new khosi and was allocated a restricted area near the Venda territory of 1896. His allies were similarly allocated land. The Boers now planned to open up the mountains to white prospecting and settlement.

In February 1899, the ZAR erected the town of Louis Trichardt. 'As a sign of Boer permanence, the government erected the town they had long sought to place at the foot of the mountains, and gave it an ironic piece of historical backdating by naming it Louis Trichardt, after the early Boer traveller whose arms had helped decide Venda succession in 1836.' [12]

At the start of the 2nd Anglo Boer War, many of the Venda who remained south of the Limpopo still viewed Mphefu as their leader and paid taxes and homage to him. It was clear to the British that the Venda would form an invaluable source of intelligence in the area. The ZAR had specifically stated that the British should not recognise Mphefu as the paramount chief of the Venda, whilst Mphefu had sent word south across the Limpopo that the Venda should assist the British. Lieutenant T. G. Trevor of the intelligence department claims that Venda emissaries came to him in late 1899. Lt Trevor also claims Alfred Taylor accompanied him on an infiltration mission into Zoutpansberg in late 1899. [13] It is easy to see, in this environment, the value to the British forces of 'Bulala' Taylor, who had a working knowledge of the Venda and Shona languages and of this remote area.

Zoutpansberg being in the extreme north of the Transvaal remained in Boer hands until well into 1900 and with most of ZAR's attention being directed towards the British farther to the south, peripheral areas like Zoutpansberg were left largely to their own devices. Venda farmers began to re-occupy and rebuild homesteads on the mountains and foothills, many believing that the British administration would restore their ancestral rights to lands, cattle and perhaps allow them to keep cattle taken from the Boers. [14]

Mphefu had been persistently lobbying Herbert Taylor, chief Native Commissioner of Matebeleland, for permission to return across the Limpopo to his capital of Luatame. Permisson was granted in April 1901 once he had offered the scouting services of his loyal following in Zoutpansberg and Belingwe. Mphefu offered to accompany Captain Keith across the Limpopo on his own mission amd the military authorities agreed. [15]

Mphefu crossed the Limpopo in late April with some of his people and a small British detachment. He soon re-established himself in his capital of Luatame in the foothills of the mountains. [16] Alfred Taylor is believed to have arrived in Zoutpansberg from Rhodesia about two weeks before Colonel Johan Colenbrander arrived in Louis Trichardt on 10 May, which would mean he crossed the Limpopo at about the same time as Keith and Mphefu. [17] Taylor would later claim that Mphefu came across after him. [18] In an interview with the *Bulawayo Chronicle* in October, Colenbrander wrote, 'There we met Bulala Taylor, by the way, and Keith. They were holding the Zoutpansberg with five men. The sixth had been shot.' [19] The sixth man was R. H. Summers and Colenbrander is clearly recounting the same story as outlined at the beginning of this chapter.

Taylor in his own account of his actions written in 1905 [20] says that: 'On my recovery [from dysentery] I got a wire from HQ Pretoria saying I was to report to Col Wood at Bulawayo where I would get instructions. I there met a man named Keith who informed me that Lord Kitchener wanted me to find a way back into Fort Botha which was situated in the Makato Mountains. I went down with six men following the Crocodile River…' Fort Botha was a moveable iron structure, previously one corner of a triangle of such structures linked by stone walls at Louis Trichardt, which the Boer republic had placed in a strategic position at Songozwi west of the mountain, now known as Hanglip, near Mphefu's deserted city. It was re-located here to prevent the chief returning to his city after the Boer force that had ejected him had left. [21] Another corner of the triangle had been blown up in an accident whilst the third would become infamous as Fort Edward. Taylor and the group of six men captured the two Boers named Lottering and Erasmus who manned Fort Botha.

Why did Kitchener order Taylor to capture Fort Botha, a tiny fort garrisoned by two men on a remote mountain at the time that Mphefu was returning to his capital? L. F. Braun summarises the situation: 'In the short run … Mphefu was in a key position to aid the British advance into the Zoutpansberg between April and July 1901, and by mobilising his mahosi and their fighting men dissuade Boer guerrillas from occupying the difficult terrain of the mountains.' [22]

After capturing Lottering and Erasmus, Taylor claims he found the rest of the Commando to be in the foothills operating a telephone link to Louis Trichardt. Taylor smashed the machine and cut off telephone communications to Pietersburg. [23] Shortly after this, Taylor and his group visited C. J. van den Berg resulting in the death of R. H. Summers. Owing to the local Boer Commando hearing the firing at van den Berg's Farm, Taylor's group had to make off into the mountains.

Then ensued some form of standoff. Johan Colenbrander, the commander of the KFS, stated in the *Bulawayo Chronicle*: 'We found "Bulala" Taylor with five men holding the mountains against heavy odds, the biggest piece of bluff and cheek I ever heard of, He lost one man, however, called Summers shot from behind by a man who had given him coffee. We added the sugar since, and the murderer is now in the happy hunting grounds.' [24] Colenbrander continues 'You see the country here may be compared to a frying pan being surrounded by hills, the handle being the only outlet. The outlet was a pass that one man could defend against an army. Bulala made out he had a devil of a force. I never saw such a piece of cheek in all my life.' [25]

Modesty deserts Taylor when he wrote of the incident to a friend on 14 May: 'Safe at last, relieved by Colonel Colenbrander. I believe I have done wonders – held the Boers' stronghold with six men for six days. [26] I got about 60 Boers to surrender and took 100 odd guns, all through bluff and bounce.' Wonders perhaps, bluff and bounce, probably, but Taylor still seems pretty relieved to have been found by Colenbrander and Grenfell!

Charles Leach, author of *The Legend of Breaker Morant is Dead and Buried* (2012) assumes that Taylor had shot van den Berg, which may well be true. However Colenbrander's use of 'we' suggests Kitchener's Fighting Scouts may also have been involved and this may well be the origin of Morant's later claims at court that KFS had shot prisoners. It seems that Colenbrander had already captured Louis Trichardt when they came across Taylor, Keith and their group but they soon took a leading hand in the fate of that town.

Taylor and Keith's relief had taken place on or around 9 May 1901, the day that Colenbrander and his column had attacked and captured the town of Louis Trichardt. [27] Colenbrander's troops found the town stricken with fever, many of the inhabitants bedridden and in filthy conditions. About forty people surrendered, and around fifty were arrested. On 11 May the inhabitants were told to collect a few things and leave their houses. [28] Having loading the inhabitants into wagons, the troops looted the houses. The residents, many of whom were sick with malaria, were to be transported to Pietersburg, though it seems they were dumped about two miles out of town and travelled on foot the rest of the way. The troops took livestock and killed trek animals for food. Almost a month later on 6 June [29] 'Captains' Taylor and Keith ordered the town to be burnt. This was apparently carried out by local natives, some of whom were Venda, with what L. F. Braun refers to as 'understandable enthusiasm'. Returning inhabitants two years later found 'not one stone left upon another'. [30]

Seen in the light of Taylor and Keith's re-establishment of Mphefu and the Venda in his mountain home (which the ZAR had burnt in 1898), the total destruction of Louis Trichardt, the symbol of Boer permanence in the area and established only a year earlier, not only suited British aspirations but also represented reward to the Venda for their expected services in the wider area. Had this been part of a deal with Mphefu? Venda interviewed in the 1960s and 1970s were unanimous in stating that those Venda who had opposed Mphefu's succession had been secretly 'tried', found guilty and shot by Taylor during this period. [31] One of these was probably Chief Madumetsa. Taylor had suspected him of collaborating with the Boers. [32]

Louis Trichardt was still smoking when 'A' squadron of the Bushveldt Carbineers arrived in Zoutpansberg, under the command of Captain James Huntley Robertson. Taylor was assigned with Robertson to set up camp at Sweetwaters Farm belonging to the Bristow family. Taylor had also been appointed as acting Native Commissioner and along with others of the British Military Intelligence Department set up his headquarters in Sweetwaters Hotel.

For many who had lived in South Africa for any length of time, the 2nd Anglo Boer War presented a dilemma in terms of allegiances. The Bristows were friends with the Boer leader Assistant Commandant, General Beyers, who was actually at the farm when he got wind of the British detachment heading there. Rather than cause a fire fight at the farm, Beyers and his men vacated to observe the situation. [33]

Had General Beyers been able stay close enough to observe the dynamics of the command structure of the incoming detachment, he would have found a rather curious situation. The ambiguity in the military relationship between Captain Robertson and 'Captain' Taylor has been much discussed, it being evident that the men of the BVC were not clear who was in command and it seems that the authorities were not entirely sure either. Later, in September 1901, when Taylor's behaviour towards the natives of the area led to attempts to replace him, Colonel David Henderson expressed the wish that any replacement should 'have control of Taylor's present force, about 100 men, as police and for protection'. [34] Yet two weeks before, Francis Enraght Mooney, who became Native Commissioner to Zoutpansberg, wrote 'Taylor ... is not in Military Command, I believe.' [35] Whilst he may not have been officially in command of the Spelonken detachment, it is certain that in effect he was.

The true character of Captain James Huntley Robertson has been obscured over the years. The blame for this must lie to some extent with a man named Alexander John Horatio Herbert Robertson, who in postwar years in Victoria lived a Walter Mitty style existence claiming to be James Huntley Robertson. Although James Huntley Robertson signed up to the West Australian Mounted Infantry, where he had been working as a mine manager, he never returned to Australia after the 2nd Anglo Boer War. He left South Africa on 25 April 1902 aboard the *Orotava* [36] for England initially, and later to Mexico, the country of his birth. He was aged 29 when he signed up and was soon promoted to sergeant. Robertson had been born in Miraflores, Mexico, in 1875 [37], the son of a Scottish mill owner

John Robertson and his Peruvian wife, Paz Beeserer. By 1891 he was working as a cotton machinery fitter in a mill in Accrington in the north of England. [38] After the Anglo Boer War he worked on the Peruvian railways [39] and his World War 1 service record, which shows he won the Military Cross on the Somme in September 1916, gives his occupation as Mining Engineer. [40]

It is difficult to reconcile the image often presented of Huntley Robertson as an effete officer with lace cuffs standing on a plank so as not to dirty his polished boots with that of a West Australian Mine manager or cotton mill machinery fitter in the industrial north of England. The image of the effete dandy appears to originate largely from the account of him given by Trooper Muir Churton in an interview with Frank Shields, when Churton was in his eighties. [41] Some parts of Churton's (very much) later account are directly contradicted by his testimony in 1902. Whatever Robertson's true character, it is clear that it was Taylor who was really in command of events in the Spelonken prior to early July 1901.

On 2 July 'Captain' Taylor received a report from his network that a party of six Boers were trekking toward Fort Edward with two covered wagons and a large herd of cattle, to surrender. The 65-year-old J. J. Geyser and the rest of his party were in fact probably heading towards the Swiss Mission clinic Valdezia, since according to one of the party, Geyser was already bedridden in one of the wagons with fever, probably malaria. Three others were also suffering with the same condition, though being younger, were still ambulant. [42] The fact that at least one was bedridden was corroborated by the testimony of troopers of the BVC.

A notable feature of the Morant story is that the BVC who perpetrated the murders, whilst claiming that the victims were killers, train wreckers and marauders, never identified them by name. The victims of the BVC have been referred to as 'the six Boers', 'the eight Boers' by Morant's admirers, as they are reluctant to humanise the victims of their hero. Besides Geyser, the men were J. C. Greyling 25 and J. F. Vercuil 31, both of whom were alleged to have been feverish. These men had enlisted the help of 18-year-old F. G. J. Potgieter and 12-year-old P. J. Geyser, youngest son of J. J. Geyser, to help them to the mission. They had been joined along the way by a stranger named van Heerden who was described by J. J. Geyser's daughter as feverish and totally destitute. [43]

The troopers of the BVC had allegedly been presented with a different story by their officers; that these men were murderers and train wreckers [44] and this, it has been claimed, was the reason for what transpired when these men were intercepted by part of 'A' squadron. Why this party actually met a different fate to the other 41 prisoners taken around this time [45] is most likely contained in a later letter of complaint by fifteen BVC troopers to Col Hall written in October 1901. It stated that 'In the wagon there was supposed to be a box containing £2000.' [46] After the war J. J. Geyser's daughter claimed that her grandfather had around £800 of gold and a large number of five pound notes in a wooden box in the wagon. [47]

The events of the group's meeting with the BVC are best described by those present. Extensive quotes from those witnesses will be given here. Too often in the retelling of the Breaker Morant saga, short sound bites, taken out of context, have been used and vital lines have been omitted to follow an author's own agenda, be that agenda to romanticise or even actively deceive.

Trooper Ernest Browne stated:

> I was one of the patrol that left Sweetwaters Farm under Capt Robertson. When the patrol fell in under Sergt Major Morrison I saw Capt. Taylor and Capt. Robertson talking together. Shortly afterwards we moved off. SSM [Squadron Sgt Major] Morrison coming direct from the officers then called Sergt Oldham on in front of the troops. They talked together some few minutes, then Sergt Oldham started off at a gallop. Sergt Major Morrison came back to the troop and called out troopers Eden, Arnold, Brown, Heath and Dale and spoke to them for a few minutes. They then followed Sergt Oldham. SSM Morrison then came back to me, I at the time being at the head of the troop with Sergt Stevens. SSM Morrison told me he had issued orders to Sergt Oldham and his party to shoot six Boers who were reported to be coming in to surrender. Sergt Oldham refused to shoot them until he was told it was an absolute order. This conversation between SSM Morrison and myself took place some considerable time before the shooting could possibly have taken place. [48]

The conversation between Morrison, Robertson and Taylor was relayed at the military court of Alfred Taylor by SSM Morrison. He stated that he had asked Captain Robertson if he should take orders from Taylor. Captain Robertson said, 'Certainly, as he is commanding officer at Spelonken.' Morrison asked Taylor to repeat his order, which he did, saying that, if the Boers showed the white flag, the witness was not to see it.

Trooper George Arthur Heath deposed as follows:

> About half a mile north of Bristow's Farm (Sweetwaters) I was told off on or about the 2nd July to go with Sergt Oldham to meet six Boers with two wagons who were alleged to be murderers and train wreckers. SSM Morrison told us that. The patrol consisted of Sergt Oldham, Corpl Primrose, Troopers Brown, Eden, Dale, Arnold and myself. Arnold and I went on in advance and met the Boers leaving the rest of the patrol at a

> farmhouse. When I saw the wagons coming I hid in the grass and Trooper Arnold returned for the rest of the patrol. We fired two or three shots at the wagons wounding a bullock in the shoulder. Immediately a white flag went up. Before shooting we had been warned by SSM Morrison that we were not to take notice of the white flag and that the Boers were to be shot. SSM Morrison said these were Capt. Taylor's orders. When SSM Morrison told us this we asked where the orders originated from. He repeated 'They were Capt. Taylor's orders'.
>
> The patrol, as soon as the white flag was hoisted, ceased firing and went up to the wagons. We took their rifles, bandoliers and all ammunition. Sergt Oldham said to the patrol 'you know your orders and they must be carried out.' We then lined the five Boers up alongside the road. Sergt Oldham told one man off to each Boer, Corpl Primrose having previously been sent in to report the surrender. We all fired and shot them. They all fell dead. There was one Boer lying sick in the wagon and to the best of my belief Trooper Eden shot him in the wagon.
>
> The Boers never made the slightest resistance. [49]

After the killings, according to the letter of complaint of October 1901 written by the fifteen BVC troopers, the bodies had been re-united with their weapons and ammunition in an attempt to give the appearance of resistance, though in the haste and confusion some of those wearing bandoliers of Mauser ammunition had been given Martini Henry rifles and vice versa. J. C. Greyling, J. G. Potgieter and J. C. Vercuil [sic] are listed on the Roll of Honour of the Zoutpanberg Commando [50] indicating that they had been combatants but were unlikely to have been involved with the killing of Captain Hunt, which happened as a result of the fight with the Viljoen Commando.

> Perhaps an hour and half afterwards Corpl Primrose galloped back and reported to the officers in charge. I heard him say to SSM Morrison the Boers have been taken prisoner. Immediately afterwards we got the order to canter and continued at that pace until we came up with the wagons when Sergt Oldham came to meet us and reported something to the officers. I heard the word 'murder' and 'after they had surrendered'. [51]

A number of other troopers who were in the patrol with Trooper Browne, which arrived on the scene after the shootings, give similar accounts. It was immediately obvious to them, from the uniformity of the wounds – a bullet hole in the forehead of each – though one had a neck wound, and from the position of the bodies that the Boers had not died in any kind of fair fight. Another observation made by more than one of the troopers is that these men were wealthy, having with them 100 or more oxen in splendid condition. [52] Trooper Solomon King would depose:

> In the Wagon lay an old man shot through the head. I saw Lt Handcock walk past carrying the cash box which had been taken from the wagon. He held it up and said; 'There is over £100 here in paper money.' I said 'I thought there was over £1000. Can't you divide it amongst us?' He said 'No I can't do nothing like that.'

Major W. N. Bolton would later write 'No trace was ever found of the gold but the notes I know were distributed amongst the men as curios. During the enquiry previous to the trial, I was shown many of these notes, most of them value five pounds.' [53]

It is interesting that of all the accusations made against the BVC, that of looting roused some of the greatest indignation among those returned troopers who wrote to the Australian press, though the sheer weight of evidence provided by various trooper's statements, and others who saw the loot, makes it clear that looting occurred on a large scale. Lieutenant George Witton, who had yet to arrive in the area, however, claimed in his book 'It has been stated that these men had a large sum of money in their possession, but the money was all a myth. I have never heard of any money being taken from them.' [54] Trooper James Christie explains how it went with the surrendered:

> Generally the escort to refugees, which were sent to Bermuda, though they surrendered and never lifted a rifle, had no tucker, and so had to depend on the natives en route, or the charity of the people who were bringing in. Generally if you were decent to the men and women, as they invariably were to you, the chances were you would be given some biltong, as well as perhaps, some skins or horns they might have with them. Lion skins or elephant tusks, or anything grand that way were generally snapped up by the officer in charge and some were paid for and others not. [55]

This assertion is supported by the fact that in late 1901 a Katrina Grobler and Cecilia Duvenhage were questioned regarding six elephant tusks alleged to have been taken from them by BVC members. [56]

It was not only Boers who suffered at the hands of the BVC. Arthur Davey records that 'Same day black spies were shot'. Charles Leach suggests this is a dating error and the two black men named Njoba and Mattungen, who were attending a social function, were shot not on the 2nd but 27 July, when

Captain Taylor returned to Valdezia with a patrol of either BVC men or his own intelligence scouts. [57]

Although the two sergeants, Oldham and Morrison, carried out Taylor and Robertson's orders, it is clear that there was some unease from these first killings among the men of the BVC, some more than others. One who was clearly troubled was Trooper B. J. van Buuren. Van Buuren was a Boer 'joiner'. The number of these within the Bushveldt Carbineers was not insignificant. Trooper James Christie recorded among his initial thoughts on his new unit that 'The office was placarded with B.V.C., Britain's Valiant Colonials, Bushveldt Carbineers etc. I thought from what I had seen of the recruits that Boer Volunteer Corps would be a more appropriate reading of the initials, or Boer Vagrant Crowd.' [58] He would later develop a considerable respect for the Boers.

Van Buuren had made the mistake of expressing his concerns, and worse, being seen talking to prisoners and pointing out Sergt Oldham's Patrol. Captain Robertson and/or 'Captain' Taylor decided that van Buuren could not be trusted and should be shot. Robertson ordered the ever willing Lieutenant Peter Handcock to deal with the problem.

Again, the circumstances are best described by those who witnessed them. Trooper Edward Powell:

> On the day that Trooper van Buuren was killed he came up to my fire at breakfast to grill some steak. He told me he had got into trouble through being more or less drunk and talking to the Boers [other captives] about the slaughter of the six. He said 'I do not care what the officers say. I will not see murder passed by and nothing said about it.' The words were to this effect. Later in the day Lt Handcock was detached with four troopers, one of whom was van Buuren, to scout for some Boers alleged to be on the left. Captain Taylor was in charge of the whole patrol and Captain Robertson was also present. I was on observation post when we outspanned. [To unhitch draught animals; here, to dismount.] I climbed a tree to get a better view and took a pair of glasses up the tree with me. I had a complete view of the country all around except as to one depression. When Lt Handcock came up I said 'I see you came in with a led horse and an empty saddle.' He said 'Yes, we had a brush with the Boers. They ambushed and killed one of our men.' Then he added 'We beat them off and they were making for that kopje.' Indicating the one by Hayes Farm. I thought at the time that it was improbable that they could have passed without me seeing them from my observation post up the tree. I swear that I saw no Boers and no one else saw any. I do not believe that there were any Boers present in the neighbourhood that day, certainly not in the direction indicated by

> Lt Handcock for when we passed under this kopje they would certainly have opened fire, whereas the facts are that Trooper Churton went right on top of the hill. I came to the conclusion that there had been foul play and that Lt Handcock had himself shot Trooper van Buuren, because he had spoken to the Dutch about the slaughter of the six.[59]

New Zealand-born Trooper Muir Churton:

> I was on patrol the day Trooper van Buuren was killed. I was on the observation post close by Trooper Powell who was up a tree with glasses and therefore had a greater vision than I had. Still I commanded a wide view. When Lt Handcock returned, Trooper van Buuren who had started out with him was missing. I saw no Boers that day, neither did anyone else on the patrol. And I am convinced that there were none in the neighbourhood. I agreed with the opinion expressed by others that there had been foul play. If anyone had been sent out to find the body there would have been a good chance of following the spoor and finding it. I am nearly certain that I could have found it. No one was sent to look for it. Very shortly after, Lt Handcock returned. I was sent by Capt. Robertson right on the hill where Lt Handcock said the Boers who shot Trooper van Buuren were located. I saw no Boers. I am confident that there were none there. I am confident that there had been no Boers in that neighbourhood for some time. The Kaffirs also reported the country quite clear. There is a kaffir kraal close by and when I asked the kaffirs they said the country was absolutely clear of Boers. [60]

Compare Trooper Muir Churton's account above given in 1901 with one he gave in the 1970s:

> On moving out, Lieutenant Handcock split the patrol into two flanks taking the left flank himself with four men including Troopers van Buuren and Muir Churton. Once into the bush Handcock ordered the left flank to fan out, while Churton saw van Buuren turn to observe him as he rode up alongside. Before he could utter a word the lieutenant drew out his revolver and put three shots in quick succession into the Dutchman, then without slackening his pace, he rode on. [61]

Besides the fact that in the latter statement Churton curiously refers to himself in the third person, this and his 1901 statement are incompatible. In the 1970s version he actually witnesses the murder. His 1901 account appears perfectly consistent with Trooper Powell's and given that Muir

Churton was in his 90s in the 1970s and had lived the life of a boxer, it is easier to believe that he had not witnessed the murder of Trooper van Buuren, and this must also call into question the other statements made by him in the 1970s.

Even less reliable, however, was the official report of van Burren's death sent to Pietersburg, which was written by Lieutenant Peter Handcock and passed to Captain Robertson. Deeming this version unsuitable, Robertson edited the report to record that van Buuren had been killed in contact with some Boers. [62] This was the version which was sent to Major Lenehan in Pietersburg.

'B' Squadron who arrived at the Spelonken on 13 July 1901 commanded by Captain Percy Frederick Hunt, assisted by Lieutenant Harry Morant, were sent to Fort Edward, by some accounts to instil some semblance of discipline into 'A' Squadron. The oft told story of Morant and the BVC contrasts the poor discipline and misdeeds of 'A' squadron with the greater discipline of 'B' squadron. This is based largely on the statements made by Lieutenant George Witton [63] and Sergeant Frank Eland. [64] The discipline of 'A' squadron may well have been poor, but with the benefit of hindsight (which Frank Eland would be denied by a Boer bullet), was 'B' Squadron's much better? Lieutenant George Witton's 'hindsight' was coloured by his own motives. Trooper John Silke:

> We relieved Captain Robinson [sic] and a party (BVC) who had to go to Petersburg to attend an inquiry on four charges: murder, cowardice, rape and robbery. The first charge was founded on fact and, with his knowledge and maybe his consent and approval, six surrendered Boers were shot after their arms were taken from them. But the other three charges were not brought up against him at the enquiry. [65]

Ultimately, little came of this enquiry. Robertson was dismissed and according to George Witton denied further military service [66] though it is known that he joined Kitchener's Fighting Scouts on 26 February 1902 as a Lieutenant resigning around two months later. [67]

The clamp-down on discipline has been highlighted as being the cause of resentment among the men of 'A' Squadron, which led to their reporting of Morant and Handcock, whom they supposedly despised. Witton:

> Captain Hunt found affairs in a very disorganised state at Fort Edward, and immediately set about to rectify them. He had the stock collected and handed over to the proper authorities, and the stills broken up. These reforms were carried out by Lieutenants Morant and Handcock, and this

was one of the reasons why these two officers were disliked (or 'detested', as a returned Carbineer put it) by certain members of the detachment. [68]

What undermines this analysis is the fact that the fifteen troopers who wrote the letter of complaint to Col Hall were mostly in 'B' Squadron, who had arrived with Morant. Secondly, there is some evidence that Handcock and Taylor were already detested. One account that appeared after the court cases:

> The news of the execution of two Australian officers for murdering Boers did not in any way surprise me, as I was told of the murders some months ago by a relative in the Bushveldt Corps. The published accounts, however, are so inaccurate—as, for instance, the story that Boers were killed because they had mutilated some Australian officers—that I feel impelled to give you an account of the murders committed by Lieutenant Hancock [*sic*] ... it was not long after the bush country was entered that Captain Robinson [sic] and the men of A Squadron found that they had peculiar people to deal with in some of the remaining officers. Captain — used to kill niggers as one would shoot rabbits. To give [an] instance [on] one occasion he was chatting with another officer. A native was standing close by. The Captain, noticing him, pulled out his revolver, and absolutely without reason shot him dead, The Captain then replaced his revolver, and went on talking as if nothing had happened. The natives called him 'balaala' – balaala being for Zulu killing or murdering.
>
> The men noticed too that when Captain — or Lieutenant Hancock had spite against a man [he] was told off to scout on the right flank, and that he very rarely returned. He may, of course, have been killed by a lion; he may have been shot by a Boer—certainly shots were sometimes heard; but they had their own views on what had happened, and when any of the men of the squadron were told off to the right flank they took great care to get some of their companions to go with them, and to watch Hancock. [68] These two officers were suspicious of the A Squadron, the men of which were very much attached to the officer, Captain Robertson. The latter remonstrated with Captain — and some of the other officers on their methods. His remonstrances failing, he made some excuse to get leave, and returned [to] the base. On hearing he was going in to Pietersburg his squadron saddled up and said they would accompany him, and it was only on his dissuading them, telling them that it would be mutiny to do so, that they remained behind. The Captain and Lieutenant Hancock did not like Robinson returning [to] Pietersburg. They were afraid he would tell tales, and had hardly reached there when he was arrested on a trumped-up

> charge and Court-Martialled. He was, however, acquitted, the Court consisting mainly of officers of the Gordon Highlanders. [69]

Besides the swapping of 'left flank' and 'right flank' in the account above, later events are recounted in the wrong chronological order, which must make the reader circumspect. It does, however, suggest that at least some of BVC saw things differently to the version of events which has become accepted.

There was certainly truth in the accusations of murder. Whether the other accusations were accurate will probably never be established. In any case Robertson was allowed to resign his position and it was probably hoped that that would be that, the BVC would be taken in hand by Captain Hunt and things in the Spelonken would return to the conventional abnormality of war.

Among Morant's apologists it has been argued that the fact that no one was charged at the time with the murder of the six Boers or Trooper van Buuren in early July 1901 constituted tacit support for the ghastly process and that nothing was done to rein in Taylor and the BVC. Certainly not enough was done; but 'nothing' is not true. Captain Robertson had been withdrawn, subject to some kind of internal inquiry and dismissed. This was an attempt to deal with the situation without attracting too much attention to the BVC. Justice it was not. It will later be seen that the authorities had good reason why they did not want attention brought to Major Lenehan's unit.

The six Boers were killed on 2 July and Trooper van Buuren was murdered on the 4th. Ten days later Captain Robertson and the 'worst of A Squadron' were on their way back to Pietersburg to face an enquiry [70] having been replaced by Captain Hunt and 'B' Squadron. Why was action against Robertson so swift when subsequent action against Morant, Taylor, Handcock and the others so slow? Was it the allegation of rape or was it that Taylor wanted Robertson out of the way? The authorities in Pietersburg must have had intelligence about events in the Spelonken which did not pass through Robertson. The most obvious route would be through Taylor's network.

Whatever the reason, Robertson was replaced with Captain Hunt, an officer who had served in the militia, irregular units and for a while in the 13th Hussars. Although inexperienced, he might have been expected to take control of the situation. Hunt should have lasted to the cessation of hostilities but this was not to be. His death within about a month would result in the BVC ending up in the command of an officer perhaps even less suited to the position than Robertson. Robertson may have been, as argued by many, a weak leader and easily controlled by Taylor but Morant was a willing accomplice, offering no counterbalance to Taylor's malign influence. The killings would multiply.

The influence of Taylor, reinforced by Handcock's willingness to obey any command, had not been removed when Captain Hunt took over the BVC at Fort Edward. Although at the later court martial it was claimed Hunt had issued orders that no prisoners were to be taken, no murders are known to have taken place under his command. In fact, as will be seen below, scores of prisoners were taken during Hunt's time as CO It is probable therefore that he had reined in the worst excesses of the BVC.

The arrival of 'B' Squadron and Captain Hunt is described by Trooper James Christie:

> Trekked on in the darkness, and at daylight crossed the sand river and halted for breakfast at Klipdam, a fortress built on the early English style, by one Captain Dahl, with high walls and towers, and courtyard after the manner of those from which the Saxons and Normans used to let fly their arrows. This was built to hold against the Kaffirs in the earlier wars, but is now a sort of farm house. Left Klipdam about 11 o'clock and then our party were put on the flanks, and we had some very rough country to scout, covered with prickly scrub. Arrived at a camping place, or 'outspan' before dark, and found my horse pretty well done up, so spoke about getting another one. Left at 3 o'clock in the morning and trekked on in the dark to Dwhars River, where we had breakfast. [71]
>
> ...From Dwharz River to the camp made a long day, but the road was good, and the mules trotted gaily along so we on the flanks had hard work to keep the convoy in sight and abreast of it at from half mile to a mile out on the flank, and rough country to get over. Into camp that night we got, tired and hungry, and with some difficulty got some scoff. Next day our captain [Hunt] decided to shift the camp there established to Fort Hendrina—a large stone wall enclosing about an acre of ground and built by the Boers in their wars against the Kaffirs in 1896, or thereabout. Our troop were first into the fort and picked our place to camp, and generally tidied things up—or rather the natives we commandeered did so under our supervision, as no one does any work he can commandeer a nigger to do. We had several days in camp and our duties were horse guard, grazing guard and find six men for two Cossack posts. [72]

Trooper McInnes' diary:

> After a rest of two or three days sixty men of 'B' and 'C' squadrons, with half a dozen waggons, started for the N.E. to join 'A' squadron, 75 miles out, starting at 12 p.m. on the 10th. We reached our destination at 5 p.m. on the 12th, and found 'A' squadron encamped on Briscoe's [Bristowes]

> farm, with about 40 Boers, with women and children and waggons, which they had captured further to the N.E. Six Boers were killed, and one man on our side, who was a surrendered burgher—Van Buhren [sic] by name. There are two fine farms here, about a mile apart, with large orchards, oranges being very plentiful, and there is plenty of good water close by. [73]

McInnes and everyone else would soon learn that the circumstances of van Buuren's death weren't quite as he had understood them at the time.

Fort Hendrina was another portable steel construction and one of the three which the Boers had positioned in the war against the Venda, one of the others being Fort Botha captured by Captain Taylor on his way down from Rhodesia. The BVC returned Fort Hendrina to one of its earlier locations and incorporated it into other defences – stone walls, entrenchments and barricades. Later in the year Trooper J. D. Pacholi of Marong, described it: 'The walls of the fort are 6ft. high, and the barbed wire fence surrounds it for about 20 yards, and is 7ft. high, with 14 wires round it, with entanglements in every direction for ten yards on either side. In fact, it appears impossible for either horse or foot soldier to penetrate it.' [74] Each of the walls was about 200 yards long. [75]

Frank Eland writing on Monday 22 July from Ellerton said:

> Last Wednesday a Patrol, of 20 Men were sent down here to watch for Boers and settle some Kaffir question.

Trooper James Christie, however, was kept back.

> Then came a patrol of 20 men to go to the low country some 70 miles further on, but I missed this, and only two of our troop went with it. I wanted our lieutenant [Morant] to let me go, but he said he did not want me to go as he might have to go out any day, and he wanted his own men with him, so I had perforce to stay. [76]

One of those who went was Trooper John Silke who went with the young Queensland Officer Lieutenant Hannam. John Silke wrote a 'diary', most probably sometime after the war, as those who don't like its contents are keen to highlight. Those same people are, however, not as sceptical about Lieutenant George Witton's book which we know was written some five years after the war ended. Silke's account is generally remarkably consistent with other sources such as Trooper James Christie's account, Frank Eland's letters and Trooper McInnes' Diary.

> I went with a patrol with Hannam down to Letaba River for the purposes of assisting the Shangaans against the Motyatyis. It was only for four days

> 'grub' and one blanket. We got down there in two days and saw a bit of a 'go' between parties of the two tribes but took no part in it. They fought with assegais and axes, also sticks and stones. The Shangaans won the day killing four of their opponents and capturing eight women. These they keep as slaves. We stayed 14 days there instead of 4, a scotch cart of rations and a demijohn of rum was sent to us. [77]

Frank Eland was still back at the fort on Thursday 18 July, when Fort Hendrina was renamed Fort Edward, after the newly crowned Edward VII. [78] Whilst the Union Flag was hoisted, a salute was fired, the National Anthem sung and according to Trooper McInnes, a bottle of whiskey broken (carefully into a bucket!) to christen the flag. [79] Frank Eland relates; 'We had a full dress parade and got a liberal libation of whiskey to celebrate the occasion. On Friday afternoon 20 men were sent to meet an incoming convoy from Pietersburg, and 4 men and a Scotch cart with rations for the Low country patrol were sent off at ½ an hour's notice' [80] to Hannam and Silke's patrol.

Having missed the previous patrol, Trooper James Christie was not particularly happy to be picked for the convoy work on Friday 19 July with Lt Picton:

> Then came a patrol to go back to meet a convoy, and two of us were unfortunately picked for this, for I hate convoy work, and away we went with 24 hours' rations, to find ourselves away nearly four days, with an experience of bad management to chronicle as the result of our patrol. At Dwharz river six demi johns of rum were looted from the waggons by the men and a lively night spent. I was on Cossack post so did not see much of it. Next day two were arrested for drunkenness, and we arrived at the fort the night after to find our lieutenant out with the balance of our troop away to the north after some 20 Boers with 14 waggon and women and children, which they subsequently got without a shot being fired. Also to find our Captain out with another patrol after another lot which they got. [81]

This not only refers to the taking of twenty Boer prisoners with their families but also to the fact that Captain Hunt, who it would later be claimed, reprimanded Morant for taking prisoners, also took prisoners himself. Lieutenant Picton's patrol with Trooper James Christie returned to Fort Edward around 23 July. Christie:

> Things were only middling the night we arrived at the fort as the Captain and all lieutenants were away, and we had only a junior with us with the

> convoy. More rum was looted, stores said to be looted, guard after guard was placed under arrest for assisting it was said, and someone clearing out with some loot was fired at by the sentry and missed. Next day a sergeant major [Morrison] and quarter-master were under arrest for drunkenness, and several others. The result of the spree was that the sergt.-major went off to Pietersburg with his kit despite orders. Six men were sent to bring him back and they went on with him. Another acting quarter-master also cleared out so there is a good time coming for them in the future. Capt. Hunt returned and squared matters up promptly with those of the arrested who remained, and they got off light. [82]

The men sent in pursuit also got drunk and Sergeant Major Morrison and Trooper Daly [83] were arrested but according to Trooper Silke got off scot free. It is claimed that the two men were discharged after giving evidence to Col Hall in relation to activities of the BVC in Spelonken and their evidence kept quiet in the interests of the corps. [84] George Witton:

> At night these men broke their arrest and rode into Pietersburg. Captain Hunt sent in a report, and made charges of a serious nature against them to Major Lenehan, who caused them to be again placed under arrest, pending court-martial proceedings. Upon a preliminary inquiry being made as to their conduct, they made disclosures regarding what was going on at Spelonken. When the matter was brought before Colonel Hall, C.B., garrison commandant, it was decided in the interests of all concerned to discharge them from the regiment and let them go. To these men may be credited the monstrous and extravagant statements and lying reports about the Carbineers which appeared later in the English and colonial press. [85]

Curiously the incident above occurred around 23 July and the two were not discharged from the BVC until 4 September 1901. Three days later Major Lenehan would arrive at Fort Edward to make enquiries into events in the area. [86]

One man who missed the drunkenness and its repercussions was Sergeant Frank Eland. Frank Eland was a local man and popular sergeant of B Squadron. Although it is often claimed that he was half Afrikaaner, based probably on the accounts of other BVC members, he had actually been born in Dublin on 13 June 1873, the son of Francis Simeon Eland and Sarah Cillborn Eland. [87] Essentially he was not an Afrikaner but a wealthy young man of the Irish 'protestant ascendency' but he had lived in Transvaal from such a young age he most probably had an accent which gave the impression of Dutch descent. His letters to his wife Dora have provided an invaluable source of information on the activities of the BVC leading up to 6 August 1901. [88]

On the morning of the 20th, the day after Picton and Christie's patrol had gone out to meet the convoy, Eland's squad was told to head out with Captain Hunt and Lieutenant Handcock of 'A' Squadron to Ellerton about 55 miles away. Hunt and Handcock rode in a cape cart while the rest of the group were on horseback. Captain Hunt had expected to meet an unnamed party at a place called Fonseca's but after waiting till 10 a.m. on Sunday the 21st it was decide to press on to Ellerton. Here, Eland heard rumours that the Majaji's people had raided one of the nearby kraals and were refusing to provide information on Boer movements. He was given information from one of 'Bullala' Taylor's intelligence agents named Schwartz. 'This feud between the Basutos and Shangaans has got to be stopped' [89] wrote Eland. Eland arranged to ride there out of uniform and on his unbranded horse 'Biting Ben' to explain to Majaji's people the danger of their situation. 'It is a bit of a risk but I don't want to see Majaji's Kaffirs wiped out as they will be if they persist in disregarding our orders. Someone must be stuffing them with false reports and I'm going to put things in a true light before them.' [90] Eland also intended to visit 'Ravenshill', his own family's farm, to see his mother.

Wearing a grey suit, Eland made his way to Ravenshill, and then on to Vredefontein. He found his mother in 'the old shanty'. He also met Revd Reuter of the German Medingen Mission. Eland hated missionaries 'as a class' but respected Revd Reuter for being good to his mother throughout the war: 'Old R. has shown up well. The Boers some time ago threatened to sjambok him when he gave a horse and he gave it saying he did not want to have their blood on his hands as he knew his kaffirs would shoot them and they would never leave the station alive if they lynched him.' [91]

Whilst at Ravenshill, Revd Reuter had warned Eland, who was unarmed; to hide in the bush as two horsemen had been seen on the road. This turned out to be two natives who had in turn seen Eland's and Reuter's horses together and were worried there were Boers around. Everyone was hiding from everyone! Eland was amongst the farms and people he had grown up with and stopped at Piet Wentzel's house at Swartkopjes for breakfast with 'the girls at Braantboontjes' [92] and found twenty Boers there. His letters reveal that although his allegiances were firmly with the British, he and his family had friends on both sides.

During his covert trip he gathered much useful intelligence and later returned to Ellerton mine with three of Majaji's 'boys' as runners.

On Thursday 26 July around 11:30 he met Lieutenant Charles Hannam and his patrol, at the mine. On this occasion Frank Eland claimed he was 'able to prevent a kaffir war'.

During Eland's covert trip Trooper John Silke relates an ominous brush between Hannam's patrol and a party of Boers under the command of Barend Viljoen. Having sent native out posts about half a mile from the camp, one morning Viljoen and party of ten Boers fired upon the natives and then 'done a "get"'. The following morning a native reported that six Boers were camped in a kraal near the Birthday mine. So Sergeant Gray, Trooper McLord, Silke and three others with one of the Shiels brothers of the intelligence department as a guide set off to get them. Arriving near Mt Labonga at dusk, they camped, setting off to surround the kraal around 4 a.m. The kraal was located but the Boers had gone. After a wild goose chase to a farm across the Molotitsi River the six men decided to head back to Hannam's main patrol. After a dispute over which direction to head in, they were sniped at by two Boers but decided not to go after them in the dark. The group returned to camp around midnight. [93]

Lieutenant Hannam had just received orders from Captain Hunt to return to Fort Edward. The patrol camped at Dadelfontein on 28 July and breakfasted again at Braantboontjes. Later they left the road, crossing the Letaba River, and rested near Memoteela's Mission Station. On information provided by natives, the patrol captured three Boers. These men were on foot and according to trooper Silke almost barefoot, 'but they had rifles and plenty of ammunition. One old Boer had his magazine full of "dum dums". He said they were for buck, but I guess he would have used them for us as well as buck.' [94] They claimed they were coming in to surrender, which subsequent events suggest they probably were.

At around midday Eland relates a 'ludicrous incident' in which some of the party attempted to extract some bees from their nest. The result was that almost the whole party was stung and could not get near their gear for nearly two hours. Eland points out that the three prisoners could easily have slipped away during the fray and if there had been Boers of a more belligerent nature nearby, the consequences could have been much more serious. [95]

Lieutenant Hannam's patrol camped for the night at Frank Hayes store, about 15 miles from Fort Edward, where 'a wagon met us with scoff and rum so we had a good feed and a nip, and turned in, and started for camp next morning in good heart. Arrived at the fort we found it has been christened while we were away and all had got drunk on whisky at the ceremony.' [96]

Trooper McInnes, at this point, was out with a patrol under Lieutenant Picton and had made prisoners of two Boers and two boys, all armed. These and some cattle had been sent in to Fort Edward. By the 29th they were at Da Tonsega to meet Hannam's Patrol. McInnes:

> 29th. We have now reached Da Tonsega, about 36 miles from camp fort, and await Lieutenant Hannam's party, who are out about 17 miles N.E. We are in the midst of our enemies at present. A party of Boers were encamped on a kopje a mile and a half distant from this place the night after we came through with the prisoners and cattle, while forty mounted Boers were in pursuit of us up to this place. Commandant Kelly is reported in the vicinity, with his commando of sixty Boers. A few days back a party of Boers raided Schiel's farm, taking away a lot of cattle ... Hannam's party passed a few miles to the south in the night, en route for the fort, so that our small party of fifteen is practically on its own. Reinforcement is expected, however.
>
> August 1st. Ten more men arrived last night, and early this morning we set out, leaving one man in camp. After riding about six miles to Ash's farm we made a halt of about an hour, and then divided into small parties, for two mounted Boers were reported in the neighbourhood, and several waggons on their way in, about a mile and a half from Ash's farm. The party on the left flank sighted the two Boers and gave chase. They, however, did not try to escape, and surrendered quietly. A few minutes later three waggons were seen, and we soon had them surrounded and the men disarmed. An ambush was laid for the other waggons, which were some distance behind. These were successfully captured in detail, and by two o'clock were all laagered at the drift close by—seven waggons and two Cape carts in all, drawn by oxen and donkeys, fourteen prisoners, and about seventeen rifles, with a quantity of ammunition, and about thirty women and children, and a number of cattle. A very promising start for the month. The whole convoy reached camp at Da Tonsega's between 8 and 9 o'clock at night, proceeding to the fort to-day [2 August] with a small escort. Our next move is already planned, for a well-known Boer farmer [Klopper], whose farm is near the Swiss Hospital, with a party of about ten men and five waggons, with some of their families, are laagered forty-five miles north-east, and probably we shall be on their trail to-morrow. On the day following the despatch of prisoners [3rd] we set out at 3 a.m., 13 all told, including the sergeant and the Swiss guide, reaching the kraal of the Kaffir chief (M'wamba), who sent in the information concerning the Boers, at midday, the guide going on with a native to locate the Boers and find out their strength, etc. He returned at midnight with a good report, having been quite close to the waggons, and heard the Boers talking. They apparently did not know there were any British in that part of their country. At 3 a.m.

> we set out, and after a tedious ride of nearly 12 miles we got near the camp. [This group were captured on 4 August.] Leaving our horses to look after themselves, we set out on foot, getting round the further side of the laager, and about 50 yards from the waggons. It was breaking day, and some of the Boers were sitting round the fire. Out we rushed, dashed through the spruit between, and with a yell of 'Hands up!' we were upon them. They were so much taken by surprise that not one of them moved. We soon turned the rest out of blanket, and made them fish out all the rifles and ammunition. There were thirteen Boers, including two or three boys, and a good many women and children. Some of the kids were only a few months old, and their mother's dead, while others were ill with fever. The Boers had killed two rhei bok the day before, and a lot of guinea fowl, so we soon had a good breakfast prepared, and the most of the Boers and the women were quite sociable before we started to trek. I think that most of the poor wretches were glad that we had taken them. Their leader, Klopper, is a fine-looking Boer of about 50, and his wife, second or third, is very pretty, and only 18 years old, and has a baby about six months old. About 9 a.m. we set out for Fort Edward, 75 miles away; four ox waggons, one donkey waggon, two light carts, and about 75 head of cattle and donkeys, and three horses, which were sorry-looking objects. The whole convoy reached the fort on the fourth day of trek. [97]

Klopper's group were captured on 4 August at Dusselboom Spruit in Low Country and included Johanna Katrina Klopper, Hans Potgeiter, John ver Maak, Anna M ver Maak, Piet Potgeiter, Nicolas Rensburg and an unnamed widow, William Roberts, Pieter Jacob Henning, (Johannes) Christian Henning, Maria Johanna Botha, Martha Johanna Petronella Venter, Susannah M. Eloff, Magdalena C. C. Venter, Johanna J. Kruger, Sussanah M. Vorster and Anna Stefina Francina Venter. J. K. Klopper later stated that Nicolas Rensberg, his wife and three children died on the road. [98]

Frank Eland was looking forward to a warm sleep after his trip, having left his blankets behind. After turning in around 10:30 he was roused to head out again with Lieutenant Handcock and a ten-man patrol to go the Schiels Farm about 6 miles away. [99] 'Colonel' Schiels was a prisoner of war and being held on St Helena; his sons Adolf and Tony, however, were working as Intelligence Officers for the British under Taylor. They still lived on the family farm with their mother. The plan was that Handcock, Eland and the ten men would lay an ambush for a party of Boers who intended to burn the farm in reprisal for the Schiels boys working for the British. The Boers had already raided the farm and stolen cattle as alluded to by Trooper McInnes. The Boer party got wind of the ambush and never turned up. [100]

Trooper John Silke returned to the Fort to find that 'they called it Fort Edwards while we had been away. Christy [sic] and two others went out scouting and located twenty Boers gathering mealies from the kaffirs about forty miles from the fort.' [101]

Trooper James Christie patrolling:

> I was sent by the captain [Hunt], in charge of two men to enquire into a report that a store had been looted by the Boers. We were only to be away a short time—a few hours and took no 'scoff' (a word equivalent to our colonial word tucker). We were given a guide to take us to the place which we found was four hours distant across some very stony broken and rough country, all scrub and bush clad. I had the captain's field glasses—a very powerful and handsome set— and reconnoitred the store before galloping up. Nothing was there but a crowd of niggers. The owner, a Scotchman, had been ordered out of the Transvaal and was in England or somewhere, leaving a Kaffir in charge. The store had been looted all right, and there was little left but 'Kaffir truck' beads, etc., and patent medicines, all articles of 'scoff' and clothing had been taken and the number of Boers was set down by the natives as twenty.
>
> After going over the wreck we followed up the trail till nightfall. We also intercepted a native runner and opened a message he had which showed us that an intelligence officer in the mountains had only escaped their clutches through being hidden by a friendly native. So I wrote an account of our doings and enclosed it with the letter and sent the boy on. At nightfall we made attempts to get into communication with the intelligence officer and it was only after much beating about and getting the confidence of the natives that we discovered him and stayed all night in a kraal and slept all night or tried to without blankets or coats round a fire, and in the morning after a further survey of the country and the direction the Boers went, returned to camp and reported.
>
> The captain must have been pleased with our work for two days after he sent for me and told me I could take two, three, or five men with me and go out and do vedette work in the Boer country, where it was alleged they were looting the natives' cattle and beating the boys. The captain [Hunt] (an Imperial officer who had been on General French's staff) questioned me about what I would do under certain circumstances, and I told him in such country if hard pressed I would abandon my horse and take to the bush. 'Very well, if you do here's a revolver and be sure you shoot your horse. Don't let them get him, and here are my glasses, if you have to do a bolt don't leave them on your saddle' (this with a smile). I selected one of the men who was with me before—a West Australian—a good bushman

and a good-humoured plucky chap, and another one who was strongly recommended.

None of us yabber much in Kaffir, but we got on all right. We were provided with horses each from the captain's stock and taking a few biscuits and riding light we set out armed to the teeth. If we found anything worth sending out a patrol to capture we were to send in word and wait at an appointed place a reasonable time and if no reinforcements came we were to return home by a different route. We passed en route, the looted store, and took some Kaffir truck brass snuff boxes (the natives are great on snuff), beads and earthenware eardrops for the Shanghans and different sorts of beads for the Basutos, who are rather mixed up in this quarter. We got a guide from an lnduhna or head man we knew, and made for the Boer haunts. Latterly we could hardly get a guide, as the natives were too frightened of the Boers, and for three men to go among them was considered the height of folly. However we persevered on being wary and taking observations from the different kopjes which rose here and there on the plain or low country which we were now on.

At night I used to lie fully armed and never stirred a foot without my rifle. We got, after being 48 hours out from camp, very close to a small Boer laager and decided to locate it and ascertain its number if possible. A friendly Induhna close by assisted us after killing a fowl for our supper and giving us some eggs and mealie pap. We planted our horses and with the native for a guide made our way towards the laager. Your humble servant, of course, close to the guide, the others in Indian file behind. I could not walk barefooted so as the gravel seemed to us to make much noise under our feet, I cut the sleeves off my jersey and slipped them over my boots and with a little grass deadened the noise. The others wore putties so I told them to wrap them round their boots, and thus accoutred with magazine cut-offs open in our rifles we toiled on. Coming near the place as we knew by the stamping and snorting of the Boer horses on the lines we ran right bang into a kraal where it seemed as if a thousand dogs issued forth and barked for all they were worth. We took cover, you bet, and lay dead to the world, but I longed to be able to silence all that dismal bark with one swoop. We heard what seemed a sentry coming over towards, us and made up our minds to pot him if necessary and bolt in different directions. However, after what seemed an age we crept closer, but found no cover, all being bare, and only solitary trees here and there. The moon had come out bright, but we could not count the men or horses, as we were in the light and they in the shade, but judged from the waggons and horses what was likely to be a fair thing, and our guide also told us there were about 20, with more

> horses than men, and 16 oxen in big waggons, six oxen in one Scotch cart, and six horses in spring waggon.
>
> This laager was being used as a collection depot for forage, etc., for conveyance to the larger laager, further over in the Majaji mountains at Barend, Viijoen's—a commandant, native commissioner, and veldt cornet, a sort of Lord High Everything in the Locality, who had some 80 to 100 men always with him. I felt inclined to do the bluff act and rush the place, firing wildly and quickly; but as our mission was to get information, not to attack, after consultation we decided that we should send in word and make further observations while awaiting the patrol, so we returned by a different route, dodging the native outposts the Boers had on, and made our way back to our horses and rode off back across the Koodoo river where the Boers, we believed, did not much frequent.
>
> My third man volunteered to go back and he got minute instructions as to where to find us, and how long we would wait until he guided back a patrol. By this time morning had broke, and, speaking for myself, I had had no sleep at all since leaving Camp, so fell dozing; while some scoff was being prepared at a kraal, only to wake with a start to think a Boer was asking me to kindly hand over my rifle. [102]

The message was relayed back to the fort. Frank Eland wrote: 'Three of our fellows went out scouting for three days patrol on Monday and tonight news has come in that they have located 18 Boers with 36 horses, 40 miles out, I think towards Buffelsberg and I may go out tomorrow, Friday morning, with a party to be sent to try to take them.' [103]

Hunt's group, including Trooper John Silke, set out on 1 August and arrived in the area of Duivels Kloof on the 5th. Silke noted the hazardous nature of the target: 'We left Reuters at 11:30 p.m. Viljoen's was only about six miles away but the Reuters warned us to be careful as the house was unassailable. It was on a rocky kloof and although only fifteen Boers were at the main homestead there were forty at Botha's farm four miles away on the other side, and there were only two ways out of the kloof once we got in.' [104]

Why Capt. Hunt decided to press on with the ill advised attack is not known but his cousin George Percy Edward Hunt had been awarded the DSO by the Governor of Gambia in July 1901; perhaps a little family rivalry had clouded his judgement.

> Hunt had a presentiment that all would not end well for he told the four Sergeants, Eland, Gray, Oldham and Robinson that if he was shot to get out of the kloof before daylight. Shiels had taken a gang of niggers on the

hill at the rear of the house. When we got within a mile of the house we left our horses and getting within two hundred yards of the house I saw Hunt for the last time alive. He told me to take fifty niggers along the road and go within fifty yards of the house and wait until I heard a shot and then to rush the house with the niggers. Well I went to where I was sent and just got to within plain sight of the house (just on the left of the stables) when the signal was fired. It was immediately answered by a volley from the house (they knew we were coming) and I shouted to the niggers 'fika' (come) but the sods went the opposite way except one old man (induna) who stopped by my side until we were seen from the house when a volley was fired at us. The old man fell dead, shot through the head. A few bullets came in close proximity to my head, too close for comfort. I could feel the breeze from them. I could not see any of our chaps going to the house and I was too well 'educated' to go myself so I went back into the ditch and waited ... There was no sign of our fellows at all, and the damn niggers were firing pot legs, bolts, nuts and various other missiles all over the place, so I went round towards the front of the house to see what the others were doing. The first found was Robinson, nearly dead with fright. He told me that Capt. Hunt was dead.

We started a search and found all but Hunt, Eland, Gray and Petrie and three others. We waited until three o'clock [a.m.] and kept firing at the house, then I was sent to bring up the horses. On the way back I saw a man sitting on the road side with a rifle. I fired at him and he fell with fright. On approaching I found it to be one of our fellows (a Dutchman) who was thought to be lost.

On getting to the horses I found two others who had cleared back when the shots were first fired. We were just starting towards the house with the horse when we met the party returning with Gray and Petrie...

We all returned to look for Hunt and Eland. Shiels and his niggers were shooting from the rear of the house. We could not find them so as day was breaking we went back to Reuters with heavy hearts, for Hunt and Eland were well liked, especially Eland. We got to Reuters at 3 a.m. and turned in for we had no sleep the night before.' [105]

Meanwhile, James Christie was coming in to Fort Edward from his patrol:

We called at the house of Mrs Scheil, a German lady, wife of Col Scheil, of the Transvaal Staats Artillery, who was captured at Elandslaagte, and is now at St Helena. The Schiel family are left untouched by the British, and although the old man is a prisoner, the two grown-up sons are in our intelligence department, and work with us. Mrs Schiel made us very comfortable, and wished us to stay all night, but when we had been out over a week without a change, and sleeping around Kraal fires, the idea of creeping into sheets and a bed was too much.

We learned that Capt. Hunt with 19 men had left to meet us, and make a descent on the various laagers we had located. We returned to the fort post haste, with the idea of getting fresh horses and following him up … It was Monday morning before we left with letters for Capt. Hunt. We hoped to catch him at Ramsden, but we found he had left there the day before for the main laager at Viljoen's house in the Devil's Kloof and that the other places we had located were being left in the meantime, also that he had left for Majagees' headquarters.

Here was a surprise. What in heaven does he want at Majagees? [the great Kaffir Queen]. We turned over in our minds what he was after, for there were no Boers there. After riding for six hours and not coming to the place, we found from a native that the Englishmen had left Majagees for Viljoens. When daylight came we made away through the mountains. We passed en route the farm of Mrs Eland, the mother of our troop sergeant. She told us to tell her son Frank – her only son – to take no risks in coming to see her. She said she heard firing that morning, and when we told her Frank was with the party, she said she hoped he would come out of it well. Little did the poor body know then that Frank was lying still in death, having been shot that morning by the Boers.

After having coffee with her we pressed on eager to be in the scrap, when we encountered the mission station in the hills, kept by the Revd Reuter [a German] for the Berlin Lutheran Missionary Society. He told us the news of the fight, so far that Capt Hunt was killed and Sergt Eland missing but he added 'the men are all around the house – the Boers cannot get away. They must get the Boers even if they have to blow the house down.' We got some dynamite and fuse from him, and we went helter skelter down the mountain, feeling now that Hunt and Eland were missing, that revenge was the only thing we were looking for. [106]

Christie and his party then met Silke and Sheils. Trooper John Silke:

…a nigger came to tell us that Shiels had the house surrounded and wanted help. So we saddled up again and started back when we met Shiels and three niggers. Shiels had his horse shot and had fired away all his ammunition and was dead beat. While we were talking we were sniped at from the rocks towards Botha's farm so we went back to Reuters again. On the way we met Christie on a scouting trip. Shiels was told by the kaffirs that there were two Englishmen dead. When we got to Reuters we found Mrs Eland and had to break the sad news to her.

> Sergeant Oldham sent a runner to the fort [40 miles] for reinforcements as the forty Boers had come from Botha's farm and joined Viljoens lot ... Next morning we saddled up again determined to get the bodies if possible. [107]

Trooper James Christie was not happy to meet the group leaving the fight:

> We eventually galloped plump right into our men coolly riding back to the mission station. We were amazed. 'We thought you were all around the house.' The sergeant in charge gave us to understand that nothing could be done. To turn back to the mission station was galling to me and my mate., but it had to be done, so back we went, and perforce had to listen to tales of valour and bravery from sundry troopers, which led us to the conclusion that the home of Bernard Viljoen must be full of nothing but dead Boers.
>
> All we hoped for was that Capt. Hunt's and Eland's death had been paid for with heads ten score. Next morning we all went back to Viljoen's house to find Kaffirs in hundreds coming away with whatever they could carry in the way of furniture, and the news that Boers were 'Namba lapa' (gone there), pointing in the direction they had gone. If any of the men had been scared to go to Viljoen's house the day before there was no scare now, and the way we trekked down that hill, leaving our horse at the top was a treat to witness. Loot, loot, loot was all the cry, and when we saw that there was nothing but a lot of smashed furniture and an empty fireproof safe, the rage of some of our men at the Kaffirs was very vivid. [108]

Trooper John Silke:

> We surrounded the house creeping from rock to rock but it was deserted. We found Hunt shot through the heart and Eland shot through the loins and both stripped naked. On entering the house we found Viljoen dead and another Boer, both stripped also.
>
> There was a large safe in one room which we blew open, but it only contained papers and books. We found a spider at the house in which we stowed the bodies of Hunt and Eland, after burying the two Boers, and with a team of niggers we started for Reuters. [109]

Trooper James Christie:

> We found the body of Captain Hunt and Sergt Eland stripped naked, and also the body of Bernard Viljoen and another Boer – that was all. These latter, too were found to be stripped. Leaving the others to search the

> house, I, with another man, lifted Eland's body out of the sluit it was in, and covered it over with branches, after finding out where he was shot, which was from side to side through the stomach. Captain Hunt's body was lying with a piece of cow hide over it. I examined the body, and found he had been shot through the heart from the front, and out below the right arm, as it were sideways when he had been crouching down. After giving the two Boers what seemed like a very indecent burial, we got the Captain's and the sergeant's bodies on to a turnover buggy that was there, and inspanned some 20 Kaffirs, and took them up to the mission station where they were both washed and dressed. [110]
>
> Captain Hunt and Sergt. Eland were the only two of our men shot in action, and neither was maltreated. [111]

John Silke describes the burial of Frank Eland:

> Arriving there we had some scoff and Petrie and I started to make two coffins. We finished one in which the body of our sergeant was placed and four bullocks were hooked into a buggy and his remains brought up to his own farm. There were Mrs Eland [Frank's mother], Mr Reuter, and Christy [sic], Petrie and I, the only three men of his troop on that patrol. We buried his [ ] close to his own house just after dark and Reuter read the burial service. [112]

Christie:

> We met Mrs Eland, mother of the sergeant, at the mission station. After the bodies were coffined and four oxen being inspanned in the buggy, we put sergt Eland's body across the front seat, and started for Mrs Eland's farm three or four miles distant. The coffin being lowered, we opened the rough plank, and Mrs Eland put the sergeant's wife's photo on his breast, and kissing him affectionately, said, 'My only son: but you never gave your mother a moment's anxiety in your life. You were a good lad.' The missionary conducted a Lutheran service at the grave.
>
> We left for the mission station, taking Mrs Elands with us. Arrived there we fell in around Captain Hunt's grave, and as a volley was deemed inadvisable owing to the proximity of the enemy, it was decided to 'snap' our rifles only. [113]

Silke recalls what might have been an amusing mistake under other circumstances: 'Sergeant Oldham who was then in command of the party gave orders to fire a 'dumb salute' [no cartridge] but only [a] chap named Hunt also neglected to put in his 'cut off' and the consequence was that when we got the order 'ready' he pushed a cartridge into the barrel, and at 'fire' bang went his rifle and just missed Marie Reuter's head. [114]

Christie:

> Then Petrie, myself, and two others lowered down the coffin, while the mission girls sang 'Shall we gather at the river' and another of Sankey's hymns, which I forget. We were subsequently ordered in to see the new commanding officer (Lieutenant Morant) to report. He was holding audience with some sergeants about Captain Hunt's death, and as they had such long winded reports to give in, and, after listening to a lot of twaddle, I begged to be excused. I was subsequently told to report myself, which I did, made my report, and was allowed to retain Captain Hunt's revolver, which he had lent me. [115]

Lieutenant George Witton, who had not yet arrived on the scene, wrote in 1907:

> Early on Wednesday morning the news reached Fort Edward, and its effect upon Morant was terrible; instead of being the usual gay, light-hearted comrade whom I had known for three days, he became like a man demented.
>
> He ordered out every available man to patrol before Captain Taylor at his office at Sweetwaters Farm, about one mile from the fort. Morant tried to address the troops, but broke down, and Captain Taylor then spoke a few words to them, urging them to avenge the death of their captain, and 'give no quarter'. Guides and intelligence agents were furnished by Taylor, and the patrol started off with Morant in command. We travelled across country, and took the most direct route to Reuter's Station. When we were about twenty miles out, we met Lieutenant Picton returning, with a number of prisoners, who were, by the order of Lieutenant Morant, handed over to a small escort, and sent on to Fort Edward. Picton and the remainder of his men were attached to the patrol.
>
> This was my first meeting with Lieutenant Picton. [116]

The alleged mutilation of Captain Hunt has often been cited as the reason for Morant's vengeance on the Boer prisoners. Perhaps it made no difference. Trooper Frank Hall of Tea Tree Gully, Victoria:

> The other point that I think should be mentioned is the fact that the late Lieut. Morant was heard by me, and in all probability by many others, to swear the bitterest vengeance on anything in the shape of a Boer, and this

> immediately on hearing that Capt. Hunt was dead. There was not at the time the least detail to hand as to how he was killed. I have the clearest recollection of Capt. Taylor saying so when he paraded us as relief for Capt. Hunt's men. Nothing was known of how Capt. Hunt was killed when the relief party set out for Devil's Kloof, under Mr. Morant and others. [117]

Trooper Hall, Morant and the rest of the relief part arrived at Reuters on 8 July. Witton:

> ...we reached Reuter's Mission Station about four in the afternoon. Here we met the men of Captain Hunt's patrol; they had just one hour before buried their captain. After visiting his grave, we returned to Mr. Reuter's house, where Lieutenant Morant interrogated several men regarding Captain Hunt's death. They were all positive that he had met with foul play; they were sure his neck had been broken, as his head was rolling limply about in the cart when he was being brought in. His face had been stamped upon with hob-nailed boots, and his legs had been slashed with a knife; the body was stripped completely of clothes and lying in a gutter when found. Mr. Reuter and Captain Hunt's native servant, Aaron, who had washed and laid out his body for burial, corroborated these statements. [118]

Clearly neither Lieutenant Witton nor Lieutenant Morant saw the bodies before they were buried, and relied on the statements of others in relation to their condition. The statements of others however were contradictory. There are still some very large question marks over the state of Captain Hunt's body and the truth will probably never be known. Witton states that at the Court of Inquiry an unnamed German farmer gave evidence that the body had not been mutilated when he saw it. [119] He was not the only one. James Christie writing in July 1902 stated:

> Captain Hunt and Sergt. Eland were the only two of our men shot in action, and neither was maltreated. Captain Hunt, though stripped had a silk khaki handkerchief round his neck, also a gold chain and locket, when I picked him up. Morant's report on Hunt's death was, 'The body of Captain Hunt when recovered was stripped, the face bashed in, the neck broken, the ankles slit, etc. This information is based on the statement of his native boy and the Revd Mr Reuter, who performed the last sad offices over the body of Captain Hunt.' This was read over to me by the president [of the court martial] and of course was not true. I was the first

> who examined Hunt's body and put him into the conveyance which took him to the place where he was buried. [120]

Trooper John Silke who was present with Christie when the bodies were lifted into the spider states that the bodies of Hunt Eland, Viljoen and the second Boer were all stripped but makes no mention of any further mutilation or damage. [121]

The *Times*' account of the Courts Martial states 'F. L. Reuter, missionary in charge of the German Berlin Mission station, deposed that Captain Hunt's and Sergeant Eland's bodies were brought to his place. Hunt's body was much mutilated. The neck appeared to have been broken, and the face bore marks of boot nails.' [122]

Revd Reuter would state in court that Captain Hunt's body had been mutilated. However, Revd Reuter did not bury the body until it was taken to his mission station more than 36 hours after death, at which point rigor mortis would have come and gone leaving the body limp. Livor mortis, the pooling of blood in the lowest parts of the body, leaving purple blotching, would have been well and truly established. Livor mortis is not uncommonly mistaken for bruising and often leaves patterning on the body left by whatever surface the body had been lying on. These post mortem effects may well account for the perception that the body had been kicked and the neck broken, if it had not been.

It has been suggested that Hunt and Eland's bodies and those of Bernard Viljoen and his compatriot had been stripped by the natives who were present. [123] It was not uncommon for the natives in the area to collect body parts for magical and medicinal purpose. Charles Leach in his book *The Legend of Breaker Morant is Dead and Buried* describes some of the beliefs behind this custom and suggests this is what happened to Hunt and Veld Cornet Viljoen.

Around twenty natives were tasked with taking the bodies to the mission station. Christie, Reuter and others then took Frank Eland's body to his farm where he was buried. Hunt was not buried until around 3 p.m. Is it possible that Hunt's body was mutilated *after* it was loaded unto the buggy or whilst Frank Eland was being buried? This appears unlikely.

One account of the mutilation of Hunt's body which appeared in the Australian newspapers is often quoted by Morant's apologists:

> But Hunt—it nearly turns me up to remember it—his head was smashed to a pulp, his teeth were broken in, his left eye had been kicked out. The ground round about where we left him wounded was kicked up, and we could see that they had simply kicked him to death. I see there was some

> yarn about the Boers tying him by the neck to a tree. That's all rot. There was no rope about that we could see, or anything like it. They must have broken his neck just by sheer kicking at him. When we got his body his Kaffir boy, Joe, was sitting beside it, crying like a baby. Joe said that he had watched the Boers jumping on Hunt's head from a bush, and he hadn't been game to come out until they cleared out. [124]

This account contains some very significant errors which must cast doubt on its veracity. Not the least of which is that the Missionary (Revd Heese) witnessed the attack from Reuter's Mission. This is nonsense. The Revd Heese did not come into the story until two weeks later, though he could be confusing Revd Heese with Revd Reuter! The clinching giveaway that the narrator was not actually present is that he claims that the Reverend – whichever it was – watched the fight from Reuter's Mission. The Mission is at least 4 miles from Duivel's Kloof, obscured by the intervening terrain and it was the middle of the night. Had the narrator been present he would surely have known this.

In the *Adelaide Advertiser* the following account was printed immediately below the apocryphal story above:

> How about the mutilation of Captain Hunt's body?
> That, from what I gathered, is quite untrue. I did not see the body myself, but I spoke to several who did see it, and they told me that except for a little blackness on the face, caused by decomposition, there was nothing wrong with it. The only mark of violence on the body was a scratch on the foot which was caused by the Boers pulling the captain's lace-up boot off. The talk about Captain Hunt being murdered is, I believe, nonsense. He was shot in a fair fight, and died instantly. [125]

This does not claim to be an eyewitness account but is therefore less likely to be that of an attention seeker. It highlights that the notion that the 'bruising' to Hunt's face could have in fact been livor mortis, was recognised by some at the time.

The whole issue of whether Percy Hunt was murdered and mutilated or not, has become a major point of dispute in the Morant myth. The question of whether this alleged mutilation was the cause of Morant's killing spree is less disputed with some suggesting that, true or not, Morant believed it and therefore that was his motivation. Trooper Frank Hall's assertion that Morant became set on vengeance before he was even aware of the circumstances of Hunt's death was made after the war had ended and

Morant and Handcock were dead. A favourite device of Morant's apologists is to claim 'animus', or motives of self-preservation, on the part of anyone who contradicted Morant's version of events. In fact it would seem there actually never was anyone in the northern Transvaal with the strength to object to the killings on moral grounds, since they find a sinister motive for all those who did, be they the courts, the high command, fellow troopers, Boers, or anyone else. It seems everyone had it in for Harry Harbord Morant. But even if Frank Hall had been one of those who were allegedly irate at Morant's crackdown on discipline, would he really have felt strongly enough about it to harbour malice towards Morant after he was back in Australia and Morant was dead?

Morant's pretensions towards the fox hunting landed gentry are well known, as is his track record as a sponger. As we have noted, Captain Percy Hunt was a member of the in-crowd. His father was rich. His American mother, Anna Benkard was even richer. Hunt was born at Pau in the French Pyrenees [126] as was his sister Lillan. [127] Pau was one of the playgrounds of the affluent English in France, where they had established the Pau Hunt Club, polo and steeplechasing. His brother Rupert had been born in the chic seaside town of Biarritz. [128] Percy Hunt was an ex-Hussar and member of the Cavalry Club. It is not hard to see why Morant saw Capt. Percy Hunt as such a good 'mate'. Was the real cause of Morant's fury at Hunt's death that his seven-course meal ticket had just been torn up by the Boers?

Whether the body was mutilated or not, and whether this alleged mutilation was the real reason for his fury, Morant became grimly set on vengeance. On hearing the news at Fort Edward, he had tried to address the men but had broken down and could not continue. Taylor had then addressed the men telling them that Captain Hunt's death must be avenged and they should 'give no quarter'. [129]

The brooding Morant was now in charge of the BVC and at Reuter's Mission Station. Runners came in from the intelligence agents who had tracked the Boers after they had left Duivel's Kloof. The runners reported that the Boers had headed in the direction of Waterburg. Morant ordered Sergeant Edwin Must to stay [130] with six men and protect the mission as the Boers had threatened to burn it down. He took 45 men with him. They travelled light taking no food. They found two graves where the Boers had camped the previous night, suggesting two more of them had died after the fight at Duivels Kloof.

Near sunset they reached Rietoel (Rietvlei) [131] where native scouts warned them that the Boer party had camped in a donga on the far side of the hills. Morant sent one party to cover the right flank whilst he led the other group. The account is taken up by Trooper James Christie:

> We halted at the Koo-doo river for lunch, and there were 30 or 40 Boers ahead of us – we were about 50 strong, or there about- an even go. It took us till dark to come up with them, and then you never saw such a 'muck up' in all your life. You could see the fires and just distinguish figures when horror of horrors we got the order from Lieut — 'at 2000 yards, volley fire'. Then 'independent firing all along the line'. Then some mad man sang out 'there goes the white flag' – it was too dark by this time to see anything except it might be the steam rising from the fires the Boers were drowning out. 'Stand to your horses' came an excited order, and I could see the Dutchmen shouting and saddling up. We pressed on and halted in a spruit, all bunched up so a volley from the Boers would have wiped every man out. Then I heard a voice sing out 'it's alright, they have gone away.' Then we swarmed the waggons. They had fled, leaving two waggons, a dead horse, a cape cart, and a wounded man or youth; we had not shot him, it was an old accidental affair, shot in the ankle. [132]

Morant had not given Picton's party the chance to get around the side of the Boers and commenced firing far too early. Consequently all of the Boers escaped except Josef 'Floris' Visser, who was wounded in the ankle. The same incident is recalled by Troopers Silke, Botha, McInnes, Christie and Lieutenant Witton. Trooper Theunis Botha attributes Morant's opening fire from such a range to cowardice, [133] Witton to excitement. [134] Trooper McInnes called it a huge piece of bungling [135] and Silke attributed it to jealousy of Picton's opportunity to capture the whole party. [136] Christie put it down to stupidity:

> We cursed Lieut — for all the born fools that ever wore a uniform for not letting another Lieutenant have time to get around on the flank before opening fire. We made sure we would follow up at daylight, but the next thing I found, was our men trekking away in the opposite direction. I sang out to Lieut — that the Boers were just up in the kopje. I thought he had gone out to stop the advance guard, but no it was only to hurry up the movement of the other cape cart, which contained the wounded Boer.
>
> We got a bit mixed up in the routes. I told the officer that by another track we could make the fort in 20 miles, but could not take the cape carts, '— the cape carts, burn them'. 'Then what about the wounded man' I asked? 'They should have taken my advice last night and shot him.' Now this sort of talk got my back up, but I said nothing but fell into the rear

guard. I arrived at the river where the rest outspanned, a bullock had been killed and the niggers were having war dances and wild goings on. Then I found myself warned for the firing party to shoot the wounded Boer, was said to have been tried by court martial and sentenced to death. 'What for?' I asked 'Oh don't know but I've warned you.' 'Well I'm not going to do it.' 'They can make you a prisoner.' 'Then I'll go prisoner, but I'll not shoot a wounded man.' I raised my voice in most emphatic protest, and a few more did the same, while others instead of refusing cleared out. I stood to my guns and said if they were dead on for shooting, they should have followed up the Boers, and come what would I would not make one of the firing party. By and bye my sergt major came up, and said, 'It's all right, we have got another man. You will not be asked to do it.' Still I protested against it, and spoke to the fellows in the same mess with me, four of whom were told off for the firing party. One of them [probably Trooper Andrew Petrie] [137] was quite willing, but the others said they would have to obey orders. A number of others stood out, and an old mate of George Arnold's in the police [Sgt Wilson] who had been a prisoner with Boers, was equally excited with me.

Then seeing the feeling of the men, one of the lieutenants sang out, `If you're so — chicken hearted I'll shoot him myself.' [138]

Lieutenant George Witton writing to his brother shortly after the Courts Martial makes it fairly clear he did not believe a 'court martial' had taken place:

Lieutenant Picton joined us again at Mamahlia Cop, when immediately on his arrival Lieutenant Morant also told him of his intentions. A consultation then followed, which has since been represented as a court-martial. At the time of this consultation no mention was made of a court-martial. At this consultation Lieutenants Morant and Handcock were in favour of shooting the prisoner. It was stated at the court-martial held at Pietersburg that the decision arrived at the consultation was unanimous, which was not so. Lieutenant Picton had objected, and I took no active part whatever. I was told at the court of enquiry that, having only recently joined, and only taken a very subordinate part, I was not responsible.

When Lieutenant Picton was ordered to the command of the firing party, Sergeant Major Clarke asked me to speak to Lieutenant Morant on behalf of the men. I quite agreed with the men that the prisoner should not be shot, and mentioned it to Lieutenant Morant. He would not listen to anything, and told me that what he was doing he was perfectly justified in, and if the men made any fuss he would shoot the prisoner himself. This is all I know

> of the Visser case. Sergeant-Majors Clarke and Hammett can bear witness to these statements. [139]

On his release from prison in August 1904 Lieutenant Witton related the incident to a journalist of the Central News Agency more concisely and in different terms, claiming the SM said: '"Some of the men don't like this cold blooded job. Will you speak to Morant?" I was pretty sick of the uncertainty of the whole job. Morant said he had his orders. What could I say? I was Morant's Junior Officer, but what I believed I actually said to the Sergt-Major was "Look here; I will shoot him myself".' [140]

Did Witton feel that, having been released, he was free to admit he had offered to shoot Visser himself? Whether he did or not, by 1907 when Witton wrote *Scapegoats* he had returned to his original assertion that Morant had offered to shoot Visser:

> I asked him to leave me out of it altogether, as I did not know anything about the orders, I had been such a short time there. Morant then walked away, and ordered Sergeant-Major Clarke to fall-in ten men for a firing party. Some of the men objected, and the sergeant-major came and asked me if I would speak to Morant on behalf of those men.
>
> I went to Morant as requested, but found him obdurate. 'You didn't know Captain Hunt,' he said, 'and he was my best friend; if the men make any fuss, I will shoot the prisoner myself.' After a little delay, men volunteered – 'to get a bit of our own back', one remarked. Lieutenant Picton was placed in command of the firing party, and Visser was shot. [141]

In relation to the lieutenant carrying out the shooting, Trooper James Christie considered that 'It is a pity for all of us he was not allowed to do it. A lad named Botha, a Boer, fighting for us, was told off too. He told me, "I know him good. I went to school with him. I don't like to do it, but they will shoot me if I don't." The wind-up was that a firing-party was called. One was a volunteer – a Victorian, the sort Victoria should be proud of. Another shootist had belonged to the Essex volunteers, and was always ready to blow any Boer's lights out.' [142]

Interestingly the more often quoted *Wellington Evening Post* article of 10 April 1902 edited the sarcastic reference to the Victorian out. This was most probably Trooper John Gill of Fitzroy, Victoria, who, it would later be affirmed by both Trooper R. M. Cochrane [143] and Trooper Sidney Staton [144] had volunteered to shoot Visser. The Essex volunteer is most probably Trooper John Wild who was the only member of the BVC known to have been a member of an Essex regiment (1st Volunteer Battalion).

New Zealander, Trooper M. A. Churton would depose 'I heard Trooper Wild volunteer'. [145]

Trooper Frank T. Hall:

> Name after name was called by the sergeant-major, but there was no answer nor man forthcoming. A party was eventually frightened into obeying. The man was carried from the cart to a donga close by, propped up and the lead pumped into his back. Shooting an innocent man that cannot stand to take his death awakes big feelings in most hearts, and more than one lanky Australian swore with a gulp that justice should peep into this. And it did. [146]

Returning to Trooper James Christie:

> I once thought of going away from the sickening sight, but instead I deliberately walked over to the cart wherein the youth sat, intending to muster up what Dutch courage I had to speak to him. He took from his pocket a piece of paper and wrote a note. A slight twitching of the face was all the concern he displayed. Some Kaffirs lifted him out of the Cape cart in a blanket and set him down some twenty yards away with his back to the firing party. He spoke no word, but clasped his hands, and as the volley rang out he fell from his sitting position backwards. Then a lieutenant stepped over to him and put a revolver shot through his head, and all was over. Just prior to the shooting Lieut. Morant addressed the firing-party, but what he said I could not exactly catch, except something about Captain Hunt's death. Morant also came to me and said, 'I know it's hard lines for him, but it's got to be done. See how the Boers knocked Captain Hunt about.' I said that Captain Hunt had died a soldier's death – that he was killed in a `fair go', and beyond being stripped there was no maltreatment of him; and anyhow the Kaffirs might have stripped him. He said no; that Captain Hunt's tunic and trousers had been found in the Cape cart. 'But' I said, 'the boy was not wearing them.' 'Anyhow, he said, `it's got to be done. It's unfortunate he should be the first to suffer.' I still held that it was not right to shoot him after carrying him so far. But as up to this time Morant and I had been good friends I said no more, but tore off my 'B.V.C.' badge and cursed such a form of soldiering. Then we saddled up and trekked for home. [147]

It seems clear that Floris Visser was not wearing Captain Hunt's clothes but was in possession of them. Lieutenant George Witton in a letter of 10 March 1902 to his brother stated: 'This prisoner was then in possession of several articles the property of the late Captain Hunt, and was wearing khaki.' Sergeant S. Robertson made a statement in the same terms at the court martial. Even if the natives had not played a role in the alleged mutilation of Captain Hunt they were certainly present during the murder of Floris Visser. Muir Churton's deposition notes that 'On looking at him I saw the Kaffirs dancing a war dance around him. Lt Handcock was watching them dance and I believe Lt Morant and Lt Picton also but I am not quite certain as to these last two.' [148]

Morant and the patrol then headed back to Fort Edward approximately 40 km away arriving there on 13 August. Lieutenant Fred Neel, who had just arrived with a supply convoy from Pietersburg, then returned there with Lieutenant Picton. Lieutenant Picton claimed during the court martial that he reported to Major Lenehan and Lieutenant Colonel Hall the events which had taken place in Spelonken and the details of Floris Visser's shooting. Lieutenant Witton claims no action was taken by Lenehan and Hall on this news which led him to believe that this kind of action was sanctioned by a higher authority. According to Trooper James Christie, however, Morant's report was: 'I regret to say that the wounded Boer, captured by us, died of his wounds the following days.' [149] This naturally would not have prompted any action. Lieutenant Picton had of course been ordered by Lieutenant Morant to take charge of the firing party, but had serious reservations about the legality of it.

On 17 August Morant wrote to Major Lenehan:

> My Dear Major
>
> A runner goes to Pietersburg this morning, so just a hasty note, as I happen to be in camp. You know how cut up we must have been over poor Hunt's death. I'll never get such a good pal as he proved to be. I wish to the Lord that I'd been out with him that night, – he might have got wiped out all the same; but the d—d Dutchmen who did it would never have left the house. We've killed 13 of them up to date now – and that crowd haven't a blanket left to wrap themselves in. It was a d—d hard job to write to Hunt's girl, which same I did after we returned. Poor old Hunt! God rest his soul! But he 'died decent'. I've lost my best mate, and you've lost your best officer.
>
> We're getting along very well up here. Whipso' work. News comes in every day of small parties of Boers; and out we go to harry them like b—dy cattle dogs. We've given this quarter a pretty hot name for the Boers, and they are drifting to the WATERBERG: gathering up there to some considerable number by this time. We're whipping them in: 'getting them together': and IT WANTS A STRONG FORCE – column – to smash them once they get consolidated there. Our great requirement is HORSE SHOES. For the Lord's

sake send up half a dozen boxes at least. We've got the shoes literally worn off the horses' hoofs – with work. I make men out on patrol walk and lead at every opportunity; and considering the work done the horses last out and look well. The Sergeant-major [Hammett] you sent up is an excellent man; has a big grip of the men; knows his work, and makes them do theirs! With the men getting 7/- per day they ought to be pretty freely 'culled' and get a better quality of soldier without damaging the numbers to any extent! By G—, there must have been some wastrels there that night when poor old Hunt went under. I suppose Mortimer has told you that his body was stripped, neck broken, etc., etc, by the Boers. I've straightened some of them up. They stand cursing! But you cannot make a crooked stick straight, or make a d—d coward a good plucked one. I fancy you've heard some fairy tales to the detriment of Taylor! You must remember the source they come from. Hunt got on with him famously right from the first, and I, Handcock, and the rest of us couldn't wish for a better fellow to work with. We work ourselves, men and horses d—d hard, but Taylor lends us every assistance, and his 'intelligence' is the most reliable I've struck in South Africa. Handcock you know, and I find him worth the other two in himself. You must excuse my apparent carelessness in the matter of letter writing, but I have really not had any chance of scribbling. If ever I sat down to write some d—d Boers bobbed up and we had to go out and 'worry' them. By the way, if there are any scattered things of Hunt's about Pietersburg camp, will you look after them personally? Poor old chap – he left his ponies and all his gear to me, and I've got something to fix up for him, as it's a very private matter, I will not write of; but will inform you privately as our C.O. when I see you. If you could only come up here for a week, I think it would do a power of good in many ways, and I hope, if you do come up, you will not be dissatisfied with our work.

Good-bye Major

Yours obediently,

Harry H. Morant 'Tony' [150]

The writer, recipient and the three men praised as being reliable in this letter – Sergeant Hammett, Lieutenant Handcock and Captain Taylor – were all later arrested for the crimes for which the BVC would become notorious.

Christie continues:

Arrived at the Fort, we found that another party had gone out to engage the Boers we had hunted away. But after exchanging shots during which one of our men was slightly wounded in the arm and another accidentally through carelessness with his own rifle, they came back to camp again. And the Boers were still at large. A section of us seemed to feel that our officers – or a leading part of them – were no good, that they did not want to catch the Boers but while away the time on inconsequent patrols, and keep clear of anything that was likely to shoot back. This was the conclusion we came to and subsequent events justified it.

I went out with another patrol to clear the way for a big convoy that was to pass along, and was left with three other men on a post, where if there had been any enemy, we should have had a good chance of being wiped out. After about 14 hours the convoy came up and laagered about midnight. With it were large numbers of prisoners (refugees I called them) – men, women, and children, who had been taken without a shot being fired … I was gradually having my suspicions aroused by these led-by-the-nose movements, but did not tumble exactly what was going on. Then I was told off to go for a three weeks patrol: no one could tell where, no kits, ride light was the order. When out some eight miles we found we were going to hold the post at Reuter's mission station, and had provisions for three weeks, there were twenty of us. [151]

This patrol was led by Lt Hannam. Christie:

On the way we met a waggon and eight Boers being brought in by our men, and here I may say this waggon was taken by two of our men, one of them a mate of mine who accidentally shot himself the previous day in the leg with a revolver he had looted. I will revert to the eight Boers some other time, as tragedy took place next morning [23 August] of which I was ignorant at the time. [152]

These men who brought the eight Boers in were Trooper Petrie and Mr Ledeboer of the Intelligence department. [153] One who was not ignorant of the fate of the eight Boers was Sergeant James Wrench:

I left the fort on 19th Aug. in charge of a patrol of nine men – Troopers Marrett, Kidd, Leeds, Ramsden, van Blerk, van der Westhuizen, Cox, Miller, and Beaven to take over from Mr Ledeboer of the Intelligence eight surrendered Boer prisoners. They had in the wagon a sack of valuable specimens of gold and each had money. I trekked with them two days. The bolts had been taken from the magazine rifles and were distributed among the troopers. I found them perfectly peaceable. I arrived at the hospital on the evening of Aug. 22nd which is about 5 miles from camp. On the morning of the 23rd before starting Lt Morant arrived accompanied by Lt Handcock, Lt Witton, Sergt Major Hammett, Trooper A. Duckett and A. Thompson. I was told when

> I heard shots to gallop back. I heard three shots apparently fired in the air from Bristow's farm, or thereabouts. We were then visible from the farmhouse. Shortly after that we heard about fifteen shots. I rode to the farm and reported to Capt. Taylor who was walking about in an excited manner. Mr Ledeboer was also present and very excited. I am sure that the three shots were signals and were not fired by Boers but by some of our own men. [154]

Four of the 'Eight Boers' shot on the 23rd were Dutch school teachers. William Daniel Vahrmeijer was a principal of the Emmanuel School in Potgietersrus, two others were also teachers at Potgietersrus. G. K. Westerhof had been the principal of the school in Pietersburg. A 45-year-old man named Edoud Boukan was a prospector. [155] The others were C. P. J. Smit, J. J. du Preez and two men with the surnames Logenaar (or Lochner) and Pauskie. [156] The Bushveldt Carbineers claimed that these men had been part of the Viljoen (or Low veld) Commando, and were therefore responsible for the death and alleged mutilation of Captain Hunt. Five of their names, however, appear on the Roll of Honour of the Zoutpansberg Commando and therefore were very unlikely to have been members of the Viljoen Commando. [157] Lieutenant Witton:

> The day following Lieutenant Hannam's departure to the Mission Station, which was the 22nd August, a report reached Fort Edward that eight prisoners were being brought in. On the following morning Lieutenant Morant came to me and requested me to accompany him on patrol.
>
> A patrol subsequently set out, consisting of Lieutenants Morant, Handcock, and myself, Sergeant-Major Hammett (who had gone out with me to the Spelonken), and two troopers. We first called at the office of Captain Taylor. Morant dismounted and had a private interview with that officer; I was not informed as to the nature of it. I was not then on intimate terms with Lieutenant Morant; I had only met him for the first time a fortnight previously as my superior officer, and had recognised him as such, and during that fortnight I had been frequently away from the fort.
>
> We went on, and Morant said that it was his intention to have the prisoners shot. Both myself and Sergeant-Major Hammett asked Morant if he was sure he was doing right. He replied that he was quite justified in shooting the Boers; he had his orders, and he would rely upon us to obey him. I also afterwards remonstrated with him for having the prisoners brought in and shot so close to the fort, but he said it was a matter of indifference where they were shot.

> We met the patrol with the prisoners about six miles out. Morant at once took charge, and instructed the escort to go on ahead as advance guard. The prisoners were ordered to inspan and trek on to the fort. I rode on in front of the waggon, and I did not see any civilian speak to the prisoners as we were passing the mission hospital. When we had trekked on about three miles Morant stopped the waggon, called the men off the road, and questioned them. Upon his asking, 'Have you any more information to give?' they were shot. One of them, a big, powerful Dutchman, made a rush at me and seized the end of my rifle, with the intention of taking it and shooting me, but I simplified matters by pulling the trigger and shooting him. I never had any qualms of conscience for having done so, as he was recognised by Ledeboer, the intelligence agent, as a most notorious scoundrel who had previously threatened to shoot him, and was the head of a band of marauders. By just escaping death in this tragedy I was afterwards sentenced to suffer death. [158]

That one of the Boers made a rush at Witton was corroborated by Sergeant Major Hammett's testimony in court though with the minor difference that the Boer grabbed Witton by the jacket rather than the rifle. Charles Leach has identified this man as C. P. J. Smit. Whether Witton is seeking sympathy or genuinely expressing righteous indignation at 'just escaping death' whilst assisting in the murder of eight unarmed men, the statement beggars belief. The notion that he was charged for being complicit in the murder of all eight and not just for shooting the one who had the audacity to attempt to defend himself does not seem to have occurred to him.

Emmanuel School in Potgeitersrus, where W. D. Vahrmeijer was on a teaching contract funded from Amsterdam, was close to a mission station at Makapanspoort run by a missionary of German descent named Reverend C. A. D Heese. Heese and Vahrmeijer were friends. [159] On 23 August, Reverend Heese was at Elim Hospital, having taken a friend of his, John H. Craig, an Australian shopkeeper and clerk in the British Army Intelligence Office [160] there from Potegietersrus. Craig had a large swelling in his neck and he had asked Revd Heese to take him there for treatment. Craig had previously been operated on at Elim for his thyroid problem, but a subsequent operation in Pretoria had resulted in an infection. Craig chose to return to Elim. [161]

Christie speaking of a later visit to Elim Hospital described it thus:

> The Elim Hospital is a Swiss Mission one, and is a fine handsome brick pile, and very well equipped. The doctor is a Swiss and his wife a German. The nurses are Swiss girls, and very charming, with a most cheery style;

> and a wholesome air of genuine Christianity hangs over the whole fabric of the institution.
>
> There is a Kaffir Hospital, also, some chains away from the larger building. The hospital is a new institution, having only recently finished. It is supposed to be self supporting, and the doctor only gets L80 a year and his keep. The salary seems small, but he loves his work of charity and mercy, and is with-all very highly qualified, as patients are sent to him all the way from Pretoria ... I thought well here is a mission that is a genuine one. Body and soul attended to and that by a gentle sisterhood devoting their lives to ease the physical pains of humanity, and bringing a balm to many a weary worn soul in distress. [162]

Heese knew the founder of the hospital, Dr Georges Liengme and as J. H. Craig worked for the Intelligence Department he and Heese had been provided with a 'spider' by Captain Ramon De Bertodano, an Australian of Spanish descent of the Intelligence Department. Heese used the spider to take Craig to Elim but unfortunately Dr Liengme was unable to save Craig from the advanced infection. He died on 22 August. [163]

Whilst at Elim, Reverend Heese had noticed the patrol and his friend Vahrmeijer among the prisoners and naturally went to speak to him. According to his wife Johanna's later account:

> ... Daniel went straight up and talked to him. The Schoolmaster said that he and the other prisoners were very uneasy as to their fate, although they had surrendered voluntarily. Daniel comforted them by telling them that nothing could happen to them. The guards became angry with Daniel for speaking to the prisoners, and ordered him to get up onto his wagon and consider himself also a prisoner. Daniel refused, saying they might have prevented his approaching the prisoners that he was in possession of a pass from a commander in Pietersburg allowing him to travel freely, and promised to report himself at the camp and bring his passport with him.
>
> The prisoners were then removed, and Daniel went to lunch with some friends. On hearing all that had happened they were terribly frightened and did their best to persuade him to stay in their house for the next two days, but he had promised to report himself in the camp that evening, and nothing would induce him to break his word. [164]

Dr Liengme wrote a report dated 9 August 1901 which stated that not only the guards but two Lieutenants also 'interrogated Revd Heese harshly. They were visibly very cross to see him amongst their prisoners.' [165]

Daniel Heese and his Ndebele driver left Elim hospital sometime after Morant, Handcock, Witton, the eight prisoners and the rest of the patrol. He later arrived at Fort Edward. Lieutenant George Witton:

> I went on with the men, and we took with us the waggon and belongings, which we handed over to Captain Taylor. I then went on to the fort. Morant and Handcock remained behind to make arrangements for the burial of the bodies. About an hour afterwards Morant came in; a few minutes later he noticed a hooded buggy drawn by a pair of mules coming along the road at the foot of the fort, and going in the direction of Pietersburg. He immediately jumped on a horse, and rode down to see who it was, as no one was allowed to travel about the country without first getting permission to do so. When he returned he informed me that it was a missionary from Potgeiter's Rust returning home, and that he held a pass signed by Captain Taylor. Morant said that he had advised the missionary to wait until a convoy returned to Pietersburg, but he decided that he would go on alone. Morant then went away to see Captain Taylor. In the meantime Lieutenant Handcock returned, had his breakfast, and also went away again. [166]

Having not been particularly reticent about using hearsay elsewhere in his 1907 book, Witton goes on: 'I have no idea of their subsequent movements, for being tired out I went to my bungalow, and slept until lunch time. I lunched alone, which was not unusual, but Morant and Handcock returned in the evening for dinner.' [167] This would seem more than a little disingenuous. By 1907 he had a good idea of their movements; indeed, if one believes his 1929 letter [168] to J. F. Thomas – and there is no convincing reason not to – then he had a greater idea than anyone else still living.

Witton says that at midday Morant called out around 40 men to Bristowe's farm around a mile away to investigate rockets he had taken to be a distress signal. They had in fact been sent up to amuse the children, much to Morant's annoyance.

Trooper van der Westhuizen:

> When the missionary, the Revd Mr Heese, passed the Fort Lt Morant jumped on his horse bare back and galloped up the road to overtake the missionary who was driving a spider drawn by two mules. After speaking to the missionary he came galloping back to the Fort. He called out for Mr Handcock. When Lt Handcock got on his horse he called out 'Mr Handcock do your best.' Mr Handcock said 'all right I know what to do.' Mr Handcock then galloped in the direction taken by the missionary. Shortly afterwards we heard the missionary was shot.

Mr Handcock was riding a chestnut pony taken from the six Boers killed on 2 July and which he claimed as his private property. [169]

At the time of Revd Heese's murder, Silas Sono, a 17-year-old from nearby Maila, was on his way back to the Kreuzburg mission station near Fort Klipdan. There he spoke to Reverend Endemann, informing him of his observations from the previous day when Reverend Heese had passed him on the road near Maila's Kop. Reverend Endemman sent a transcript of the report to Superintendent Krause in Pietersburg. Below are two versions translated from Silas' Sotho language, one being the version sent to Lt Col Hall and the other from the Berlin Mission's records.

From the records of Berlin Mission society (Charles Leach)

Mr Heese sat in the cart (spider) and read a book (most probably the New Testament.) A little while later, it crossed my mind I should have asked him whether Mynheer (Mister) would permit me to sit on his cart, in order to get home faster. I then ran after the cart as fast as I could. Mr Heese was already far ahead.

A rider came galloping after me, going in the same direction. He wore Khaki clothes, like the soldiers do, and had a light coloured hat with a cloth of many colours (red, blue, white and black) and wore the badge of a Corporal.

He was a young, sturdy man, with a clean-shaven face, except for his moustache. * He had two bandoliers crossed over his shoulders, and his breast pockets, were also full of bullets. His horse was of a red-brown colour and had a long tail. (i.e. it was not shortened) and it was not particularly fat. I greeted him and he answered: 'Mm,' with

Version sent to Col Hall (Denton, repeated in Davey)

I was in Spelonken and left there on the morning of the 23rd. in order to return home. Soon after midday I was overtaken at Mailaskop by Mr Heese. He was sitting in his spider and reading a book. A while later it came to my mind that I could ask whether Mynheer would permit me to sit with him on his waggon in order to get home more quickly. Mr Heese was already well ahead.

While I was hurrying along, a rider came galloping behind me, going in the same direction. He wore khaki clothing such as the soldiers wear, a light coloured hat with a cloth of motley colours (red, blue, white and black), and stripes like a corporal.

He was a young, stocky man; his face was shaved except for the moustache that he wore. He wore two cartridge-belts crossways over his shoulders and his breast pockets were filled with cartridges. His horse was of a bay colour, had a long tail and was not particularly closed lips. From the spoor, I saw that his horse was shod.

A little while later I came to a place from where one has a free view over the next rise. Here I saw how the rider got off his horse and led his horse by the rein into the bushes. At the same time I noticed a cart/wagon coming down from the rise in front of me. A bit further down, in the dip, Mr Heese's cart stood out-spanned.

When the wagon reached Mr Heese, the owner of the wagon van Rooyen, climbed down and had a short conversation with Mr Heese. Then they said good bye and he followed the wagon which had gone ahead. Van Rooyen was still walking when I met with him. He spoke to me and asked about 'where from' and 'where to' and whether the road to Maila's Kop was safe. I told him that I had seen nothing suspicious and that there was nothing to be afraid of.'

Through this conversation I had lost some time. Mr Heese had in the meantime inspanned and was riding up the rise. I rushed after him and was about 300 yards away from him (the distance was later accurately measured) – but I could not see his cart because of the bend in the road. That is when a shot was fired; immediately after that a second, a third and a fourth.

I asked myself, what does this mean? But I did not think anything bad. In the time from the first to the fourth shot. I had only moved

well conditioned. I greeted him and he replied with closed lips, "Mmm". From the back I recognised that the horse was shod.

A while later I came to a spot from which one has an unhindered view to the next rise. It was there that the rider had dismounted, leading the horse by the bridle, he turned off into the bush. At the same time I noticed a waggon come down from the rise lying ahead of me. A little lower down in the hollow stood Mr Heese's spider, unharnessed.

When the waggon reached the spider, the owner (Van Rooyen) alighted and had a conversation, not for very long, with Mr Heese; then he took his leave and followed on foot after his waggon which had driven ahead. Van Rooyen was still walking on foot when I met him; he addressed me and asked me about 'Where from?' and 'Where to?' and whether the road towards Mailaskop was safe. I told him that I saw nothing and also that there was nothing to fear.

Through this conversation I had lost a little time. Mr Heese had in the meantime harnessed up and drove on up the rise. I hurried after him and had come within a distance of about 300 yards from the spider (the distances were measured off later) but could not see the vehicle on account of a bend in the road, when a shot was fired, immediately afterwards a second, a third, a fourth.

I asked myself what that might mean, but did not think

ahead about 16 yards because I had slowed down my pace.

As everything was quiet after this I went on, always on the lookout for something to find.

Then I saw Mr Heese's cart standing to the right of the road; but it was turned around with disselboom/shaft pointing to the Spelonken from where he had just come. I did not see the mules in front of the wagon. But the grass was somewhat high there (3–5 feet high); yet I should have been able to see the animals: they were nowhere to be seen. Behind the cart stood a horse, bridled and saddled, its reins thrown over it. It was the same horse which I had seen just before – the red-brown horse of the rider who had overtaken me as he galloped past me just this side of Maila's Kop.

The cart was standing only 50 yards away from me in the road; yet I could not see anybody in it or near it. In me the notion/idea arose that the four shots, the empty cart and the saddled horse, all formed an unholy alliance/connection, and fear crept into my soul.'

While I slowly moved forward – scanning the areas to the side of me, with little regard for the road ahead – I noticed the lifeless body of the Black man on the left side of the road, close in front of me. I was so frightened/shocked that I called out aloud: What is this? A person has been murdered here – who has murdered him? And I recognized

anything bad. In the period from the first to the fourth shot I had only progressed 16 yards because I had slowed down my steps; however since I could hear nothing further I went on, always on, always on the lookout whether I could discover something.

Then I see to the right of the road a vehicle – spider of Mr Heese – standing, the pole however not in the direction of Pietersburg, but turned around towards Spelonken, from where he had come. I did not see the mules in front of the spider; the grass indeed was very long (3 to 5 feet high) nevertheless I would have had to see the animals. They were not there. Behind the spider stood a horse, bridled and saddled, with the reins lying on it; and the horse was the same one that I had seen shortly before, the bay horse of the rider who, galloping past me, had overtaken me this side of Mailaskop.

The spider stood only about 50 yards off the side of the road but I could see neither anyone in the spider nor anyone in the vicinity of it. But the inkling rose up in me that the shots, the empty waggon and the saddled horse had to have a sinister connection; and fear crept into my soul.

While I moved hesitatingly forward with my eyes turned sideways and took little notice of the road I caught sight of the lifeless body of a Coloured. I was so scared that I cried out loudly: What is that? Here a person has been murdered – who has murdered him? And I recognised this dead person. It was Mr Heese's wagon driver. A shot in the forehead had torn away the top part of his skull, causing a long wide wound from which the blood and brains were gushing, I put my hand on the body and felt that he was still very warm. Such horror came over me, that I could think of nothing else, than to run home and report the matter to Mr Endemann in Kreuzburg. [170]

this dead person. I recognised his face and recognised his clothing; I had seen him at Elim and seen him near Mailaskop when the spider drove past- It was Mr Heese's driver. A gun shot in the forehead had torn away the scalp and brains came forth. I laid my hands on the body and felt that it was quite warm. Such terror came over me that I could think of nothing else than to run home and report. [171]

The above description by Silas Sono has raised a number of points which have been used to argue that whoever killed Daniel Heese, it was not Lieutenant Peter Handcock. 'He wore Khaki clothes, like the soldiers do, and had a light coloured hat with a cloth of many colours (red, blue, white and black) and wore the badge of a Corporal.' Handcock was a Lieutenant and would not have worn stripes or the badge of a corporal. There is nothing to suggest that Handcock would have worn a cloth of red, blue, white and black. It has also been argued that Handcock was a tall man rather than a stocky or sturdy one, as described by Silas. One must bear in mind that this is a translation from Silas' own Sotho language. The two versions above ably demonstrate the difficulties in translating the subtleties of any language. We have no way of knowing how well the translator knew this language. How can we know if the word translated as 'sturdy' or 'stocky' implies shortness in Silas' language, or just big? Was the rider wearing stripes or some other kind of badge? And how well would Silas have known the badges and ranks of the British Army?

During the subsequent Court Martial, Handcock said he 'left on foot for Schiel's in the morning, taking the road which branched off to the Pietersburg road, and then across country. He lunched at Schiel's, and then went to Bristowe's until dusk, then back to the fort.' [172]

Morant also gave evidence:

> Morant deposed that on August 23 eight Boers guilty of train-wrecking and other crimes were shot by his orders. Heese spoke of these Boers, and was told not to do so. Afterwards the witness saw Heese in a cart. He produced a pass signed by Taylor. The witness advised him not to go on to Pietersburg because of the Boers. Heese said he would chance it, and by the witness's advice he tied a white flag to the cart. The prisoner

returned to the fort, and then went to Taylor's, and he afterwards saw Handcock at Bristowe's. Handcock went on to Schiel's. The prisoner never made any suggestion about killing the missionary. He was on good terms with him. [173]

Besides the fact that Handcock says he left 'on foot', whereas elsewhere there is much debate about the colour of his horse, Morant's depositions says that Handock went to Bristowe's first where Morant saw him and then 'Handcock went on to Scheil's.' Handcock's evidence says: 'He lunched at Schiel's, and then went to Bristowe's till dusk, then back to the fort.' This reversal could of course just be an error of reporting by the *Times* correspondent; or did Morant and Handcock give inconsistent evidence? We will never know.

New Zealander Corporal Ernest G. G. Brown of the BVC later stated in a deposition: 'On the day the missionary was shot a picket comprising Trooper Phillips, Wrangham and Benadie were at Cooksley's Farm and saw van Rooyen who told them that he had passed one of the Bushveldt Carbineers in the vicinity of Bandolierkop. This Picket was later minutely questioned by Lieutenant Handcock who was labouring under very great excitement.' [174]

Lieutenant Witton was later limited, by Morant, in the area he was allowed to search for Revd Heese's body:

Nearly a week later, I, with Lieutenant Morant, was at Captain Taylor's office, when a neighbour came in and said there was a rumour abroad that a missionary had been killed on the road at Bandolier Kopjes, about 15 miles from Fort Edward, the most dangerous spot on the road to Pietersburg. I at once volunteered to take out a patrol and investigate. I was not permitted to go as far as Bandolier Kopjes, but was sent with half a dozen men to a farm-house five miles out to get what information I could, and was given orders by Lieutenant Morant not to go any further. Upon arrival at the farm I could glean nothing. I had all the natives brought up and questioned, but they did not know anything. I then went along the road to several kraals, but could get no news; I met a native post-boy with the mails from Pietersburg, and questioned him, but he knew nothing and had seen nothing along the road.

I then returned to the Fort, and on the way back met Taylor and Morant. I informed them of my inability to get any further information, and expressed to them my opinion that it was only a Kaffir yarn.

Two days later, however, Lieutenant Handcock was sent out to Bandolier Kopjes with a strong patrol to make a further search, and discovered the body of the missionary, his buggy, and his mules, some distance off the

> road. There was every indication that he had met his death by foul play. He had been shot in the breast, probably whilst sitting in his buggy; the mules, taking fright, had galloped off the road, throwing the missionary out as they travelled along. The buggy was found jammed between some trees and a telegraph post, with the pole broken. The mules had freed themselves, and were feeding about harnessed together. Lieutenant Handcock made arrangements for the burial of the missionary, and returned to the Fort, taking the mules with him. [175]

If one believes the above version of events then no member of the BVC would have seen Revd Heese dead or alive after 23 August until about a week later. Ramon de Bertodano's account, which he states was based in his intelligence reports and his private diaries, says that in the last week of August he received a wire from Lieutenant McWilliam stating that the Mission at P.P. Rust urgently required the return of Revd Heese. De Bertodano wired Fort Edward asking for

> ...a full explanation as to why Heese had been detained for several weeks. The reply made some excuse for this, and said that he was leaving the next day, about 26th or 27th August. [Heese had been dead 3 to 4 days by then.] About the 29th of August a further wire came to say that the Reverend Heese had been shot by Boers near Bandolier Kopjes, 15 miles from Fort Edward on the Pietersburg Road ... That a Predicant [Missionary] had been shot by Boers was a yarn I could not swallow. [176]

If Fort Edward did claim that Revd Heese was about to leave on 26 or 27 August, three or four days after they had last seen him, they were lying – with the obvious implication that they already he knew he was dead. This they only admitted to knowing, to Pretoria, on 29 August, after the patrol had picked up the body.

Andries Pretorius has asked the question: Why was Lieutenant Witton permitted by Lieutenant Morant to travel to Bandolier kopjes but only as far as a farmstead 5 miles out? [177] Was it to ascertain, before recovery of Heese and his driver's bodies, who in the area knew what, so that any potential witnesses could be 'dealt with'? It is not unreasonable to ask why Morant would specifically limit Witton's movements. It also suggests Witton was ignorant of the true events at the time.

Around a week after the Reverend Heese's body was found, an even more horrific event was to unfold in the Mooketsi Valley about 5 miles from Modjadji's Kraal. A small patrol of the BVC was at Reverend Reuter's Mission station at Medingen when the officer in charge, Lieutenant Hannam, received intelligence that a party of Boers were coming in to surrender. One of the patrol at Medingen was Trooper James Christie:

> We heard Boer waggons to the south and east of us, and presumed as usual, that they were trekking in to surrender. We had been some four or five days out in camp when a corporal told eight of us that we were to go out and bring in three waggons with four men with them and some women and children. We said: 'Leave them alone; they are trekking up this way out of the fever country, and will come in.' 'No,' he said, 'we are to go out; none are to be brought in.' 'What do you mean?' 'Oh,' said he. 'We've got to blot the lot out.' 'What! Shoot the kids!' 'Yes, of course.' We all pooh-poohed the idea, but he told us seriously that such was the case. Then I opened out, and asked him what sort of men did he take us for. Others chipped in, but he still adhered to his statement, except that he softened it by saying if we brought them in we should have to feed them. Latterly, to justify his intention, he told us the old chestnut about Strathcona's Horse hanging five or six Boers; that he was there; and was up before Lord Roberts for it, and that all Roberts said was, 'He wished to God he had more men like them in South Africa.' I told him I did not believe a word of it, and that I was for no such duty. He said he could get plenty more. [178]

Trooper Jacob Hatfield, a sailor from Cheshire, England, of Nova Scotian parentage, gave an account of what ensued:

> About 6.30 p.m. we came up to the wagons of which we were to search. There were three wagons. Lt Hannam divided the patrol into two parties, himself, Trooper Hampton and Gibbald and two armed Kaffirs constituting one party which went to the right and Corporal Ashton, Trooper Maynard and myself and ten armed kaffirs went to the left. Lt Hannam called me as we were dividing and told me to tell Corporal Ashton that when we heard him fire we were to fire on the wagons. We heard his signal and started to fire. I heard a woman (it might have been a boy) screaming. I stopped firing and drew Corporal Ashton's attention to it. He said his orders were to keep firing till he got the order to stop. I heard a man shouting 'we surrender'. I drew Corporal Ashton's attention to it again and he went over to Lt Hannam. He came back from Lt Hannam and asked me to continue firing. I fired one shot in the air and then refused to fire any more. [179]

Meanwhile Trooper James Hampton was on the right:

> Lt Hannam then took Tpr Gibbald and myself to get within three or four hundred yards of the wagon. On arriving there we could plainly

> hear women and children laughing and talking. Without asking them to surrender Lt Hannam fired the signal shot. It was an understood thing that as soon as Lt Hannam fired the signal shot we were to fire. During the firing, that is to say as soon as the first shot was fired, we could hear shouts of 'we surrender'. Lt Hannam's servant jumped up and said to Lt Hannam 'The Dutchmen say they surrender, Sir.' He took no notice of this but ordered Trooper Gibbald and myself to continue firing. The women and children were shrieking all the time ... I can positively swear that from first to last not one of the Dutchmen, neither the one in the wagon or the three in the donga made the slightest attempt to fire a shot. [180]

Hampton and Hatfield's descriptions of the effect of the shooting are consistent; Hatfield:

> About five minute afterwards we closed on the wagon. There we found one man. Lt Hannam sent Tpr Gibbald and myself with three Dutchman to the donga in search of the other three men. The first to arrive was a woman with a dead child in her arms, a boy of about five or six years of age. He had been shot through the back of the neck. Then arrived a man carrying a boy of fourteen who was shot through the back but still alive. Next I saw a little girl about eight years old wounded in the neck. We put the wounded in the wagon. The boy was suffering horribly. He died in about an hour. We trekked to Bla's store. We turned the wagons and people over to Trooper[s] Christie and Coetzee. [181]

Although Lt Witton was not present at this incident, it is worth considering his treatment of these events in his book *Scapegoats of the Empire*:

> I can explain here how those infamous rumours gained currency as to the shooting of children by the Carbineers. A patrol of Lieutenant Hannam's men were out making a reconnaissance, when they suddenly came upon a Boer laager and opened fire. They heard women and children screathing, and ceased firing. Upon taking the laager they found that a child had been shot and two little girls slightly wounded.
>
> I afterwards escorted these prisoners to Pietersburg, and in conversation with the parents of the children they told me that they in no way reproached Lieutenant Hannam or his men for what had happened; they were themselves to blame for running away from their waggons when called upon to surrender. This is the only foundation for the wicked reports as to the wholesale shooting of women and children by the Carbineers. [182]

Besides the fact there was nothing sudden about the patrol coming upon the Boer waggons, Witton gets both the victims and their injuries wrong, it was not that 'a child had been shot and two little girls slightly wounded' but two boys killed and one girl shot through the neck. The two boys were Jan Dirk Grobler (Jnr) aged 13 and Jacobus Daniel Grobler, aged 5. The girl, shot through the neck was their sister Elizabeth Maria Grobler aged 9. [183]

If their parents really did not reproach Hannam and his men, as Witton claims, one must suppose that they had very high expectations of their children, for who would reasonably expect children of these ages not to run from the rifle fire of eighteen men? You would also have to suppose they were devoid of any of the normal parental devotion. Troopers Hampton and Hatfield make no mention of any call for them to surrender coming from the BVC before firing commenced, as Witton claims.

Trooper John Silke, who was not actually present, stated in his 'diary', 'one boy about ten years of age was carrying his baby brother on his back when a ball passed through the two of them killing them both ... Christie buried the children the next day.' [184]

Trooper James Christie, who had not taken part in the shooting but took over the party of prisoners the next day, takes up the story:

> Next day the patrol went out, and the sequel was that two children were shot dead—one three, and another nine years; and a girl of nine was shot through the neck and the lobe of her ear taken off.
>
> Some cows were shot. This was done about eight o'clock at night, and, although the men and women called out that they surrendered, the firing still went on, and finally when it ceased the above were the casualties. With the exception of three men, all the others told me before they went out that they would not fire on women and children. They were about 200 or 250 yards off the waggons when they opened fire. Next day I was ordered out with a Transvaaler called Cootze to go to the Koodoo River and take over the waggons from Corporal Ashton, and take them to the fort. I left the camp and met the waggons. There were a lot of armed Kaffirs with the party, who had taken part in the firing, and who had looted the blankets, utensils, etc, when the firing ceased. The Boers never fired a shot. When the lieutenant saw the extent of the damage, he said (this was told me) –'My God I didn't think this would happen.' 'What the – did you think would happen if you fire at women and children?' said Hampton, an outspoken Londoner. 'You won't get me on an outfit like this again.' Hatfield, a bluff young sailor of Nova Scotia descent, bound up the wounds and helped to stop the bleeding, and told me he had seen some sights in his time, but, he felt more sick over this business than anything he had ever been mixed

up in. The Boers were made to in span in the darkness and trek away in case the firing might have been noticed by some other Boers, and the dead infant and the living one were put aboard and trekked away to where I was to meet them. The second boy only lived two hours, and the grief of the parents was loud and pronounced. The three waggons now contained four men, four women and twenty-two children (all of tender years), and two bodies. The father, Piet Grobler asked leave to bury them and a coffin was made out of some boards lying about a store. Kaffiirs were put on to dig a grave, and the men themselves made a coffin. It was dark before the coffin was finished, and as I helped to lift the two children into it the father prayed in Dutch over his two sons, weeping profusely. When the coffin was settled in the grave, the men chanted something like a Scotch psalm. I caught something about Louis Botha and Kitchener in the father's impassioned praying, and was told that he was referring to the terms offered by Kitchener to Botha, who should have then given in and saved unnecessary bloodshed. I felt just at that moment that we were round what was one of the saddest sights of the war—sad because quite unnecessary. The men were trekking in to surrender, and had left their farms with all their worldly gear, to prevent, them from being commandeered by the Boers themselves. They told me that their commandant told them if they would not go on commando he must take their money and horses, which was done, and that if they stopped on their farms the British would maltreat the women and shoot them too. So they went into the lion veldt with their families, to be out of the way of friend and foe. The fever was now driving them in. Ten donkeys, in a big lumbering waggon, one would think, would be overweighted, but they always turned up soon after we got the ox outspanned. It took some time in the morning to get all the kids fed and at noon we always halted for at least two hours, when the women did the washing. I had in my kit some reels of cotton, buttons, needles, etc., which I gave them; and soon they were darning the few rags that adorned the children. Some of the kids were feverish, and all were thin and gaunt—even the men, they had no coffee or sugar, only mealies and biltong, and a very poor quality of salt.

The second last day of our trek I was on some two hours ahead waiting for them at the noon halt, when I heard some news which turned me sick. The eight Boers I previously mentioned had all been shot by three officers, a non-com, and two privates, under circumstances which led me to the conclusion that it was not a fair deal, and that, some foul play was at the bottom of it. They were surrendered men, and had no arms, and when I thought of my little lot coming along, I cannot describe my feelings. My informant was a neutral man, and, of course, would not speak, but later on

I had afternoon tea with his wife, and got,-though she was cautious—some hang of the story. I decided to trek still further that night, but did not let my refugees know the real reasons. Halted, outspanned, lit our evening fires, but slept not that night. I remembered how six Boers had surrendered, and were said to have attacked our men, had all been shot. I remember van Buren, one of our own men, being shot by the Boers(?) while out flanking—he was supposed to know too much. Now, here were eight blotted out, and the same old yarn—that they had grabbed at a rifle and fired at our men, and in the melee all were shot—no casualties -on our side; and here was me coming in with another lot, and 'just within the firing line,' as we called it. At daylight a Captain — the officer commanding the district, and Native Commissioner—Balala (murderer) the natives called him—drove up at a full gallop in a buggy and pair, and asked how my men were. I explained I had a wounded girl in the wagon. 'How did that happen?' I told him our men opened fire on the women and children and two little boys had been killed. 'Indeed!' he queried. 'You had better keep that quiet.' He looked at the girl's wound, and gave me an order to see the hospital doctor—we were to pass the place—and seemed quite concerned, and then drove off after telling me to get on as quickly as possible, as there was a convoy waiting to go to Pietersburg. I got to the hospital at noon, and had the child looked to, also some of the women. Had a yarn with Petrie; his leg was getting better. Broached the subject of the eight men being blotted out—he knew them all.

Heard too, that a German missionary, who had been up at the hospital with a patient, had been shot dead on his return at Bandolier Kopjes. He had been present just before or immediately after-the eight men had been shot—that one of our lieutenants had left the fort after the missionary secretly, was seen by the grazing guard to go in the direction the missionary had taken. That the lieutenant returned to the fort late, etc., etc. —much more I weeded out of him. After the patients had been attended to we inspanned, and were moving off when I sighted that same Lieutenant and two men galloping up after me, and my heart stood stock still, for I thought I was about to witness another tragedy. Quickly but mechanically I slipped a dumdum into my breach, and waited. The picture of the six Boers lying dead, as had been related to me, the eight men surrendering shot in cold blood, and van Buren shot, all came on me in an instant. My mind was made up that though it should be a crisis in my life I should shoot that lieutenant if he opened fire on the men in my charge, or else get shot, according to who might have the advantage. He galloped up with two men. When I saw the men I knew they were out for no good purposes for both of them would always do as they were told though they had no fancy for it. However, the hospital was too close, and I was told to go on to the fort.

> I said "Very good, but I have my orders from Captain —. He looked as if he doubted my having seen Captain —. 'Go on,' he said, "and I'll catch up on you.' The Boers, who saluted him, not knowing his nature, seemed hurt that he did not recognise it, or in any way notice them. Anyhow, on we went. By and by up he came, and then a conversation took place between him and me, starting with the shooting of the women and children, and its unfortunateness. 'Oh,' he said, 'they had no business there,' and went on to argue in an ignorant, brutal way that they should all be shot. I kept back my feeling that he had been mixed up in what were pure and simple murders, and argued on broad grounds that conduct such as we were pursuing would give the corps a bad name—would, in fact, make it a hissing reproach on the army. He went on to say that they were justified in shooting everything in sight; but it was a long yarn, and I got emphatic, and argued that once a man put his hands up he could not be shot unless after a proper trial. At this time I held my rifle across my saddle bow, and if he had dared to put his hand to his revolver I would have dropped him like a buck. The man I found to be an ignorant and cowardly bully. I forgot for the moment I was speaking to my superior officer, and expressed regret, etc. When he wanted me to go back and see the donkey waggon, I said: 'Oh, it's all right.' 'It's not all right,' he said. 'Well,' I said, 'it's come about 100 miles, and no one has looked after it, and it's not likely to run away now.' However, I called out on Cootzee to wait for the donkey waggon. Thinks I, my fine fellow, if you think to get me away from these waggons you have struck the wrong party. That was how the others were always 'done in'—party came out from the fort: 'Oh, you can go home; we'll take the waggons in.' Result: Every one of the surrenderers butchered. 'Not me I'm going to take those refugees in, or there will be a scene.' And take them in I did. And then I learned fuller particulars from some of my chums as to the goings on. The arrival of the refugees and my safe arrival were the cause of much joy amongst a section of us who did not hold with the carryings on; and as our mates were coming in, with another lot, we speculated on their success, and how we could get word out to them as to what had taken place but to no purpose. We were watched like hawks by the officers and their minions. We swore that if anything came over 'Charlie' and 'Jake' we would 'hands up' the officers and put them in irons, or, if necessary, take the law into our own hands and shoot them. The trouble was to get a sufficient force of our view to take a step. One had to move warily in the matter. [185]

Trooper James Christie was not the only one who thought the BVC officers were nervous about things getting out. Writing to his mother on 20 November 1901 Australian Trooper Ham Glasson expressed the view that: 'I know you did not receive too many letters from me, although I wrote fairly often. Have an idea that letters written from where we were stationed used to be opened by some of our own officers, & were then destroyed, fairly strong, but never the less fact.' [186] Glasson would later express even stronger views on the BVC officers.

Christie continues his description of the increasing discontent which led to fifteen of the troopers writing a letter of complaint about their officers:

> The night I got my lot in it started to rain and blow, and the men were to be taken and put in a cage barb wire enclosure about 20 feet by 10 feet with an iron roof. I offered to guard and be responsible for them in the waggons. All of no use. The sick man was, however, left in the waggon. The others were put in the cage and a guard with fixed bayonets put round them. It blew and rained all night. Some of us got some sacks and cavalry cloaks for them, and they sat and shivered in the rain all night, and these were the men who had come in and voluntarily surrendered and whom we had escorted for five days through the veldt without a guard. It turned some of us sick to see the treatment, meted out to them. The next morning they were to trek for Pietersburg, but I was not allowed to go with them. I told them that they could take the sacks—three of them were my own—as it was still raining. Soon after an officer came to me in a tearing passion, and wanted to know what right I had to give Government property to prisoners. I told him that some of the sacks were mine, but that if I had given away any Government property inadvertently I would get them back, so I went and got two Government sacks back. The corporal fell out with me for taking them back, and said, 'If he (the lieutenant) wants to get you and me into a row let him. I'll put him up as high as a kite.' And so we took comfort in the fact that together we would help to hang him before we were much older unless we shot him. At the time of writing our mission is nearly fulfilled, for he is in 'clink' with seven others, charged with murder. But that story is yet to tell. [187]

The ultimate line of the above has been used, in isolation, by some authors to suggest animosity on the part of Trooper James Christie towards Morant. One avers that Morant's letter to Lenehan claiming that those who had left Hunt and Eland to their fate at the Viljoens farm were wastrels, etc., had angered Trooper James Christie who was purported to be one of these wastrels. In fact, as is evident from the accounts of Christie and Silke, Christie, despite his efforts to get there, was not present at the Viljoens farm until after the fighting had stopped and the party returned to collect the bodies. In fact, Christie was, himself, scathing of those who were present.

Besides the fact that it is not clear, in the passage above, that the Lt in question is actually Morant and not one of the others, Christie said that up until the shooting of Floris Visser he had got on well with Morant. Both were accomplished horsemen and both had a love of literature. [188] The following mildly amusing incident as related by Christie, indicates something of the nature of the relationship between Christie, Silke and Morant prior to the killings. Trooper Silke's account of the same incident confirms the Lieutant in the story was Morant. Christie:

> July 1st 1901 A Sydneyite and myself had an experience the other day. We were sent escort to a Cape cart with two Wilts sergeants and two Kaffirs to get barb wire at a farm. Arrived there, while the niggers were getting the wire we had a small shooting match, which we generally had when out on a patrol and far enough away from the camp. We had a target at the end of the brick house, and were boring holes in meat tins at 150 yds and after, to prove the penetrating power of the Lee Enfield, we put holes in half-inch steel plate, and also through 12in solid wood. We were quite engrossed in our experiments when, lo, and behold, I heard a tramp of horses at the gallop, and here up comes the lieutenant with all available men at his heels in warlike array, some looking jubilant at the idea of a brush, and some looking scared. Lieutenant rides up to me, 'Were you shooting,' 'Yes, sir.' 'What at?' 'Target, sir, and trying our rifle's penetrating power, etc.' He looked half mad, half amused; then he said, 'You ought to know better, Christie. The Wilts outposts reported heavy and continuous firing, and here we are out on a wild goose chase. Where are the Wilts men, have they been firing?' Fortunately they were away just then, and I told him where they were without saying whether they were doing any shooting or not. I had my ordeal over, and was only scared about the Wilts, because, being Imperial men, they might get jacketed over it. So when the column turned to ride back, my mates saying they knew well it would be Christie and Silke before they left camp, they went back their five miles having had an alarm for nothing. To make matters easy for the Wilts, if it came to bandolier inspection with them when they got back, my mate and I gave them all the cartridges we had to complete their number—they are not supposed to carry less than 150 but nothing came of it, and the matter passed off pleasantly. [189]

This story hardly suggests any particular hosility on either man's part prior to the first killings in which Morant was involved. The incident hardly reinforces the story that Morant was despised by the men for his cracking down on lax discipline either.

In any case, James Christie had plenty of reason to be angry at the killing of the Grobbler Children. As Christie had recounted, he had helped to place the bodies of the Grobbler children into coffins while their father wept over them. This must have been an even more agonising experience for Christie since, only a year previously, he had lost his own four children when his farm, Keithmore, in Otago, New Zealand had burnt to the ground. [190] By his own admission it was the ensuing sense of loss and lack of direction which had resulted in him drifting to the war in South Africa. [191] He was now back among burning farms and the senseless death of children.

Although Lieutenant Witton in his 1907 book *Scapegoats of the Empire* claimed that the killing of the Grobbler children 'is the only foundation for the wicked reports as to the wholesale shooting of women and children by the Carbineers'. This is not true. Only two days after the death of the Grobbler children, Roelf van Staden and his two sons were killed by a patrol of the Bushveldt Carbineers. One of these, Chris van Staden, was claimed in court to be 14 years old. Lieutenant Witton claims he was 18 to 20. Charles Leach in his book *The Legend of Breaker Morant is Dead and Buried* states that 'The age of young Chris is generally given as about 12 years. His older brother Roelf (jnr) was said to be about 17 years old…' Although their ages are not certain and they were not so tragically young as the Grobbler children, unlike them, there is not the remotest suggestion by anyone that their deaths were accidental.

The *Times* coverage of the Courts Martial concentrates on the subsequent reporting of the case to Major Lenehan in the mess on 7 September. The deposition of Trooper Ernest Browne relies on hearsay in that the version of events related was passed to him by Troopers Hodds and McMahon. Hodds, who had gone out with the patrol, was sent back to Fort Edward with two mules before the murders took place. According to Browne he stated that Lt Morant's orders were, 'When I say "dismount", dismount and load your rifles; when I say "lay down your arms" then shoot them down.' McMahon who was actually present during the killings told Browne that Morant had spoken to the three Boers before the signal to shoot and had given the sick boy a drink of brandy. He then gave the order and the Boers were shot. McMahon claims to have shot over their heads. [192]

Trooper John Silke stated in his 'diary'; on 7 September 'News then came to the Fort that three Boers on foot, one a sick boy, were coming in to surrender. Morant, Handcock, Whitton [sic] and Botha set out and met them within half a mile of Captain Taylor's [Intelligence] house and shot them down in cold blood. (Botha shot the boy.).' Silke appears to be incorrect when he states that Witton was present at the killing of the 'three Boers,' he was in fact on convoy duty, escorting prisoners to Pietersburg during which time he met

Major Lenehan heading to Fort Edward. [193] Witton, who was not charged with any part in this crime, states with a somewhat disingenuous lack of detail '...while I was away from Fort Edward on convoy escort, three armed Boers were reported coming in. Upon Lieutenant Morant being informed, he went out, taking with him Lieutenant Handcock and two men. The Boers were met and shot.' As Australian historian Craig Wilcox has pointed out, Witton uses the passive tense, a device he uses more than once to suggest a crime without a perpetrator. [194]

During his efforts to secure monetary compensation for the victims, Major Bolton wrote: 'I have it on the best information that these men had not fought during the war but had been hunting in Rhodesia and considering that hostilities were over were trekking in quietly to report themselves at Fort Edward.' [195] Research by Charles Leach suggests that Roelf van Staden (senior), fearing that his youngest son Chris would not survive another of the recurring bouts of malaria from which he was suffering and was taking him to Elim Hospital for treatment. At Elim hospital he was informed that they should proceed to Sweetwaters to obtain a military pass for Chris to be admitted to the hospital. The group, travelling under a white flag, were only a few hundred metres from Captain Taylor's office when they were met by Lieutenants Morant and Handcock, Sergeant-Major Hammett, Corporal McMahon and Troopers Botha, and Thompson.

Some greater detail of the circumstances in which the van Stadens were killed may however be known. Charles Leach relates an account, passed down in the family of the current owners of Sweetwaters Farm. In this version of events a black man named Scotch Mahange told a government delegation in 1919 that he had actually witnessed the murders. He had hidden in an acacia tree to avoid the BVC patrol. From this vantage point, he claimed he had seen the killings in clear view. He stated that Roelf van Staden (senior) and his older son Roelf were forced to dig their own grave while Chris, probably due to his fever, remained in the waggon. When the grave was about waist-deep the father of the two boys was shot, Roelf junior tried to run but was chased and shot, dragged back and thrown into the grave on top of his father. By this time Chris van Staden had climbed out of the waggon and was holding the wheel when he was also shot and thrown into the grave.

Such handed-down accounts should always be treated with some caution but Scotch Mahange's final comment was that, should the grave be opened, in order to verify his version, then the father would be found buried the deepest with his older son in the middle and Chris van Staden, the youngest, on top. Given that the government delegation was there specifically to investigate and record the graves of Boers killed during the war, the exhumation of the three bodies was not out of the question at the time. Exhumation of the grave by forensic archaeologists is probably the only way that this account may be verified.

One detail of the killings which is noted with some certainty is that during the trial of Major Lenehan for not reporting the killings, Trooper Theunis Botha admitted that it was he who had shot Chris van Staden. [196] Sometime after the courts martial and executions of Morant and Hancock, Theunis Botha was shot from his horse by an unknown marksman. Perhaps Morant and Handcock were not the only ones executed for their part in the murders.

Major Lenehan had arrived at Fort Edward on the day the van Stadens were shot. Lieutenant Witton wrote in 1907 that Lenehan had found Morant

> ... gloomy and morose, and was still brooding over the manner of the death of Captain Hunt. Morant fancied that if he had been out with Hunt it would not have happened. The major thought, as did others, that Morant's mind had become unhinged with grief. [197]
>
> During dinner, at which were present Major Lenehan, Captain Taylor, Lieutenants Morant and Handcock, and Surgeon Leonard, an argument arose regarding the trustworthiness of Dutchmen on British service. Captain Taylor said they were not trustworthy, but Morant maintained the affirmative. In support of his arguments he sent for Botha, and in reply to questions put by Morant, he said he was a good soldier, and had done his duty and shot Boers. [198]

It would seem unlikely that in a conversation in which Morant was trying to convince Lenehan that Botha 'was a good soldier, and had done his duty and shot Boers' that he would fail to mention that he had done so that very day.

When he returned from Pietersburg around 9 September Witton learned that two significant forces of Boers were reported in the district, and the 'outlook at Fort Edward was not a bright one'. [199] Field-Cornet Tom Kelly, a formidable Boer Irregular, was moving in from the Portuguese territory and was reported to have a number of artillery pieces with him. Commandant Beyers, with a strong force, was threatening on another side. Morant had been wishing for months for a chance to capture Tom Kelly, and he now entreated Major Lenehan to allow him to go in pursuit. The major hesitated for some time, but finally gave permission. This brightened Morant up considerably. [200] Major Lenehan had indeed hesitated, for Morant's Patrol did not leave until Monday, 16 September. [201]

Morant and Witton left the Fort with thirty men in search of Kelly, proceeding in the direction of the Birthday Mine [202] which they reached about three days later. On reaching the village of a local chief named Baniella, the patrol learned that Kelly had been there sharing palm wine only two hours before. Having boasted that if a thousand Englishmen came for him he would wipe them all out, he would shortly be in the bag.

Trooper James Christie, who had previously refused to take part in killing Floris Visser, was apparently not welcome on this patrol:

> After the refugees I had brought into Spelonken had been sent off to Pietersburg, a patrol of 30 of us were sent out to take 'Tom Kelly' who had 11 men and his family with him somewhere east towards the Portuguese border. We were lined up and the names called out. After I had answered to my name one of the officers thundered out 'as you were'. I had been enrolled against his order. I was not sorry but a lot of my mates went, and if that officer had only known that it was their fixed intention to 'blot him out' if any 'funny business' was likely to take place, he would have made a more judicious selection. However they got Tom Kelly without a shot being fired and brought him in alive. He was too great a target to 'blot out'; besides hints had been received by the officers that their game was not appreciated by the men. [203]

Morant's version of events, which he recorded in a letter to Major Lenehan and published in Frank Renar's book *Bushman and Buccaneer* in 1902:

> At 10:20 p.m. I arrived in the near vicinity of the Boer camp. Halting the men, I made a personal reconnaissance of the laager with CONSTANTEON, of the Intelligence Department, and found out the exact situation of the waggons and surroundings. As there were women in the camp I refrained from shooting. I divided the patrol into three troops of 10 men. Leaving one with Sergt-Hammet at 150yards from the Boer camp, I took the other with Lieut. Witton into the river bed, which ran under a steep bank around Kelly's waggons. There we lay quietly until 4.30a.m., Monday 23rd instant, when we charged the camp with rifles loaded. The camp was taken completely at a surprise. I took Kelly's rifle whilst he was still in bed, and the camp put their hands up sulkily as the B.V.C collected their rifles etc. [204]

Trooper John Silke presented a different picture:

> We journeyed four days and got within five miles of the laager where we left our horses and went cautiously on foot and got within 50 yards of the camp at 11 pm. Morant was in charge and wanted to fire on the

> camp right away although he knew there were women and children in the camp. However Constantin, a Swiss intelligence scout, restrained him and induced him to wait till morning. We were then spread out in three parties and laid in the grass all night and at dawn we rushed silently into the laager completely surprising the Boers. I got to a tent door when Kelly himself poked his head out and put the muzzle of my rifle under his chin and told him hands up. He opened his mouth that wide I thought I would fall into it so I stepped back a pace but he never showed fight at all. [205]

One can only assume that Chief Banniella's palm wine was some powerful stuff, since Kelly would have had considerable problems wiping out a thousand men with his force, which was certainly not a Commando. 'There were ten men, thirteen women and about 50 kids, four waggons and oxen, three horses, twenty rifles, about 10 cwt of ammunition but no pom poms.' [206]

Lieutenant Witton's version of 1907 includes: 'Morant rushed to Kelly's tent, and called upon him to surrender, and when he showed his head through the doorway he was looking straight down the barrel of Morant's rifle. The others, as they rolled from under the waggons, put up their hands very sulkily, while we collected the rifles.' [207] Which version of the taking of Kelly one believes is probably down to one's views on Silke and Morant.

The patrol arrived back at Fort Edward where the BVC officers were already nervous about the men in their charge. It would soon transpire that they would be British forces and not those of Kelly and Beyers which would surround them.

A number of factors probably came into play leading to the officer's arrest including De Bertodano's investigations into Taylor's activities at Fort Edward. At the fort, fifteen members of the BVC, including Christie, had had enough of the senseless killing anyway and decided to do something about it. Possibly frustrated by Major Lenehan's perceived complicity in covering up the extent of the shootings they, headed by Trooper Robert Mitchell Cochrane, wrote a letter for submission to Colonel Hall.

Getting the letter to Colonel Hall however was not a simple affair as the BVC officers were now a little cagey. James Christie recounts that 'In the fort we had rather a trying time, and orders about leaving the fort, or holding any communication with anyone outside were rather stringent. We could see they were afraid anything would leak out, and you may be sure we were the very pictures of innocence.' After a patrol to Louis Trichardt and another patrol repairing telegraph lines from Pietersburg, Christie's group were allowed to go to Pietersburg: 'After several refusals, some of us who were nearly time-expired got leave to go to Pietersburg with the convoy and

Kelly's waggons. We got in without mishap, and there laid our complaint before the Provost Marshal.' [208] The letter given to Major Bolton on 8 October was passed on to Colonel Hall. [209] Major Poore and Capt. Bonham started to take depositions on the 9th, which continued until at least 15 October. The revelations of these depositions resulted in a Court of Inquiry being convened on 16 October, though the officers of the BVC had not yet been arrested.

Subsequent to the capture of Commandant Kelly, Lieutenant Morant spent two weeks leave in Pretoria signing himself into The Transvaal Hotel as 'Capt.' Morant on 6 October 1902 [210] during which time he was supposedly sorting out Hunt's affairs. Morant then returned to Pietersburg. Handcock, Witton, Lenehan and the BVC who were still in the Spelonken left for Fort Klipdan, arriving on the evening of 22 October. The following morning they covered the further 15 miles to Pietersburg with Witton as an advance guard and about three miles out of Pietersburg, Witton was met by two mounted officers who informed him that the camp commandant wished to see him. The main convoy was still behind. James Christie:

> The whole affair of the arrest was managed beautifully. Two officers came in with a convoy from Spelonken, and it was promptly 'jugged'. Then it was read out in orders that no message was to be sent by the Kaffirs to Spelonken under pain of court martial – all communications must go through the authorities. Then the garrison at Spelonken was relieved, and the officers came quietly in with their convoy. When within four miles of Pietersburg, the 20th Mounted Infantry swooped down upon the convoy on all sides: took the carbines, revolvers, and bandoliers off the officers, and took them to the fort under escort right before their own men, who had a shrewd idea of what was coming. Nominally every man with the convoy was a prisoner, and the M.I.'s had orders to shoot anyone leaving the convoy. Carrier pigeons were taken out by the arresting officers so that the authorities at Pietersburg could be advised if any hitch occurred. But the men of the BVC were only too pleased to see the officers off; they had endured things long enough. The arrests comprise one major, one captain, five lieutenants, and one sergt major. Such a spectacle has never, I hear, taken place in the annals of the British Army.
>
> It was only after much thought, of what the consequences might be to ourselves that we took the final step. In fact on one occasion the men, or a section of them, were nearly driven to the desperate course of putting their own officers in irons, so you see we were going on what we believed good grounds when we got away from them into Pietersburg, and laid a full written account of their doings before the authorities. We now have the satisfaction of knowing that our actions have been appreciated by the

> few remaining officers who were not mixed up in the scandals which have made us notorious. A colonel in authority told me personally that he could quite appreciate the difficulties that were around us in Spelonken, and that how we had come out of them was a credit to us. From the open bare faced way in which things were done which ought not to have been done, he could understand that we could believe they were countenanced by higher authorities. The officers are placed under arrest in different parts of the garrison. We are now attached here awaiting the court martial. More has come out at the preliminary investigation then we ever imagined. [211]

Trooper James Christie would probably not have been aware that the letter of complaint by the fifteen troopers was not the only means by which the authorities had become aware of the trouble in the northern Transvaal. It is clear that the authorities were aware of events up north in early September since Major Lenehan himself stated he had been sent up to the Spelonken specifically to investigate them. Neither is it the case that the killing of Boers and Revd Heese was the only cause for the authorities to be scrutinising the activities of 'Captain' Taylor. The authorities were closing in on 'Bullala' Taylor in early September 1901, if not before.

By late August Lord Milner had appointed Sir Godfrey Yeatman Lagden as Secretary of Native Affairs, Transvaal. Lagden had appointed Francis Enraght Mooney as Native Commissioner, Zoutpansberg. Around the end of August 1901, Enraght Mooney, ordered by Lagden at Lord Kitchener's request, [212] travelled to Pietersburg to take general charge of Native affairs in the Northern Transvaal.

On 31 August 1901 Lagden wrote to Col Henderson, Director of Military Intelligence:

> Referring to my conversation with you and with Lord Kitchener about Taylor who is holding an appointment under you [Intelligence Officer] in the Spelonken.
>
> Mr Mooney has arrived at Pietersburg and seen Col Hall. They concur in thinking that Taylor should receive instructions from the Commander-in-Chief to communicate with Mooney on matters relating to Native affairs up there. He will not do so unless under instructions from those who appointed him.
>
> Lord Kitchener suggested that we should take Taylor over, but I think it would be undesirable to do so, so long as he is in command of men performing Military service whose usefulness might be impaired at this juncture by conflicting instructions.
>
> Please advise me in this matter. [213]

Although Taylor was operating as an intelligence officer, Lagden clearly believed he was in command of men 'performing military service'. In relation to Taylor reporting to Enraght Mooney, Col Henderson acted two days later. He wrote to 'Captain' Taylor informing him that Lord Kitchener desired him to

> ... keep Mr Enraght Mooney informed generally of the state of affairs in the district in which you are operating, and that in the event of any serious complications between different tribes, or of civil cases of importance, you will, if possible, consult with him before giving any decision.
>
> With regard to the recovery of Boer cattle hidden by Natives, the G.O.C. in chief does not consider this a matter of importance at present. He desires you to confine your attention as much as possible to two duties, keeping the Natives in hand, and preventing any concentration by the enemy. Your success as shown by the considerable captures sent in by you is much appreciated, and Lord Kitchener hopes to hear of your further successes. [214]

This praise for the 'considerable captures sent in by you' is hardly suggestive of a 'take no prisoners' policy. On 11 September 1901 Francis Enraght Mooney wrote to the Minister for Native Affairs:

> These instructions are noted, but appear to imply a desire from a military point of view, to retain the services of Taylor in the Spelonken. This is to be regretted. From all reports I have heard regarding the actions of this man, in his dealings with the Natives, the more I am convinced that he should be removed without delay. Some of the charges are so serious as to practically amount to murder. It is also reported that under the pretext of looking for Boer cattle hidden by the Natives he has seized numbers of their cattle which have since been misappropriated. I believe this matter is in the hands of the military. [215]

Is Enraght Mooney referring to investigations, including Maj. Lenehan's enquiries, which had supposedly commenced in the Seplonken four days earlier? Mooney continues:

> Taylor is very rough and arbitrary in his treatment of the Natives and flogs freely. From all I can hear the Natives of the Spelonken and Zoutpansberg were very friendly disposed towards the British upon our occupation and the reports of their lawlessness were exaggerated; but, I fear, Taylor's

> administration is fast dispelling this friendly feeling and will in its place sow sullen antipathy...
>
> I hope that you will be able to arrange with the Commander in Chief for the removal of Taylor from the District at the earliest possible date, also for the removal of Schiel and Schwartz. [216]

The situation with the natives had indeed deteriorated. Taylor's initial support of Mphefu and brutality towards his enemies had alienated much of the native population which had been favourably disposed towards the British; but Mphefu himself had also become a problem. A few days before the killing of Captain Hunt, around a month earlier, Taylor had reported that Chief Mphefu

> ... is turning out to be a public nuisance. He has been steadily trying to acquire an influence over the neighbouring Chiefs and to pose as a Paramount Chief in this part of the country ... If allowed to remain here, I foresee infinite difficulty in managing native affairs. I would therefore suggest that M'Pefu be immediately sent back to Rhodesia, and not allowed to return. [217]

Taylor was not going to attribute the deterioration in relations between the British and the native peoples of the northern Transvaal to his own actions, but Enraght Mooney believed Taylor to be at fault. On the same day as he wrote to the Minister for Native Affairs, Francis Enraght Mooney wrote to Sir Godfrey Lagden, The Secretary of Native Affairs:

> I have written re Taylor again. This is a most important matter hence my insistence. I think that if we sent up a man who could cooperate with the officer in charge of troops up there he could render as much assistance as Taylor to the military. He should have tact to be able to get on with the irregular forces – Bushfelt [sic] Carbineers – which is stationed there, in trying to put a stop to the irregularities practiced by those men. Col Hall is in accord with me regarding the desirability – nay – necessity, of removing Taylor. He would send the best officer he could to take command and work with our man. This is of course confidential and not to be used in discussing the matter with the C-in-C [Kitchener], Taylor was sent up without reference to Col Hall. [218]

So the reprehensible activities of the BVC and the malign influence of Taylor were recognised at least by Francis Enraght Mooney, Col Hall and

Sir Godfrey Lagden in early September 1901. At this time Major Lenehan was already at Spelonken supposedly investigating the irregular activities of the BVC.

On 24 September Col David Henderson informed Lagden:

> The Chief wishes to remove Taylor, who is making trouble in the North. Lord K. thinks it is time for your department to take over the Native control of the Zoutpansberg, which is very nearly clear of Boers, and suggests that you should send up the man whom you intend to have the district finally, and let him take over now. The intention is that he should have control of Taylor's present force, about 100 men, as police and for protection ... Please keep this as quiet as possible as I do not wish Captain Taylor to have much warning. [219]

By 27 September Colonel David Henderson had ordered Taylor to return to Pietersburg, though he had not yet arrived there. [220] Taylor was to demonstrate his slippery nature, which probably played some part in his avoiding more serious consequences around six months later. On 28 September, in a letter to Enraght Mooney, he placed the blame for the alienation of Mphefu's enemies squarely on the mysterious Keith and Mphefu himself. [221]

Discussions were held between Enraght Mooney, Sir Godfrey Lagden and Lord Kitchener on or shortly after 29 September, on subjects including the removal of Taylor, Mooney's future relations with the BVC and other troops at Spelonken and Col Hall. Also on the agenda was the removal of Mphefu. Evidently, Taylor's recall to Pietersburg was as much to do with his stirring up trouble with the Native populations as it was with the murder of Boers by the BVC. [222]

Mphefu and three Mahosi were escorted to Pietersburg on 28 October and were later held in Pretoria until cessation of hostilities. [223] Taylor would be placed under arrest and later subject to a military court.

The machinations within the authorities outlined above were clearly not in the public domain. Major Lenehan, commanding officer of the BVC, had been sent to the Spelonken and arrived on 7 September with orders to make an inquiry into events there, to set his house in order. The last murders occurred on the day he arrived. It was too late to keep things quiet. Too many stories had been heard. The Troopers were now too disillusioned to maintain silence and frustrated with Lenehan's attempts to cover things up. Others were probably too worried about their own role in the events. When the fifteen troopers managed to get their letter to Col Hall it was clear that something had to be done.

Dr Kay, a Pretoria-based civilian doctor, claimed that he had heard the story of the BVC killings from the Portuguese Consul. Due to the Consul's concerns that Kitchener was trying to hush things up, Kay wrote to Joseph Chamberlain, Secretary of State for the Colonies. [224] On 8 January 1902, Lord Roberts cabled Kitchener, requesting information and asking for Dr Kay's bonafides, since Kay was suspected of being a deserter in September 1900. [225] So Chamberlain had passed Kay's letter to the War Office. On the 9th Kitchener cabled back saying that charges against the BVC Officers had been framed and that the case was being tried. [226] Kitchener confirmed, on 14 February, that there was 'no ground for suspicion as to Kay. He is said to have done good work at Ladysmith during siege'. [227]

Several stories appeared claiming that Silas' account of the death of Revd Heese was 'reported to his chief, who, in turn, communicated it to the heads of the German mission. They, accompanied by the German Consul at Pretoria, waited on Lord Kitchener, the British Commander-in-Chief, and-informed him of the outrage, and insisted on a thorough enquiry being instituted concerning the affair.' [228]

However in the House of Commons on 9 April: 'Viscount Cranborne, Under-Parliamentary Secretary for Foreign Affairs, stated that no communication had been received from Germany 'or the German Consul at Pretoria regarding the death of Mr. Hesse [sic], the German missionary'. [229] If the Secretary for Foreign affairs had received no communication from Germany it would seem the military authorities had. Baron Von Richtofen in the Reichstag was quoted in British and Australian newspapers:

> A Berlin telegram, dated April 2, says:—'In connection with the alleged murder of Herr Heese, a Berlin missionary, by Australian officers in South Africa; the German papers recall the following statement which was made by Baron von Richthofen, Secretary of State for Foreign Affairs, in the Reichstag on January 13 last. [Three days before the commencement of the first Court Martial,] The Minister on that occasion said: 'many missionaries have no longer German nationality, or only in addition to being citizens of the Boer Republics. In such cases the British Government has refused to permit any intervention. I have, for instance, been informed of the following case: A missionary named Heese, belonging, I believe, to a Berlin mission, was murdered, apparently by soldiers of the British Army. The German Consul immediately placed himself in communication with the British military authorities, who instituted a most searching inquiry into the matter.

> Upon the Consul writing to Herr Hesse's father, who is also a missionary in South Africa, the father replied: 'My son is a British subject. I can therefore not claim intervention on his behalf by Germany.' [230]

If Viscount Cranbourne was being truthful, it may suggest that Kitchener did not pass on details of the German Consul's inquiries to his political masters, perhaps giving some credence to the Portuguese Consul's concern that Kitchener was trying to keep things under wraps at that point. [231]

On 18 February 1902, however, the Secretary of State for War had sent a telegram to Kitchener saying 'Further serious reports have reached me about the conduct of the Bushveldt Carabiniers. What has been done to them. What was the result of the Trial?' [232] The origin of these reports is not known.

If any level pressure was being applied by a foreign government by the time of the courts martial, it would seem likely that it was from the Portuguese Government and not the Germans, who appeared to lose interest once they were made aware that Revd Heese was a British subject. Since Heese was not Portuguese, and the Portuguese at the time were on relatively good terms with the British allowing troops and materiel to pass through their ports into Transvaal, this pressure would not have been a major concern for Kitchener. Public relations and inquiries from the British Government were a different matter.

10

The Rise of the Tenterfield Star

In the popular myth of Breaker Morant much has been written on the plucky and heroic defence put up by embattled bush lawyer J. F. Thomas in the face of overwhelming odds. The opinion of many of the legally trained, and some of the untrained, is that his defence was naïve, inept and it might be argued somewhat preposterous. Australian historian Dr John Bennett considers that 'He hectored the court with extraneous remarks of a political flavour; he allowed the prisoners to volunteer unguarded and prejudicial testimony; and his attempts to address questions of military law (of which he had scant knowledge) were demolished by the prosecution as "being perfect nonsense ... a mere twisting of words".' [1] John Francis Thomas may have thought he was doing the BVC officers a favour by stepping in but as with some of his other ventures, he may have been self-deluding.

Thomas was born in 1861 in St Marys, NSW and educated at The King's School, Paramatta in Western Sydney. Like many schools in the days of empire, King's School had a military ethos which nurtured Thomas's love of sport. His love of poetry however was probably self-driven and would later gain him some appreciation in Sydney's literary circles. The late Victorian thirst for poetry enabled him to get a number of his poems published. On leaving school Thomas had no desire to follow in his father's farming footsteps, preferring to embark on a legal career and he signed the solicitors roll on 28 May 1887 after a period serving articles of clerkship.

What drew Thomas from Sydney to the tin mining town of Emmaville, New England, NSW is not known, though this venture does not seem to have been particularly successful. A law practice eluding him there, Thomas moved to Tenterfield, a town near the Queensland border of New South Wales, in 1890. He became the town's first permanent lawyer and here built up a good clientele. [2] This success apparently owed more to his 'outgoing personality and overweening self-confidence' [3] than to a sound knowledge of conveyancing, methodical mind and rigorous record keeping, all of which were conspicuous by their absence in his disorganised office in Tenterfield.

Thomas devoted considerable energy to local activities, building on the military character of his schooling by joining the Tenterfield arm of the Upper Clarence Light Horse, becoming a 2nd Lieutenant in 1891 and Captain in 1895. For those disposed to see the Masonic glove on Lord Kitchener's hand in the Courts Martial of the BVC officers it is inconvenient that James Francis Thomas was initiated to the Tenterfield 55 United Grand Lodge of New South Wales on 18 November 1891, 'passed' on 16 December the same year and became a Master Mason on 10 February 1892. [4] He was a Junior Warden of the Lodge from 11 January 1893 to January 1894 and senior warden for the subsequent year, a responsibility he discharged again for the year leading up to his departure for South Africa. [5]

Thomas was fiercely in favour of the federation of the Australian states and in 1889 had played a role in organising the visit of Henry Parkes to Tenterfield at which he delivered a keynote speech on federation. Buying the *Tenterfield Star* in 1898 gave him a mouthpiece for passionate editorials in support of federation. Thomas rebuilt the print works incorporating his presumably still chaotic office into the new building.

Heeding the call of the Boer War, Thomas raised a squadron of mounted infantry, which he commanded himself. Thomas's military career in South Africa was marred by a Court of Enquiry into the loss of a convoy at Rhenoster Kop on 11 January 1901. [6]

Thomas had been the Commanding Officer of a convoy of 2 officers and around 106 men from Vlackfontein to Rhenoster Kop, which had been attacked by elements of a Boer Commando. Some of the men were unarmed and were outnumbered. A Corporal Mason of the West Riding Regiment raised the white flag. During the engagement Thomas seems to have taken on the role of military doctor, tending to the wounded underneath a wagon when he should have been commanding those still able to fight. Thomas told the board he had done a good deal of doctoring and acted as squadron doctor. He always carried a small selection of simple remedies and bandages with him. Thomas also told them that he declined to wear a Red Cross badge because he was a combatant officer.

The result was the loss of 8 Ox wagons loaded with stores, medical supplies, 1 span of oxen sent to fetch a Boer wagon, 4 buck wagons with their spans loaded with ordnance stores, clothing, mess stores, 1 telegraph wagon with span of mules, £852 in gold and 1000 sheep.

A letter from Gen. Evelyn Wood to the Commander in Chief stated: 'Please see Court of Enquiry on Captain Thomas of the Australian Bushmen. One cannot expect quite the same line of conduct from a man who has never been a soldier previously but there can be no doubt that he was wrong to attend to the wounded instead of doing his proper work. I do not think there is much blame to be attached to him for not having a reserve when he only had 100 men altogether and some apparently not armed.' Kitchener considered that whilst Captain Thomas 'was apparently not responsible for the hoisting of the white flag, his dispositions were most faulty and his conduct in leaving the firing line to attend to the wounded men under the wagons cannot be commended. (14-02-01.)' [7]

No serious action appears to have been taken against Thomas and in April 1901 when his unit was notified that they would be relieved, Thomas put down his name for further duty. He ended up returning to Australia. Regarding his trip back, Thomas claimed, as if the Australian soldiers could not look after themselves, that 'finding on arrival at Cape Town that none of the Regimental Staff were returning, it was my bounden duty to go back with the men and see them paid off and I applied for leave to do so and said if I did I would probably return with a detachment.' [8]

In the short term his poor performance at Rhenoster Kop did his military career little harm since Captain Thomas was promoted to Major in the NSW Citizens Bushmen in June 1901, replacing Maj. Henry Phelps Dangar, who had been invalided back to London with malaria. [9] Dangar was an ex-13th Hussar and friend of Captain Percy Hunt. [10]

It is clear that Major Thomas had the interests of Australian soldiers at heart and his desire to assist the Empire is genuine; but his sense that everything would fall apart if he were not present seems to pervade everything he did. Thomas set himself up as a guardian angel of all things Australian. In September 1901 Thomas returned to South Africa under his own steam, or at least that of the SS *Britannic*, with 250 indulgence passengers for which he paid all the expenses, advancing to the men their passages: 'It would be impossible to ask a Transport Ship's Captain to bring over 250 men without any officer in control of them.' On arrival in Cape Town on 20 September the men were snapped up and distributed to various units. Thomas complained that 'the very few indulgence passenger officers (myself included) who accompanied them were overlooked. I could not even get a squadron of my own men … I reported myself for duty and have been waiting ever since.' [11]

In November 1901 he was the prime mover in setting up, organising and promoting an Australian Association in Cape Town of which, according to Thomas, all those who accompanied him over on the *Brittanic* became members. [12] By December Thomas had devised a scheme for Australian soldiers to invest part of their pay rather than blow it all on whatever distractions the Cape had to offer. He wrote to Sir Ian Hamilton:

> ... I am apparently in the unfortunate position of being only a civilian in this country at the present time, though still an Australian officer in N.S. Wales...
>
> I should specially like to see you. Morally I feel bound to do my best for all Australians, amongst whom I have hundreds of friends from all parts of Australia. Last August I called Lord Kitchener offering the services of 'several hundreds' of them and he accepted and I have come over with 250 arriving by the *Britannic* on 20 Sept last. About 150 more have followed me over since. The men came over to settle after the war and many have re-enrolled.
>
> My Govt stopped my war gratuity and allowance on the grounds that I had come over on further service, but I am advised that I have no status here.
>
> I have now been living at my private expense for three months and my funds are about exhausted.
>
> Meantime I have been continuously at work in the interests of the men and have helped (unofficially) to get an Australian recruiting system at the Cape put in order.
>
> I have planned out a Scheme for the benefit of the large numbers of Australian Soldiers here which is evoking the greatest enthusiasm amongst them and all I am going to ask is for your aid, as far as you can accord it, in enabling me to carry out my plans which I think will benefit the service too. I cannot do it single-handed under all the disadvantages of a quasi-civilian and private cost. I have carried it this far, that I have all in readiness to start within a fortnight at least, but this is a bad country to live in at private expense – and I begin to fear failure – and this will mean great disappointment to many.
>
> I feel sure you will do what you can when I explain – if I may – the scheme. We have sent thousands of Australia's best men here – and so far no one seems to have considered their future welfare, unless it is myself.
>
> I have the honour to be
> Sir, Your obedient servant J.F. Thomas (Maj. Aust Mntd Forces, lately commissioned 1st Bushmen)

Thomas's scheme was in fact described in Australian Newspapers. [13] On 31 December 1901 he wrote to Sir Ian Hamilton again. Thomas requested that from the date of 20 September 1901 he should receive his rank as a NSW Officer claiming 'I have at least done good service as a "Recruiting Officer"' Thomas continued to fight the case for Australian soldiers who stayed on in South Africa, arguing that they found themselves unable to find employment or go to any rest camp and that if provided with some rest and support they would probably re-enrol. 'It is a pity to send them off to Cape Town to waste their pay.' Thomas recognised that his scheme could not be officially recognised but requested that the CiC provide facilities to assist him in a scheme 'for the acquirement of farming and horse and cattle breeding land, &c for them so that after the war they will have some assets in the country'. Thomas proposed that he organise a short-service, three-month corps of Australian Scouts from time-expired Australians. The men would be allowed to go to a rest camp for six weeks on half pay or 'whatever is thought fair in these respects'. Afterwards they could be assigned to any column. 'Later on they might buy such a farm, which would add to the interests of my proposal.' [14]

Thomas was to be disappointed. Sir Ian Hamilton replied: 'He [the Commander in Chief] directs me to say that the ideas put forward in Paragraphs (2) and (3) are inadmissible, in view of the fact that Lord Kitchener feels himself bound to return every man of overseas contingents to their colonies before he accepts fresh contingents from these Colonies. This is a tacit agreement Lord Kitchener has with the Australian Government and he is bound to adhere to it.'

It was not only in South Africa that Thomas met resistance to his scheme. A Special Correspondent for the Adelaide *Advertiser* wrote from Cape Town on 8 November 1901: 'Mr Thomas was associated with some similar movement at your end before he came to this country, but was discouraged by the authorities on the very reasonable plea that, even for South Africa, the Australian States should not be depleted of their best blood and sinew.' [15]

In relation to his own employment, Lord Kitchener was unable to provide Thomas with 'employment suitable to [his] rank and position'. Although Sir Ian Hamilton had passed on Thomas's letter Col Adye replied: 'I have a great surplus of Officers, as you know, and a Major is particularly hard to find employment for.' It is noteworthy that the Court of Enquiry in relation to Rhenoster Kop was not mentioned at all in the above exchange. Not being able to secure a position in the Australian units, Thomas signed up with the Canadian Scouts, but 'at once broke off his connection with them as they could not give him the rank of Major'. [16]

Thus it was that in early 1902, Thomas found himself not wanted by the army, at least as a Major, his schemes for an Australian Association in South Africa and his investment fund for time-expired Australian soldiers were meeting with apathy and resistance both in South Africa and Australia, and his own resources were almost depleted. Thomas was still touting his investment fund in March 1902. 'Among ventures suggested for the employment of accumulated capital are breeding of horses for remounts, timber trade with Australia, forestry, loans on landed properties, prospecting and so forth'. [17] The opportunity to defend the BVC officers must have seemed like an opportunity to unfurl his guardian angel's wing but also to find a purpose and perhaps make a name for himself.

Lieutenant Witton claimed that Major Lenehan requested Maj. J. F. Thomas to represent him, and that he agreed to act 'for us all'. [18] Dr John Bennett doubts this, suggesting that being an experienced solicitor himself Lenehan would never have entrusted a bush lawyer with a case on which lives depended. [19] It must be remembered, however, that the charges were such that *Lenehan's* life did not depend on it. However it came about, J. F. Thomas was to act for all of the accused.

Above: 1. Bridgwater Workhouse c 1880. (Blake Museum)

Below: 2. Malt Shovel Inn, watering hole of Bridgwater rugby clubs. (Blake Museum)

3. The grave of Edwin Murrant Snr, the Breaker's real father. (Authors' collection)

Right: 4. Field Marshal Horatio Herbert Kitchener, 1st Earl Kitchener, KG, KP, GCM, OM, GCSI, GCMG, GCIE, PC, pictured in 1914. (Library of Congress)

Below: 5. The RMIB building today. (Peter Ibbett, RMIB Old Boys)

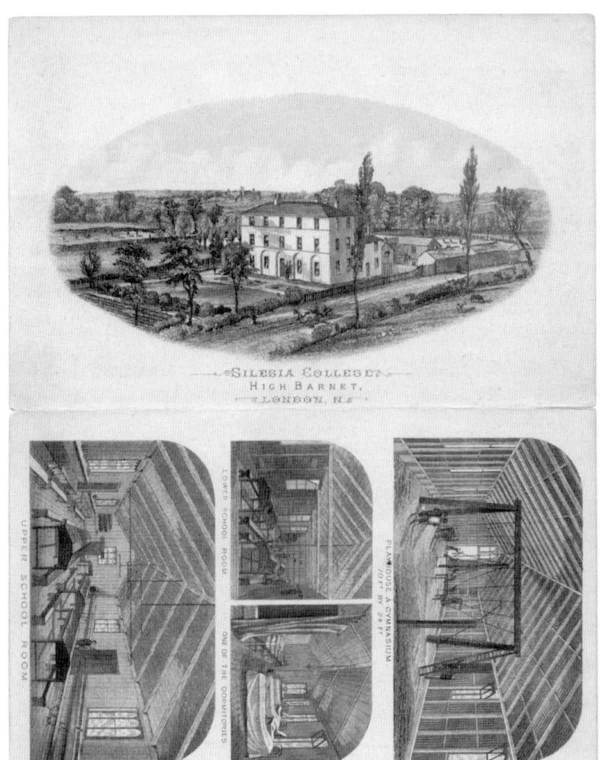

Above: 6. The RMIB with girls from RMIG in 1865. (Peter Ibbett, RMIB Old Boys)

Left: 7. Silesia College Barnet. Edwin's first job was here. (Authors' collection)

Above: 8. Silesia College after a visit from Hitler. (Dr Gear, Barnet Museum)

Below: 9. Silesia College first form, Breaker front left, George Baker next to him and James Russell rear centre. (Dr Gear, Barnet Museum)

EMIGRATION TO QUEENSLAND.

FREE PASSAGES to bonâ fide Farm Labourers and Domestic Servants.
ASSISTED PASSAGES to Skilled Artizans and others approved by the Agent-General.

GOVERNMENT LAND

TO BE OBTAINED UNDER DEFERRED PAYMENTS.

The next Vessels will sail from PLYMOUTH for QUEENSLAND in JAN., and Two will be dispatched each following month.

For Handbook and Forms of Application, apply to

THE AGENT-GENERAL FOR QUEENSLAND,
1, Westminster Chambers, Victoria Street, S.W., or to

DISTRICT AGENT:—J. J. TREMEER, 65, Boutport-street, the Square, Barnstaple.

10. Advertisement for emigration to Queensland. This advert ran every week during January 1883 in the *North Devon Journal*. (Authors' collection)

11. Cooktown 1887. A Chinese Investigation Commission arrived from Canton to investigate the conditions of Chinese living in the colonies. They were pleased with what they found. (Cooktown Historical Society)

12. Cradling for gold outside Charters Towers. (John Oxley Library, State Library of Queensland)

13. Daisy Bates when she snared the Breaker. (*Northern Miner*)

14. Daisy Bates in later life. (Authors' collection)

15. Admiral Digby Morant (left), Capt. Lord Charles Beresford (right), Alec seated. (Authors' collection)

Above left: 16. A famous portrait of Morant. (Creative Commons 2.0)

Above right: 17. 'Captain' Alf Taylor seated, the shrewd and manipulative intelligence officer operating in Zoutpansberg at Kitchener's behest. (Authors' collection)

Below: 18. The Salisbury Field Force, 1896. Taylor is third from right, and Cecil Rhodes is seated in the centre. (Zimbabwe Archives)

Above: 19. Morant enlists with mates in 2nd SAMR. (Bill Woolmore)

Below: 20. Sgt Frank Eland. (Margaret Barrett)

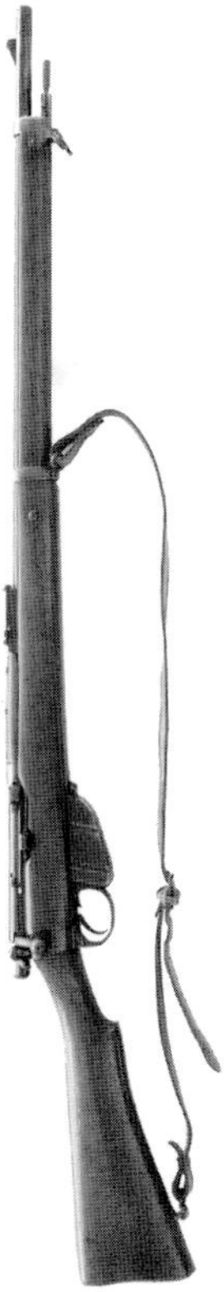

Right: 21. 1895 magazine Lee-Enfield, the type Trooper Christie describes 'testing' on page 174. (Courtesy John Hutchins, from his *Conquest of Empire, Defence of the Realm: The British Soldier's Rifle 1800 to 2014*, ISBN 978-0-9928776-0-6)

Above: 22. Fort Edward today in Louis Trichardt. (Charles Leach)

Below: 23. 2nd Wiltshire Officers. Col Carter, Capt. Evans, Maj. Bolton, Maj. Beatson and Lt Matcham all served on the Courts Martial. (Wardrobe Museum)

Above: 24. Maj. Wilfred Nash Bolton and family c 1914. (Andrew Bermingham)

Below: 25. W. N. Bolton in the England rugby team 1884, seated on the ground, left. (Rugby Football Museum, Twickenham)

Above: 26. Ramon De Bertodano on horseback. (Zimbabwe Archives)

Right: 27. Robert Montague Poore takes an unconventional guard. (Hampshire CCC)

28. Robert Poore c 1908 in military uniform. (Hampshire CCC)

Above: 29. Edward VII's mistress Mrs Keppel sought the release of Lt Witton. (Authors' collection)

Right: 30. *The Bulletin* – 'Australia for the white man'. (Authors' collection)

The Bulletin

The National Australian Newspaper.

" Australia for the White Man."

31. Diarist John Silke (second from right) and friends. (Authors' collection)

32. Kitchener at the peace conference that led to the Treaty of Vereeniging, signed on 31 May 1902, that ended the Second Boer War. The terms of the settlement meant that all combatants were to be disarmed – and included the commitment that no death penalties would be passed. (Library of Congress)

11

Arrest to Execution

For the last century the Courts Martial of Morant and the other BVC Officers has formed the central core of the story of 'Breaker' Morant, both cinematic and literary, though it is the film *Breaker Morant* that has had the greatest impact on popular perception. The film was adapted from the novel *The Breaker* by Kit Denton, who later felt it necessary to publish an investigative account [1] of the episode, entitled 'Closed File' to correct some misconceptions that his novel and the film had created. The book could never have the same impact as the film of course. Recently some have sustained the myth in historical novels [2] and TV documentaries. [3]

As with all conspiracy theories, those relating to the Morant affair have been built in the gaps in our knowledge created by a lack of surviving evidence, sometimes bolstered by an unwillingness to look for evidence which might not suit the story. The proceedings of the courts martial are lost to us, providing the conspiracy theorists not only carte blanche to speculate but also proof of a government cover-up by their very disappearance. If this were so, then the British Government should be bombarded with pardon campaigns, since only a single set of court martial proceedings exists for the period between 1850 and 1914. [4]

Consequently the period from the arrest of the BVC officers up to the execution of Morant and Handcock has become contentious, with those in support of a pardon for Morant and his co-convicted arguing that the defendants were kept incommunicado with no chance of contact with their families and with totally inadequate legal representation in cases conducted in absolute secrecy. Many have sought to portray Morant as an embattled David slinging stones against the gold-braided Goliaths of the British Army. Some are deeply critical of the court cases' fairness and impartiality. Others grudgingly conclude that Morant and the co-accused were guilty but got a raw deal because others were also guilty. These assertions can be shown to be false except the last. It is true that others were certainly guilty. Less has been written defending the impartiality of the courts, some by Australians – notably Craig Wilcox, historian for the Australian War Memorial – and some by South Africans. Almost nothing has been written on the subject in Britain. To the dispassionate observer, some of these debates may seem superfluous, since Morant and his co-defendants admitted to the shootings, which were murder.

When asked whether his drumhead 'Court Martial' of Floris Visser, one of the murdered Boers, was similar to the one he now found himself in, Harry Morant answered 'No; it was not quite so handsome. As to rules and sections, we had no Red Book.' [5] The 'Red Book' to which he refers and which has come under considerable scrutiny recently by those seeking a pardon for Morant was The Manual of Military Law 1899. It is not particularly handsome. Recently, some have tried to shift the focus away from whether the defendants were guilty or not to whether they received a fair trial, by which they mean, were the correct legal procedures rigidly adhered to? Faced with incontrovertible evidence that the men were guilty of murder they scour the 'rules and sections' for legal procedures which the Courts Martial of 1902 may not have followed, highlighting any perceived deviation as a deliberate perversion of justice, any lack of evidence as a cover-up and any inaccuracy as a deliberate deception. Whilst it would be naive to suggest that there was no politicking going on in the background, it can be shown that many of the elements of the conspiracy theories are false or at least grossly exaggerated.

The main objections to the Courts Martial are:

1. The court cases were conducted in secret.
2. The defendants were prevented from communicating with their families in Australia and Britain.
3. Lt Colonel Hall, seen as a key witness, was suddenly and conspiratorially sent to India.
4. The defendants had inadequate legal representation whilst the prosecution was a crack legal team.
5. Lord Kitchener deliberately delayed the commencement of the Courts Martial so 'Captain' Taylor could be tried under a military court rather than a court martial.
6. When Major Bolton wanted to withdraw charges against Morant for instigating Handcock's murder of Revd Heese, the senior authorities prevented him from doing so.

All of these will be shown to be false.

Returning to Pietersburg in October 1901, after his arrest Lieutenant George Witton was escorted to the Commandant's Office. Here Witton was met by Major Neatson who instructed the accompanying officer to take Witton to the Garrison Artillery fort. At this point he was still in the dark and Lieutenant Beattie shed no light on the situation. Major Neatson later informed him that he was under arrest pending a court of inquiry: [6] 'The officer commanding the fort informed me that I was a military prisoner under his charge, and if I attempted to escape, or went outside the wire entanglements, I would be shot; that I was not to communicate with anyone outside, and all correspondence was to be sent through him. At this time I had not the faintest notion of the charges against me, or for what reason I was made a prisoner.' [7]

The other BVC officers were distributed amongst the British garrison in Pietersburg. Major Lenehan was initially handed over to the officer commanding the Gordon Highlanders and detained in a tent in a small fort in their lines. Later, around 10 December, the Gordon Highlanders left Pietersburg and Major Lenehan was transferred to the lines of the 2nd Wiltshire Regiment.

Captain Taylor and Lieutenant Handcock were kept in the blockhouses close to the Wiltshire Lines and Lieutenant Hannam and Sergeant Major Hammett were placed in the garrison prison. Lieutenant Picton was with the Royal Field Artillery. As with Major Lenehan, Lieutenant Morant was first kept with the Gordon Highlanders but later taken to the garrison prison. [8]

Instructions to convene the official Court of Inquiry were issued to Lt Colonel Hall on 16 October at Pietersburg. The Court of Inquiry assembled on the 25th. [9] According to the Manual of Military Law 1899, a Court of Inquiry is not technically a court at all but 'an assembly of persons directed by a commanding officer to collect evidence with respect to a transaction into which he cannot conveniently himself make inquiry'. The main purpose of the inquiry is for the convening officer to make a decision as to whether there is a case to answer. A court of inquiry could be made up of any number of officers of any rank and had no judicial power. [10]

It might be argued that the Court of Inquiry should have started when Major R. W. Lenehan arrived at Spelonken on 7 September 1901 to make investigations in to the alleged crimes. Owing to the troopers' apparent belief that Major Lenehan was complicit in a cover-up however, he himself became a subject of the inquiry. In the week preceding 16 October, Major R. M Poore, Provost Marshal at Army Headquarters and his assistant Captain W. Bonham took sworn statements from NCOs and troopers of the BVC. The statements of Corporal Browne, Trooper Jacob Hatfield, Trooper

Hampton and Trooper van der Westhuizen were formally examined prior to the issue of orders to convene. [11]

President of the Court of Inquiry was Colonel H. M. Carter of the 2nd Wiltshire Regiment. He was assisted by Major Bolton, Provost Marshal at Pietersburg. Captain Evans, adjutant of the 2nd Wiltshires who Witton claimed was the most knowledgeable officer at Pietersburg on matters of Military Law acted as secretary of the court. [12] The burden of collecting evidence fell on Major Bolton. He employed Trooper Robert Mitchell Cochrane and Corporal Herbert Sharpe to assist. Corporal Sharpe had a chequered history with the BVC having once been reprimanded by Handcock for selling his uniform. [13] In his defence of the BVC officers, J. F. Thomas would emphasise this fact and point out that Sharpe had once stated to Trooper Hodds that he would walk barefoot from Spelonken to Pietersburg to be in the firing party to shoot Morant and Handcock. It is quite possible that Sharpe is the Corporal Trooper James Christie refers to in the passage above. Inevitably, these indiscretions would be used by pro-Morant authors to attack his credibility. He had, however, formerly been a detective of the Boer republic, which at least gave him some qualification for the role bestowed upon him.

Robert Mitchell Cochrane has also become demonised in the Morant myth since, besides being one of the signatories to the troopers' letter of complaint, he also submitted an additional memorandum that expanded on that document. Whilst many of his allegations were factual, he also ventured into the realms of hearsay and supposition. Some of his assertions turned out to be false and this, combined with an apparently meteoric rise from obscurity and an equally speedy descent, has been used to undermine his character and credibility. Recent research [14] has, however, revealed that Cochrane was a capable man whose primary failing was an annoyingly over-enthusiastic approach to everything he did combined with an aura of pomposity. He was neither in obscurity prior to the BVC episode nor after, but a prominent figure in his community wherever he ventured. The *Daily News* in Perth described him in 1908: [15]

> Mr. Cochrane is one of those men—in some, respects exceedingly desirable men—who have a habit of becoming absolutely overwhelmed with the immense importance of the district in which they happen to reside—at the moment. A few months ago Mr, Cochrane succeeded in persuading himself that Bunbury was the pivot of the universe. At that time he resided in that place. Since then he has gone to Geraldton, and behold the pivot of the universe has suddenly changed to his new place of residence ... Seriously, however, enthusiasts like Mr. Cochrane have their uses, and no doubt some

> of the wrongs, oppressions, and injustices he has succeeded in unearthing at Geraldton will be attended to and removed.

Cochrane was in fact everything he said he was, a Justice of the Peace in Coolgardie, W.A., a mine manager [16] and actually much more. He had gone to South Africa to learn more of the metallurgical processes used in the mines of the Transvaal [17]. The war drifting into the guerrilla phase had delayed his plans and he had signed up with the BVC whilst waiting for the war to finish, or perhaps to do his bit in speeding the process up.

Cochrane had arrived in Cooktown, Queensland from Plymouth on 21 September 1882 on the ship *Dorunda* eight months before Edwin Murrant arrived in Queensland. [18] After a period working as a surveyor working for the Queensland Government, in which he determined the latitude and longitude of all the major Queensland towns, [19] he had become editor of *The Eagle* in Charters Towers in 1892/3. [20] Although this was long after Murrant had left the area, it is not impossible that he had heard tales of Edwin Murrant whilst there.

Much scorn has been heaped upon Cochrane because some of the allegations he passed to the inquiry were false; but any criminal investigation commences with the consideration of all possibilities, no matter how far-fetched; many of which will be dismissed quickly, others only after further investigation. The evidence is gradually filtered and analysed until it is presented to the court where it undergoes the final test of validity. Here, the adversarial justice system, in theory at least, subjects it to its final test of fitness. This iterative process appears to have been lost on those who seek to belittle the contribution of Cochrane and Sharpe whose roles were, after all, to cast a broad net to capture all possible pertinent information to be sifted by the Court of Inquiry, and then the Courts Martial. It is not surprising that evidence presented would be called into question, not least by the defendants. By a number of accounts no small amount of irrelevant information to the charges in question was presented. [21] It is not known how many witnesses provided evidence to the Court of Inquiry, though according to Trooper John Silke, twenty BVC Troopers were ordered to remain in Pietersburg potentially to provide evidence at the Courts Martial. [22]

Were the Court of Inquiry and the Courts Martial conducted in absolute secrecy as claimed, thus preventing the defendants' families and the Australian authorities from learning of them and protecting their citizens? It will later be shown that of the Courts Martial themselves, only the Heese case, in which the defendants were acquitted, was not held in public. As to the Court of Inquiry, Lt George Witton in his 1907 pro-Morant book *Scapegoats of the Empire* states, 'This court of inquisition sat daily for nearly a month, and was supposed to be held in camera, yet statements made during the day, with additions, were freely discussed at garrison mess, and were the common talk of the town during the evening.' [23] Clearly, Witton felt the Court of Inquiry was not private enough. Since Witton claims to have been kept in 'solitary confinement' during the Court of Inquiry one must assume that his knowledge of what was discussed at garrison mess and in town was based on hearsay; or that his 'solitary' wasn't.

One author [24] has argued that Witton, who mentions attending the Court of Inquiry twice, the occasions separated by a few weeks, must therefore have been prevented from attending at other times. The Manual of Military law states that a defendant could neither be forced into, nor be prevented from, attending a court of inquiry. [25] If Witton did only attend on those two occasions then some of his assertions about what went on must also be taken as hearsay: '...in some cases questions and answers would be taken down in writing without their knowledge; a day or so later they would be sent for again, and a long statement read over to them, which they were ordered to sign.' [26] Rules of procedure no. 4, Manual of Military Law 1899, actually requires that the witnesses' statements are read back to them and that they sign them. [27]

A Court of Inquiry, it should be reiterated, is not strictly a court at all and its purpose is to determine whether there is a case to answer. So much of the 'evidence' submitted to the inquiry is likely to be of a less secure and possibly more fanciful nature than the evidence allowed in the actual Courts Martial. Witton claims: 'Some of the statements were made by men who knew nothing whatever personally, but had only heard the case was as they represented; some even had merely heard that someone else had heard and so on. These men's statements were taken as evidence. Others who were called, and said truly that they knew nothing, were treated as hostile, and were bullied and badgered, and even threatened with arrest.' In fact, the authorities recognised that much irrelevant evidence had been taken and this had to be filtered out when the Summary of Evidence was prepared. [28]

Witton was of course one of the accused and he would write a letter in 1929 to J. F. Thomas in which he stated that he had learned prior to the Courts Martial that Handcock had murdered the Revd Heese at Morant's instigation. [29] If one believes this letter, then the whole premise of his 1907 book must be called in to question. If one finds reason to disbelieve his letter of 1929, as some authors do, then one must believe that in 1929 he was willing to besmirch the reputation of the two executed men and deliver a shattering blow to J. F. Thomas for his own purposes. This letter will be considered later; but either way, Witton's 1907 account on which much of the Morant myth is based, should be treated with caution.

Unfortunately, the evidence taken at the Court of Inquiry does not survive but statements taken before the inquiry began do. Typical of the statements made is that of Trooper Staton:

> I Sidney Allen Staton hereby make oath and swear as follows:
> I remember the second of July when the six Boers were shot. The patrol was drawn up at Sweetwaters Farm and I saw there Capt. Taylor, Capt. Robertson and Lt Handcock. Then we rode on until we came across five Boers lying in the road dead and one lying dead in the wagon under his blankets never having left his bed. The five lying in the road were shot in the head save one who was shot in the neck. They had no arms and from the position in which the bodies were lying it was evident they had not died fighting. It looked to me just like an execution. I saw both Capt. Taylor and Capt. Robertson ride on the scene while the bodies were lying there unburied.
>
> I remember the shooting of the captured Boer prisoner F. Visser who was severely wounded when captured. This happened on or about Aug. 11th. This Boer was carried in a cape cart about fifteen miles. After we outspanned we heard the Boer was to be shot. On looking at him I saw the Kaffirs dancing a war dance around him. Lt Handcock was watching them dance and I believe Lt Morant and Lt Picton also but am not certain as to these two latter. He was carried close to the river and placed sitting with his back to the firing party. A short time after we started in the morning, that is several hours before the Boer was shot, I heard Lt Morant tell Trooper Botha to translate to the Boer this sentence: 'You might tell me something about the Boers for as your doom is sealed anyhow you needn't tell any lies.' The words were to that effect. Before the wounded Boer was shot, Lt Picton called for volunteers to shoot him. The men murmured and Lt Picton said 'it was no crime to shoot him as he was outlawed'. I saw trooper Gill volunteer.
>
> The wounded Boer was then shot and immediately fell backwards. I was going to see him when Lt Picton said 'as you would not help to shoot him you cannot go to see him.' Shortly after either Lt Handcock or Lt Picton went up with a revolver and blew out his brains. I cannot swear positively as to which it was. I saw Lt Picton go close up to the Boer with the revolver in his hand but I think at the last minute Lt Handcock took it out of his hand and fired blowing out Visser's brains.
> Sgd Sidney Allen Staton
> Witness: R. M. Poore
> Provost Marshal
> Army Headquarters
> Pretoria
> 11 Oct. 1901 [30]

The above is illuminating in relation to Witton's claims about the taking of evidence. Twice Staton admits uncertainty: 'but am not certain as to these two latter' and 'I cannot swear positively as to which it was.' Is this the statement of a man who has been coerced? Other statements express similar uncertainty. At least prior to the Court of Inquiry, there appears to be no pressure applied to the witnesses.

It was part of the Court of Inquiry's role to provide a summary or an abstract of evidence and recommendations to Colonel J. St Clair, Deputy Judge Advocate General of Lord Kitchener's Staff. The inquiry concluded its work on 23 November. The last of the proceedings were received at headquarters on the evening of the 28th. [31] St Clair's legal opinions on the main cases were provided on 13 and 22 November, with opinions on Taylor's alleged mis-appropriation of cattle and Lenehan's failure to report provided on 3 December. [32] Claims that the last 'staff action' on the case occurred on 21 November, which suggest that there was an unnecessary delay in bringing the BVC officers to court [33] are incorrect.

In all, Colonel St Clair considered at least fifteen cases relating to the BVC. St Clair's early recommendation was that Lieutenant Hannam should not be prosecuted. According to some accounts this was because the Boers in the party shot at had not been disarmed, [34] thus it could be argued that in theory their surrender had not yet been accepted, though it seems questionable whether a party which comprised more children than adults and as many women as men would have needed to surrender at all. In consequence, Lieutenant Hannam was released on 1 January 1902 [35] along with Sgt Major Hammett.

His other recommendation was that Lieutenant Witton was an accessory to murder and should be charged with 'the capital offence'. [36] He further stated:

> I agree generally with the views expressed by the court of Inquiry in their opinions of the several cases. The idea that no prisoners were to be taken in the Spelonken appears to have been started by the late Captain Hunt and after his death continued by orders given personally by Captain Taylor.
>
> The statement that Captain Hunt's body had been maltreated is in no way corroborated and the reprisals undertaken by Lt Morant on this idea were utterly unjustifiable.
>
> Lt Morant seems to have been the prime mover in carrying out these orders and Lieut. Handcock willingly lent himself as the principal executioner of them. Lieut. Witton acquiesced in the illegal execution of the wounded Boer Visser and took a personal part in the massacre of the 8 surrendered Boers on 23 August. The two N.C.O.'s [37] acted under

> orders but were not justified in obeying illegal commands. After the murder of van Buuren the officers seem to have exercised a reign of terror in the district which hindered their men from reporting their illegal act and even prevented their objecting to assist [sic] the crime. I think the charges may be preferred as under:
>
> Lieut. Morant For Murder or being accessory to murder in cases 2-4-5 and 6.
> Lieut. Handcock For murder in cases no 2-3-4-5 and 6.
> Lieut. Witton For being accessory to murder in case 3. For murder in case 4.
>
> As to Sergt Oldham the C of. [sic] I recommend no prosecution, and I think taking all circumstances of case no 1 [the 'six Boers'] into consideration the responsibility should rest with the officer 'Captain Taylor' who gave the order to this N.C.O through Sgt Major Morrison.
> I will report separately on Capt. Taylor's case. [38]

In the case of Taylor, St Clair wrote:

> Case No 1 I agree with opinion of the court of inquiry. The order given by Captain Taylor that no prisoners were to be taken was against the usage of modern warfare, this in my opinion rendered him personally responsible for the shooting of the 6 Boers who were trying to surrender, who made no defence when fired on. As being an accessory before the fact he is liable to a charge of murder.
>
> Case No 2. The shooting of trooper van Buuren by Lt Handcock was authorised by Captain Taylor and Captain Robertson. Both these officer were accessories before the fact to Lt Handcock's act which in my opinion was murder.
> Even if van Buuren was shot because he was suspected of being a traitor there appears no reason why he should not have been arrested and tried either on the spot or at Pietersburg.
>
> Case nos 4 + 6 The verbal orders given by Captain Taylor to the officers and men of the BVC at various times not to take prisoners rendered him primarily responsible for these massacres and I think he is liable as an accessory before the fact.
>
> Case no 8 The shooting of van der Berg without trial was an illegal act, however guilty he may have been. There appears no sufficient reason this man should not have been made a prisoner and tried for his alleged offence. I think Captain Taylor has rendered himself liable to a charge of murder. [39]

Presumably the offence alleged to have been committed by 'van der Berg' was the killing of R. H. Summers.

> Case no 9 Captain Taylor should have been aware when he ordered these natives to be shot that he was exceeding his powers. It is possible however that he may have been acting in good faith in this instance.
>
> Case 10 The summary shooting of these two natives as spies does not appear to have been warranted by the evidence against them, and Captain Taylor should have known that he was exceeding his powers in ordering their summary punishment.
>
> Some kind of investigation seems to have taken place and Captain Taylor may have acted in good faith.
>
> Case 11 I think a charge for manslaughter will lie against Captain Taylor in this case.
>
> 22-11-01 [40]

As will become evident, not all of the recommendations made by Col St Clair as a result of the court of inquiry were taken further, particularly in the case of Alfred Taylor. The 'summary of evidence' was also to be provided along with charge sheets to the defendants when they were warned for court martial. It has been claimed by some that there is 'every indication' [41] that no formal summary of evidence was produced, on the basis that Witton makes no mention of it when discussing being served with the charge sheets. [42] Witton may have just assumed that the summary formed part of the charge sheets. The same source quotes Colonel St Clair writing to the Adjutant General that: 'The summary has been carefully taken and should, I think, be sufficient to prove the several charges. As copies of the summary will have to be given to the accused when they are warned for trial I would suggest that they be made at once by the typists who have been engaged for the trial. They should be sworn to secrecy.' [43] It is then argued by the same person that to gain the approval of the Adjutant General and signatures of up to 41 witnesses, proof reading and copying etc would have taken longer than the time available and that therefore, it was unlikely that this summary actually existed. So, the summary doesn't exist because Witton doesn't mention it – and it doesn't exist because St Clair does.

The Courts Martial commenced on 16 January 1902. Colonel St Clare gave the above advice on 10 January. This is not a lapse of 'four days' but in any case instructions had been issued to O.C. L. of C. (Officer Commanding Lines of Communication), North, on 26 December 1901 'to have the Summary taken as quickly as practicable and forward it to Head Quarters' [44] and the summary had been already been sent to the Adjutant General and AHQ on Monday 6 January 1902. [45] It is not known how many witness statements were referred to in the summary and therefore how many signatures were required, neither how many typists were employed.

Further evidence for existence of the Summary of Evidence is revealed in Col St Clair's response to Major W. N. Bolton's doubts in relation to his own level of legal experience being sufficient to prosecute in the Heese Case. On 6 February 1902, St Clair wrote '...from what I remember of the summary of evidence, I do not think it is too complicated a case for Major Bolton to conduct.' [46] On 10 February after the first four trials had been completed the DJAG (Deputy Judge Advocate General) wrote, 'I think that reason is shown for a new court and recommend that it is assembled at Pietersburg ... If a fresh summary is taken every effort should be made by the prosecutor to procure further evidence.' [47] This also suggests that new evidence was being collected up to and during the Courts Martial.

It is clear that a Summary of Evidence did exist. Of course Morant's apologists only adopt this rather desperate argument in order to suggest that Lord Kitchener invoked special powers under Rule 104 to dispense with the requirements for one. In fact, the defendants themselves had the right to waive the requirement [48] though they actually requested a formal summary. [49] The use of Rule 104 would have also allowed Rule 13 to be dispensed with, which states that a defendant must be allowed 'proper opportunity of preparing his defence, and shall be allowed free communication with his witnesses, and with a friend or legal adviser with whom he may wish to consult'. [50]

Much has been made of the fact that J. F. Thomas was a small town solicitor and only arrived the day before the Courts Martial started. Major J. F. Thomas had been about to return to Australia in January 1902 when he got wind that Major Lenehan needed someone to represent him in court. According to Nick Bleszynski, he received a telegram from Major Lenehan and cables on 6, 7, and 9 January [51] requesting that he defend him and arrived at Pietersburg on 15 January. Dr John Bennett, a legal historian, doubts this, on the basis that Lenehan as a prominent Sydney solicitor would have known that Thomas had very little experience in such serious cases and would have been very unlikely to request him specifically. [52] Lieutenant Morant also requested legal representation from Captain Purland, (then Director of Prisons), on 7 January 1902. Purland declined on 9 January saying he hardly knew Morant and his official position prevented him from undertaking such a duty even if wanted to. [53] A week before the Courts Martial were due to start, Witton approached Captain Evans about representation but then, on Evans' advice, did not worry further until the Courts Martial began. [54] With the short time between Thomas' arrival and the commencement of proceedings, Thomas was entirely within his rights to seek an adjournment [55]. There is no record that he did so.

In any case, considerable legal expertise was on hand prior to Thomas' arrival, in the portly form of Major R. W. Lenehan. Major Lenehan had experience of both courts martial and the New South Wales Supreme Court. In 1895 Lenehan had been the defence solicitor in two high-profile courts martial, both of which would have a bearing on future events: Hutton vs Close and Captain Johnson vs Surgeon Lea [56]. Lenehan's experience in the Supreme Court of NSW was as a solicitor instructing barristers, who in simple terms, do the talking in court. Lenehan once instructed J. H. Want QC, Attorney General in the Supreme Court of NSW. [57] Based on this and probably on the adage that 'a man who represents himself in court has a fool for a client', Lenehan allowed J. F. Thomas to represent him whilst no doubt briefing him thoroughly on a previously considered defence, at least for himself.

Major Lenehan however had even more recent and pertinent legal experience than this. In a letter to the Australian Prime Minister [58] he stated that Kitchener had availed himself of his legal knowledge in detailing him to prosecute the case of Jacobus Spoelstra in a military court in Pretoria. This case took place between 26 and 31 April 1901 [59] whilst Lenehan was C.O. of the BVC. J. Spoelstra was a Hollander who had written accounts of the deplorable conditions in the concentration camps and also of alleged ill treatment and rape of Boer women by soldiers of the British Army. One of Spoelstra's letters had been intercepted and Spoelstra was charged with 'Evasion of Censorship'. At the military court it seems Spoelstra made little or no real attempt to prove himself innocent of the charge but produced a number witnesses to reinforce the claims he had made in the letter to the Dutch press. [60] Major Lenehan was successful in his prosecution and Spoelstra was found guilty. He was sentenced to imprisonment with hard labour but Lord Kitchener immediately commuted his sentence to a year's imprisonment as a Prisoner of War. Spoelstra was sent to Bermuda. [61]

Lenehan's involvement in the Spoelstra case is not discussed by any of the Morant biographers though Carnegie and Shields quote Lenehan's claim to have prosecuted the case in the letter he wrote to the Australian Prime Minister. [62] A transcript of the proceedings of the Spoelstra case was published in London by W. T. Stead, a well-known investigative journalist and pacifist. [63] These proceedings had to be smuggled past the censors written on tissue paper and hidden in a cocoa tin. [64] The name of the prosecutor in this document however is given as 'Maj. Lingham – Australian'. No record of an Australian officer named Major Lingham has been found [65] and there seems no reason to disbelieve Lenehan's claim that he prosecuted the case, especially as it was made in a letter to the Prime Minister. '*Die lotgevalle van die burgerlike bevolking gedurende die Anglo-Boereoorlog, 1899–1902*' also gives the prosecutor's name as Lingham. Lingham is a quite plausible mis-reading of Lenehan. (A Lieutenant Lingham arrested Emily Hobhouse).

The DJAG Col St Clair and Maj. Montagu Poore, having advised in the Spoelstra case, would have been well aware of Lenehan's legal abilities. These talents were also known in the lower ranks. It may well have been Lenehan's success in the Spoelstra case that prompted Lieutenant D. J. Stewart of Woolongong, NSW, who was temporarily attached to the BVC, to write in May 1901 'Rumor says [it's] not unlikely that Major (or Lieutenant-Colonel as I understand he is about to become) Lenehan will one of these days be appointed a judge of the Supreme Court.' [66] Since Lenehan had been sent to Fort Edward to investigate the alleged crimes of the BVC Officers, he would have had a very good idea of what the charges would be. He would also have had plenty of time to think about a defence during his three-month incarceration.

Neither were Thomas and Lenehan up against the crack prosecution team that has sometimes been suggested. On 5 February Major Bolton who feared, in relation to the case against Morant for getting Handcock to kill Revd Heese, his legal knowledge to be insufficient for 'such an intricate case' sent a request to the Adjutant General that a civilian barrister or solicitor be appointed to prosecute. [67] The following day he asked the Provost Marshal at AHQ Pretoria to make arrangements for a civilian lawyer to be sent up informing him that he had already been requested to do so to the Adjutant General. On 6 February St Clair replied ' I am informed that a Solicitor's charges will be at least 10 guineas per diem, and from what I remember of the summary of evidence, I don't think it is too complicated a case for Major Bolton to conduct. If no more evidence can be procured, I do not think a conviction will be obtained. But I advise the prosecution of Lt Handcock being proceeded with. Mr Weeber, a Solicitor employed by the Law Department might undertake the case, but I have not seen him about it.' [68] On the 7th his request was turned down by the AG. This response hardly sits well alongside the story of the poor country solicitor bravely defending his clients against a crack prosecution team employed by an administration hell-bent on crucifying Morant and Handcock. Furthermore, Major Bolton in his request to the Provost Martial for a civilian lawyer, begs 'Could you try and arrange this and let me get back to my work at Bloemfontein. I have already been away four weeks.' [69] This raises the oft-forgotten point that the members of the courts were all soldiers in the midst of war with other jobs to do. The fact that at least five members of the Courts Martial came from the same infantry unit, the 2nd Wiltshires who happened to based in Pietersburg at the time, hardly suggests that they were a cherry-picked legal elite.

In view of his experience and knowledge, was Major Lenehan likely to let the court slip up on any point of procedure without calling 'foul'? Lenehan kicked up a considerable fuss after the court cases in relation to the nature of his incarceration and subsequent expeditious deportation from South Africa but did not raise any point of procedure. The DJAG James St Clair and Major Poore [70] would have been keenly aware of Major Lenehan's accomplishments. Would they have allowed any errors of procedure knowing one of the defendants would take them to task over it? It will be seen that the Courts went to extraordinary lengths to comply with the correct procedures.

That the administration was wary of the BVC officers' knowledge of their own rights is demonstrated when the St Clair provided his final comments on the charges for the Courts Martial Case 4, the murder of the eight Boers on 20 December 1901:

> This was in my opinion the most serious crime of the series and there is ample evidence. The question whether a charge of being accessory after the fact to these crimes can be brought against Major Lenehan is one I think for the Civil Lawyers – the objection to trying the officers conjointly is that they may at the last moment claim to be tried separately under RP15. [71]

This further refutes the claim that the last 'staff action' on the case occurred on 21 November and therefore there was an unnecessary delay in bringing the BVC officers to court. [72] In fact, it was precisely the need to comply with procedure before defendants who knew their rights which contributed to that delay.

Whilst arguing that the Courts Martial were perfunctory, rushed affairs, the conspiracy theorists have seized upon the time lapse between arrest and arraignment as excessive. The coincidence of this three-month period with the period after discharge for which an officer is still subject to military law has been used to suggest that Kitchener, who clearly cannot win either way, deliberately delayed the commencement of the Courts Martial to allow Alfred Taylor to be tried by military court rather than a court martial.

In fact there is compelling evidence that Kitchener wanted things to move faster. The following memo is in fact the only evidence found of Kitchener applying pressure of any kind on those involved in the court process. Major Kelly's response also delivers the coup de grace to the notion that a formal Summary of Evidence did not exist. [73]

Army Headquarters, South Africa
A.G./
The Chief has desired me to address you regarding the delay which has taken place in bringing the trial of those men of the Bushveldt Carabiniers who stand charged with murder. In view to the necessity of bringing in witnesses from the north of the Zoutpansberg, Lord Kitchener quite understands that a certain amount of delay was unavoidable. Nevertheless, the importance of this trial is so great and the lapse has been so exceptional, that he will be glad if you will favour him with a written statement bringing out clearly the circumstances which have contributed to this delay.
Hamilton
C of S
Johannesburg 4.1.02 [74]

The response from Major General Kelly provides a timeline of events between October 1901 and January 1902.

Army Head Quarters.
Pretoria, 5th January, 1902
The Chief of Staff

With reference to your letter C.of S. 189 of the 4th instant:-
1 The following telephone message was sent to the General Commanding-in-Chief yesterday in reply to an inquiry as to the progress of the SPELONKEN case:-.
'Case is proceeding; the Court will probably assemble next (i.e., this) week'.
2 The circumstance which gave rise to the present proceedings were reported on 8 October 1901, and after formal examination of certain sworn statements, instructions were issued on 16th October, 1901, to the O.C., L. of C., North, Pietersburg [then Colonel F. H. Hall, R.F.A] to hold an exhaustive inquiry into the alleged conduct of certain officers of the Bushveldt Carbineers, which comprised at least eight separate transactions in the months of July, August and September, 1901.
3. A Court of Inquiry was assembled at Pietersburg on 25th October, 1901.
4. This inquiry concluded its work on the 23rd November, 1901, the last of the proceedings being received at Head Quarters on the evening of the 28th November, 1901.
5. The proceedings are voluminous, and were carefully reviewed, with the result that it was decided to arraign certain of the officers concerned before a General Court-Martial, and on the 6th December, 1901 instructions to this effect were sent by telegraph to the O.C., L of C., North, (Colonel S. H. Harrison).

Inquiries were then made in accordance with R.P.8 [Rules of Procedure 8 MML] as to whether the accused waived their right to have a formal Summary of Evidence taken, and were willing to accept an Abstract of Evidence from the proceedings of the Court of Inquiry instead. They claimed their right to have a formal Summary taken, and in consequence the proceedings of the Court of Inquiry had to be carefully gone through a second time with a view to making certain extracts for the guidance of the officer taking the Summary, much of the evidence given at the inquiry being wholly irrelevant to the main points at issue. The claim of the accused to have a Summary of Evidence taken is therefore the main cause of the delay in assembling the Court-Martial.

6. On 26th December, 1901, instructions were issued to O.C. L. of C., North, to have the Summary taken as quickly as practicable and forward it to Head Quarters.

7. On the 2nd January, 1902, a telegram was despatched to O.C. L. of C., North, asking him to report progress, and his reply was to the effect that the evidence was being taken daily but that the delay was caused by the non-arrival of witnesses from Pretoria.

8. From this it appears that the witnesses who gave their evidence at the Court of Inquiry have been allowed to leave Pietersburg before any decision had been arrived at, and without reference to Head Quarters.

Such witnesses as are required and who are now in Pretoria have been despatched to Pietersburg.

9. The late Assistant Provost Marshal at Pietersburg, Major W. N. Bolton, was removed at short notice and transferred to Bloemfontein. He was thoroughly conversant with the whole case from its beginning, his absence cannot fail to have had a disadvantageous effect upon the regular and continuous conduct of the inquiry.

10 Until this Summary has been received the charges cannot properly be framed, and any attempt to do so would only lead to possible failure as the result of the hurry, which was depreciated in your 156 of the 2nd January, 1902.

M Kelly
Major- General,
AG

Lord Kitchener's handwritten response is recorded at the foot of this document: 'Very unsatisfactory[,] military justice should be prompt and in this case most unusual delays appear to have taken place. K'. [75] The Summary of Evidence was sent to the Adjutant General and AHQ on Monday 6 January 1902. [76]

The essential difference between an Abstract of Evidence and a Summary of Evidence is that a Summary is taken in front of the accused and must be signed by the witness. The fact that the defendants demanded a Summary of Evidence rather than an abstract after the witnesses had been allowed to leave Pietersburg would have meant that the key witnesses would have been recalled to give their evidence again in front of the accused and to sign the written copy. Given the distances involved this would have been a time-consuming process, involving considerable effort. Allowing them to leave after giving their statements was a mistake – but given that some were being paid a pound per day, understandable.

It has also been argued that undue delay occurred in informing the defendants of their respective charges. Lieut. Witton was given his charge sheets 24 hours before he was arraigned, the minimum allowable under the Manual of Military Law for a general court martial. [77] The charges were 'murder by inciting instigating and commanding certain trooper to kill and murder one named Visser' and 'murder by inciting instigating and commanding certain trooper to kill eight men, names unknown'. However, around 4 November 1901 Witton attended the Court of Inquiry and the President read out that he was charged 'with Complicity in the death of a prisoner of war named Visser, with complicity in the death of eight others names unknown, also with complicity in the death of C.H.D. Hesse [sic], a German Missionary'. [78] In relation to the Heese case Witton states 'I proved even to the satisfaction of this court that I knew nothing of this case, and the charge was immediately withdrawn.' [79] So with the charge in relation to the Heese Case immediately withdrawn the charge sheets reflected exactly the information relayed to him almost 11 weeks earlier.

One of the abiding elements of the Morant myth is the notion that Lieutenant Colonel Hall, perceived to be a key witness, was hastily and mysteriously posted to India to prevent him from giving evidence shortly before the Courts Martial. Lieutenant George Witton is the source: 'Hall was suddenly recalled by the War Office, relieved of his Command, and sent out of the country to India.' [80]

In reality there was nothing mysterious about his posting. South African author Arthur Davey suggested that Hall's posting resulted from the deployment of five batteries of artillery to India in late 1901: 'It is just possible that Hall's transfer there was a routine move to bring a detached officer back to his normal duties in gunnery command.' [81] An artillery brigade in 1901 comprised three batteries, and Lieutenant Colonel Francis Henry Hall was the commanding officer of 3rd Brigade Royal Artillery comprising the 18th, 62nd and 75th batteries. [82] These batteries under Lt Colonel Hall had excelled themselves at Modder River and Magersfontein in the last two months of 1900. [83]

It was announced in *The Times* of 23 November 1901, during the BVC Court of Inquiry, that:

> The 18th, 62nd, and 75th Batteries Royal Field Artillery are under orders to proceed immediately in the transport *City of Vienna* from South Africa to India, to be stationed at Kirkee, Bombay. Among the units to be exchanged are the 2nd Batt. Gordon Highlanders and the 1st Batt. Devonshire Regiment, but the exact dates of sailing cannot be given. [84]

The same publication later announced 'The Steamship *City of Vienna* left Port Natal for Bombay November 25, having the following on board:- 3rd Brigade Divisional Royal Artillery – Col [sic] Hall ... *The City of Vienna* is due at Bombay on December 13'. [85] Hall actually debarked on 12 December.

This was not a rushed decision. The Proceedings of the Draft Committee, no. 185, 27 June 1901 under the title: 'Amendments necessary to bring the Indian and Colonial Reliefs, enumerated in No 172. Proceedings of Draft Committee, into Harmony with the arrangement of trooping season, 1901–1902.' stated: 'The scheme takes into consideration the reliefs already proposed in the Proceedings Drafts Committee, No 172, of the 30th May 1900, which has now been modified; (1) by the addition of another year's Indian reliefs; (2) by the proposal to move from South Africa those battalions on their colonial tour which have been there too long, and (3) by the creation of certain battalions of the Royal Garrison Regiment...' [86] The proceedings then include a large table of battalion movements, an extract of which is shown below:

Royal Field Artillery			
Brigade Division	From	To	Remarks
III Brigade Division - 18th Battery 62nd Battery 75th Battery	South Africa.	India	Vice XXXIV. Brigade Division
XXXIV Brigade Division - 22nd battery 50th battery 70th battery	India	Home	Due Home 1900-01.

The press release announcing the above was written on 20 November 1901 by the Under Secretary of State, India office and was approved by Lord George Hamilton [87] on the 21st.

The above entries in The Proceedings of the Draft Committee, No 185 of 28 June 1901, five days before the first murders attributed to the BVC occurred, show that the intention to send Hall's 3rd Brigade to India had actually been made on 30 May 1900, almost a year before the BVC had been formed and indeed *The Times* of 14 September 1900, announced: 'The programme of artillery reliefs shows that the ... the Field Artillery brigades which go to India from South Africa are the 1st Brigade, which includes the 13th, 67th, and 69th Batteries, and the 3rd Brigade, which consists of the 18th, 52nd, and 75th Batteries.'

Lt Col E. A. Lambart and 67th and 69th batteries of his 1st Brigade were moved to India on 3 November 1901, three weeks before Lt Col Hall and his own three batteries.

There is absolutely no doubt therefore that these were planned routine reliefs. There was nothing sudden, mysterious or conspiratorial about Lt Colonel Hall's departure for India.

One commentator [88] questions Arthur Davey's original allusion, asserting that there was little correlation between the rank of colonel and five batteries of artillery, arguing that officers with the rank of colonel and above lose their corps identity; therefore the fact that Hall was an Artillery Officer was irrelevant to a posting of artillery batteries. [89] Given that in late 1901 Hall was actually Lieutenant Colonel (and Brevet Colonel) and only attained the substantive rank of colonel in 1903, this argument can be refuted.

The writer also suggests that Lt Colonel Hall's fortunes in India rose when Lord Kitchener arrived in India later in 1902, claiming that his service on half pay ended on 21 July 1902 followed shortly by the award of Companion of the Order of the Bath on 29 July 1902. In fact the *London Gazette* 1 August 1902 states: 'Royal Horse and Royal Field Artillery, The undermentioned Brevet Colonels, on completion of five years' service as regimental Lieutenant-Colonels, are placed on half pay. Dated 21st July 1902'. Lt Col Hall was one of these. Therefore his stint on half pay did not end but started on this date. Whilst it is true that Hall was awarded the Companion of the Order of the Bath in July 1902, Kitchener did not arrive in India until late November. Hall came off half pay seven months later when he became 'a colonel on the Staff to command the Royal Artillery 11nd Army Corps, with substantive rank of Colonel in the Army. Dated 6th February, 1903'. [90] He would be acting as Commandant of the Artillery Practice Camp on Salisbury Plain in England by March 1905.

Whilst there was nothing conspiratorial about his posting at this time, it is probably fair to say that he should have been made available for the Courts Martial and would have been today.

Were the defendants kept incommunicado prior the Courts Martial and prevented from writing to loved ones or anyone else? Stories appeared in British newspapers as early 4 April 1902 [91] apparently originating from Witton's fellow travellers to England on the *Canada* that the prisoners had all their letters returned to them undelivered and consequently their families could not lobby the newly formed Australian Federal Government on their behalf. However, only around a week before this article, the *Argus* in Australia reported:

> When the cable message announcing that two members of an irregular corps had been shot in Pretoria was published in *The Argus* on March 10, Lieutenant Witton's relatives manifested some anxiety but they could not bring themselves to believe that he was one of those who had suffered the penalty because in all the letters in which he had referred to the impending court martial he treated the matter very lightly. He expressed the opinion that the worst that could happen to them all would be the loss of their commissions and, he added that Lieutenant Morant intended if that were the result of the court martial to re-enlist as a trooper in one of the Australian Commonwealth contingents, which were expected shortly to arrive. [92]

So George Witton, at least, contacted his family on several occasions before the courts martial. His brother Ernest Witton had received a number of letters prior to the court case, one of which was referred to in a number of Australian newspapers:

> The letter was written from Pietersberg, under date December 4, 1901, to the writer's brother in Melbourne. It states that there had been some trouble with the officers of the Bushveldt Carbineers, to which he belonged, and that at the time of writing, four of them, including the writer, were under arrest on a charge of shooting unarmed Boers, but he did not regard the position as serious, feeling that the most extreme punishment to which they were likely to be subjected was cashiering. [93]

The date of writing was six weeks after their arrest and about the same before the Courts Martial started. Clearly Lieut. George Witton was lying when he claimed that the prisoners had all of their letters returned [94].

Peter Handcock's wife also received letters during the period of incarceration, prior to the Courts Martial. 'Mrs. Handcock stated that she received the last letter from her husband three months ago. Prior to that, in November, [he was arrested 24 October] he wrote saying that he had been having a very rough time.' [95] Some authors have implied that this three months corresponded to the three months between the defendants' arrest and the start of the Courts Martial, however given that Handcock's wife complained that her husband had been dead for over a month before she was informed, she could not have said this before around 27 March 1902 and 'three months ago' [96] was therefore around Christmas 1901, around two and half weeks before the Courts Martial started and two months after the Court of Inquiry assembled. She had also heard from him in November, 1901, during the Court of Inquiry.

Not only were the defendants writing to their families during their incarceration pending trial but so were others. The *Windsor and Richmond Gazette* for Saturday 29 March 1902 stated: 'About three months ago we heard that private letters had been received from South Africa by a resident of this district telling that Lieut. H. H. Morant ('The Breaker') had got himself into serious trouble with another Australian officer. The news was never officially confirmed until Thursday, when particulars of the unhappy affair appeared in the daily press.' [97]

Some of the witnesses were also writing letters back home. Although the Courts Martial had been conducted in public in Transvaal and letters were allowed home, the press had almost certainly been silenced. One of the most lengthy and detailed accounts of the crimes to appear in the newspapers after the executions was in a letter by Trooper James Christie, who wrote to the *Clutha Leader* in Otago, New Zealand. These accounts have been referred to extensively in Chapter 11. Christie was a farmer, schoolteacher and local councillor who had in 1893 [98] stood for election, unsuccessfully, as the candidate for Mataura to the New Zealand House of Representatives. Although it appeared in April 1902, the letter had been sent in October 1901. The *Clutha Leader*:

> We may mention that we had a full report of the tragedies, at the time, but our correspondent asked that the report should be kept private till the conclusion of the war, and we felt in honour bound to comply with his request. Further, we felt sure that the secrecy that had been observed in connection with the whole matter was the work of the press censor in South Africa, and although we could not see why he should suppress all reports regarding the matter, we felt he must have some good and valid reason for so acting, and we respected his decision. Thus it is that we lave hitherto been silent on the subject. But as various reports have now been published, and the War Office having published a statement regarding the crimes and the execution of the officers referred to, we see no reason for further reticence. We, therefore, in this issue give the first instalment of our report received upwards of four months ago. [99]

The details contained within the letter corroborate the October date. Christie wrote a series of letters to the *Clutha Leader* before, during and after the Court of Inquiry, published between 11 October and 24 December under the titles 'With the Bushveldt Carbineers 1 to 8', though these did not mention the murders. [100]

On 19 January, three days after the start of the Courts Martial, BVC Trooper Ham Glasson wrote home:

> Well since landing in South Africa I have had some very funny experiences & the funniest of all was my six months at the front. Saw what is called British warfare, soldiering alright enough with good officers, but our officers were a lot of rotters, & the same applies to great many officers of the South African Irregular Corps, & the song[?] That is made of these Boers shooting our soldiers cowardly, when it has been done on our side is simply disgusting. I have seen enough to satisfy me that the Boers are not so bad as they are painted, when you take into consideration some of our actions. A lot of our Bushveldt Carbineers officers are at present shut up at Pietersburg waiting a Court Martial, & for my part would like to see some of them shot, but would not be a bit surprised to see it hushed up, among the men they were some of the finest fellows I ever met, several of them had studied for law, & had been in banks & that sort of thing. [101]

The BVC officers were also writing to each other in this period [102] though clearly the authorities were keeping an eye on any collusion. The nature of the prisoner's confinement has been the subject of much discussion, started by Witton describing it as 'solitary confinement'. Although it is quite likely the prisoners were kept in relative isolation it is doubtful that it approached the true meaning of the phrase. Jarvis says that prior to the Court of Inquiry Morant and the others were under 'open arrest' [103] and that 'During this period he was advised by friends, who had some inkling that matters might prove far more serious than he suspected, to desert and make for the Portuguese Border.' This conflicts with Witton who states that they were immediately placed under 'close arrest'. Since Jarvis's account was written in 1943, weight should probably be given to Witton, even though he cannot be viewed as an impartial witness and many of his assertions are questionable. It certainly appears that Major Lenehan was allowed relative freedom. Major Bolton wrote a letter in 1905 in response to a request for information following complaints by Major Lenehan about his treatment:

> ...Major Lenehan was handed over to OC Gordon Highlanders and placed in a tent in a small fort in their lines where he was detained as a prisoner.

During the time he was in the fort I visited him on several occasions and often found many others visiting him. About 10 December 1901 the Gordon Highlanders left Pietersberg and Major Lenehan was transferred to the lines of the Wiltshire Regiment where he was allowed to see anyone he wished. On the 14 December I was transferred to Bloemfontein as APM ORC. [104] From the time of his arrest until I left Pietersberg on19/12/01 I never heard of anyone being refused to visit him except for the other prisoners. I returned to Pietersberg in January for the trial and then found that Lenehan was a prisoner in a fortified house known as the Pietersberg Railway Restaurant. I may state here that at the time that all troops in Pietersberg were at that time under canvas.

When he was arrested I received orders to search his belongings, which was done in the presence of two officers of his own corps but nothing was taken. I also went through the Regimental documents with the adjutant. Whilst he was under arrest to the best of my knowledge he was requested to leave his letters open but only when they were to the other prisoners were they read. The letters received by post except local ones I believe were not interfered with. During the whole time he was under arrest he was allowed to take exercise and this was generally with an officer as an escort. He was also allowed horse exercise and I believe on several occasions no officer being available an NCO was sent out with him. After Major Lenehan was arrested and handed over to OC Gordon Highlanders (Col Scott CB) I had nothing to do with him but to the best of my beliefs he was treated with great leniency considering he was under close arrest. The following officers will be able to corroborate this Col Scott, Major Bethune, Capt Simpson adjt Gordon Highlanders, Col Carter CB, Capt Evans DSO (adjt) Wilts Regt. There are many officers of both regiments who constantly went out with him...

There are still two or three gentlemen in the area who were officers in the BVC to whom I have spoken and they state they were never refused leave to visit Major Lenehan when under arrest and one of them informs me that he on several occasions remembers Major Lenehan visiting him in town during this period.

Signed W N Bolton
Major Wilts Regiment
Resident Magistrate [105]

Overall it seems unlikely that the prisoners were kept in solitary confinement though it does seem that they were kept in relative isolation. Is this really so surprising? Would the authorities really be expected to allow the prisoners to collude and concoct evidence? They were after all under investigation for very serious crimes. There are enough statements by contemporaries, however, to show that the nature of their incarceration raised some indignation. Ex-trooper C. E. Barber for example wrote in his copy of George Witton's *Scapegoats of Empire* 'I cannot accept the author's account of the BVC affair as complete or wholly accurate according to my knowledge of the incidents he narrates. I agree that the treatment of Morant, Handcock, Picton and himself after arrest and before sentence was abominable.'

Even James Christie who had been among those who helped bring the officers to justice wrote: 'After the first blush of feeling against them, when the business was going on, I felt nothing but the sincerest pity when I used to see Handcock walking round his fort inside the barb wire surroundings with a guard over him. I felt that surely he must feel lonely and miserable during the months he was there. We were under orders not to hold communication with either of them…' [106]

Some claim that the Courts Martial were held in total secrecy; but Witton states, referring to the Heese case, 'For some unknown reason this case was heard privately in the garrison, and not publicly in the town, as the others had been.' [107] This is corroborated by Kit Denton in his book *Closed File*. At the time of writing he was in possession of a pamphlet published in Pretoria after the trials which considers the life and death of Revd Heese. This pamphlet includes the note: 'It remains striking that only the case of the murder of the missionary took place behind closed doors.' [108] There is no reason to doubt Witton on this point so it is reasonable to believe that the only case to be heard behind closed doors was the Heese case, the only one in which Morant and Handcock were acquitted. A conspiracy theorist might read something into this but the reason will become apparent. Officially the court cases were promulgated in Army Order 497 of 12 February 1902 [109] though this would have reached a mainly army audience. Although the press was silent on the matter until after the Courts Martial were complete, as the *Clutha Leader* highlighted. The Courts Martial were clearly not conducted in total secrecy as Morant's apologists claim and the evidence for this has been in plain sight since 1907 and before.

The above articles are illuminating in another respect. The cutting off of the defendants from the outside world has been cited as the reason the defendants' families did not seek help from the Australian Government. Clearly Ernest Witton knew his brother was in some trouble but George Witton had assured him it was not serious. This might be interpreted as admirable protection of his loved ones from a distressing situation, were it not for the fact that he wrote the same in his book *Scapegoats* published in 1907, in which he states that they did not realise the seriousness of the situation until they were placed in irons to be transported to Pretoria.

As we have seen, Witton '...expressed the opinion that the worst that could happen to them all would be the loss of their commissions'. [110]

C. S. Jarvis also stated: 'Though under close arrest, he [Morant] had no idea that he would be sentenced to anything more severe than dismissal from the Army, which as a temporary officer was of no importance to him. Close arrest of an officer does not mean that he is locked up in a barred cell, and it would have been the simplest matter for Morant to evade his officer escort and make his escape to Portuguese territory, where he might have remained in safety until the war ended and with it the responsibility for all crimes committed during hostilities.' [111]

Patrick Picton, son of Lieutenant Harry Picton, said in the 1970s 'His [Morant's] friends, and there were many of them, repeatedly offered him horses so that he could escape over the border into Portuguese territory, but neither Morant nor his friends felt that they were in any danger.' [112]

Even Banjo Paterson, quoting J. F. Thomas in an article in 1939, says '...I never believed the execution would be carried out. When I found that the thing was serious I pulled every string I could; got permission to wire to Australia, and asked for the case to be reopened so that I might put in a proper defence.' [113] Clearly this comment needs to be treated with caution being so long after the fact and related by a third person but in the light of Witton's assertions, it cannot be disregarded. Did Thomas feel he had not put in a 'proper defence'?

How then, could the defendants not take the charges seriously if they had been subjected to the kind of brow beating and interrogation at the Court of Inquiry that Witton claims? Witton says Handcock had been pressured and broken to the point that he wrote a confession, which he later retracted. They had, he claimed been kept in solitary confinement for months. If these things were as bad as he claimed, it seems difficult to believe that they did not realise they were in serious trouble.

Witton claims: 'The sentences were decided upon evidence taken at the court of inquiry, at which no one was given an opportunity of making a defence or even of denying the slanderous and lying statements made by prejudiced and unprincipled men.' He contradicts himself, having previously stated 'I proved even to the satisfaction of this court [the Court of Inquiry] that I knew nothing of this case [the Heese case], and the charge was immediately withdrawn.' [114]

Regarding Lieut. Picton, a witness to the court cases stated 'At the court of inquiry he was accused of having drawn a revolver, and put a bullet through one Boer [Visser], who was lying on the ground with seven other bullets in his body, but he swore that he fired into the earth; and this statement was accepted by the court. He was subsequently freed from all blame.' [115] Since Picton was only cashiered, this looks to be true. So Witton's claims about the harshness of the Court of Inquiry needs to be treated with considerable caution.

One should also ask why Witton attacks the Court of Inquiry with such venom whilst remaining silent on the actual Courts Martial. After all, the Court of Inquiry had no judicial power. Witton quotes *The Times*' 17 April account of the evidence given in court largely verbatim, adding certain depositions made by the defendants and some quotes presumably from memory. He must therefore have considered that *The Times*' account was accurate, at least as far as it went. Was it because the Courts Martial had been held in public that he felt he could not refute newspaper account? The Court of Inquiry was held in camera and a record of the evidence presented doesn't survive, offering much less chance of his own account being refuted. Lt Col Caligari:

> The questionable activities of the court of inquiry to intimidate, exhaust and entrap the accused differ markedly from the attitude of the courts-martial. Many of the members of the courts-martial were stationed in Pietersburg and would have been friendly with the accused in better times. The members appear sympathetic with, and at times supportive, of the accused. The leeway given to the defence frustrated the prosecution and the Judge Advocate of the court on a number of occasions. The Not Guilty verdict in the Heese case prompted two members of the court-martial to send champagne to the accused! [116]

If the Courts Martial, which allegedly differed so markedly from the Court of Inquiry, found the Officers guilty, then could the Court of inquiry have been so wide of the mark, given that its role was mainly to determine whether there was a case to answer? Witton and Morant's apologists have another reason for attacking the Court of Inquiry, which will be addressed later.

In viewing the whole Morant case, one must consider certain aspects of contemporary Military Law. The 'Red Book' Chapter 3, Section 10 defines a lawful command.

> 'Lawful command' means not only a command which is not contrary to the ordinary civil law, but one which is justified by military law; in other words, a lawful military command, whether to do or not to do, or to desist from doing, a particular act. A superior officer has a right at any time to give a command, for the purpose of the maintenance of good order, or the suppression of a disturbance, or the execution of any military duty or

> regulation, or for any purpose connected with the amusements and welfare of a regiment or other generally accepted details of military life. But a superior officer has no right to take advantage of his military rank to give a command which does not relate to military duty or usages, or which has for its sole object the attainment of some private end. Such a command, though it may not be unlawful, is not such a lawful command as will make disobedience to it criminal. In any case of doubt, the military knowledge and experience of officers will enable them to decide on the lawfulness or otherwise of the command.
>
> Duty of Obedience 11. If the command were obviously illegal, the inferior would be justified in questioning, or even in refusing to execute it, as, for instance, if he were ordered to fire on a peaceable and unoffending bystander. But so long as the orders of the superior are not obviously and decidedly in opposition to the law of the land, or to the well-known and established customs of the army, so long must they meet prompt, immediate, and unhesitating obedience. [117]

Just following orders was clearly not, even in 1901 or a long time before that, a defence in the eyes of the law. The issue of whether orders existed not to take prisoners, which will be discussed later, should always be viewed in this light. Even proof that orders were given, if it were found, would not be the Holy Grail that Morant's supporters proclaim it to be. It may be a mitigating circumstance, in sentencing, it would certainly suggest guilt on the part of the issuing authority, but it would not confer innocence on Morant, Handcock and the others.

The Manual of Military Law states in Ch VI 14:

> Where it is proved that an unlawful act has been committed, a criminal intention is presumed, and the proof of justification or excuse lies on the prisoner. On the charge of murder the law presumes malice from the fact of the killing, and throws on the prisoner the burden of disproving the malice by justifying or extenuating the act. [118]

The prisoners did not dispute the fact of the killings and there can be no denying that they took place; therefore the burden of proving justification, that it was not murder, was on them. In this light, was Morant's behavior in court really a 'plucky defence'? His supercilious behavior in court may have seemed like a plucky defence to a naïve young subaltern but may well appear as plain stupid to others.

In fact it appears that the hot-headed Morant may have disregarded his best defence, since Lieutenant Hannam stated: 'You may imagine how much

Morant was thought to have changed when his counsel at Pretoria wished him to plead insanity for his defense'. [119] It was a defence he did not make, as far as we know. The legal system has almost always and everywhere recognised insanity as a legitimate mitigation. Lieutenant Murchison who murdered a Special War Correspondent in November 1899 has been used by the pardon lobby as an example of a defendant being released on the grounds of 'Condonation'. In fact, his death sentence was first commuted to penal servitude and he was later committed to Broadmoor Lunatic Asylum where he died in 1917. [120]

Much has been written about the lack of official transcripts of the court proceedings. There is nothing suspicious about this, as has been claimed, since, as mentioned earlier, only one record of court martial proceedings survives from the period 1850 to 1914. The best available evidence of the court proceedings is the report from *The Times* of 17 April 1902. This has been reproduced below, interspersed with the additional words of Lieutenant Witton as indicated in italic, much of this Thomas' defence and the prosecutor's reply. Witton quoted some of the *Times*' report verbatim.

The first case to be tried was the murder of Floris Visser.

> Court-martial held at Pietersburg, Transvaal, on the 16th day of January, 1902, by order of Lord Kitchener of Khartoum, commanding the forces of South Africa. The court was constituted as follows:- The president was Lieutenant-Colonel Denny, 2nd Northampton Regiment. The members were Brevet-Major J. Little, same regiment; Brevet-Major Thomas and Major Ousely, of the Royal Field Artillery; Captain Brown, of the 2nd Wiltshire Regiment; Captain Marshall, 1st Gordon Highlanders; Captain Nicholson, 1st Cameron Highlanders. Waiting members: Captain Matcham, 2nd Wiltshire Regiment; Captain Jobson, Royal Garrison Artillery. Major C. S. Copeland, 2nd Northampton Regiment, acted as Judge Advocate; Captain Burns-Begg as Crown Prosecutor. Major Thomas, New South Wales Mounted Rifles, was counsel for prisoners.
>
> The prisoners were charged with the murder of a wounded Boer prisoner named Visser. They pleaded 'Not Guilty' and were defended by Major Thomas, New South Wales Mounted Rifles.
>
> *After the preliminary proceedings of the court and the swearing of the members, an adjournment was made until the following morning to enable a telegram to be sent to headquarters asking authority for Major Thomas to undertake our defence.*
>
> *The necessary authority being obtained, the court assembled the following morning, and the first charge, that of murdering a prisoner*

named Visser, was proceeded with. On the plea of 'Not Guilty', witnesses for the prosecution were called. These described the fight at Duival's Kloof, and how Captain Hunt was killed, and the state of his body when found, and also gave particulars as to the capture of Visser, who was wearing a portion of Captain Hunt's clothing.

The prosecution called Sergeant S. Robertson, who stated that he remembered the fight at Devil's Kloof, when Captain Hunt and Sergeant Hunt [sic] were killed. Captain Hunt's body was found to have been stripped. He took the bodies back to Reuter's farm, where the party was reinforced by Lieutenants Morant, Hancock, Picton, and Wilton [sic]. Next morning they went in pursuit of the Boers, overtook them, and captured their laager, finding one wounded Boer there. Next day the Boer accompanied the force some distance. During the dinner hour the accused held a conversation in which the Boer prisoner, who was in a Cape cart six yards away, appeared to take no part. Morant and an Intelligence officer named Lady-bore went to Visser (the Boer prisoner) telling him that they were sorry, but he had been found guilty of being in possession of the late Captain Hunt's clothing, and also of wearing khaki. The witness did not catch what further was said, but was told to warn two men for duty. He refused, asking Picton by whose orders this man was to be shot. Lieutenant Picton replied that the orders were by Lord Kitchener, naming a certain date and were to the effect that all Boers wearing khaki from that date were to be shot. The witness said he had never seen any such orders, which should have been posted or read regimentally.

Cross-examined, he said that Captain Hunt's body bore marks of ill-treatment. The prisoner had a kind of khaki jacket on. Captain Hunt had previously told the witness that he had direct orders that no prisoners were to be taken. On one occasion Captain Hunt abused him for bringing in three prisoners against orders. The outrage on the train when Best was killed had embittered the men very much. Morant had previously been considerate to prisoners. He was in charge of the firing party that executed Visser. Trooper Botha corroborated the previous witness, and said he was one of the firing party who carried out the sentence on Visser, who was carried down to a river and shot. The witness had previously lived with Visser on the same farm. He objected to forming one of the firing party. Corporal Sharp gave corroborative evidence, and said that after the firing party had fired Picton discharged his revolver apparently at the dead man's head. L. Ledeboer deposed that on 10 August last year he translated the sentence of a Court-martial that condemned Visser to be shot. Morant, Picton, Hancock, and Wilton formed the Court-martial.

The prisoners elected to give evidence on their own behalf. Morant stated that he was under Captain Hunt with the force charged with clearing the northern district of Boers. It was regular guerrilla warfare.

Captain Hunt acted on orders he got in Pretoria, which were in effect to clear Spelonken and take no prisoners. Captain Hunt had told him that Colonel Hamilton, military secretary, had given him the orders at Lord Kitchener's private house where he had gone with a pair of polo ponies, just prior to his departure for Spelonken. All the detachment knew of the order given by Captain Hunt not to bring in prisoners.

On one occasion he brought in 30 prisoners, when Captain Hunt reprimanded him for bringing them in at all, and told him not to do it again. The witness took command after Captain Hunt was killed and went with reinforcements. When he learnt the circumstances of Captain Hunt's death, and the way he had been maltreated, he followed the Boers and attacked their laager. The Boers cleared, leaving Visser, who had on a soldier's shirt, and was using Captain Hunt's trousers as a pillow. He was court-martialled and shot on this account. The others knew of Captain Hunt's orders. Morant told them he had previously disregarded them, but after the way the Boers had treated Captain Hunt, he would carry out the orders which he regarded as lawful.

After the death of Captain Hunt he took command and went out with reinforcements, and when he learned the circumstances of his death, and how he had been maltreated, he told the others that he had previously disregarded the orders of Captain Hunt, but in future he would carry them out, as he considered they were lawful. The orders had only been transmitted verbally by Captain Hunt, and he had quoted the actions of Kitchener's Horse and Strathcona's Horse as precedents; he never questioned the validity of the orders, he was certain they were correct. He had shot no prisoner before Visser, and the facts in Visser's case had been reported to Captain Taylor, also to Major Lenehan and Colonel Hall.

Cross examined, the prisoner said that Captain Hunt's orders were to clear Spelonken and take no prisoners. He had never seen these orders in writing. Captain Hunt quoted the action of Kitchener's and Strathcona's Horse as precedents. The prisoner had not previously carried out the orders because his captures were 'a good lot'. He had shot no prisoners prior to Visser. No witnesses were called, as they were all eye-witnesses. Picton raised an objection to Visser being shot, on the ground that he should have been shot the night before. Captain Hunt told the witness not to take prisoners. He never questioned their validity. The prisoner was asked whether he knew who gave the orders, but the Judge-Advocate protested against the question, and was upheld by the Court after consultation.

On the resumption of the trial next day, however, the Court allowed the question, and the prisoner Morant stated that Colonel Hamilton, Military Secretary, was the one who had given Captain Hunt the orders that no prisoners were to be taken. Others, including Hancock, received these orders from Captain Hunt. The Court-martial was reported to Colonel Hall within a fortnight after it was held. A report was also sent to Captain Taylor. The prisoner had only Captain Hunt's word for it that Colonel Hamilton had given those orders. He had made no attempt to get his report of the Court-martial as evidence.

'Was your court at the trial of Visser constituted like this?' asked the President, 'and did you observe paragraph — of — section of the King's Regulations?' 'Was it like this!' fiercely answered Morant. 'No; it was not quite so handsome. As to rules and sections, we had no Red Book, and knew nothing about them. We were out fighting the Boers, not sitting comfortably behind barb-wire entanglements; we got them and shot them under Rule 303.'

Morant made a plucky defence; he openly admitted the charges, and took all responsibility upon himself, pleading custom of the war and orders from headquarters. He did not express any regret, or have any fear as to what his fate might be. Driven almost to desperation, and smarting under the recent unjust acts of the court of inquiry, he, in his usual hot-headed manner, made disclosures which he believed would in all probability 'stagger humanity'. He vowed that he would have Lord Kitchener put into the box and cross-examined as to the orders given to officers, and his methods of conducting the war. The folly of all this was apparent to everyone, as Lord Kitchener held Morant's life in his hands; but Morant would not be restrained, and was prepared to suffer.

Picton, another of the accused, deposed that he had previously done two years' service in this war, and gained a D.C.M. under Le Gallais. *He had commanded the firing party that had shot Visser, and had carried out the execution in obedience to Morant's orders. He had reported the matter to Major Lenehan and Colonel Hall. He also had received orders from Captain Hunt not to take prisoners.* After the capture of Visser, Morant said he was perfectly justified in shooting him. The prisoner said it would be hard lines to shoot him, and asked Morant to call the other officers together. A meeting was held, and it was decided to shoot Visser. Picton corroborated the statement that he also had received orders from Captain Hunt not to take prisoners. He never questioned the orders, and had been reprimanded by Hunt for bringing in prisoners.

Captain Hunt was very bitter about the death of a friend of his, a lieutenant in the Gordon Highlanders, who had been killed in a train

> wrecked by Boers. The prisoner reported the execution of Visser to Major Lenehan verbally immediately after, and then to Colonel Hall. Morant and Hunt had been old friends, and after Hunt's death Morant was inclined to be more severe to the enemy. He had never previously shot a prisoner or seen one shot: Visser was not informed of the nature of the trial that was taking place. Prisoner opposed the shooting of Visser at the Court-martial. He had never obeyed the orders to take no prisoners, because he did not like the idea. He was in command of the firing party, and merely obeyed orders. On the whole Visser would be aware of the charge against him, as the prisoner had previously told him of the seriousness of his position. Hunt never had any chance to carry out his own orders about taking no prisoners.

The final paragraph states that Picton reported Visser's court martial and execution to Major Lenehan 'verbally' immediately afterwards. We have already seen that this was disputed by Trooper James Christie, who claimed in a letter of August 1902 that the report made to Lenehan and Hall took the form 'I regret to say that the wounded Boer, captured by us, died of wounds in the following days.' [121] Christie furthermore stated that 'their reports to headquarters classified all these murders as engagements'.

Frank Renar [122] and Bill Woolmore [123] both reproduce Morant's letter to Lenehan of 17 August 1901, which suggests they had not seen each other in some time and in which he conspicuously makes no mention of events. Frank Renar suggests this silence in relation to the killing implies Morant was fully aware of the darkness of the deed. Returning to the Courts Martial:

> Major Neatson, staff officer to Colonel Hall, Officer Commanding Lines of Communications, deposed that he had received certain reports from Captain Taylor with regard to engagements with Boers, but remembered nothing about a summary of a Court-martial. P. J. Hancock, another of the prisoners, deposed that he had attended the trial of Visser at Morant's request. He corroborated the previous evidence as to the reasons for executing Visser and the orders not to take prisoners. Prisoner Witton gave corroborative evidence, and said he was present at a conversation with a Mr. Reuter, from which he gathered that Hunt had been murdered. Reuter said Hunt's neck was broken, and his eyes gouged out. The prisoner was guided by his superior officers in regard to the finding of the Court-martial. He believed Visser knew that he was being tried, but he was given no opportunity to speak or make a defence.
>
> *Lieutenant Handcock corroborated previous evidence as to the reasons for executing Visser, and also as to the orders not to take prisoners.*

> *I also supported the evidence as to the information received from the Rev. F. L. Reuter about the maltreatment of Captain Hunt.*
>
> F. L. Reuter, missionary in charge of the German Berlin Mission station, deposed that Captain Hunt's and Sergeant Eland's bodies were brought to his place. Hunt's body was much mutilated. The neck appeared to have been broken, and the face bore marks of boot nails. *The body had been stripped, and the legs gashed.*

Captain Hunt's body had of course already been buried by the time Witton arrived on the scene.

> Civil Surgeon Dr Johnson testified that he had heard Hunt reprimand Morant for bringing in prisoners. He was of opinion from the evidence that the injuries to Hunt's body were caused before death. Captain Taylor stated that he had received a message from the Boers through natives that if he were caught he would be given four days to die, which meant torture, because he had previously been hunting in the country. The Boers in that part of the country were more outlaws than part of a legal commando. He had heard Hunt reprimand Morant for bringing in prisoners. Morant had always behaved well to the Boers. He had transmitted a report of the expedition in which Hunt was killed, but did not know what was in it. Field Cornet Tom Kelly sent him a message saying that the first Englishman who came near his wagon would be shot.
>
> Major Lenehan, in command of the Bushveldt Carbineers, was next called. He said he had no direct control over the corps, which acted under headquarters at Pretoria. Captain Hunt took over the command from Robertson and got orders from the officer commanding the line of communication. From his knowledge of Morant be thought him incapable of murder or inciting thereto. Picton reported the shooting of Visser, and the witness reported it to Colonel Hall. He knew nothing of any order not to take prisoners. Major Bolton denied any knowledge of a proclamation that Boers taken in khaki were to be shot. Major Lenehan had never heard of orders that no prisoners were to be taken the evidence of Colonel Hamilton, taken in Pretoria, emphatically denied the issue of any order that no Prisoners were to be taken.

In his version, Witton omits this paragraph in which his co accused, Major Lenehan, states he knew of no orders that no prisoners should be taken. [124]

> *Next day [125] the court adjourned to Pretoria to take the evidence of Colonel Hamilton, military secretary to Lord Kitchener. My escort*

(or 'tug-boat,' as these individuals were termed in nautical phraseology by Lieutenant Morant) was a newly commissioned lieutenant in the Pietersburg Light Horse.

The fact that the whole Court Martial moved from Pietersburg to Pretoria in order to hear the evidence of Colonel Hamilton and then moved back again undermines the notion that the Courts were rushed and perfunctory affairs.

Fully armed and equipped, we proceeded by rail to Pretoria. Quarters were provided for all the prisoners at the Mounted Infantry Depot, about a mile from the town. The following day the court, which was constituted as at Pietersburg, assembled at the Artillery Barracks to take the evidence of Colonel Hamilton; all the prisoners were present, and when this officer appeared every eye was upon him. He was stern and hard-featured, and looked just then very gaunt and hollow-eyed, as though a whole world of care rested on his shoulders. He was apparently far more anxious than those whose fate depended on the evidence he was to give. The following is his evidence:

Examined by the Court:- Lieut. Morant, in his evidence, states that the late Capt. Hunt told him that he had received orders from you that no prisoners were to be taken alive. Is this true?

Ans.: Absolutely untrue.

Examined by Counsel for Prisoners:-

Do you remember Captain Hunt taking two polo ponies early in July last up to Lord Kitchener's quarters; at which time you came in, and had a conversation with Capt. Hunt?

Ans.: No. I have no recollection whatever. I have never spoken to Capt. Hunt with reference to his duties in the Northern Transvaal.

The Counsel for the Prisoners then made the following address:- As regards the evidence of Colonel Hamilton, just called, I wish to state that the defence do not regard his evidence, one way or the other, as having any real bearing on the defence; in fact, I submit to the court that it is really illegal evidence. It really amounts to this: a certain conversation is stated to have taken place between Colonel Hamilton and the deceased, Capt. Hunt, which conversation was mentioned by Capt. Hunt to Lieut. Morant, apparently in a confidential or private way. This, having been obtained by the court from the prisoner Morant, is then sought to be contradicted by the evidence of Colonel Hamilton, which, I submit, is quite contrary to the laws of evidence. It really does not matter much, from the point of view of the defence, where Capt. Hunt got his instructions. The fact is clear from the evidence that Capt. Hunt did tell his subordinates, not once, but many times, that prisoners were not to be taken. This fact is admitted by witnesses for the prosecution. The chief value of these instructions, as given by Capt. Hunt, is that they go to show that he, being a man of some standing, and a personal friend of Lieut. Morant, they were entitled to weight, and go to remove any question of malicious intent.

It is difficult to see how Thomas could argue the absence of malicious intent when Morant himself stated that he had acted in a spirit of revenge.

Now, the four prisoners are jointly charged with the crime of murder—not as principals, but as accessories before the fact. The principals, or actual perpetrators of the alleged murders, are four troopers named Silke, Thomson, Botha, and Honey, according to the indictment. As a matter of fact, the evidence for the prosecution shows that there were ten, and that they formed a firing party, which under orders shot Visser, the man alleged to be murdered. It is charged that the prisoners committed this offence, by wilfully, feloniously, and with malice aforethought, inciting, instigating, and commanding these four persons to kill and murder one Visser, and that the persons mentioned accordingly did kill and murder him. This should be borne clearly in mind all through the case, that these prisoners did not actually commit the murder, nor are they charged with such, but with instigating others to do it. Now, under the law, it is clear that he who instigates or procures another to commit a felony is himself liable to the same punishment as the actual felon. But persons charged with being accessories to the crime cannot be convicted as such unless the guilt of the principals be first established. Nobody can be an accessory to a crime which is not proven. Under the old Common Law of England it was absolutely necessary that before an accessory could be found guilty there should be an actual verdict of guilty against the principal, so that if the principal managed to evade justice the accessory escaped also. But under existing English law, I believe the accessory may now be tried and convicted, although the principal is not before the court, and has not been convicted but, I take it, it would be only in very special circumstances that this would be done, where it is absolutely impossible to obtain the principal, in order to bring him to justice. It seems proper that if we suppose one man instigates another to murder a third, and the murder takes place, and the actual murderer flies the country before trial, if the fact of the murder is clear and beyond all doubt, the accessory should not escape. But in this case all the alleged principals are easily obtainable, yet we find that not one of them is before the court, except that inferentially it is averred in the charge-sheet that they actually murdered Visser. If that is so, and they are murderers, why are not these four actual perpetrators charged before the court? However, be that as it may, this must be very clear to the court, that this court cannot convict the four prisoners of inciting, instigating, or commanding the four troopers to commit the murder, which murder it is alleged these four troopers actually committed, unless they are satisfied that the troopers are malicious and felonious murderers. The court must, therefore, I submit, clearly in its mind say these four troopers are murderers, who may now or at some future time be brought before a court of justice and tried for their lives as murderers. That is the extraordinary position in which the court finds itself, because these four troopers have merely been inferentially set down as murderers. They must be convinced on these two points:-

(1) That they are murderers.

(2) That the prisoners now before the court incited them to commit that murder.

If the court is not satisfied that they are men who should suffer death, the charge against the prisoners, as accessories, must fall to the ground.

Now, has the prosecution attempted to show that the murder was committed by these troopers? I submit the contrary. Two were brought as witnesses by the prosecution. They were not even warned to be careful lest they should incriminate themselves, and, really, I submit to the court that the assumption that these troopers are murderers is simply monstrous, and cannot by any possible means be substantiated. Clearly, they only obeyed the orders of a superior officer, and formed a firing party for the execution of Visser after their officers had held a summary court-martial and convicted him. There is not the slightest evidence that these troopers were in any way a party to the shooting of Visser, except that they obeyed their orders as soldiers. They are, therefore, not murderers. How can they be called such? If they are not murderers, there can be no accessories to the alleged crime. Even if the court-martial was improperly constructed, its proceedings informal, or its decision illegal, how could these four troopers, against none of whom there is any suggestion of crime, be regarded as murderers, simply because they fired the shots which killed Visser. The guilt of the four prisoners depends entirely upon the guilt of the four troopers. The troopers have been stigmatised as murderers, so as to found the charge against the four prisoners. If it was desired by the prosecution to shift home a malicious and unwarrantable act, resulting in the death of this man, it seems to me that the four prisoners should be charged with conspiring together to bring about the death of Visser by unlawful means. It should have been made a conspiracy amongst themselves, and the troopers should have been left out of it. Instead of which these men are called murderers.

Thomas' argument here is a typical lawyer's mobius strip, with nothing to latch onto. The troopers who shot Visser were not guilty of murder because they had been ordered to do so. Therefore because they were not guilty of murder, the officers could not be guilty of being *accessories* to murder – though those officers had given the orders. Even a country solicitor must have been able to see the ludicrous nature of this argument! The prosecutor certainly did, as expressed in his response. Thomas continued:

> *Suppose these four troopers were now on trial and said they simply obeyed their orders, the court could not have convicted them, and I say that the charge, if any, against the prisoners should be a conspiracy amongst themselves to do an illegal act. Yet another difficulty arises when we come to deal with the prisoners individually. Lieutenant Morant, no doubt, is primarily responsible, being senior officer at the time when the trial took place, and the court has to be satisfied in his case, as in that of the others, that he deliberately and feloniously ordered the men to commit murder. There is no doubt that Captain Hunt did give certain very definite orders to Lieutenant Morant, and on his death Mr. Morant took over command. There is no doubt that his conduct was largely influenced by the treatment of the body of his friend, showing circumstances of barbarity, even if the injuries inflicted upon Captain Hunt, as clearly shown by Mr. Reuter's testimony, were done after death, although the medical evidence goes to show they were committed before death. There is no doubt that this did prompt him with the spirit of retaliation against the Boers who had done this thing. In war retaliation is justifiable, revenge is justifiable. Rules applicable in times of peace are quite inapplicable in times of war. In the Manual of Military Law it is stated, 'Retaliation is military vengeance;' it takes place when an outrage committed on one side is avenged by a similar act on the other. I am free to admit that this maltreatment of his friend did exercise an influence over him when he came to deal with this man Visser, and it is natural he should be so influenced. He pursues these Boers, which ends in the capture of Visser, whom he finds wearing clothing the property of the late Captain Hunt. I go so far as saying that under the circumstances Mr. Morant would have been perfectly justified in shooting Visser straight away. The fact of wearing British uniform is altogether against the customs of war, and I know that this man Visser was present when Captain Hunt was killed from the evidence. At the request apparently, of Mr. Picton, it was decided to give Visser a court-martial – such a court-martial as is frequently held in the field, under the circumstances in which this was held. Informal, no doubt; how can we expect formality in the field, in the*

> *immediate vicinity of the enemy, and when Visser himself admitted that the Boers had promised to recapture him? All this is provided for in the Manual of Military Law. We claim that substantial justice was done, and I submit that there is nothing whatever to satisfy the court that Mr. Morant ordered a wilful or felonious murder. On the contrary, under the Rules of War, I consider that he was quite justified in confirming the sentence. The evidence of Captain Taylor shows that these men were the offshoots of commandoes and mere outlaws, who went about looting from Kaffirs, and, what I say now I wish to apply to all the prisoners. They were dealing in that particular district with a party of irresponsible outlaws, under no recognised control, sending in threats of torture, &c. In July, 1901, trains were wickedly wrecked, and numbers of men wounded. Such men forfeit all rights to be treated as prisoners of war. When irregulars are sent out to deal with an enemy of this kind, marauders and train wreckers, the officers should be allowed a wide discretion in dealing with them. If they err technically, or even make serious mistakes, they must be upheld. We cannot afford, in dealing with people of this description, to go into nice points of sentiment. I submit the irregular troops, sent out to deal with the people in this particular district, were entitled to deal with them as outlaws. I do not ask for proclamations to say we must do these sort of things, but we must take it for granted that we must do so. Departures from the usual customs of war have, in many instances, been visited by the troops by methods which they merit. No one denies that chivalric actions have been done by the Boers, but I say also that there are districts where that sort of thing does not occur at all, and notably in the particular district in which Visser was caught.*

Notwithstanding the extremely questionable notions that certain kinds of enemy should not be entitled to be treated as prisoners of war, or that irregulars should not be subject to military law, this argument flies in the face of Morant's statement that he had not shot prisoners previous to Hunt's death because they were a 'good lot'. Were they not captured in the same district under similar circumstances? What had changed other than the death of Capt. Hunt?

> *If the prisoners have been mistaken in their views as to what they were entitled to do, then it must be assumed that they erred in judgment; they may be even open to censure, but not charged with committing murder.*
>
> *I claim from this court that the prisoners shall not be stigmatised as inciters to murder, because, acting on a responsibility which was naturally their own, they did carry out what I submit is only martial judgment.*

Lieutenant Picton undoubtedly gave the order to fire to the firing party, and in doing so simply obeyed his orders. Witton and Handcock simply, on being summoned to the court-martial, coincided with the views of their superior officer; further than this they took no place in the proceedings. They cannot be charged with inciting and instigating, even if they concurred in the verdict; the verdict was of no effect until confirmed by Mr. Morant.

I submit to the court that this charge is improperly made, or, if it is ostensibly correctly made, then it must fall to the ground, for the simple reason that this court cannot, I submit, say that the crime of murder against the troopers is proved to the court's satisfaction, and if that is not proved, then nobody can be found guilty of being accessory.

The prosecutor in his response expressed surprise if not incredulity at Thomas' arguments to the point that he spends a significant portion of his response answering what he thought Thomas' defence should have been, rather than what it was.

The Prosecutor replies:-
The defence has made a good deal of the fact that the court must hold the four troopers guilty of murder before they can hold the four prisoners now before them guilty of accessories. That is perfect nonsense. The Manual of Military Law says that where a person has been guilty of killing another the law presumes the killer to be guilty of murder (page 125), and on that the court must necessarily rest content, in so far as the guilt or innocence of the troopers is concerned. This is borne out by the statute law of England, which enables an accessory to be tried before, after, or with a principal felon, irrespective of the guilt or innocence of the latter.

The defence also raises the question, on the indictment, whether or not I have succeeded in proving that the prisoners each and all incited and commanded the troopers under their command to kill Visser. As regards that, I have no doubt the Judge Advocate will direct you that where a common criminal intent is proved to be shared by several persons, any criminal action by any one of these persons in furtherance of that criminal intent, may be visited on any one of them, and could any clearer proof of common intent be submitted than the prisoners' own description of what took place at the so-called court-martial. I thought that the prisoners would rely mainly on the alleged orders of Captain Hunt, and on this so-called court-martial for their defence. To the first contention I would point out, a complete answer is returned by the Manual of Military Law, which says that an officer is responsible for the carrying out of even lawful commands which result in injury, and is a fortiori responsible for the carrying out of obviously illegal and improper commands from superiors. As regards the so-called court-martial, the court cannot hold that it was a court-martial in any sense of the word. It was anything that the court pleases except a tribunal, martial or otherwise. It was a consultation, a conspiracy, a measure to mature a criminal purpose, but it was not a court. And even if it were, and even if the court were fully and properly constituted, still, according to the Manual of Military Law, the members of such court would be liable to be hanged if they had illegally carried out a sentence of death.

But these defences have really hardly been urged by the defence at all seriously. Counsel for the defence appears to rely mainly on the technical objection to the indictment raised first of all, on the nature of the warfare waged against the Bushveldt Carbineers, and on the fact that Visser was shot in retaliation for Captain Hunt's death. Now, the latter point is the strongest possible point in the case for the prosecution. It proves conclusively the malice of the prisoners. Captain Hunt, so far as they knew and had reason to suppose, was killed in fair fight, and there was even then nothing whatever to connect Visser with his death, and yet every one of the prisoners, as well as the counsel for the defence, admits that the real reason for shooting Visser was because Hunt had been killed. Could proof of malice conceivably be clearer?

Counsel for the defence urges that retaliation is recognised as legitimate by the Manual of Military Law. That is a mere twisting of words, and I think it is hardly necessary for me to urge on a body of military men the danger of acknowledging the right of subaltern officers to avenge their private grievances on prisoners of war who happen to fall into their hands. Retaliation has a perfectly definite meaning in military law, and means the deliberate and authoritative taking of measures of reprisal, as answer to some action on the part of the enemy contrary to the customs of war, but it certainly does not mean that subordinate officers are entitled to shoot prisoners who fall into their hands because an officer of their regiment has been killed. There is not a grain of evidence to connect Visser with Hunt's death, nor to show that Hunt was not killed in fair fight. As to Major Thomas' (counsel for defence) argument, based on the state of the country, could anything be more preposterous than to say that minor officers are entitled to make war on principles of barbarity approved only by themselves? If they do so they must abide by the consequences.

The Judge Advocate summed up as follows:- With reference to this case, it would appear that the prisoners considered that they had justification (in virtue of their instructions from the late Captain Hunt regarding the treatment of Boer prisoners of war) for the course they adopted, also that they acted under provocation and in ignorance.

The general rule is that a person is responsible for the natural consequences of his own acts. If several persons meet with a common intent to execute some criminal purpose, each is responsible for every offence committed by any one of them in furtherance of that purpose.

A person is in all cases fully responsible for any offence which is committed by another by his instigation, even though the offence may be committed in a different way from the one suggested. The fact that the blame is shared by another will not relieve a person contributing to the death from responsibility.

If a person has unlawfully caused death by conduct which was intended to cause death or grievous bodily harm to some person, whatever the intention of the offender may have been, he is guilty of murder. It may be taken generally that in all cases where a killing cannot be justified or excused, if it does not amount to murder it is manslaughter, and a person charged with murder can be convicted of manslaughter. Again, the offence is manslaughter if the act from which death results was committed under the influence of passion arising from extreme provocation; but it must be clearly established, in all cases where provocation is put forward as an excuse, that at the time when the crime was committed the offender was actually so completely under the influence of passion arising from the provocation that he was at that moment deprived of the power of self-control, and with this view it will be necessary to consider carefully the manner in which the crime was committed, the length of the interval between the provocation and the killing, the conduct of the offender during the interval, and all other circumstances tending to show his state of mind.

Ignorance of law is no defence to a criminal charge, but such ignorance may be properly taken into consideration in determining the amount of punishment to be awarded.

The essence of the crime of murder is malicious intent. I would point out that the prisoners did not carry out the order they allege to have received re the shooting of Boers in khaki until after the death of Captain Hunt, which they admit biassed their minds.

The right of killing an armed man exists only so long as he resists; as soon as he submits he is entitled to be treated as a prisoner of war.

As regards the treatment of an enemy caught in the uniform of his opponent, it would have to be shown that he was wearing such uniform at the time with the deliberate intention of deceiving.

Enemies rendered harmless by wounds must not only be spared;but humanity commands that if they fall into the hands of their opponents the care taken of them should be second only to the care taken of the wounded belonging to the captors.

The prisoners, their escorts, and counsel then retired to the corridor while the court consulted upon a verdict; in a little over half an hour we were recalled. Glancing round the court, I noticed one of the members in tears. My attention was arrested, but I did not then attach any significance to it.

On our appearance in court we were requested to state our military service, which was as follows. Statement as to service by Lieutenant H. H. Morant, B.V.C.:-

I have held a commission since 1 April, 1901, in the Bushveldt Carbineers.

Prior to this I was in the South Australian Second Contingent for nine months. I was a sergeant in that corps, and was promoted to a commission out of that corps into the Transvaal Constabulary, but went home to England for six months. I came out again and joined the B.V.C.; since then I have been serving on detachment the whole time. I hand in a letter from the O.C. South Australians.

In March, 1900, I was carrying despatches for the Flying Column to Prieska, under Colonel Lowe, 7th D.G. I was in the general advance to Bloemfontein, and took part in the engagements of 'Karee Siding and Kroonstadt and other engagements with Lord Roberts until the entry into Pretoria. I was at Diamond Hill, and then was attached to General French's staff, Cavalry Brigade, as war correspondent with Bennet Burleigh, for the London 'Daily Telegraph,' and accompanied that column through Belfast and Middleburg to the occupation of Barbeton, when I went home to England.

The letter from the O.C. South Australians read:-

My dear Morant – There seems to be an immediate probability of the S.A. Regiment returning either to Australia or going to England, so I hasten to send you a line wishing you 'Au Revoir.' I desire to wish you most heartily every success in your future career, and to express my entire satisfaction with your conduct while with the South Australians. Your soldierly behaviour and your continual alertness as an irregular carried high commendation – and deservedly – from the whole of the officers of the regiment. I trust that in the future we may have an opportunity of renewing our pleasant acquaintanceship.

Statement by Lieutenant Picton:-

I have been in South Africa two years on service. I hold my commission in the B.V.C. since last May. Previous to that I was attached to the 8th M.I., and served under Colonel Le Gallais. I have received the Distinguished Conduct Medal, and been mentioned in despatches. I have been three times wounded since the outbreak of the war.'

I produce three letters from different commanding officers under whom I have served, and could refer the court to Col Hodgson, commanding 9th Area, Cape Colony.

During the month I was in Spelonken under Capt. Hunt I took 37 prisoners, 50 rifles, 15 waggons, and 500 head of cattle, mules, horses, &c.

Letter (1) from Captain Savil, O.C. Loch's Horse:- Sergeant Picton came out with Loch's Horse as a corporal in February, 1901. He has given entire satisfaction to his officers, and I am very pleased to state I have found him not only very plucky when in action, but steady and painstaking in the execution of his duty.

He has been recommended for the D.S.M. Having been under my personal command for some time, I cannot speak too highly of his good conduct.

Letter (2):- This is to introduce to you Sergeant Picton, of my corps, Loch's Horse. He is a worthy fellow and well connected, and is seeking a commission. Could you help him in getting such, in your regiment? I understand you have some vacancies.

Letter (3) from Lieut.-Colonel Hickee, O.C. 8th M.I.:- I am sending Sergeant Picton, Loch's Horse, for discharge. He has served with the 8th Corps M.I. for the last eleven months, and has been under my command since 9th November, 1900. I am able to say that he has carried out his duties in a most satisfactory manner.

He is a most efficient interpreter and a good man in the field, and was recommended to the C. in C. for his behaviour at Bothaville.

Statement by Lieutenant Handcock, B.V.C.:- I have served about twelve months in the New South Wales Mounted Infantry as a farrier; about two months in the Railway Police, Pretoria; and from the 22nd February last year in the Bushveldt Carbineers as veterinary lieutenant.

Statement by Lieutenant Witton, B.V.C.:- I have held a commission since June last in the B.V.C. I was previously in the 4th Contingent Imperial Bushmen (Victorian) as Q.M.S. for fourteen months. Formerly I was in the Victorian Permanent Artillery about twelve months as a gunner.

I have also served nearly two years in the Victorian Rangers, Volunteer Corps. I received my commission for raising a gun detachment for the B.V.C.

The issue of whether orders to 'take no prisoners' existed has been central to the Morant controversy for over a century. Some are adamant that the order did exist and came from High Command, despite the fact that there is no written evidence for these orders and that thousands of prisoners were taken during the period in question, hundreds by the BVC. Some authors express bewilderment at this obvious paradox whilst maintaining an unshakable belief that the orders did exist. Some simply ignore it.

From the evidence presented at the Courts Martial there seems little doubt that Taylor and probably Captain Hunt had expressed the opinion that taking prisoners should be avoided. In Hunt's case the witnesses quoting him suggest the inability to feed them was a driver. No known murders took place during Hunt's time in command. In any case a distinction needs to be made, one which may seem somewhat academic but has very real implications. Even if there were an order to 'take no prisoners' to 'take no prisoners' is not the same as to take them and then shoot them in cold blood days later. Surrendering is a risky business. A combatant is not obliged to accept a surrender. He may accept it, at which point he becomes responsible for the prisoner and his delivery to a safe place. He may choose not to accept it by maintaining belligerence – with such 'belligerence' proscribed of course: the Convention with Respect to the Laws and Customs of War on Land, part of the later Hague Convention of 1907 but based on the US Lieber Code formulated during the American Civil War, expressly forbids the killing of enemy combatants who have surrendered. He may even, as did Australian Lieutenant Steven Midgely, [126] cease hostilities but not accept the surrender advising the enemy to find someone else to surrender to. It seems clear that at least some of the BVC officers were aware of this distinction. The *Times* account of the Courts Martial tells us that: 'Picton raised an objection to Visser being shot, on the ground that he should have been shot the night before.' [127] Witton by his own admission did not understand this at the time:

> The men were told to go out and meet the waggon in which were the six Boers; they were to make the Boers fight, and on no account were these to be brought in alive; if the white flag was put up the men were to take no notice of it, just fire away until all the Boers were shot. This, I afterwards learned, was the correct interpretation of the orders not to take prisoners… [128]

Some have cited an entry in the diary of Robert Montagu Poore as proof that orders to 'take no prisoners' did exist and that they came from a higher source than Taylor and Hunt. The quote in question is the entry for 7 October 1901:

> At about 6 p.m. Bolton [Wilts Regt] arrived with some papers about some rather bad things which have been taking place north of Pietersburg. The BVC accepted surrender of 8 Boers and after taking them along for several

> days shot them. If they intended doing this they should have not have accepted their surrender in the first instance. A German missionary was close by so to prevent his saying anything they shot him too. I have just given the outline of the case to Lord K but the case is a bad one especially as it's officers who are implicated. [129]

This has been taken by some as confirmation that orders to 'take no prisoners' existed. In fact it confirms nothing other than the normal rules of war outlined above; that a soldier does not have to accept surrender but if he does then he becomes responsible for the prisoner's safety. Those who maintain that this is proof of orders to 'take no prisoners' argue that the order existed and was intended to operate within the normal rules of war, i.e. that those attempting to surrender were to be shot in the attempt, rather than be taken prisoner or taken prisoner and then shot. Consider other quotes from Robert Poore's diary:

> Monday 8 April 1901
> The BVC have done very well indeed, they have captured several prisoners, among whom were some men who have been blowing up the railway line...
> Wednesday 10 April 1901
> The BVC have been doing extremely well, they have been getting more prisoners and Lord K is pleased with them. [130]

Given that these comments are in a private diary, it is unlikely that there is any agenda behind them. They do not chime with any 'take no prisoners' policy on the part of Lord Kitchener, at least that Robert Poore knew about.

We don't have to venture too far from the Courts Martial to find evidence that there were no such orders. Could the court have really been expected to believe the claims of the BVC officers relating to these alleged orders when Lt Picton in his deposition to the court stated: 'During the month I was in Spelonken under Capt. Hunt I took 37 prisoners...' Lt Witton in his book in the chapter entitled 'No Quarter', claimed that Headquarters' perceived lack of reaction to reports of Visser's shooting had '...tended to convince me that the orders and the interpretation of the orders regarding prisoners as transmitted to me by Lieutenant Morant were authentic, and that such proceedings were not only permitted, but were approved of by the headquarters.' Immediately below this he writes, 'Lt Hannam captured a large number of prisoners and sent them in to Fort Edward.' [131]

Whilst the defendants claimed that Captain Hunt had given the orders to take no prisoners, none of the killings took place in the month he was in command. The words used by Captain Hunt when reprimanding Morant were related by a witness as: 'What the hell do you mean by bringing these men in? We have neither room nor rations for them here.' [132] Others claimed that they had overheard Hunt berate Morant for bringing in prisoners and that they should be fed and watered from his own pay. These reprimands sound much more like a local commander with a logistical problem rather than an order from the Commander-in-Chief.

There is a letter relevant to the BVC but produced before the issue had come to a head. The following was written on 5 August 1901, the day before Captain Hunt and Sergeant Elland were killed, but published in the Bendigo *Advertiser on* 14 October:

> LETTER FROM THE FRONT. Private J. D. Pacholi has written to his sister from Pietersburg under date of 5th August. He states:- '...Some of our lads met a number of Boers and encircled them. We had one killed and two severely wounded, but the Boers had to surrender. We captured 41 prisoners, and six of them were shot before they reached the camp. I intend to kill every Boer I get a chance at, for they sent word that they intend to shoot all the Bushveldt Carbineers who fell into their hands. So there will be no surrender now. If there are only 10 of us left we have determined upon fighting to a finish.
>
> 'If we are caught as prisoners death is certain, so we may as well die in arms as submit to treachery or positive murder. I have seen so many of their tricks and blood-thirsty rapacity that instead of fear I only seek revenge, and an opportunity of lessening their number ... This letter was written a long time before it could be posted. With best wishes, and God bless you.' [133]

So 41 were taken, 6 were shot. If there was a decision not to take prisoners, then in this instance it was taken at a much lower level than High Command. The following letter is dated 16 August 1901, ten days after the killing of Captain Hunt, five days after the killing of Floris Visser and before the killing of the 'eight Boers' and Revd Heese. The following account of the taking of prisoners has also been related in Chapter 11, based on the diary of Trooper McInnes:

> From the Front. Trooper R. McInnes of Nook, who is now attached to the Bush-Veldt Carbineers, S.A.F.F., writes from Spelonken, August 16:- 'Just as I finished my last letter we were ordered out after some Boers We went N.E. about some 50 miles and captured the Boers, who had a wagon and

> cart and a lot of cattle. Sending these in with a small escort, the rest of us camped to wait for some more Boers who were on the trek that way, and one morning 20 of us set out and made another haul of seven wagons, with ox and donkey teams, a lot of cattle, rifles, ammunition, and 14 Boers. When these were on their way to the fort, a dozen of us made up our minds to go after a notorious character named Klopper, reported to be a great hunter and crack shot, who had said he would shoot every Englishman who came within a mile of him. He had five wagons and 12 other Boers with him, which made them equal to us, as we were 13. They were camped about 70 miles from the fort. We dropped on them about daylight and surprised them, catching them without firing a shot, and got them safely to the fort. The prisoners have left for Pietersburg, numbering about 43, with 30 wagons and about 800 cattle, most of which were captured by our small party of 15 men! Capt. Hunt, with 15 men and a sergeant, rushed Viljoen's house in the night. It was full of Boers; Captain Hunt and the sergeant were killed as well as Viljoen, another Viljoen, and four other Boers. A stronger party followed the Boers and had a fight, with one wounded on each side. There is some talk of us going to Lydenburg shortly; there are not many Boers in this part now. I do not know where all the mails get to as with the exception of one letter I have not heard from Tassie since January. I have three months to put in with the B.V.C.'s yet. This war seems to be going on for ever; a great many Boers are in the field yet, and seem to be doing well enough; it's good fun, anyway!' [134]

McInnes is proud of 'catching them without firing a shot, and [getting] them safely to the fort'. If there had been an order in place to take no prisoners, would this not have been the perfect opportunity to wipe out a few more Boers? McInnes refers to three separate groups of prisoners being taken and sent to the fort. Are we to believe that the commander of his detachment was reprimanded three times for these alleged acts of disobedience? McInnes tells the same story in his diary but in more detail. This version is given because it was made before the troubles came to a head.

If any legitimate order to take no prisoners existed it is difficult to see how it could be so widely disobeyed. Morant himself had ignored it up to the moment when Captain Hunt, the man who he claimed gave him that order, was killed. He then changed his position and began to shoot prisoners. This was a conscious decision. Lt Hannam took a large number of prisoners and sent them in to Fort Edward after the killing of Floris Visser. [135] Assuming for a moment that this order existed, both men disobeyed it. In such an environment an instruction which can be ignored with impunity is by definition not an order. Two possibilities present themselves: one, the order never existed; or two, the order existed but both they and their superior officer knew it be an illegal order, and therefore unenforceable, in which case they were allowed by The Manual of Military Law to refuse to carry it out. If they followed the 'order' they were knowingly guilty of a crime. It is not suggested that it would be easy to disobey the order of superior officer, even if it were clear to both parties that the order was illegal, but it ought to be easier than committing murder – and a good number of the BVC troopers had the courage to disobey.

The only member of the Bushveldt Carbineers to receive any kind of recognition or award for distinguished service whilst serving in the BVC was Sergeant Charles Forbes, who Lord Kitchener 'Mentioned in Despatches' on 8 August 1901, just as Morant's killing spree was about to start: 'on own initiative, on hearing of presence of Boers, marched 80 miles, surprised and captured the party'. [136] We don't know which officer of the BVC recommended Sergeant Forbes for a 'Mention in Despatches' but rewarding an NCO for taking prisoners on his own initiative once again gives the lie to the idea that orders not to take prisoners came from High Command. Neither was it going to make life easy for any officer trying to convince troopers that these orders existed.

There undoubtedly were cases of Boers being shot whilst surrendering and after they had surrendered but not on the scale of that of the BVC. So it is ironic that the example quoted by Morant of Lord Strathcona's Horse appears to be bogus. The story was doing the rounds in the Army rumour mill that near Twyfelaar on the Komati River in the Eastern Transvaal on 15 August 1900, 'The cavalry [the South African Light Horse] encountered a force of enemy on the south bank of the Komati River, being fired upon from a house flying a white flag. Burnt the place and proceeding crossed the river and bivouacked on the N. bank at Twyfelaar.' [137]

The Strathconas then, according to the rumour, hanged six Boers in retribution. Brian Reid, author of *Our Little Army in the Field: The Canadians in South Africa, 1899–1902* researched this episode. In fact there was no record of any Boer casualties in this area at the time. Some of the BVC troopers didn't believe it. James Christie referred to the 'old chestnut about Strathcona's Horse hanging five or six Boers ... I told him I did not believe a word of it and that I was for no such duty'. [138]

Trooper Frank T. Hall wrote from Teatree Gully, South Australia, after the war:

> What I would refer to as of the greatest importance is the fact that we were fed up with false proclamations from Lord Kitchener to the effect that no quarter whatever was to be shown captives after such and

such a date, and this even previous to the death of Capt. Hunt. I am surprised that Mr Lenehan has made no reference to this. These bogus proclamations were accepted by the men in various spirit. By the very green with absolute credulity; by the older hands with hard contempt; while others, still seeing the required daring on the one hand, and the inhumanity on the other, had no opinion, and were consequently the most miserable. [139]

The Lenehan case has understandably received less attention than the others as the charges were ostensibly considerably less serious. Australian press reports from 1904, when Major Lenehan was attempting to claim recompense from the British government for his harsh treatment, said the charge was purely 'technical'. [140] It should be borne in mind that Lenehan had 'come down to Spelonken expressly to make enquiries concerning rumours of the shooting of prisoners, and statements were taken' and on the day of his arrival (7 September, 1901) [141] a Boer man and two boys had been shot, probably within his earshot. He was charged with failing to report this fact to his senior officer. Perhaps during the normal operation of his unit, failing to report an incident may be considered purely 'technical' but when he was specifically sent to investigate such incidents, it was in essence a charge of attempting to pervert the course of justice, a cover-up. In only charging Lenehan with 'Culpable neglect' Kitchener was letting him off the hook. Kitchener may have had his own reasons for not wanting Lenehan charged with covering up war crimes.

The Lenehan case was conducted between 21 and 24 January 1902. The *Times*' account and in italic, Witton's:

Major Lenehan. The charge against him was that, being on active service, he culpably neglected his duty by failing to report the shooting by men of his regiment, the Bushveldt Carbineers, of one man and two boys, these being prisoners and unarmed. The prisoner pleaded 'Not Guilty.'

Trooper Botha deposed that three Boers were being brought in by Captain Taylor's Police, and were shot at close quarters by fire of his own corps. He reported what had been done to Morant in [the] presence of Lenehan. Trooper Bonny testified to hearing the last witness make his report to Morant. In his defence the accused denied having heard any such report made to Morant.

Although *The Times* uses the term 'report' in the paragraph above this actually refers to a conversation in the mess when Morant called Botha into the conversation to demonstrate his loyalty. Botha had no need to report what had been done to the van Stadens to Morant, as Morant was present when they were murdered:

The main evidence in this case was given by Trooper Botha, a Dutchman, who had been Lieutenant Morant's favourite servant, though he was proved to have been at heart a traitor, for as soon as Morant got into trouble he immediately turned round and did him every harm in his power. There are men who could testify to hearing Botha ask Morant's permission to shoot Visser; he was allowed as a volunteer to form one of the firing party that did shoot him, yet at the court-martial he stated in evidence that he had objected to forming one of the firing party, which was absolutely untrue.

Some time after the conclusion of the trials Trooper Botha was 'accidentally' shot. His death could not be attributed to the condemned officers, as two had taken their departure to another world, the rest for other lands.

This Botha stated 'that the three Boers were being brought in by Captain Taylor's Police, and were shot by five of the Carbineers; he reported what had been done to Morant in the presence of Major Lenehan.' The five Carbineers of the patrol were Lieutenants Morant and Handcock, Sergeant-Major Hammett, Corporal McMahon, and Trooper Botha.

He had heard Morant say to Taylor that he had had a scrap with the Boers and had got three. The accused told them that he had come down to Spelonken expressly to make inquiries concerning rumours of the shooting of prisoners, and statements were taken. He had never had any reason to believe that these three Boers had not been killed in in a fair fight. Lieutenant Edwards, who took down the evidence in connexion with the inquiry made by Lenehan said that the report on the shooting of these three Boers was included in papers sent in on the subject. Civil Surgeon Leonard deposed that Morant and Taylor were having an argument regarding the trustworthiness of the Boers, Morant maintaining the affirmative. He sent for Botha, who, in reply to questions by Morant, said he was a good soldier and had done his duty and shot Boers. There was no special mention of any particular Boers being shot.

Major Lenehan had arrived at Fort Edward on the very day that these three men were shot. I had met him going out as I was on my way to Pietersburg with prisoners. During dinner, at which were present Major Lenehan, Captain Taylor, Lieutenants Morant and Handcock, and Surgeon Leonard, an argument arose regarding the trustworthiness of Dutchmen on British service. Captain Taylor said they were not trustworthy, but Morant maintained the affirmative. In support of his arguments he sent for Botha…

It would seem unlikely that in a conversation in which Morant was trying to convince Lenehan that Botha 'was a good soldier, and had done his duty and shot Boers' that he would fail to mention that he had done so that very day. Returning to Lieut. Edwards' evidence:

> Lieutenant Edwards deposed that he received a confidential letter from Captain Hunt, of which a copy was made, the original being forwarded to Pretoria. A postscript to the original had since been torn off. The postscript read:- 'Will also write details of death of van Burend; Hancock shot him.' The detachment in which van Burend was, was only nominally a detachment of the corps. No details of van Burend's death were ever received. Lenehan sent word by witness that he would make a confidential report. It was Hancock who reported the death of van Burend. Major Bolton gave evidence as to the searching of the prisoner's kit and the finding of the letter produced, minus the footnote.
>
> *Major Lenehan was further charged with having failed to report that a trooper of the Carbineers, van Buren, had been shot by Lieutenant Handcock. He pleaded 'Not guilty.' Ex-Captain Robertson was the principal witness for the prosecution in this case. He said he knew van Buren, who had been shot; he had been warned that he was not to be trusted, and men refused to go on duty with him. He, Taylor, and Handcock had a talk over it, and decided he was to be shot. He said that he made a report of this occurrence, and also of the shooting of six men, to Major Lenehan. The report made of van Buren's death was not a true one; he had concealed the true facts in the interests of the corps.*
>
> *Major Lenehan, in his defence, said that he had never been informed of the actual manner of van Buren's death.*
>
> Ex-Captain Robertson said he knew van Burend, who was shot on 4 July last. The witness had been warned about van Burend as one who was not to be trusted and was suspected of thefts of whisky from an officer and of money from Kaffirs; and men refused to go on duty with him. He was always creating disturbances and abusing khakis. The witness, Taylor and Hancock had a talk over the man and it was decided he was to be shot. Hancock and four men went out on the left flank, and when it was finished the witness told Lenehan he was prepared to stand a Court-martial, as he had 30 prisoners, and Boers were near, and the man might give them the slip and give them away. The witness was superseded by Hunt. He made a report of this occurrence and of the shooting of six men to the accused. The report made to Lenehan of van Burend's death was not a true one. He concealed the true facts in the interest of the corps. Taylor also knew the true facts. The witness also

reported the true facts to Hunt. Lenehan had come down to inquire into the charges against the witness.

The prosecution was closed, and the defence claimed the discharge of the prisoner on the ground that it had not been shown who was the superior authority to whom the prisoner should have reported and that it was not shown, therefore, that a report had not been sent. The Court decided that the case should proceed. The accused in his defence denied that Robertson had ever informed him of the manner of van Burend's death. It never occurred to him that the postscript in Hunt's letter indicated anything suspicious.

Captain Taylor denied that he was a party to the conversation when it was agreed that van Burend must be shot. Robertson mentioned casually that he would have to shoot him, but the witness never heard till afterwards that he was shot. The accused asked the witness if he knew anything about van Burend's death. The witness replied, 'Not personally'. The accused said he would have to report the murder when he returned to Pietersburg.

Lieutenant Hancock denied that a meeting was held which decided on the shooting of van Burend. The witness carried out Robertson's instructions in this matter, and Robertson ordered him to report, making it appear that van Burend had been shot in a brush with the Boers. The report which he prepared did not suit Robertson, who wrote one himself. The witness reported the true facts to Hunt asking him to inform Lenehan. He told Robertson, who said he was a fool to have anything put in black and white. Robertson's evidence was all a fabrication. *The verdict and the sentence were not made known.*

The counsel for the defence referred to the fact that the prisoner had already been under arrest for three months, and protested against an officer's being kept so long without trial. The prisoner was commander of the corps in name only. Robertson was the man who should have reported, and had done, so falsely. He and Taylor were the men who should have been prosecuted, but Robertson had been allowed to resign unconditionally. The prosecutor maintained that, Robertson having reported to the accused, the latter should have reported to his superior.

The fifteen troopers who signed the letter of complaint also accused Lenehan of being privvy to the murders [142] and R. M. Cochrane accused him of falsifying evidence. [143] This is also important since the conspiracy theorists have claimed that the fifteen BVC troopers were attempting to cover their own misdeeds and that they had some personal animus towards Morant, Handcock et al. [144] What hostility might they have towards Lenehan, the absentee commanding officer? Their contact with him had been minimal.

Furthermore they stated that they were nervous about taking the matter to the authorities for fear of them siding with the officers. Would it not have been the case that the higher the rank of the officer they complained about, the more dangerous it would be? There would have been good reason to leave Lenehan out of the accusations, especially as the accusations were not as serious as those against the more junior officers. The most likely explanation is that their letter of complaint was born out of frustration at Lenehan coming to Fort Edward to do something about the situation and their finding him complicit.

Lenehan arrived at Fort Edward on 7 September 1901, the day the three Boers were killed.

> Trooper Botha deposed that three Boers were being brought in by Captain Taylor's police, and were shot at close quarters by five of his own corps. He reported what had been done to Morant, in presence of Lenehan. In his defence the accused denied having heard any such report made to Morant. He had heard Morant say to Taylor that he had had a scrap with the Boers, and had got three. The accused told them that he had come down to Spelonken expressly to make enquiries concerning rumours of the shooting of prisoners, and statements were taken. He had never had any reason to believe that these three Boers had not been killed in fair fight. [145]

Lenehan was charged with not reporting this incident. He claimed he went specifically to 'make enquiries concerning rumours of the shooting of prisoners' and in the NSW legislative assembly it was later stated that 'He was sent away by his superior officers with sealed instructions to the district in which they occurred. His instructions eventually turned out to be that he was to make an inquiry, and to see that there was no recurrence of these murders.' [146] Relating to an apparently tedious lecture given by Lenehan in Sydney in July 1902: 'Representations had been made respecting the matter in Germany, and a serious scandal was caused. Major Lenehan did not know all that was going on, but he received orders to go to the district to put a stop to such conduct. Nothing more was heard of the matter, till the officers of the corps were arrested.' [147] He probably could not have stopped the killing of the three Boers but there were no more killings afterwards.

The fifteen troopers did not sign their letter of complaint until 4 October. Lenehan had had almost a month to report the van Staden murder. So why did he not report it? It might be argued that he did report it and the charge was trumped-up. If this were the case, why was this not his defence rather than claiming that he was not present when it was discussed with Morant? There were very good reasons why the authorities would not have wanted

Lenehan implicated. If, as is suggested here, Lenehan was guilty of covering up the crimes of the BVC, why was he only charged with failing to report the two shootings? The DJAG had written on 3 December 1901: 'I think there is evidence to justify charges under the same section for failing to report certain evidence made in his presence during an inquiry into certain events which had occurred in the Spelonken, in which his corps was implicated ... The question whether a charge of being accessory after the fact to these crimes can be brought against Major Lenehan is one I think for the Civil Lawyers.' [148]

Why Lenehan was not charged with more serious crimes may be explained by his activities in late April 1901 during his time as commanding officer of the BVC when he prosecuted the Spoelstra case.

The reporting of the Spoelstra case had become a thorn in the side for Kitchener. The case had been watched by the Consul General of the Netherlands in Pretoria, F. J. Domela Nieuwnehuis and had been discussed in various Dutch newspapers, the *New York Times* and other American newspapers. Even Arthur Conan Doyle felt it necessary to address Spoelstra's claims. [149] If Lenehan, the prosecuting officer in this case, was to be implicated in covering up war crimes in his own unit, a whole new can of worms would wriggle their way across the pages of the world's press. There was every reason for Kitchener to drop the 'cover-up' charges against Lenehan, merely retaining the charge of 'culpable neglect'. There is no hard evidence that this is the case. It is however no harder to believe than the notion that the whole affair was to appease the German Government for the murder of Revd Heese, who was in fact a British citizen. [150]

If Lenehan was guilty of attempting a cover-up, did he therefore feel there was something to cover up? He had himself stated in court that he had not heard of any orders not to take prisoners.

During the Lenehan case the Boer General Beyers attacked Pietersburg. There had been a general resurgence of activity by Beyer's Commando leading up to this point and Morant biographers have put this down to the reining in of the BVC and the incarceration of their heroes. In fact, as Kitchener points out in his dispatch of 8 March 1902 [151] it is much more likely to have been due to the departure of Colonel Colanbrander's Column, which moved South on 22 December to avoid African horse sickness. Colonel Dawkins' mounted infantry left the area at the same time.

Between about 2 and 3 in the morning of 23 January 1902, General Beyers advanced towards the British camp at Pietersburg with a force of two to three hundred men. His intention was to capture horses from the remount depot and strengthen his commando with men from the burgher camp. [152]

The Hon. Isaac A. Isaacs, K.C., M.P., in his petition for George Witton's release, relayed an account provided by Trooper Heath:

> From the sources available to me, and which I accept as correct, and particularly the personal explanation given to me by Mr Heath, who was a trooper in the Bushveldt Carbineers, the position as far as material now, was that Beyers advanced from the East with about 200 or 300 men. Close to the town of Pietersburg was an armed camp of British, containing 800 or 900 men. The town and camp were enclosed in a huge ring protected by blockhouses. At or near the Eastern side of the town was the remount depot, and not far from this, but of course, outside the ring, was the blockhouse held by the Wilts. About the centre of the ring was a prison and not far from that was a fort with a gun, familiarly called a Cowgun. Near the town stood a Burgher camp with some 150 Boers. Beyers with no artillery, and a comparatively small commando, could not, and did not, as it would seem, place the British camp itself in any danger. The lives of Morant and Witton were not imperiled, even though they remained unarmed. Handcock, with the time at the disposal of the British Commander, could easily have been withdrawn from the blockhouse to the prison or the fort. So small was the danger to the camp that some of the men in the camp nearer than Witton's fort to the Wilts' blockhouse, which practically repulsed the attack, did not think it necessary to go to the trenches. According to Heath, some of the men stayed in bed. Not a shot, so far as Heath knows, was fired from the camp except from the gun at the fort. The only British rifle fire was from the Wilts blockhouse. It is understood that Handcock actually fought but that is immaterial to Witton's case. What is material to him is that, some little time before the attack, the prisoners were allowed to bear arms, they received rifle and revolver, and Witton (for I confine as far as possible my observations to his case) moved among his fellow soldiers prepared and permitted, if need were, to do perilous and honourable service for his country. [153]

Witton's account:

> Beyers now turned his attention to Pietersburg. During the trial of the Visser case, on the night of 22nd January, the soldiers who were in the blockhouses guarding the camp were enticed from their duty by the Boer women. Beyers, with a strong force, then rushed the Burgher camp, and, unchallenged, entered it, looted a quantity of provisions, and took away 150 men who had previously surrendered and had been allowed to remain with their families in the camp.

> Upon an inquiry being made into the conduct of the soldiers on guard, several were court-martialled and sentenced to terms of imprisonment ranging from six months to two years.
>
> It was anticipated that the Boers, having secured a large number of recruits, would require remounts and equipment, so on the following day arms were returned to the late officers of the Carbineers, and we were ordered to be ready for duty when called upon. Next morning, just as the day was breaking, the Boer force rushed upon the town, making for the Remount Depot. This necessitated breaking through the ring of block-houses at the point where Handcock was confined, and close to the garrison prison where Morant was located. From my position near the cow-gun I saw the Boers galloping madly over the sky-line, making for the town, doubtless thinking that the forts were only dummies and unoccupied, and expecting to annex the remounts as easily as they had the recruits.
>
> They were allowed to come within fifty yards of the block-houses, when they received a warm welcome from within in the shape of a shower of bullets. They made a desperate effort even then to get through, firing as they charged. Handcock was at the block-house nearest the point of attack. This had originally been a small brick building, and had been converted into a fort by being loop-holed and sangered.
>
> Morant joined Handcock as soon as the firing commenced, and they climbed together on to the flat roof of the fort, in the most exposed position. Disregarding any cover, they fought as only such brave and fearless men can fight. Handcock in particular, in his cool and silent manner, did splendid work, one of his bullets finding its billet in Marthinus Pretorius, Beyers' fighting leader. Handcock was the only man armed with a Mauser rifle, and when Pretorius was brought in, dangerously wounded, it was found that he had been struck by a Mauser bullet. [154]

Handcock being confined in the blockhouse near the point of attack clearly took part in the hostilities. Mention of Morant, however, is conspicuously lacking when Isaacs says 'It is understood that Handcock actually fought but that is immaterial to Witton's case.' One might ask if some men didn't even feel it necessary to leave their beds why would the prisoner Morant, who was close to the fort at the centre, be released and allowed to run to the blockhouse at the perimeter of the ring?

General Beyers succeeded in liberating about 150 of the burghers in the camp but more than 100 simply returned the following day.

The eight Boers Case:

Lieutenants Morant, P. J. Hancock, and G. Witton were then charged with having murdered, or instigated others to murder, eight men whose names were unknown. They pleaded 'Not guilty.' Major Bolton prosecuted.

The Visser case was now over. Not the slightest hint was given that we had been found guilty, and a sentence passed; I was never informed as to the finding of the court regarding this case, but three years later I read in a newspaper summary of the evidence that I had been found guilty of manslaughter and cashiered. The case had barely concluded when Captain Burns-Begg, who had acted as prosecutor, was ordered to England. It seemed as though he was required at the War Office to give particulars personally of the trial and of the disclosures that had been made there. Major Bolton now took the place of Captain Burns-Begg; Major Ousely, D.S.O., and Captain Marshall were also relieved as members of the court, and their places were filled by Captains Matcham and Brown.

Witton continuously complains that he was not informed of the sentence in each case as it finished, as do some of Morant's apologists. This is however in complete compliance with Section 52 of the Army Act in the Manual of Military Law 1899. This required every member of the Court Martial to swear an oath that contained the words: '...and you further swear that you will not divulge the sentence of the court until it is duly confirmed, and you further swear that you will not on any account at any time whatsoever disclose or discover the vote or opinion of any particular member of this court martial, unless thereunto required in due course of law. So help you GOD.' [155] One sentence should be passed on all charges. So the sentences could not be confirmed until all of the cases had been completed. The defendants therefore could not be legally informed of the findings of each case until all had been completed. Returning to the court case:

The reconstituted court started from Pretoria for Pietersburg on the 31st January. When we entrained it was evident our social status had undergone a decided change. The accommodation provided was the same for the return trip as when going down, but this time we were not permitted to enter a carriage. After considerable delay a small, dirty, covered-in truck was attached to the train, into which we were crowded, with our escorts, servants, and baggage. It was a sweltering day in January, and the effect it had upon us is more easily imagined than described.

When nearing Warm Baths Station the train pulled up; it was reported that a party of Boers were crossing the line. A member of the court came to our little sheep-truck, and for the second time during our trial we were ordered to stand to arms. Morant prayed, as I am sure he never prayed in his life before, that we might get into action. The members of the court did not reciprocate his feelings, but did their best to avoid action, and kept the train at a standstill for over an hour while they carefully examined the surrounding country through their field-glasses, giving the Boers ample time to get out of sight. Then, moving on slowly from block-house to block-house, we safely passed the point of danger.

We arrived at Pietersburg on 1st February, and the court assembled again on the 3rd to adjudicate on what was called the eight Boers case. Morant, Handcock, and myself were arraigned on the charge of shooting or instigating others to shoot these. The main facts, as adduced by the evidence for the prosecution, were not disputed. At the close of the evidence for the prosecution, Major Thomas, the prisoners' counsel, made the following protest:- 'I submit the charge of inciting to murder has not been proved. The prisoners are alleged to be accessories before the crime of murder. They are not charged with being conspirators, and I submit that the alleged charge of murder against the principals has not been established, and, if so, there can be no accessories. I submit that the proper way to have brought this case before the court should have been in the form of a charge for conspiracy.'

The court ruled that the case must proceed. Major Thomas then said that he did not propose to put the prisoners in the box, as the main facts were not disputed, but statements would be handed in, and the evidence he would call would be confined to three things – orders received, the customs of the war, and the practices adopted in other irregular corps against the enemy when breaking the customs of war.

Did Major Thomas feel that Morant's histrionics in court were damaging to the defence? Intelligence agent L. H. Ledeboer then gave evidence:

L. H. Ledeboer deposed that about August 20 last he was in charge of a party who captured eight Boers. He handed the prisoners over to a patrol, and did not know what became of them. Trooper Thompson stated that he and Troopers Duckett and Lucas were sent for by Morant, who asked if they were friends of the late Frank Eland; if they knew the late Captain Hunt; and if they had seen Lord Kitchener's proclamation to the effect at 'those who take up the sword shall perish by the sword.' The Lord, he added, had delivered eight Boers into their hands, and they were going to shoot them. Lucas objected, but Morant said, 'I have orders and must obey them, and you are making a mistake if you think you are going to run the show.' On the morning of the 23rd the witness saw a party with eight Boers. Morant gave orders and the prisoners were taken off the road and shot, Hancock killing two with his revolver. Morant afterwards told the witness that they had to play into his hands, or else they would know what to expect. The witness said that the evidence which he had given at the Court of Inquiry was given under pressure and was untrue. He only knew about Hunt's orders by hearsay. Witton was present at the execution.

Sergeant-Major Hammett corroborated the evidence as to the shooting of the prisoners. Morant informed him on the previous evening that prisoners were being brought in and were to be shot. The witness asked Morant if he was sure he was not exceeding orders. Morant replied that he had hitherto disregarded them, and would do so no longer. The Boer prisoners were first asked to give information about Tom Kelly, and one of them made a rush at Witton and caught him by the jacket, whereupon he was shot dead, and all the rest afterwards. Morant had always treated prisoners well till Hunt's death, and then he became a different man altogether. Witton shot the prisoner who seized hold of him.

Sergeant Wrench said it afterwards appeared that some objected to the shooting. Morant told him to find out who did not agree, and he would soon get rid of them, adding that he had been 'congratulated by headquarters over the last affair, and meant to go on with it'.

The prosecution was then closed. The counsel for the defence claimed the discharge of the prisoners on the ground that the charge was not proven, arguing that they should, if charged with anything, be charged with conspiracy. The Court overruled the objection. The counsel for the defence then said he did not dispute the facts, but would call evidence to show (1) the orders received; (2) the prevailing custom, having regard to the enemy they were fighting; (3) the practices adopted by other irregular corps against an enemy breaking the usages of war.

This is the statement made by Lieutenant H. H. Morant:-

'I do not feel called upon, nor am I advised by my counsel, that it is necessary for me to enter the witness-box in this case. In the case of Visser I gave the fullest explanation of my position and my instructions regarding the Boers captured in the Spelonken district. I was distinctly and repeatedly told by my late friend and commanding officer, Capt. Hunt, on our arrival at Spelonken, which happened a few days after the train-wrecking occurrence, that no Boer prisoners were in future to be taken. I have already shown in Visser's case, and can bring further evidence in this case, to prove that Capt. Hunt gave these orders not only to me, but to others under his command, that is, "that no prisoners were to be taken", and he reprimanded me for not carrying out this order.'Capt. Hunt had

been my most intimate friend in South Africa. We were engaged to two sisters in England. He joined the B.V.C. in order to be in the same regiment as myself, and he practically asked Major Lenehan that we might be together in the same squadron. Capt. Hunt had Imperial service in the 10th Hussars [Hunt was actually in the 13th Hussars], and some colonial service in French's Scouts, and I had implicit confidence in him and regarded his orders as authoritative and bona fide. Until Capt. Hunt's body was found stripped and mutilated I shot no prisoners, though I maintain it is generally known that Boers who had been concerned in misdoings and outrages, such as the nomadic Dutchmen of the Spelonken, had been executed summarily by many Irregular Corps who have done good work in South Africa. After Capt. Hunt's death and the brutal treatment of him, alive or dead, I resolved as his successor and survivor to carry out the orders he had impressed upon me, orders which other officers have in other places and in other corps carried out, with the provocation we had received. The Boers had left my friend's body, the body of an Englishman and officer, lying stripped, disfigured, and not buried – thrown into a drain like a pariah dog. Moreover, I had heard so much about the deeds of these particular Boers that I have [been] charged with murder[ing], reports which connect them with train wreckings and maraudings. I also know they belonged to the same gang that had maltreated and dishonoured the body of my friend and brother officer. I considered I was quite justified in not treating such men with the amenity usually accorded to prisoners of war, and I am quite satisfied that they fully deserved the summary execution they received. In ordering these Boers to be shot, I did so fully believing that, in view of what Capt. Hunt had so distinctly ordered me, and what I myself knew had been done elsewhere, I was practically right and justified by the rules of guerrilla warfare.

'I was Senior Officer of the B.V.C. in the Spelonken, and for the ordering of the shooting of these Boers I take full and entire responsibility. I admit having sent in an "edited" report, but I did so for reasons which have actuated higher military authorities than myself. I have been told that I was never myself after the death of Capt. Hunt, and I admit that his death preyed upon my mind when I thought of the brutal treatment he had received. This treatment of Capt. Hunt's body, coupled with the train wreckings which had occurred, made me resolve to act on orders and do as other officers have done under less trying circumstances than myself.

'The alleged conversation between myself and Sergeant Wrench is absolutely untrue; No such conversation ever occurred. It is an entire fabrication.'

Statement made by Lieutenant P. J. Handcock:-

'I am Veterinary Lieutenant. I have had a very poor education. I never cared much about being an officer; all I know is about horses, though I like to fight. Capt. Robinson said it was right to shoot traitors. Capt. Hunt told us when he came out that no Boers were to be taken. I had often heard that Boers were to be shot if they sniped or wore khaki or smashed up trains. I do not know what the rule under such things is, but we all thought that Capt. Hunt knew the correct thing. I did not much believe in Capt. Robinson, and when he ordered the man to be shot I told Capt. Hunt all about it. When he came to Spelonken, Capt. Hunt did not say it was wrong; he said we were not to take prisoners anymore, so I thought he was doing his orders. I did what I was told to do, and I cannot say any more. No conversation ever took place between Sergeant Wrench and Lieutenant Morant in my presence, as stated by Sergeant Wrench in court.'

Statement by Lieutenant Witton:-

'I had received my commission as a Lieutenant about six weeks before the 23rd August. I was told what the orders about Boers were as received from Captain Hunt, and I took it they were correct; I did whatever I was told, and raised no question one way or the other, as it is customary to obey orders.

'Capt. Hunt and Lieut. Morant were great friends, and I supposed that all orders were correct that Capt. Hunt gave. He was greatly relied upon by all when he came to reform matters at Spelonken, after Captain Robinson left.

'On the 23rd August one of the Boers rushed at me to seize my carbine, and I shot at him to keep him off.'

Lieutenant Picton gave evidence that he was moving out with a patrol towards Scinde, when Captain Hunt gave him instructions not to bring back any prisoners. He got some prisoners on this patrol and brought them back to Fort Edward, and was reprimanded for doing so. One of the prisoners was a man named Venter. He was sent to the Burgher Camp, and was one of those who escaped from there and went on commando with Beyers. 'He was shot during the attack on Pietersburg, and I recognised him.'

Captain Taylor was called to give evidence for the defence, and stated that he remembered one time when Lieutenant Morant brought in prisoners; he was asked by Captain Hunt why he brought them in; Capt. Hunt said they should have been shot...

The prisoners having handed in their statements of defence, Civil Surgeon Johnson deposed to reprimands administered by Captain Hunt to men who brought in prisoners. Lieutenant Hannam stated that when he was a trooper in the Queensland Mounted Infantry, on one occasion at Bronkhorst Spruit in 1900 his squadron took some prisoners, and was reprimanded by Colonel Cradock for taking them. Lieutenant B. F. Guy, R.S.O, handed in a statement as to trains wrecked on the Pietersburg line by Boers. J. E. Tucker testified to Boers breaking into a refugee camp and carrying off 141 of the inmates. Their evidence showed that Captain Hunt gave distinct orders to sergeants not to take prisoners. Sergeant Walter Ashton deposed to Brabant's Horse receiving orders to take no prisoners in consequence of specific acts of treachery on the part of the Boers. The Judge Advocate objected to such evidence as irrelevant.

The Judge Advocate twice protested that the evidence that was being produced was extremely irrelevant, and the rule was that nothing should be admitted as evidence that did not tend immediately to prove or disprove the charge in criminal proceedings.

Sergeant McArthur testified to seeing one Boer summarily shot for being caught in khaki. Lieutenant Colin Philip said the Queensland Mounted Infantry were in disgrace on one occasion for bringing in prisoners caught sniping. Boers caught breaking the customs of war were shot summarily. Instructions were published in the orders in Colonel Garrett's column that Boers caught in khaki were to be shot. Captain King, of the Canadian Scouts, stated in evidence that Boers guilty of wearing British uniforms, train wrecking, or murdering soldiers were dealt with summarily. Another witness deposed that Hunt and Eland's bodies were found stripped and maltreated. Sergeant Roberts said that on one occasion Hunt gave him orders to lead a false attack on a fort, during which some prisoners were to be shot. The witness objected, and the orders were not carried out. Further testimony as to the good character of all the prisoners and their kind heartedness was given, and the case then closed.

If Sergeant Robert's testimony is true, if there were orders to shoot prisoners, then why would there be a need for the pretence of a false attack? The answer is that there were no orders to shoot prisoners. Secondly, how could Sergeant Roberts refuse to carry out this order with impunity? The answer must be that both he and Captain Hunt knew Hunt's order to be illegal and therefore that he could ignore it. This leaves the possibility that there *were* orders not to take prisoners; but this has different implications than taking prisoners and then shooting them afterwards, which is what the defendants were charged with. That some units shot prisoners under circumstances of dubious legality and complete illegality is almost certain; but as the prosecution would point out, two wrongs don't make a right and there is scant evidence that any had done it on the same scale as the BVC.

Cable messages also appeared in the Australian press, dated November, 1901, that Lord Kitchener had issued orders that all Boers who were captured wearing the khaki uniform of British troops should be shot.

It was also stated in another cablegram received a short time before this that a number of Boers wearing khaki belonging to the commando of Commandant Smutz had been captured by Colonel Gorringe, and had been shot.

The ordinary regulations provide that in time of peace any person found wearing a military uniform of the British forces, when not entitled to do so, may be fined £10, while for the same offence in time of war the death penalty can be exacted.

The counsel for the defence pleaded justification, on the ground that the Boers in that district were gangs of train wreckers without a head, and their conduct had brought reprisals. The prosecution submitted that the evidence was not denied. The eight men had been shot.

The Judge Advocate refused the plea of justification. The contention that other corps had done similarly did not make two wrongs right.

In the face of this Major Bolton went into the witness-box, where he said that he had 'no knowledge' of a proclamation that Boers taken in khaki were to be shot.

This was the time Lord Kitchener should have been put in the box, and the facts of the case and all necessary information obtained direct from him in the interests of justice and the Empire generally.

(This incident came under my notice while we were being tried at Pietersburg. A small patrol of the Pietersburg Light Horse, mostly raw recruits, went out scouting. When approaching a farm house they saw several men walking about dressed in a similar fashion to themselves; they rode up, dismounted, and entered into conversation. They were greatly astonished when they were covered by the rifles of the others, and ordered to hand over their arms and ammunition. Upon this being done, they were requested to hand over their uniforms; when they were stripped they were allowed to return in a nude state to Pietersburg. The party into whose hands they had fallen were a party of Irish-Americans fighting with the Boers.)

The Court was cleared, and on its reopening Major Lenehan was asked if he could give evidence regarding the character of the Prisoners. He gave an excellent account of the pluck, and good services, of Morant who was responsible for the capture of Tom Kelly. Hancock, he said, had an excellent record and was simple minded and with a strong sense of duty, obeying order implicitly. Witton was also a good soldier and officer.

Major R. W. Lenehan, late of the Bushveldt Carbineers, gave evidence that Lieutenant Handcock was a veterinary officer, and that he had not wished him to go to Spelonken, but upon representation being made he allowed him to go. Mr. Handcock had a very strong sense of duty, and anything he was ordered to do he would do without the slightest question, no matter what it might be.

Major Thomas, the prisoners' counsel, then handed in his address, as follows, which was read and attached to proceedings:-

'The main facts, as adduced by the evidence for the prosecution, are not denied by the defence. The long statement, alleged to have been made by Lieutenant Morant to the witness Wrench is denied, and the court must form its own opinion, from the attitude of Wrench, as to whether or not he has not drawn considerably upon a rather vindictive imagination for his glibly told story. But even if true, this does not affect the real issue. Apart from any question of law, such as was raised at the conclusion of the evidence for the prosecution, and which this court perhaps can scarcely deal with, the prisoners' defence is that, no matter in what way the charge against them has been, or might have been framed, the action they respectively took in the summary execution of these eight Boers was justifiable, or, at any rate, not criminal. That which would be a crime, a felony, or a malicious act in time of peace may be quite justifiable in time of war, and doubly so in guerrilla warfare, waged against men who cannot be regarded as lawful belligerents, but only as lawless bands of marauders, who carry on desultory hostilities, combined with train wreckings and other uncivilised practices. Upon such an enemy I maintain our troops are justified in making the severest reprisals, and are entitled to regard them, not as lawful belligerents at all, but as outlaws.

'But having regard to the immensely wide area over which the present war in South Africa has for more than two years extended, the nature of the country, and the peculiar class of people who keep the fighting going, it happens that, whilst in one part of the theatre of war the enemy's methods may be such that we cannot take great exception to them, however senseless and infatuated the prolongation of the strife may seem to us, yet in other parts of the country quite a different kind of operations are in vogue, operations of such a nature that they must be treated as uncivilised and often barbarous. In one district we may meet a large organised body of Boers fighting under a recognised and honourable commandant, whilst in another district we find ourselves pitted against roving bands under no recognised leader. It was against the latter class, and especially during the months of July, August, and September last, that the small Spelonken detachment of the Bushveldt Carbineers, to which the prisoners belonged, were sent out to operate under special orders. A small body, about 100 strong, they had to work over a vast area of difficult country, where, in

small patrols and parties they had literally to hunt down the shifting bands of the enemy, in kloofs and almost inaccessible places, taking their lives in their hands. And sufficient evidence has come out during these cases to show how excellently their work was done. Practically they cleared the Spelonken district of Boers, many of whom found harbour there after their exploits against trains on the Pietersburg line. Even the prosecution admit that these Boers were of a bad class, and that this was the character of some, if not of all, of the eight men alleged to have been murdered.

'We have shown that train wreckers were in the district at this particular period, and we have put in an official return of their doings in this respect, starting from 4th July last. On that date a train-wrecking occurred, in which an officer and a number of men were killed – the officer being a friend of the late Captain Hunt. Closely following upon this, Captain Hunt was sent to take charge of the Spelonken detachment, and it is abundantly proved that his orders were "No prisoners" after this – no quarter. He impressed this upon his officers and non-commissioned officers, and reprimanded them for non-observance of his orders. He had been in the regular army, and his instructions, coming as he did to institute a new order of things at Spelonken, were entitled to weight from irregular subordinates. It was quite evident that they were guided by him, but it was not until Hunt himself was killed, with rather brutal surrounding circumstances, that his directions were fulfilled. After this his successor, Lieutenant Morant, as he says, resolved to carry out previous orders. Up to this Morant had been particularly lenient towards prisoners, and there is no proof (but the very opposite) of his being of a malicious or cruel nature. It is true that after Hunt's death he changed a good deal, and adopted the sternest measures against the enemy. In civil life, and if trying a civil offence, under civil and peaceful conditions, it might be said that he became revengeful, but in time of war revenge and retaliation are allowable. It would be cant and hypocrisy to maintain otherwise. War makes men's natures both callous and, on occasions, revengeful. What is the object of war? Simply to kill and disable as many men of the opposite side as possible. In pursuing these objects, soldiers are not to be judged by the rules of citizen life, and often, as soldiers, they do things, which, calmly regarded afterwards or in time of peace, appear, and are, unchristian and even brutal. The more civilised the foe we deal with the more chivalric the methods of warfare, and the brutal element is absent or rarely apparent. But when the civilised rules and customs of war are departed from by one side, reprisals follow from the other, and then the bad, the bitter, the revengeful side of war is seen. If in every war, especially guerrilla war, officers and men who committed reprisals were to be brought up and tried as murderers, court-martials

might be kept going all the year. Such might be the case in the present war, if all the reprisals, summary executions, slaughters, were dragged before formal courts, argued over by counsel and prosecutor as to points of law, and all the gruesome details exposed to the light of day.

'We cannot judge such matters fairly unless we place ourselves amidst the same surroundings, and with the same provocations as obtained with the men whose actions are to be tried. What are our irregular troops for? To ride down, harry, and shoot the enemy, and I submit, if the latter deserve it, to adopt strong retaliatory measures. These irregular combatants of the army are really charged now with the bulk of the fighting, and if they are to be restrained and tied down by strict rules, such as might obtain were they fighting French or German soldiers instead of guerrillas, then the sooner they are recalled from the field the better, or, at any rate, let definite instructions be issued for their guidance. Do not let them have indefinite, hazy instructions as to what they may do. Do not let us have officers reprimanded by their seniors for hampering the column with prisoners, and at another time, and another place, haul them up as murderers because they do the opposite. I fear there is a great deal of rather mawkish sentimentality about some of these Boer bands, who do so much to keep this prolonged war going in spite of the marvellously good treatment the British have extended towards their people, wives and children.

'I refer again to the class of Boers which had to be combated in the Spelonken in July, August, and September, and I maintain that it was to be presumed, and the actions of other irregular corps elsewhere show, that the Bushveldt Carbineers were not singular in this respect, that if the foe committed outrages, and departed from the customs of war, punitive measures might be adopted. If these officers have overstepped the mark they should be upheld. The Boers brought these measures on themselves, and should take the consequences of their collective acts in the district. We cannot discriminate as to who did this or that; they must all be regarded as involved in, or countenancing nefarious practices which provoked reprisal. Their own countrymen are beginning to become disgusted with the prevailing methods, and in hundreds are joining the British, in hope of stopping the useless fighting which is desolating their country, and keeping all South Africa chafing under martial law. South Africa is a cosmopolitan country, and what affects the British affects large numbers of Germans and other foreigners, who are excluded from their homes or from settling here. For the interests of the foreigner, and even the Dutch themselves, as well as the British our troops are fighting, and on our irregulars falls the brunt of it. Are we to recognise them as, irregulars or as regulars? From irregulars irregularities are to be expected, and cannot be avoided. Let us, if we employ

them in guerrilla tactics, either definitely instruct them by clear orders and proclamations as to how far they may go, or uphold them if they have not been so instructed and thus fallen into error. If these arguments apply in ordinary cases, they have especial force in the present case, where Lieut. Morant acted under express directions conveyed to him by his deceased superior officer, and if he followed these instructions when he himself took over command, believing that he was justified in following them, then any "criminal intent" is disproved, and if this applies to Lieut. Morant, it applies again with still greater force to his subordinate lieutenants, Handcock and Witton. Lieut. Morant honourably acknowledges in his written statement the responsibilities of his position as senior officer, but that he also takes upon himself the burden of a crime is repudiated and denied.

'In conclusion, I would quote the following passages from the Chapter on Customs of War, as comprised in the Manual of Military Law, issued for our guidance by the Army, remembering, however, that no precise rules can be laid down to meet all the varying styles of warfare. Such rules can be but guides as to our actions, and in default of clear orders abrogating these, I submit that they are to be followed as far as applicable.'

Thomas again argues that effectively the Manual of Military Law should not apply because the enemy did not deserve it, a position he maintained after the war. Thomas wrote a letter to George Witton's brother in March 1902. The letter concludes 'War is war, and rough things have to be done. Only yesterday news came in of horrible barbarities on the part of the Boers towards some of our colonials. I say they deserve all they (the Boers) get, and with less nonsense and sentiment the war would be over.' [156] Returning to the Court Martial:

'"The first duty of a citizen is to defend his country, but this defence must be conducted according to the Customs of War." Further, "War must be conducted by persons acting under the control of some recognised Government, having power to put an end to hostilities, in order that the enemy may know the authority to which he may resort when desirous of making peace." Under ordinary circumstances, therefore, persons committing acts of hostility who do not belong to an organised body, authorised by some recognised Government, and do not wear a military uniform, or some conspicuous dress or mark, showing them to be part of an organised military body, incur the risk of being treated as marauders and punished accordingly.

'Persons, other than regular troops in uniform, whose dress shows their character, committing acts of hostility against an enemy, must, if they expect

when captured to be treated as prisoners of war, be organised in such a manner, or fight under such circumstances, as to give their opponents due notice that they are open enemies from whom resistance is to be expected.

'Retaliation is military vengeance; it takes place where an outrage committed on one side is avenged by the commission of a similar act on the other.'

As reference was made by Major Thomas to a witness named Wrench, I attach his evidence:-

'On the 19th August you were sent out to take charge of some prisoners?'

'On the 19th August I went out with nine men to bring in some prisoners. The prisoners were handed to me by Ledeboer, of the Intelligence. Five bolts were also given to me, taken out of the prisoners' rifles, and these were distributed amongst the men. We returned, and arrived at the hospital on the evening of the 22nd August, and camped there for the night. On the morning of the 23rd August, at about 7 a.m., Lieuts. Morant, Handcock, and Witton, Sergt.-Major Hammett, and Troopers Duckett and Thompson, came out. Mr. Morant informed me that Tom Kelly, with about forty Boers, was in the immediate vicinity. Mr. Morant gave me orders to saddle up and inspan the waggon at once, and get on the road. I was to extend the men well away in the bush, and keep in the centre of the road myself, and to skirmish at least a mile ahead of the waggon.

'Mr. Morant said I was to keep a sharp look-out, as no doubt I would hear firing, and when I did so I was to immediately gallop back to him. When we first came in sight of Bristow's Farm, one shot was fired by somebody hidden. I then gave orders to dismount, and then two other shots were heard in the same place, the farm. I did not go back to report this to Mr. Morant. Shortly afterwards about fifteen shots, as far as we could make out, were fired in our rear, at least 1000 yards behind. I then gave the order to mount, and we went on to Bristow's Farm, to report to Captain Taylor, having received instructions to do so from Mr. Morant. I reported the arrival of the patrol to Capt. Taylor, who was walking about in front of the house in a very excited state. I told Capt. Taylor I had handed over the eight Boers to Mr. Morant and his party. Some time after this I was sent for by Mr. Morant. Mr. Morant and Mr. Handcock were lying each in their beds. Mr. Morant had a letter in his hand, and said to me that I had made a fool of myself, and that this was the letter reporting me, and that it would very likely mean a court-martial for me. After a little conversation Mr. Morant said "Don't let us beat about the bush. From what I can see of it, there are several men here who don't agree with this shooting. I want you to go round to the men and find out those who are willing to do it and those who are not, and then we will soon get rid of those who don't

agree. I had orders to weed out the Fort, which you know I did, but I still find there are a lot of sentimental [men] left. I have had several letters of congratulation from headquarters over the last fight, and now I've started I mean to go on with it. From what I can see of it, you had a rotten lot of men, but we will give you another chance. I shall send out a small patrol in a few days; I shall pick my own men this time, and send you with them." When Mr. Morant spoke of finding the men who were agreeable and who were not, Lieut. Handcock said, if he could only get ten men, that would be sufficient for his purpose.'

'Did Mr. Morant say why you were to be tried by court-martial?'

'Yes That three parties of our people met the Boer prisoners returning to the Fort, who were not guarded, which was not true. He said the first party were Kaffir scouts. I said that that did not amount to much. The next party were our own Intelligence. I then asked who the third party were. He said, "Don't let us beat about the bush," and then the subject started.'

'Do you know who fired the three shots that were heard?'

'No. They were fired from the farm.'

Wrench was cross-examined by the Counsel for the Prisoners.

'This conversation you refer to, is it related exactly as it occurred?'

'Not exactly, but words to that effect. I have not added to it. I may have left something out. It occurred about 8 o'clock. I was not in bed. We were playing cards. The two officers were in bed when this conversation took place. It occurred about a week after the Boers were shot – about the 30th August.'

'You once got yourself into trouble in the Spelonken with Captain Hunt?'

'No, never.'

'Is it not a fact that you were reported for insolent conduct to Sergt.-Major Clark, and were reprimanded for it?'

'I did not get on well with Sergt.-Major Clark.'

'On account of your bad conduct, were you not threatened to be tied up to a waggon by Captain Hunt?'

'No, never.'

'Did you not ask Mr. Morant to save you from that taking place?'

'No, but I spoke to Mr. Morant, and reported the conduct of Sergt.-Major Clark on patrol to Saltpan.'

'Was anyone else present except Mr. Morant and Mr. Handcock?'

'No; only those two.'

Wrench was examined by the court:-

'How many prisoners did you hand over?'

'Eight. They were voluntary surrenders.'

'Were you present when they surrendered?'

'No. I was not present when they surrendered.'

'Then you do not know whether they were captured prisoners or had voluntarily surrendered?'

'Ledeboer said they had surrendered to him.'

A statement of the trains wrecked in the district from 4th July, 1901, was also put in:- The first wreck occurred on 4th July, about five miles north of Naboomspruit. There were killed and died of wounds: One officer (Lieut. Best, Gordon Highlanders) and fifteen men, three natives. Wounded: Seven Gordon Highlanders, one native.

The second attempt at train-wrecking occurred on 10th August, 1901, 3½ miles N. if Groon Vlei (about 12 or 13 miles N. of Nylstroom). Lieut. Burnett, Gordon Highlanders, beat off Boers. No record of our casualties, which were very slight.

The third train wreck occurred on 3ist August, 1901, at Kilo 35, between Waterfall and Haman's Kraal. Killed and died of wounds: One officer (Col Vandeleur), twelve men, and two natives. Wounded: Twenty officers and men.

The Prosecution handed in a written reply as follows:--'

'I submit to the court that the witnesses have shown by their evidence, which is very clear, that on the evening of the 22nd August the prisoners Lieut. Morant and Lieut. Handcock sent for Troopers Thompson and Duckett and warned them for a patrol the following morning, telling them at the time that they were going out to shoot eight Boer prisoners or surrenders.

'About 5 a.m., 23rd August, the patrol, consisting of Lieuts. Morant, Handcock, Witton, Sergeant-Major Hammett, and Troopers Duckett and Thompson, left Fort Edward and proceeded towards Elim Hospital, where they met Sergeant Wrench in charge of the eight Boers. Lieut. Morant told the members of this patrol that these men were to be shot, and that the signal for this would be when he said, "have you any more information," or some words to that effect. Sergt. Wrench was ordered to proceed then with his patrol to the Fort, Lieut. Morant taking charge of the prisoners with his party. About half way back the convoy halted, and the eight men, who were unarmed, were ordered about twenty paces off the road and questioned by Lieut. Morant, and on his giving the signal were shot down by the members of this patrol. The defence do not in any way question these facts materially, but try to justify them in three ways:-

'Firstly: That they were only carrying out orders from superior authority. All I have to say on this head is that such orders, if given, do not constitute a lawful command and need not be obeyed.

'Secondly: That other irregular corps had done the same thing. Even if so, two wrongs do not make a right.

'Lastly: That the character of these men was such that they did not deserve any other treatment. I must submit to the court that, even if these men had been caught red-handed committing some outrage, they, once having surrendered or been taken prisoners and disarmed, were entitled to our protection until such time as they would be brought to trial.

'I have nothing further to say, and so leave it to the court to say if the prisoners are guilty of the crime of which they are charged, or if their acts were such as are customary in civilised warfare.'

The following is the summing-up by the Judge Advocate;

'In the case now under consideration the prisoners practically admit having committed the offence with which they stand charged, but maintain that they had justification for the course they pursued, and that there was palliation for their action owing to the fact, as alleged by them, that similar occurrences have taken place during the course of this war, and have been ignored or condoned.

'I would point out that two wrongs do not make a right, and that the commission of a wrongful act can scarcely be urged as a justification for the repetition of that act.

'I would point out that war is not a relation of man to man, but of State to State, and of itself implies no private hostility between the individuals by whom it is carried on.

'The object of war is the redress by force of a national injury. Wars are the highest trials of right, and it is scarcely seemly that they should degenerate into a medium of personal revenge. Retaliation is military vengeance. It takes place when an outrage committed on one side is avenged by the commission of a similar act on the other.

'Retaliation is the extreme right of war, and should be resorted to only in the last necessity, and then only by someone in authority. The first principle of war is that armed forces, so long as they resist, may be destroyed by all legitimate means.

'The right of killing an armed man exists only so long as he resists; as soon as he submits he is entitled to be treated as a prisoner of war. Quarter should never be refused to men who surrender, unless they have been guilty of some such violation of the customs of war as would of itself expose them to the penalty of death, and even when so guilty they should be put on their trial before being executed, as it is seldom justifiable for a combatant to take the law into his own hands against an unresisting foe.

'Where an act complained of is itself unlawful, bona fides or honesty of purpose is no excuse; how far a subordinate could plead the specific

commands of a superior, such commands being not obviously improper or contrary to law, as justifying an injury inflicted, is doubtful.

'The rule is that a person is responsible for the natural consequence of his acts.

'If several persons go out with a common intent to execute some criminal purpose, each is responsible for every offence committed by any one of them in furtherance of that purpose. A person is in all cases fully responsible for any offence which is committed by another by his instigation.

'If a person has unlawfully caused death by conduct which was intended to cause death or grievous bodily harm to some person, whatever the intention of the offender may have been, he is guilty of murder. If a person is proved to have killed another, the law presumes prima facie that he is guilty of murder.

'It will be on the accused to prove such facts as may reduce the offence to manslaughter, or excuse him from all criminal responsibility. It may be taken generally that in all cases where a killing cannot be justified, if it is not murder it is manslaughter; again, the offence is manslaughter if the act from which death results was committed under the influence of passion arising from extreme provocation, but it must be clearly established in cases when provocation is put forward as an excuse that at the time the crime was committed the offender was so completely under the influence of passion arising from the provocation that he was at that moment deprived of the power of self-control, and with this view it will be necessary to consider carefully (1) The manner in which the crime was committed, whether deliberately and with premeditation, and also (2) the length of the interval between the provocation and the killing, so as to establish the fact that the alleged provocation was a justification of the crime.

'I must further draw the attention of the court to the fact that much irrelevant evidence has been allowed to be produced, which will require careful sifting before they can arrive at a just finding.'

The conclusion of this case was similar to the first, our military service being again taken. No *intimation was given as to the nature of the verdict or the sentence.*

This concluded the charges against me, and I was not required to attend subsequent sittings of the court; my guard was now more relaxed than hitherto. Often I went about the garrison unattended, and in the company of an unarmed non-commissioned officer frequently visited friends in the town.

On the afternoon following the conclusion of the 'eight Boers' case I attended a cricket match, which took place on the town cricket-ground, mingling with, among others, the president and members of the court, who had only the previous day, though I was not then aware of it, passed upon me the extreme penalty of the law, 'To suffer death by being shot.' With the exception of a surprised kind of stare from the haughty president, my presence there was unheeded. Incidents such as these tended to convince me that the penalty hanging over me could not be a very serious one. We were often provided with horses, and permitted to take riding exercise in the morning before breakfast.

The three Boers Case:

Lieutenants Morant and Hancock were next charged with murder in instigating the killing of two Boers and one boy names unknown. They again pleaded 'Not guilty'.

Sergeant-major Hammett deposed that he was one of the patrol which the prisoners accompanied in search of three Boers. It was reported that the Boers were discovered, and it was then agreed that when Morant asked, 'Do you know Captain Hunt?' that was to be the signal for shooting them. This was done. The youngest Boer was about 17. Other members of the patrol corroborated this evidence. The Boers, they stated, were discovered at a native kraal, were sent on, and at the signal shot. It was understood that no prisoners were to be taken.

In this case Lieutenant Morant again chose to go into the witness-box, and gave evidence on oath. For the defence, Morant deposed that he went out to look for the three Dutchmen. He found them, and never asked them to surrender. As they were Dutchmen with whom they were at war and belonged to the party which had stripped and mutilated a brother officer, who was a friend of his, he had them shot. Hancock gave evidence as to Hunt's orders that no prisoners were to be taken. The Boers in that district were simply a scattered band of marauders. The counsel for the defence urged that it must have been a matter of military knowledge that the Boers in this district made no pretence whatever of being under a leader or carrying on recognized warfare.

Major Bolton was asked if he wished to cross-examine the witness, and upon replying in the affirmative Morant sprang up, and passionately exclaimed, 'Look here, Major, you are just the "Johnnie" I have been waiting to be cross-examined by; cross-examine me as much as you like, but let us have a straight gallop.' In the cross-examination Morant's retorts were so straight and so bitter that they resulted in the collapse of the Prosecutor after a very few questions had been asked.

The Heese Case:

The trial of the last, and what was considered the most important case, that of the murder of the alleged German missionary, was opened on the 17th of February. Lieutenant Handcock was charged with having killed Mr. Hess; Lieutenant Morant was charged with the offence of inciting to murder. For some unknown reason this case was heard privately in the garrison, and not publicly in the town, as the others had been.

Another court was also constituted, with Lieutenant Colonel McVean, C.B., Gordon Highlanders, as president. The members were: Major L. L. Nichol, Rifle Brigade; Major E. Brereton, Northampton Regiment; Captain E. Comerwell, York Regiment; Captain Stapylton, Royal Field Artillery; Captain Rhodes, Welsh Regiment; and Captain Kent, Northampton Regiment.

On 17 February the Court-martial sat to hear a charge of murder preferred against Lieutenant Hancock in having killed Mr Heese, a German missionary, while Lieutenant Morant was charged with the offence of inciting to murder. The prosecution stated that witnesses would be called to prove that on 23 August 1901, Missionary Heese left Fort Edward for Pietersburg, and the motive for killing him was that he had got to know of the killing of eight Boers, and was on his way to Pietersberg to report the occurrence when he was shot by Handcock under orders from Morant.

Morant and Handcock pleaded 'Not guilty,' and the following evidence was adduced:-

Trooper Phillips deposed that on August 23 last he was on duty at Cossack Post when a Cape cart containing the missionary and a Cape boy was going in the direction of Pietersburg. The missionary showed a pass signed by Captain Taylor. He was greatly agitated, saying there had been a fight that morning and several had been killed, but he did not say whether they were British or Boers.

Corporal Sharp said that he had seen Morant addressing Heese, and had afterwards seen Hancock riding in the same direction as the missionary. It was about 10 or 11 am when the missionary went past, and Hancock went about 12. The latter had a carbine. He did not take the same road as the missionary. Cross-examined, the witness admitted that he had gone a long way to fetch one van Rooyen, who, he thought, was an eye-witness of the killing of the missionary. He did tell Hodds that he would walk barefooted from Spelonken to Pietersburg to be of the firing party to shoot Morant. He admitted that Hancock had issued an order against soldiers selling their uniforms in consequence of the witness having done so. He had made it his business to collect notes of what was going on at Spelonken.

Two witnesses said that Hancock had left the fort that day with a rifle. He was on a chestnut horse. It was not unusual for an officer to carry a rifle. A native deposed to having seen an armed man on horseback following the missionary. The man was on a brown horse. The witness afterwards heard shots, and then saw the dead body of a coloured boy. He took fright and fled. This was about 2 p.m. Trooper Thompson testified to having seen the Missionary speaking to the eight Boers who were shot. Other witnesses gave evidence as to having seen Heese speak to Taylor, while Morant was present after the shooting of eight men. H. van Rooyen gave evidence as to having spoken to the Revd Mr. Hesse on the road about 2 p.m. The witness trekked on with his wagon till sundown, when he saw a man on horseback coming from the direction of Pietersburg. The man turned off the road. Afterwards a man came on foot to the witness. He could not say if it was the same man that he had seen on horseback. The man on foot was Handcock, who advised the witness to push on, as Boers were about. Trooper Botha deposed that he was one of the patrol of which Handcock had charge and which found the missionary's body. The case for the prosecution then closed.

The accused, Morant, deposed that on August 23 eight Boers guilty of train-wrecking and other crimes were shot by his orders. Heese spoke to these Boers and was told not to do so. Afterwards the witness saw Heese in a cart. He produced a pass signed by Taylor. The witness advised him not to go on to Pietersburg because of the Boers. Heese said he would chance it, and by the witness's advice he tied a white flag to the cart. The prisoner returned to the fort and then went to Taylor's, and afterwards saw Handcock at Bristow's. Handcock went on to Schiel's'. The Prisoner never made any suggestion about killing the missionary. He was on good terms with him.

The accused, Handcock, made a statement as to his doings that day. He said he left on foot for Scheil's in the morning, taking the road which branched off to the Pietersburg road, and then across country. He lunched at Schiels, and then went to Bristow's till dusk, then back to the fort. Further witness proved that Handcock was at Schiel's and Bristow's when the Missionary was shot.

Mrs. Schiels, who lived on a farm about three miles from Fort Edward, the wife of Colonel Schiels, an artillery officer, who had fought with the Boers, and had been captured and sent as a prisoner to St. Helena, gave evidence that Lieutenant Handcock had lunch at her house on the 23rd August, and left during the afternoon.

Mrs. Bristow, who lived about a mile from Fort Edward, and was not on speaking terms with Mrs. Schiels, was the wife of an old settler in the

> *district who had not taken any part in the war. This witness deposed that Lieutenant Handcock had been at their place on the afternoon of the 23rd August, and had returned to the fort in the evening.*
>
> *The Court returned a verdict of 'Not Guilty' in the case of both prisoners.*

It was acknowledged by the prosecution, immediately before the Courts Martial that the case against Morant in the Heese Case was weak. [157] Previously however, according to both one of the accused, Lieutenant Witton and the Prosecutor Major Bolton, [159] Handcock had confessed to the murder, under duress or otherwise. Handcock later retracted this confession shortly before the Courts Martial and it was therefore not allowed in court.

If we take at face value Witton's claims that Lieutenant Handcock had made a confession to killing Revd Heese at Morant's instigation and then in January 1902 withdrew this confession, also at Morant's instigation, then it is easy to understand why Major Bolton, on 5 February, had asked to drop the Heese case against Morant, though not Handcock.

> From To
> Bolton A.G., A.H.Q.
> 5th Feby C.1 In case of missionary I can obtain no further evidence stop. Can I withdraw charge against Morant absolutely no evidence in this case.

To Which the Adjutant General replied:

> Feby 5th A.8845 Your C.1 not clear X If trial of Morant in missionary case is in progress charge cannot be withdrawn, but Court must deal with it according to the evidence X If trial has not begun you may use your own discretion as regards him X Proceed with charge against Handcock in Missionary case. [160]

So the AG gave him leave to drop the case against Morant if it had not already started but advised him to proceed against Handcock. [161] This exchange has been widely misrepresented by Morant's apologists; one simply writes that Major Bolton's 'request was denied'. [162]

It is important to note that there were two cases here. Handcock was being charged with the murder. Morant was being charged with inciting Handcock to commit murder. In fact, Bolton never asked to drop the case against Handcock for the murder of Revd Heese, merely the case against Morant. Without Handcock's confession there was really no evidence against Morant in this case.

The widespread belief that Morant and Handcock were only tried at all because of pressure from the German Government in relation to the Heese case makes the truth about why the case against Morant actually went ahead all the more interesting. This is provided by none other than the defence lawyer, Major J. F. Thomas himself. In a letter dated 4 April 1902, to *The Age* newspaper, he stated:

> ...at the last moment the prosecution, fearing that they would fail to prove their allegations against Morant, asked him on two occasions to let them withdraw the charge (which he refused to do saying, 'I will stand my trial'); ... the president of the court-martial (a special court demanded by the defence) stopped the evidence for the defence and acquitted the prisoner ... apart from the court-martial. [163]

So Morant was tried on the charge of inciting Handcock to kill Revd Heese by a 'special court ... apart from the court martial' by his own demand and that of his defence. This 'special court' almost certainly explains why Witton stated 'For some unknown reason this case was heard privately in the garrison, and not publicly in the town, as the others had been.' [164]

This goes to the very heart of the Morant myth in a number of ways. Not only does it fly the face of the notion that these were kangaroo courts hellbent on a conviction to appease the Germans, but also demonstrates the lengths to which the authorities went to respect the defendants' rights according to law. They actually asked the defendant's permission to drop the case, twice. Surely if the military authorities were half as nefarious as some suggest, they would have just dropped the charges without asking for permission. If they prosecuted Morant with the aim of appeasing the Germans (who in any case had already expressed their indifference), then wouldn't the Heese case also have been conducted in public? A 'show trial' is not much use if it's not on show! Thirdly, it has a bearing on the reliability of Witton as a witness to the court cases. His phrase 'For some unknown reason...' shows that even in 1907 he either did not know why the Heese case had been tried separately or that he did know and chose to misrepresent events. So what else did he not know or understand? Or what else does he misrepresent?

Handcock was provided an alibi by both Mrs Schiel and Mrs Bristowe. [165] Many authors claim the two women were not on speaking terms and were therefore unlikely to have colluded. A number of authors also note the fact that Mrs Schiel, was in fact being protected by the British Army, although her husband had been a member of the Staats Artillery and was a prisoner of war in St Helena, whilst her two sons Tony Schiels and Adolf Scheils were intelligence agents for the British working directly under none other than Captain Alfred Taylor. [166] Witton makes no mention of this. [167] Taylor's office was also literally only a few metres away from Bristowe's Farm at Sweetwaters. [168]

Noting that there was a perception among some that the only case that really mattered was the Heese case, it seems quite possible that one of Taylor's cronies influenced Mrs Schiel and her two sons to provide Handcock with a false alibi under the misapprehension that if acquitted of this charge, no serious action would result from the other charges. There would have been plenty of leverage against Mrs Schiel since the Boers were breathing down her neck and had already attempted to burn her farm for her collaboration with the British. To apply pressure, all Taylor's confederates had to do was threaten to withdraw protection. She and her sons may have even provided a false alibi of their own volition. Once Morant knew that Handcock could get an alibi he may have convinced Handcock to withdraw his confession leaving the prosecution with very little to work with, a position they certainly found themselves in. Taylor and his cronies may have influenced Mrs Bristowe in any number of ways. Of course this is only a theory but it is one that the pro-Morant lobby cannot entertain, since it would imply guilt on the part of Handcock and Morant and would in turn imply that they had reason to hide the events in the Spelonken from the authorities in Pietersburg; thus giving the lie to the 'superior orders' theory. It may be that Handcock did not shoot Revd Heese but the letter written in 1929 by George Witton [169] to J. F. Thomas, discussed later, suggests not.

The real injustice in the whole Morant affair was not in the guilty verdicts on Morant, Handcock, and Witton but in the acquittal of Captain Taylor and, to a lesser extent, the leniency shown to Major Lenehan. Taylor was the driving force behind many of the crimes of the BVC. This was certainly the view of the DJAG, who, based on the evidence of the Court of Inquiry, considered him 'primarily responsible' for cases 4 and 6. [170]

Taylor was not tried under Military Law but under Martial Law by a military court as he had 'not been subject to Military Law for more than three months'. In simple terms, Military Law applies to members of the military as they perform their duty. Martial Law is the law imposed by the military on others during periods in which it is declared. The three months exemption, it has been suggested, explains why Taylor resigned his commission, to escape Military Law. The argument is that the Courts Martial were deliberately delayed to allow this amount of time to pass. The deliberate delay theory has already been shown to be false – and in addition there was more than a little confusion in relation to Taylor's legal status. Prior to the military court the DJAG St Clair wrote:

> 1Sec 175 (4) applies more especially to officers of colonial forces raised by order of His Majesty. Captain Taylor was employed as I understand by the Military Intelligence Dept with the equivalent rank of an officer and should I think be considered as subject to Military Law under sec 175 (7).
>
> Is there not some general order as to the employment and pay of intelligence officers who are specially employed during the campaign? Some such order would be necessary to cause his description under this subsection. [In] its absence he should be brought under sub section 4. [171]

Section 175 (7) of the Army Act states:

> Every Person not otherwise subject to military law who under the general or special orders of a Secretary of State or of the Governor-General of India accompanies in an official capacity equivalent to that of an officer any of her majesty's troops on active service in any place beyond the seas, subject to this qualification, that where such person is a native of India, he shall be subject to Indian military law as an officer. [172]

The DJAG refers to Taylor serving with the 'equivalent rank of an officer' and that to charge him under military law a general order concerning the employment of intelligence officers would need to be produced. If it couldn't be produced then he suggests going back to 175 (4) of which he had already expressed doubt concerning its applicability. If Taylor was an Army Officer during his time in Spelonken, no record of his resignation has been found, though it ought to have been in the *London Gazette*. Some have therefore argued that news of his resignation had been deliberately suppressed. [173] This is a moot point since, if he had been allowed to resign in order to justify his being tried by military court rather than a Court Martial, then the resignation would need to be ratified and known. If he was tried by military court without it being known why he was no longer subject to military law, this would be seen as being illegal, which is exactly what the conspiracy theorists argue the authorities were trying to avoid. Why, if they were being underhand, would the authorities suppress a piece of information when their allegedly dubious actions would only appear legal if that information were widely known?

If the general order referred to above could not be produced then technically he was outside of Military Law the whole time he was an Intelligence Officer and would always have had to have been tried under

Martial Law. This may on the face of it seem an unlikely explanation but at the start of the war the 'Local Intelligence Organization' attached to the British Army had been raised on a very ad hoc basis. [174] No unit smaller than a division had an intelligence officer; and even then, many divisions had a vacancy. Only around July 1900 did the organisation become recognised as the 'Field Intelligence Department'; and intelligence personnel were still employed as and when needed. At this time Colonel Hume, now Director of Intelligence, produced a paper on the Field Intelligence Department in which he wrote about the more junior intelligence personnel: 'The terms of engagement must be a private arrangement with each man, and should be of liberal value.' [175] It is quite possible that this kind of arrangement existed with Taylor, though not certain. On 10 January 1902 the DJAG wrote 'I think that A. Taylor's trial should be postponed until last and that he should be tried by a military court – if he was a native commissioner at the time of the offences, some such description will be advisable on the charge sheets.' Why would he not be described as an Intelligence Officer?

There is one other point which may also suggest why Taylor was not subject to Military Law whether or not he had resigned his commission. 'The discharge of duty involves condonation: and if the crown, with full knowledge of an offence, permits an officer to resign his commission, that would, I apprehend, be such a condonation, that he could not be put upon his trial before a Court-martial.' [176] This would suggest that if Taylor had been allowed to resign in the last few months of 1901 he might never have come to court at all. This may also be a contributing factor as to why Captain James Huntley Robertson was not charged at the same time as the other BVC Officers. He had been allowed to resign before the letter of complaint by the fifteen troopers, the point when it became obvious that the misdeeds of the BVC could no longer be kept under wraps. He was allowed to turn King's Evidence.

A suggestion that J. F. Thomas understood Taylor to be a civilian is provided by Banjo Paterson; 'This was the story of the Morant affair, told me by Thomas, and confirmed by reference to his bundle of papers: "Morant," he said, "was detached from his own command in South Africa, and was acting under the orders of a civilian official named Taylor, who knew the country and had been appointed by the Army to go round the outlying farms requisitioning cattle. They knew that Morant was a good hand with cattle, so that was how he was put on the job. He had a few men under him, and pretty well a free hand in anything he did." [177]

The court of inquiry appears to have recommended at least nine charges against Captain Taylor. The charge of misappropriating cattle was dismissed by the DJAG on the basis of insufficient evidence.

In his review of the findings of the Court of Inquiry in relation to the other charges, see page 201 [178]

Despite the DJAG's recommendations, Taylor was, it appears, only tried on two of the eight remaining charges, those of the murder of the six Boers and the killing of the native man which is presumed to be Case 11. The events of the military court were reported in *The Times*:

> On February 7 the military court sat to hear the charges against Alfred Taylor, who was accused of murder by inciting Sergeant Major Morrison, Sergeant Oldham, and others to kill and murder six men, names unknown. The prisoners pleaded 'Not guilty.'
>
> Sergeant-major Morrison, Bushveldt Carbineers, deposed that on a certain day in July last he paraded his patrol and reported to Captain Robertson. The accused was present, and said he had intelligence that six Boers with two wagons were coming in to surrender, but that he would take no prisoners. The witness asked Captain Robertson if he should take orders from Taylor. Captain Robertson said, 'Certainly, as he is commanding officer at Spelonken.' Morrison asked Taylor to repeat his order, which he did, saying that, if the Boers showed the white flag, the witness was not to see it. The witness repeated these orders to Sergeant Oldham, and warned six men and a corporal to accompany Oldham as an advance party. Six Boers were shot by the advance guard. These were the only ones met with that day. 'The patrol went on, and the following day a larger party of Boers with women and children was brought in, Taylor and Picton going to meet them.
>
> Sergeant Oldham stated that the previous witness warned him of six Boers, and told him he was to make them fight, and on no account bring them in alive. The Boers were ambushed. There was a man in front of a wagon holding a white flag, and a great noise in the wagon. Oldham stopped the fire, thinking there might be women and children, but since he found only six men, as described in the orders, they were taken out and shot. He believed the flag was put up after the firing commenced. The Boers were armed, and their rifles loaded. A good many prisoners were afterwards taken and sent in to Pietersburg. The witness addressed his report of the affair to Captain Taylor, by Morrison's orders. Captain Robertson complained, and the report was readdressed to him. Neither Taylor nor Robertson was present at the shooting of the Boers.
>
> Trooper Heath corroborated this. He said the Boers were disarmed, lined out on the road, and shot. Ex-Captain Robertson corroborated and said that he had told Morrison he must take his orders from the accused. Oldham reported, 'All correct; they are all shot,' and the witness saw the bodies.

Cross-examined, the witness admitted having had to resign and having been refused admission to any other corps. Morrison reported that he was threatened with arrest. Morrison demanded an inquiry, but broke his arrest and went into Pietersburg. Taylor asked for the patrol, as six armed Boers with two wagons were reported. Morrison did not receive instructions from Taylor in the witness's presence. It was usual for patrols to get orders from Taylor.

Major Lenehan deposed to receiving orders to supply 50 officers and men to proceed to Spelonken with Taylor. An inquiry was held in regard to charges in which Robertson and Morrison were mixed up. Colonel Hall decided that it was better that Morrison should go. This closed the case for the prosecution.

The accused elected to give evidence in his own defence. He said that during July last year he was in charge of natives and Intelligence work. He was formerly a lieutenant in Plumer's Scouts and came down on special service. No part of his instructions authorized him not to take prisoners. He had no military command. His instructions went to the officer commanding the detachment of Bushveldt Carbineers. Colonel Hall's instructions were that a detachment of 60 men were to assist him in the Zoutpansberg. He gave instructions to the officers, telling the number of men required for patrols if any Boers had to be fought or captured. He never interfered with non-commissioned officers, but once, when Lieutenant Picton placed Morrison under arrest and the witness refused the latter permission to go to Pietersburg, although he nevertheless broke his arrest and went. The witness received intelligence of certain Boers coming in to surrender, but never of the party of six. He never gave Morrison any orders, and knew nothing about the six Boers, nor had he asked for a patrol to meet them. That patrol took three days' rations with it. The patrol afterwards brought in parties of Boers of which the witness had been advised. The first intimation he had received of the charge of six Boers having been shot was made yesterday in Court.

Davidson, clerk to the accused, deposed to the fact that letters addressed to the latter giving intelligence of the Boers were missing from the office after someone else took the witness's place. The empty file was found at his successor's office. Otto Schwartz, an Intelligence agent, [said he] reported to Taylor the intention of two parties of Boers to surrender, but said he had never mentioned a party of six. Taylor was angry about the shooting of these Boers. Further evidence for the defence was taken to show animus on the part of Morrison.

The counsel having addressed the Court, a second charge was preferred against the same prisoner in respect of the murder of a native. Corporal

> McMahon deposed to being out on patrol when he sighted some Boers, but the latter evidently had wind of his coming, for when the place where they had been seen was rushed no Boers were there, but some opened fire from a kaffir kraal. The Boers were driven off. The witness heard a report, and somebody said, 'Taylor's shot a nigger.' He walked over and saw Kaffir and Taylor standing by with a pistol in his hand Trooper Lucas stated that after the engagement with the Boers he rode to the kraal. Captain Taylor questioned a native, who said 'I konna.' The witness heard a report, and the native fell dead. Taylor had a pistol in his hand. Trooper Sheridan corroborated this.
>
> The accused stated in his defence that he had received his appointment as Native Commissioner in the north on account of his knowledge of the natives and went on condition that he would have a free hand. On this occasion the natives had warned the Boers of the approach of the party, and one native was brought in and recognized as one of them who had been assisting the Boers. He refused to give any information and was threatened with trial as a spy. He refused to show or say anything, and was going off when he was called back, but would not return. Witness then fired meaning to frighten him, had unfortunately fired too low, and the native was killed. The shooting of this native had had a salutary effect. Corroborative evidence was called, and the counsel for the defence pleaded justification.
>
> The Court deliberated, and on its reopening the prisoner was informed that he was acquitted of both charges.

The best indication of why Taylor was acquitted on the charges of inciting the murder of the six Boers is provided by Major Lenehan, who says he was acquitted because he had 'no military command'. [179] Technically this is true; but the men who carried out the shooting clearly believed he had military command.

His acquittal over the murder of the native man is indicative of the inherently racist standards of the time. Military command or not, he pulled the trigger and the 'salutary effect' is the justification. These were the decisions of the military court. The decision to drop the other charges which the DJAG had recommended, however, was made by the convening officer, Lord Kitchener. Prior to the Courts Martial the DJAG had recommended that Taylor be tried on eight charges. [180] He was only tried for two of these. In the light of the acquittal in the six Boers case however it is unlikely that Taylor would have been found guilty of the murder of the other Boer prisoners. He had not pulled the trigger and, rightly or wrongly, the same defence of him having 'no military command' would apply. Justice in its moral sense was not carried out in the case of Captain 'Bulala' Taylor.

Why were many of the charges against Taylor not pursued? The simplistic argument presented is that Taylor was British whilst Morant, Handock, Witton and Lenehan were Australian. This does not hold water. Taylor had been born in Ireland and had spent much of his adult life in Rhodesia. He was as much a colonial, if not more so, than the English-born Morant. As to the 'British' officers, James Huntley Robertson [181] was born and his family lived in Mexico, his mother being Peruvian; Percy Hunt was born in France to an American mother [182] and his family lived there, and even Kitchener himself was born in Ireland. The truth is that all of them – Morant, Handock, Witton and the others – were British officers.

One possible explanation may lie in Taylor's relationship with Chief Mphefu and the Venda. Mphefu had been allowed back into the northern Transvaal and occupied the mountain ranges there, effectively denying this refuge to the Boers. Taylor had facilitated this. Mphefu had later, in the eyes of the British, started to become a nuisance and had been taken to Pietersburg in October 1901 and held until the end of hostilities. Taylor had been removed from the Northern Transvaal partly due to his arbitrary dealings with the Venda and other native peoples.

There had been a tacit agreement between the British and the Boers that the native peoples should not be armed. [183] This had clearly been ignored by the British in the northern Transvaal. [184] It has been suggested that Kitchener spared Taylor for fear of him revealing the use of armed natives and his secret negotiations with the Venda. Armed natives, though not necessarily Venda, had been present at more than one of the BVCs engagements with the Boers and enough Boers had escaped these engagements for this to have become generally known. But if this was the reason it would have been safer to drop all charges rather than just some. In any case, in the event of a guilty verdict, sentence could, as shown by those of Morant and Handcock, be carried out quickly enough to silence him.

It seems more plausible that a guilty verdict and possible death sentence against Taylor would have delivered a message to the native people of northern Transvaal that Kitchener did not want to send. Taylor as we know was feared by the natives as 'Bulala', 'Killer'. The authorities may have wanted to rein in Taylor's often cruel and arbitrary treatment of the native peoples, but a death sentence may have been seen as a step too far in the opposite direction. He may also still have been useful. For all his cruelty, Taylor was clever, shrewd and had an invaluable knowledge of the area, its peoples, their languages and military operations.

The Heese case had ended on 19 February 1902 with a verdict of Not Guilty. The proceedings of the courts martial were sent to Col St Clair and Col Pemberton for their legal opinions, which were given the next day. [185]

Both legal advisors generally agreed with the verdicts though in relation to the Visser case Col Pemberton wrote of Morant: 'A stronger case of implied malice aforethought has rarely been represented before any tribunal.' As for Handcock, Picton and Witton, 'I fail to understand on what grounds the other three prisoners were found guilty of manslaughter only – I disagree with their finding.' Col St Clair agreed but had plenty to say about the overall procedure:

> The Procedure followed on these trials was by trying the prisoners jointly on each charge of murder and conducting each trial to its conclusion, including the sentences.
>
> It resulted from this mode of procedure that Lieut. Morant has been convicted three different times of murder and sentenced three times to death.
>
> Lieuts. Picton, Handcock and Whitton [sic] have been convicted once of manslaughter and sentenced to cashiering; Lieut. Handcock has been also tried, convicted and sentenced to death twice.
>
> Lieut. Whitton has been also once convicted of murder and sentenced to death.
>
> From the above it appears that the responsibility for these illegal acts was in the following order: 1. Morant 2. Handcock 3. Whitton 4. Picton.
>
> According to the rules of procedure 48 and 62 the trial on the separate charge sheets should have proceeded up to and including the findings – but that one sentence should have been awarded each prisoner for all the offences of which he was convicted.
>
> This irregularity has not in my opinion inflicted any injustice on Lieut Morant; but I am not prepared to say that it has not done so in the other three cases. A heap of irrelevant evidence was admitted by the Court on the part of the defence despite the rule of the Judge Advocate who I consider was justified in protesting. [186]

Army Act Section 54 (2) and Rules of Procedure 51 (a) and 52 (a) make it clear that irregularities or errors in sentencing do not necessarily affect the findings. [187] Revisions to sentencing are allowed before and even after confirmation. Section 54 of the Army Act in the Manual for Military Law 1899 states: 'The authority having power to confirm the finding and sentence of a court-martial may send back such finding and sentence, or either of them, for revision once, but not more than once, and it shall not be lawful for the court on any revision to receive any additional evidence...'

Rules of Procedure 51 (a) states: 'A confirming officer cannot send back a part of a finding or sentence for revision; if he thinks that part only requires revision on account of invalidity or otherwise, he should return the whole, pointing out the part which he considers to require revision.' [188]

So an invalid sentence, as pointed out by DJAG St Clair, can be returned for revision, which appears to have been the case with the BVC officers.

It may have not been only Pemberton and St Clair who reviewed the findings of the Courts Martial. A handwritten telegraph message to an unknown recipient held with the Chief of Staff's papers [189] reads:

> All sentences of death and P.S before required confirmation by me. Then before confirmation were reviewed by the DJ.A.G who is a competent barrister who wrote a precis and legal opinion on each case. Proceedings were then passed to A.G. for his minute and subsequently to Sir Richard Solomon the legal adviser to the Transvaal Administration and late Attorney General C.C. for his opinion. In every case of death and in most others serious cases I have discussed matter with Sir R. Solomon before confirmation.
> Kitchener H. H.

The opinions of Sir Richard Solomon, who had been Attorney General to Cape Colony and was legal advisor to the Transvaal Administration, have yet to be found.

We are reliant on Witton for the wording of the verdicts:

> The following is a true copy of the findings of the court, and furnishes a complete answer and direct contradiction to Lord Kitchener's statement that there were 'no extenuating circumstances':-
> CASE I. VISSER CASE.
> SENTENCE.
> Lieut. H. H. Morant, Bushveldt Carbineers, to suffer death by being shot. Death.
> Signed at Pretoria this 29th of January, 1902. H. G. DENNY,
> Lieut.-Col., C. S. COPLAND, President. Judge Advocate.
> RECOMMENDATION TO MERCY.
> The court strongly recommend the prisoner to mercy on the following grounds:-
>
> 1. Extreme provocation by the mutilation of the body of Capt. Hunt, who was his intimate personal friend.
> 2. His good service during the war, including his capture of Field-Cornet T. Kelly in the Spelonken.
> 3. The difficult position in which he was suddenly placed, with no previous military experience and no one of experience to consult.

Signed at Pretoria the 29th day of January, 1902. Confirmed H. C. DENNY, Lt.-Col.,

KITCHENER, General. President. 25th February, 1902.

Promulgated at Pretoria, 26th of February, 1902, and extracts taken.

Sentence carried out at Pretoria on the 27th February, 1902.

H. W. HUTSON, Asst. Prov. Marshal, Pretoria, 27th February, 1902. Pret. Dist.

EIGHT BOERS CASE.

SENTENCE.

Lieut. H. H. Morant, Bushveldt Carbineers, to suffer death by being shot. Death.

Lieut. P. J. Handcock, Bushveldt Carbineers, to suffer death by being shot. Death.

Lieut. G. R. Witton, Bushveldt Carbineers, to suffer death by being shot. Death.

Signed at Pietersburg, this 4th of February, 1902.

H. C. DENNY, Lt.-Col., C. S. COPLAND, Major, President. Judge Advocate.

RECOMMENDATION TO MERCY.

The court recommend Lieut. H. H. Morant to mercy on the following grounds:-

Provocation received by the maltreatment of the body of his intimate friend, Capt. Hunt.

Want of previous military experience and complete ignorance of military law and military procedure.

His good service throughout the war.

The court recommend Lieut. P. J. Handcock and Lieut. G. R. Witton to mercy on the following grounds:-

1. The court consider both were influenced by Lieut. Morant's orders, and thought they were doing their duty in obeying them.
2. Their complete ignorance of military law and custom.
3. Their good services throughout the war.

Signed at Pietersburg this 4th day of February, 1902. H. C. DENNY, Lt.-Col., President.

I confirm the finding and sentence in the case of Lieuts. Morant and Handcock.

I confirm the finding in the case of Lieut. Witton, but commute the sentence to one of penal servitude for life.

> 25th February, 1902. KITCHENER, General.
>
> Promulgated at Pretoria on the 5th [sic] February, 1902, and extracts taken. Sentence carried out at Pretoria on the 27th February, 1902.
>
> H. W. HUTSON, Capt., Court Provost Marshal, Pretoria District. 27th February, 1902. [190]

On 21 February the prisoners were ordered to Pretoria Gaol and Kitchener sent a telegram to Broderick, Secretary of State for War informing him of the verdicts:

> Morant of 3 separate murders, Handcock, 2 murders and 1 manslaughter; Whitton [sic] 1 murder and 1 manslaughter; Picton 1 manslaughter; Lenehan neglecting to report knowledge acquired after fact. The murders were of Boer prisoners, in a spirit of revenge, for alleged ill treatment of 1 of their officers, Lieutenant Hunt, who was shot in action. No such ill treatment was proved. Sentence, the first 3 to death; Picton cashiered; Lenehan will be removed. As corps had been disbanded some time ago for irregularities, dismissal of Lenehan not necessary, and he will be ordered to Australia. I propose to confirm sentences on Morant, who originated the crimes, on Hancock who carried out several cold blooded murders, and, in the case of Whitton, who was present, but under influence, commutation to penal servitude for life. Do you concur? There are other cases against Morant and Hancock, including charge of murder of German. Plea in evidence was not sufficient to convict. [191]

Broderick replied on 24 February:

> The circumstances, and the evidence which has led to the conviction of these 5 officers, are not before us in sufficient detail to enable a judgement to be formed here of the relative guilt of those convicted. We are prepared to support the conclusions you have arrived at. If you have any doubt as to reprieving Whitton, I could only express our opinion if all the facts and circumstances were communicated, which would cause delay, and I fully rely on your judgement. As the incident will probably become public, I should like to be furnished with the fullest particulars and the evidence by mail. Meantime, please telegraph the number of murders committed in all, the authority responsible for the appointment of the officers, and the name of the General to whom they were responsible at the time. Were the murders all committed at one time and how long time elapsed before the accused were placed under arrest? These disclosures will greatly

> affect the confidence felt in the administration of Martial Law by Colonial Officers. Can you restrict this by more stringent regulations? [192]

This exchange has been used by some to suggest that Kitchener did not comply with the requirement of his warrant. His warrant was in effect the licence by which he was allowed to convene courts martial and confirm their sentences and these took several forms allowing different commanders different levels of authority.

Lt Col Caligari accuses The DJAG of being careless in his opinion in presuming [193] that Lord Kitchener's warrant took form IV, as detailed on Page 765 of the Manual of Military Law, 1899. But that is exactly the form of warrant that Kitchener held at that time. On 6 November 1901, Lord Kitchener sent a letter to the Adjutant General to the Forces in London, received by the War Office on 30 November:

> ...under the Provisions of the Form of Warrant Number IV (pages 765, 766 and 767, Manual of Military Law), I am debarred from confirming a sentence of 'Cashiering' or 'Dismissal' in the case of an Officer whether of the Regular Forces or of the Colonial or Irregular Forces serving in South Africa, and all such sentences have to be referred for confirmation by His Majesty The King, thereby causing considerable delay ... Considering the manner in which these Officers are appointed I beg to request that I may be given authority to confirm sentences of 'Cashiering' or 'Dismissal' passed by General Courts-Martial upon Officers of Colonial or Irregular Corps, and that a Warrant with amendments to that effect may be issued to me. [194]

This request was debated. F. H. Jeune, Judge Advocate General, suggested that discriminating between regular officers and colonial or irregular officers was inadvisable. J. K. Kerry, Adjutant General, went further writing on 7 December 1901: 'I agree with the JAG that it is not advisable to make a distinction between Home and Colonial Forces. I would therefore either go further than Lord Kitchener asks, that is – I would give the same warrant that the Commander in Chief in India has, or refuse altogether. I am in favour of the first course.' [195]

The Adjutant General held sway and on 17 January 1902, a day after the first Court Martial commenced, Kitchener was granted a warrant giving him the same powers as the Commander-in-Chief in India. He could now confirm the sentence of any court martial within his jurisdiction without referral to the King. This was considerably more than he had requested.

The Judge Advocate General's objections to the escalation of the proposed change were recorded, after the grant of the warrant, in the Judge Advocate General's Minutes No 14 of 24 January 1902.

> This appears to me to be a proposal to deprive soldiers of a most important constitutional right. The confirmation of the C. in C. does not provide any adequate safeguard against illegality in sentences of a very grave character, certainly no safeguard at all comparable to that afforded by confirmation by the Sovereign after an examination of the case by the authorities in this country. [196]

The JAG's concerns were certainly valid but it is also true that it was quite usual for the warrant of the CiC on 'Active Service in the Field' to be as that of the CiC in India. In relation the Morant myth it is important to note that Lord Kitchener had not requested the power to confirm the death sentence. He had merely asked for the power to confirm sentences of 'Cashiering' and 'Dismissal' on officers of colonial and irregular forces.

If Kitchener had wanted the fate of the BVC Officers to be a fait accompli right from their arrest, as some have suggested, he would have been thwarted by the fact that his warrant at that time would not have allowed him to confirm the death sentences himself. They would have been referred back to the Crown and therefore out of Kitchener's control. They could have been challenged by petitions from Australia or anywhere else. This would also have been the case if Kitchener had been granted the warrant he had requested. If capital sentences had been Kitchener's intention right from the arrest and Court of Inquiry, would he not have requested the power to confirm the death sentence and not just 'cashiering' and 'dismissal'? He had expressed his frustration at the delays in the preparations for the Courts Martial before he had confirmation of his new warrant, so he was happy for the courts martial to go ahead without him having the power to confirm the death sentence.

If the BVC cases were at the forefront of Kitchener's mind when he requested extended powers, his request for powers to confirm sentences of 'Cashiering' and 'Dismissal' suggests that he did not expect sentences of death or penal servitude to be passed. Was it the Leneham case that was his primary concern? Lt Col Caligari states that:

> There was no requirement for Kitchener to refer the proceedings of the Courts-Martial under Form II for Crown concurrence, unless he chose to do so. In the case of Form IV he was obliged to 'transmit the proceedings of any General Court-Martial to our Judge- Advocate-General, in order that he may lay the same before Us'. But Kitchener submitted his

preferred sentences for crown concurrence without submitting the actual proceedings. [197]

The form of his warrant at the time of the sentencing (Form II) allowed Kitchener to confirm the sentences himself and it also allowed him to defer to the King for confirmation of a sentence, if he so chose, in which case he was required to send the full Court Proceedings to the Judge Advocate General. Kitchener's telegram above is not a request for Royal confirmation of the sentences. Broderick, Secretary of State for War, was not Judge Advocate General. Kitchener's telegram amounts to no more than a report and request for advice from his boss, as he might reasonably be expected to make. Although he requested Broderick's opinion he was in no way obliged to do so and Broderick's response to the report was certainly not in the form of a confirmation of sentence. [198] Kitchener confirmed the sentences himself as his warrant allowed.

The verdicts were promulgated in Army Order No. 506, 28 Feb. 1902, from which the following extract has been taken. As the promulgation speaks of only one sentence for the multiple charges, this suggests that the multiple sentences, as highlighted by the St Clair on 20 February, were returned to the Court Martial for revision as allowed by Section 54 of the Army Act [199] in the Manual of Military Law and Rules of Procedure 51 (a) 52 (a). [200] The initial mistake in sentencing did not invalidate the finding of the court.

1. Discipline
   The following extracts from the proceedings of General Courts-Martial held at Pietersburg, Transvaal, between the 16th January 1902, and 19th February, 1902, for the trial of the undermentioned prisoners are published for information:
2. H. H. Morant, P. J. Handcock, G. R. Witton and H. Picton, of the Bushveldt Carabiniers, were charged with
   Charge: When on Active service, committing the offence of murder.
   Finding: The Court find the prisoner Morant guilty of murder, but find the prisoners Handcock, Witton and Picton guilty of Manslaughter.
3. H. H. Morant, P. J. Handcock, and G. R. Witton, of the Bushveldt Carabiniers, were charged with:
   Charge: When on active service committing the offence of murder.
   Finding: The Court find the prisoners guilty of the charge.
4. H. H. Morant and P. J. Handock, of the Bushveldt Carabiniers were charged with:
   Charge: When on active service committing the offence of murder.
   Finding: The Court find the prisoners Guilty of the charge.

Sentence; The Court sentence the prisoners Morant, Handcock, and Witton to suffer death by being shot, and the prisoner Picton to be cashiered.

Confirmation: The General Commanding- in-Chief has confirmed the sentence in the case of the Prisoners Morant, Handcock, and Picton, but has commuted the sentence awarded the prisoner Witton to one of Penal Servitude for life.

The sentences awarded the prisoners Morant and Handcock have been carried out.

5. Major R. W. Lenehan, Bushveldt Carabiniers, was charged with:
Charge: When on active service by culpable neglect omitting to make a report which it was his duty to make.
Finding; The Court find the prisoner guilty of the charge. [201]

According to Witton in the period after the Courts Martial the officers of the BVC whiled away time together in the prison garden hurling peaches at unsuspecting passers-by – including one of the native chiefs working for the British Intelligence Department. On the night of 20 February they met for dinner and spent a pleasant evening made more enjoyable by the news that they had been exonerated of the murder of Revd Heese. The following morning the reality of their situation sank home with the news that they were to entrain for Pretoria at 7 a.m. After breakfast an apologetic sergeant arrived to handcuff the four men; Morant remarked 'This comes of Empire building,' before breaking down and weeping. They then endured the 30-hour train journey to Pretoria standing in cattle trucks under guard. [202]

Major Lenehan was sent onto Cape Town whilst the others were driven to the Old Pretoria Gaol. After Broderick's telegram of 24 February Kitchener took another day before the prisoners were told of their fate on the 26th. On that Thursday Morant was called to the governor's office first. On his return Morant's pallid countenance prompted Witton to exclaim 'Good God, Morant, what is the matter?' 'Shot tomorrow morning' was the response. Handcock was more resigned 'Oh, the same as Morant.' Witton was next called to Captain Hutson, Provost Marshal of Pretoria. According to Witton, Hutson said 'George Ramsdale Witton, you have been found guilty of murder and sentenced to death.' After a pause he continued, 'Lord Kitchener has been pleased to commute your sentence to Penal Servitude for life.' Lieutenant Picton was told he was 'found guilty of manslaughter and cashiered'. [203]

As Floris Visser had done six months previously, Morant requested writing material. He petitioned Kitchener in the hope of a reprieve, a hope Visser could not have entertained. Handcock also wrote to his sister and to the Australian government asking that they look after his children. Since Mrs Handcock later complained that her husband had been dead for a month before she found out, through the newspapers, he did not write to her that night. It appears that the military authorities did not write to his wife either.

Morant's supporters have attributed that lack of communication with Handcock's wife to the callousness of the British authorities, as did Mrs Handcock herself, though the reason that Handcock's wife was not informed of his death is simply that Handcock had not listed her as his next of kin on his attestation papers, preferring to list his sister. [204] Those associated with the case simply didn't know her address. Major J. W. Kelly, Acting for General Commanding in Chief, South Africa, wrote: 'I may add that Lieutenant Handcock before his execution begged that the Australian Government would befriend his children. The address of the nearest known relative of the deceased is that of his sister, Mrs. J. Dempsey, post-office, Peel, via Bathurst, New South Wales.' [205]

It would appear that Handcock spoke more of his sister than his wife when at the gaol, since his last warder (and friend), J. H. Morrow, also wrote to Mrs Dempsey shortly after the executions.

Hansard (Australia) 3 October 1901, seven months after Handcock had joined the BVC:

> Mr. YOUNG asked the COLONIAL SECRETARY (1.) Will he try to find out whether Peter Joseph Hancock, who left with the mounted infantry, Second Contingent, is still in the service of this state in South Africa? (2.) If not, when did he quit the service? (3.) Will Mrs. Hancock and children be entitled to support from the Patriotic Fund, should he not be found? (4.) If not, will the State Board for the Relief of Destitute Children make provision for their support? [206]

On the day that Robert Mitchell Cochrane and the other fifteen troopers were signing their letter of complaint, the response appeared in the Australian press:

> The Premier, in reply to Mr. Young, said that Peter Joseph Hancock, who left for South Africa with the second contingent of Mounted Infantry, was transferred to the Bushveldt Carbineers as veterinary lieutenant on the 20th of February. If Mrs. Hancock applied to the State Children's Relief Board, her case would receive full consideration. The Government had nothing to do with the administration of the Patriotic Fund. [207]

It would appear then, that for almost the whole of the time that Peter Handcock was a serving Lieutenant in the BVC his wife did not know where he was. If anyone was guilty of neglecting his wife, it was Handcock himself!

Harry Morant, who had not seen his wife for about eighteen years, wrote a will on the eve of his execution and not surprisingly left nothing to her, or for that matter to anyone else in Australia:

> I Harry Harbord Morant declare this to be my last will and testament.
> I leave all money in my possession, due to me as pay and any money now lying in my account in the Standard Bank of South Africa to Mary Ella Wickett, wife of George Augustus Wickett, residing at Holmewood House, Bideford N, Devon, England.
>
> I leave my gold cygnet ring to Maud Murray of Rowena, Westward Ho, N, Devon England.
>
> I leave a ring with turquoise stone and gold chain to Lilian Hunt of 64 Avenue de Bois de Boulogne, Paris. I leave my Mauser Carbine in the possession of Civil Surgeon Johnstone Pietersburg to Francis Morant, Brockenhurst Park, Hants, England.
>
> I leave a pair of Zeiss Field glasses and compass case to Lieutenant Barker 2/ Wiltshire Regiment.
>
> All my other personal property, horses and arms and baggage whatsoever in Pretoria and in Pools Hotel in Capetown I bequeath to civil surgeon Johnstone in Pietersburg Pool's Hotel; and I also wish this said Dr Johnstone to act as my Executor.
>
> Harry Harbord Morant
>
> This 26th day of February 1902 at Pretoria Transvaal. [208]

Francis Morant did not live at Brockenhurst Park and neither did the Admiral, Morant's 'adopted' father. Although Francis Morant had once lived at Brockenhurst, the Brockenhurst Morants were a different branch of the family from the Admiral.

By 29 March 1904 Mary Ella Wickett had not claimed Morant's bequest of money since on that date the *London Gazette* issued a notice of 'Soldiers Balances Unclaimed'. The estate of H. H. Morant of the Bushveldt Carbineers was unclaimed and worth £123 6s 1d. This is roughly equivalent to £14,000 today. More than a few lodging house keepers, hoteliers and disgruntled barflies must have raised an eyebrow at the amount. Whether any of them attempted to claim against the estate is not known.

J. F. Thomas on learning of the sentences attempted to reach Lord Kitchener. He was, according to Witton, told by Colonel Kelly that Kitchener was 'away on trek'. [209] Kitchener was at Harrismith. Thomas begged

Kelly to stay the executions to allow for enough time to appeal to the King. The reply from Kelly was that the sentences had already been referred to England, and approved by the authorities there. There was no hope of an appeal. Morant had written a petition to Lord Kitchener but the reply came from Colonel Kelly and was that the sentence was irrevocable. [210]

The detailed account of the executions was revealed to the Australian public by George Aldridge, who had been a member of the Second South Australian Contingent. He passed a letter from Mr. J. H. Morrow, warder in the Pretoria Gaol, to the press:

> Dear George—I write these few lines to you on behalf of Lieutenant H. H. Morant, who was shot here on February 27, two days ago, by order of court-martial. His last word was that I should write and tell you. There were four officers, one South Australian, one Victorian, one New South Welshman, and one New Zealander, all Australians concerned. The South Australian and New South Welshman were shot, and the others transported. It is quite a mystery here. Regarding the deed, all I know is they shot 38 Boers, and there are rumours in circulation that the Boers surrendered to them. Morant told me he was guilty of shooting the Boers because they shot his captain. I was the warder who was in charge of the officers the last week they had on earth, and they faced their doom as brave as men could do. Everyone said it was a pity to shoot two such brave men. Morant came out here with the South Australian Mounted Rifles, with which you and I enlisted. He got a commission in the Bushveldt Carbineers, and I went on the railway here, and I only transferred to this prison about six weeks ago. I was not here when they came here. They had been in prison at Pietersburg for four months and they were transferred to Pretoria where sentence was passed upon them to be shot next morning at 6 o'clock and buried at 5 o'clock in the evening. There were a large number of Australians at the funeral, there being no fewer than 30 Australian officers. We got a hearse and mourning coach and there was a very nice funeral. I felt it very much. The only reply given by the men when asked if they were ready was 'Yes. Where is your shooting party?' and the men marched out hand in hand. The firing party went to blindfold the men, when Morant said, 'Take this thing off,' and pulled it off, and as the two sat down in chairs awaiting death he remarked 'Be sure and make a good job of it.' Morant folded his arms across his chest and looked them straight in the face, and said if they didn't fire he would look down the barrels of their rifles for the bullets. The firing party fired, and Morant got it all in the left side, and died at once, with his arms folded and his eyes open. You would have thought he was alive. [211]

There is no evidence for Morant saying 'Shoot Straight You Bastards,' which formed the title of a book. The misquotation originated from Kit Denton's 1973 novel *The Breaker*.

There are strong counter-arguments to the notion that Lord Kitchener deliberately scapegoated colonials, specifically Australians. There is plenty of evidence that he had a considerable respect for Australians and New Zealanders. Besides the fact that the gaol register at Pretoria listed Morant as English, which he was, Lord Kitchener (though it may have been penned by his chief of Staff Ian Hamilton) in a telegram of 25 February 1902 mentioned his belief that Morant had been in the Royal Navy. [212] He must have heard of Morant's yarn about this, which almost certainly went hand-in-hand with the claim to being the son of Admiral George Digby Morant. It seems likely that Kitchener believed he was executing a scion of the English landed gentry rather than an outback Aussie.

12

Aftermath

> TWO MURDERERS SHOT. London March 9.
> Two troopers belonging to the irregular forces operating with the British army, having been tried by court martial and convicted on a charge of shooting Boers who had surrendered, have been shot at Pretoria. [1]

This brief note is how the news of the Courts Martial was broken to readers of the Adelaide *Advertiser* in early March 1902. Two-and-a-half weeks later the *Advertiser* followed up:

> A cablegram appeared in *The Advertiser* of March 10, stating that two members of an irregular corps fighting in South Africa, who had been convicted by court martial of shooting a Boer who had surrendered, had been sentenced to death and had been shot at Pretoria. Little notice was taken of the news at the time, but a painful interest has been awakened in the event by some additional particulars which have been supplied, showing that the men thus punished came originally from Australia. At the time when the incident occurred they were serving in one of the many irregular corps which had been locally raised in South Africa, and were entirely under Imperial authority. This accounts for the fact that the Australian military authorities received no official particulars with regard to the trial and punishment. The information which has now come to hand is entirely unofficial. Major R. D. [sic] Lenehan, who was in command of the corps with which the convicted men were connected, arrived in Melbourne on his return from South Africa by the steamer *Aberdeen* on Monday. [2]

So in late March, one of the co-accused, Major Lenehan, had brought back the news that the two men shot by firing squad in South Africa had come from

Australia. The accounts of Maj. Lenehan and letters received from Lt Witton by his brother around the same time were about to set in train a controversy which would spark an immediate media frenzy, a book published within two months, [3] and Witton's own book five years later. Over the next 115 years there would numerous other books, stage plays, articles and documentaries.

It is hardly surprising that in the years after the executions, public opinion in Australia would turn in favour of the defendants. After all, one of the defendants was a celebrity of sorts and there were three middle class families with an interest in creating the impression that they had been hard done by. Major Lenehan, with his military career in tatters, felt that he had been badly treated in being bundled out of South Africa so expeditiously. Lieutenant Witton was still incarcerated with his family fighting for his freedom and Major Thomas, his ego battered and reputation somewhat tarnished, still passionately believed he was right. Set against the general anti-British feeling fostered by publications such as the *Bulletin* there was really only one outcome. Those BVC troopers such as Frank Hall and Hamline Glasson who thought that Morant and Handcock had got what they deserved were never going to create as much noise.

They were never going to make as much of an impact as Morant's mates at the *Bulletin* either. On 12 April 1902, five days before the detailed account of the Courts Martial appeared in *The Times*, the *Bulletin* wrote:

> The Australian Officers were in part victims at least of their ignorance of Military Law and of the brutal homicidal carelessness or worse of the Kitchener gang in appointing blacksmiths, drovers and what not as responsible military officers in disturbed districts ... we repeat, the chief responsibility must rest with the persons who were guilty of criminal carelessness, or the sanguinary design, of letting irregulars loose on the Boers. [4]

Notwithstanding the fact that Kitchener had appointed Major Lenehan and he and Major Poore had receuited the 'blacksmiths, drovers and what not', any implication of 'the Kitchener gang' in the Morant affair would be pounced upon and sung from the Blue Mountains when it came. Many would make judgements based on their perception of the character of the defendants and Morant's press connections and fellow-poets were about to pipe up with their 'Sketches of Lt Morant'.

Some expressed the opinion that the Morant that they knew would never have been capable of such acts as were being described in the newspapers; others found scarcely a good word. The Breaker's mate, J. C. L. Fitzpatrick, wrote in the *Windsor and Richmond Gazette* on Saturday 5 April:

It is not the intention of the writer here to canvas the justice of the sentence passed and carried to its dread conclusion upon Harry Harbord Morant and his companion, but merely within the brief space allotted to pen a sympathetic notice of a man who possessed many excellent characteristics of head and heart, and who, but that he was human and had his fair share of this frailties of the world, might have made his mark in the literary world, and, according to the verdict of quite a number of 'very proper' people, have occupied an honored place in the community. Let not those judge him harshly however, whose knowledge of the man was but of a superficial nature – who saw him casually and knew nothing of the trials and tribulations by which he was beset. Under a rough exterior there existed an abundant good nature, and a kindliness of feeling towards all mankind, which appealed to those who enjoyed his confidences; whilst his merry laugh and his perennial good humour scarce sufficed to hide at any time to such as knew the sorrows within him. How easy it is to be sure, to prophesy what he 'might have been' as, no doubt, many will most readily do whose lots have been cast in pleasant places – how comforting to suggest that the victim himself is alone to blame for the trouble which has cost him his life. Perhaps tis true; yet, knowing Morant, as I did, I believe that he fully endorsed the sentiments of Adam Lindsay Gordon when he wrote –

'For gifts misspent and deeds undone and resolutions vain I care not now to trouble – this I know, I would live the same life over if I had to live again And the chances are I go where most men go.'

A courageous rider and a writer of strong and vigorous verse; a man imbued with many lovable traits of character and a high sense of respect for the opposite sex, Harry Morant made himself popular wherever he ventured; and there are today, scattered throughout this young continent of ours many one-time acquaintances of his in every circle of life, who will feel sincere regret at hearing of his untimely end. From Walgett to Windsor, from Penrith to Parkes, and from Muswellbrook to Mungundi he was known by the quaint title bestowed upon him during the period when he was engaged 'out back' in the somewhat hazardous occupation of taming young horses. And if the good folk in country parts had never witnessed his exhibitions of prowess in this direction they had at least heard of his feats of horsemanship or had read in the press those poems from his pen which bore the signature of 'The Breaker'. Absolutely unafraid, absolutely careless of danger, and with his face in a condition of perpetual smiles, it took little time for Morant to ingratiate himself with the men of the bush; and his charm as a raconteur did the rest. He was a welcome guest at farm and station-homestead, and the inexhaustible fund of general information upon which he was ever able to draw at a moment's notice made him an interesting companion at all times. Hard living, and the buffeting he had received during a chequered career, rendered him somewhat cynical and endowed him with a wholesome repugnance for many institutions claimed to be cherished by folk more favorably situated; and yet he was wont to recognise in a generous spirit the most trivial kindness shown him, and to distinguish readily between 'a real white man' and that snuffle busting and unctuous person who turns up the white of one eye at the bare thought of the world's wickedness – and keeps the other fixed all the time on 'the main chance'. A keen sportsman, he had followed the hounds in the best of company on his native moors in Devonshire, and I have by me at the present time a copy which was his of Whyte Melville's 'Katerfelto', a story of Exmoor, which is marginally marked here and there and from which a few quotations may be appropriately made, as showing how devoted he was to his native country and how strong his penchant for the sport of the chase:-

'I might ride through Exmoor half a summer's day and never set eyes on a human face, but the curlew seems to know me as he flits by, with a quiet call of greeting and a wave of his wide brown wing – the red herds, leading their calves along the ridges, look kindly over their shoulders, and turn their handsome heads to gaze after me, till they disappear. Why, the very breeze, whispering amongst the rushes, pilfering in my own garden, not so many miles away. You know no more than a blind man what morning means till you've seen the sun rise in North Devon. I wish I was back there now. I will be back there next week, if I'm alive.'

'If I'm alive!' Also, the poor old 'Breaker's' eyes have closed upon all North Devon's charming sunsets for ever – unless he be born again.

It was delightful to breathe a free, fresh air, untainted by the smells of London – to see the sky come down to a wide horizon uninterrupted by streets and houses – to feel beneath him the strong elastic action of his good bay horse.

The man cannot be morally crooked or mentally depraved who realises the beauty and appreciates the charm of ... pictures such as that quoted – no doubt it commended itself doubly to Morant by reason of the fact that he was reminded of his own favourite mount, 'Cavalier,' in the reference to the 'good bay horse.'

Talk of the music and the organ in Exeter Cathedral – thirty couple of such voices (the hounds) as those would silence a battery of cannon. They spread like a Lady's fan, they swarm like a hive of bees, soon they settle into their places and stream across moor, like horses in stride and speed, like lions in strength and energy and fierce desire for blood. Now's your

> time, old man. You sit down in your saddle and say to yourself there is nothing on earth worth living for compared to such moments as these. And now into the story is introduced a sporting parson of the good old English type, the sort who would sooner ride fifty miles to a fight than five to a prayer meeting, who knew a good dog when he saw him, or a game cock, could tell the points of a pacing nag, and was an excellent judge of strong ale – by name the Rev. Abner Gale and he preaches to himself, riding homewards one dark night, on a test which apparently appealed strongly to the sympathies of 'The Breaker' – 'Keep your own counsel – and take a good hold of your horse's head.' But enough! The end has come and the writer here pays his meagre tribute to the memory of a comrade who no matter what his faults and failings were, ever proved himself a manly, good natured, ruggedly honest fellow, and one who has got as good a show as the average man of being well treated in the Great Beyond! [5]

Exactly a month earlier in the same publication, 'H. F.' wrote a lengthy letter from a different standpoint:

> In the Gazette. 27/2 '04, a long quotation is given of an alleged report of the trial and execution of Harry Morant. On the face of it that account is fabulous, and of itself is unworthy of serious comment; but it is quite likely to be a symptom of a reaction of ignorant public sentiment, towards defecation of an unworthy object. Morant was not Australian born, bred, or by adoption. Though many years in this country, his vices and virtues were not of us; but of the class of English gentleman blackguard to which he belonged. The man, after a worthless life, met with courage a soldier's death. Let the dead bury its dead! The writer, for one would not rake up old stories were it not that ignorant busybodies were striving to make an Australian hero out of an English scamp. Now for a picture of the man as he really was A shortish man, large features, small eyes (too close together), clean shaven, his skin red with alcohol, a horsey look about his dress, the manners and speech of a gentleman, of surprising physical courage (particularly on horseback), quite destitute of moral courage or moral principle; fond of exercise in the way of sport, he would never willingly exert himself to earn an honest shilling if he could borrow it off no matter whom; a confirmed dipsomaniac. During the many years he wandered about Australia, Morant brought the art of being a sponge on other men's generosity to a fine art, and for bilking hotelkeepers and tradespeople he was unsurpassed. Probably no man this side of the world ever owed so many unpaid accounts, most of them paltry. From North

Queensland to South Australia there appears to be hardly a town that he did not bleed. His mode at a new place, as with a new acquaintance, was to introduce himself as the nephew or son (he gave both versions) of Admiral Morant, as a visitor to Government House, and as a contributor to the "Bulletin." He has been known to convey all this personal information within ten minutes of meeting an utter stranger, and this not in the way of boasting, but as part of a consistent plan for getting credit. He had the ability to have made a decent living as a drover, horse-breaker, or sporting newspaper reporter; he could write fragmentary verse above the average in merit. But he lacked all desire for honest earnings—to best someone, by lying inventions to take someone down, was a perfect delight to him. One of his common tricks for exciting charity was to say he had been robbed. The writer has known him to have been robbed—according to his own account—three times within a week of sums varying in amount from twenty to forty pounds. If they would take him in he always put up at the best hotel in a town. As he never meant to pay, price was no object; also such hotels rarely prosecute defaulters, and residing there gave him credit with tradespeople, As in some hotels he was no doubt an attraction to the bar, and caused other people to spend money there, many of his victims did not think hardly of him. In any part of Australia if you mention Morant's name you will be asked 'What did he take you down for?' The wholesale nature of his operations would gain a certain respect were it not for their general meanness; no sum was too small for him to borrow, no person (male or female) too poor for him to bleed—for under a superficial politeness he was utterly selfish, It is true he was careless with money when he had it; he is reported to have shared a considerable sum with a comrade; but when he was short of cash then someone else must pay, no matter whom. Free and easy back-block Australia stood such a creature for many years; it is a mark of his genius that the Hawkesbury being had by him once, and knowing his character quite well, allowed itself to be had again in exactly the same way. But latterly he was getting old, his beery face and red nose were not so attractive; and going south his luck deserted him. Melbourne was too hot for him in a month; and Adelaide was his Waterloo. They did not appreciate him in the city of the churches. After three days trial of Mr Morant, and no cheque or promised luggage arriving, one of Adelaide's leading hotelkeepers took Harry by the scruff of the neck and the seat of the pants and threw him violently into the middle of the dusty road. Late the same night he received exactly the same treatment from the back door of a house of ill repute; the following day he was arrested at the instance of an acquaintance for attempting to gain money by false pretence.

> Mr. O'Kane of the Adelaide 'Critic' very generously offered to pay his rail fare out of the colony, and prevailed with the police to see him to the station. It is well to recall this softened picture of a worthless personality when it is sought to put him on a pedestal of honour or martyrdom. As a horse soldier under strict discipline he might have been a success; as an officer in independent command he was bound to be a failure; for he could not command himself. In his sober moments, those who knew him best would not credit the acts of cold blooded cruelty laid to his charge; but drunk, with unlimited drink under his hand for months, everything was possible; and the man was a moral coward who having committed one crime when drunk would not have hesitated at other crimes for self protection. A crooked mind, not perhaps wholly responsible; heroic on the physical plane, a dastard on the moral plane, Australia wants no such heroes foisted on her. His leading brought some of our boys into deserved odium. His dramatic death was fitting and probably welcome to him, as a right climax to a life of vagabondage he found year by year harder to play. Repudiated by his own people, Australia has nothing to thank him for. In his better moments he was genial and friendly, with a healthy love of the open air, joined to a thin vein of poetry; those who only saw that side of the man may remember him with sorrow and regret. Let us hope that in a future life it will be the side to survive from a character so chequered and deformed. H. F.' [6]

Such were Morant's powers of deception that both of the above writers, notwithstanding their opposed views on his character, believed him to be an English gentleman of Devon beset by trials and tribulations and repudiated by his own people. One can only wonder at their reaction if they had known he was most probably just another economic migrant.

J. F. Thomas was another beguiled by Morant. In his article 'Doubting Thomas' in the Law Society Journal (NSW, Australia) of October 2001, Dr John Bennett observes that Thomas 'committed the most basic error of advocacy; that he identified himself with the cause of his clients'. [7] The degree to which Thomas identified with, or had been taken in by, Morant and the other BVC officers is revealed by the letter he wrote to George Witton's father from South Africa. It was published in a number of Australian papers:

> Dear Sir— have a painful duty—though I am glad it is not so painful as it might have been—to perform, in giving you some particulars of the conviction, for instigating to murder, of your son, of the Bushveldt Carbineers. I may say at once that I believe, when the facts become known

to your Government, it will not be long before your son is released. But, in any case, I anticipate he will be kept prisoner till the war is over, or, possibly, till the King's Coronation. I am seriously dissatisfied with the severe punishment meted out. It has astounded, I think, every unbiased person. I cannot say much here, but to one, at least, of the officers who were shot—a New South Wales man—I owe a sacred duty, and that is to let Australia know all the circumstances. Lieutenants Morant and Handcock, who were shot here on the 27th ultimo, were convicted, together with your son, by a court-martial consisting of Imperial officers, of ordering their men to murder, as the charge alleges, several Boers who had been captured under the following circumstances. Briefly stated, the evidence distinctly shows that their senior officer Captain Hunt, formerly a Hussar officer, gave his junior officers and his sergeants orders that after a train-wrecking episode in which an officer and a number of men were killed near Pietersburg, they were to take no prisoners. Hunt was soon afterwards killed himself, and Lieutenant Morant, his personal friend for years, succeeded to the command of the detachment. Hunt's body was badly maltreated by the Boers, Morant swore vengeance, and swore to carry out Hunt's orders. He pursued the party of Boers, who had done this to Hunt, and captured one who was hit through the heel, and had portion of Hunt's clothing in his possession. It was decided to hold a drumhead court-martial, and the Boer was found guilty of wearing khaki, and of being implicated in the barbarities to Hunt. He was shot by a firing party. Subsequently eight Boers, who had been captured in some outlying place, were, under Morant's orders, all shot for being wreckers, bandits, and concerned in Hunt's maltreatment. Your son was present, and a Boer who rushed at him was shot by him. It was considered by the court-martial that these executions were illegal, and that all the officers present were equally to blame for the shooting of these Boers by their men. The defence maintained was that under the customs of war the shooting these Boers was allowable, as they were merely running bandits or marauders. It was proved that in other cases exactly the same procedure was adopted and approved of by other officers. Consequently you will see that from a soldier's point of view, at any rate, the crime was not so dreadful as might appear, although, technically, it was a crime. I only regret that poor Morant and Handcock did not receive a sentence of penal servitude, but, poor fellows, they were shot at about eighteen hours notice. Over Handcock's death I have suffered the deepest grief. It may be that before long I shall be back in Australia, when I shall make it my business to let the Government know the position. Your son has been sent a prisoner to England, and I think it

> will be wise to defer any active steps concerning him till the Australian Commonwealth Government is in possession of the facts. As counsel for your son and other officers I should like to see that all the facts from the prisoners' point of view are fairly brought forward. When everything is known you will not think the disgrace amounts to much or anything. War is war, and rough things have to be done. Only yesterday news came in of horrible barbarities on the part of the Boers towards some of our colonials. I say, they deserve all they (the Boers) get, and with less nonsense and sentiment the war would be over—(Signed) J. F. Thomas, Army Post Office. Pretoria, March, 1902. [8]

Just as he had in court, Thomas argued that the normal rules should not apply since these particular Boers did not deserve such protection. He had no way of knowing whether the Boer victims had committed any indiscretions. He just took Morant, Handcock and Witton's word for it. Morant's 'drumhead court martial' of his victims did not happen and there was nothing to suggest that the eight Boers had anything to do with train wrecking or the death of Hunt. In any case the JAG had made a judgement that train wrecking was a perfectly legitimate military activity and no more a crime than attacking a supply column.

It seems more than a little ironic that the pardon lobby argue that the BVC officers were scapegoats for the barbarities of the British Empire when their defence counsel states: 'I say, they deserve all they (the Boers) get, and with less nonsense and sentiment the war would be over'. Was he suggesting the British forces should have been more brutal? Remember he had, himself, survived falling into Boer hands. There were many in Australia and elsewhere however, having been bombarded with tales of Boer brutality, who agreed with this sentiment. This probably more than any legal argument accounts for any sympathy for Lenhehan and Witton.

Contrary to the assertions of the pardon lobby, Ernest Witton, Lieutenant Witton's brother had known that his sibling was being tried for being complicit in the shooting of unarmed Boers, since he had received a letter telling him so. The letter was later reported in the Australian press:

> Lieut. G.R Witton, writing from Pietersberg under date December 4, 1901, to his brother in Melbourne, states that there had been some trouble with the officers of the Bushveldt Carbineers, to which he belonged, and that at the time of writing four of them, including the writer, were under arrest on a charge of having shot unarmed Boers; but he did not regard the position as serious, feeling that the most extreme punishment to which they were likely to be subjected was cashiering. [9]

Some of the content of a letter from George Witton to his brother prior to the Courts Martial, which is probably the one referred to above, was reported in *The Evening Star*:

> We can prove justification for dealing with them summarily. The lives of these Boers were already forfeit if they wear British uniform. In the Franco-German war the Germans made no scruple about shooting 'Franc tireurs' who, masquerading as harmless persons, were yet carrying on their tactics of guerilla warfare! The two cases were precisely parallel; in fact, several Boers have already been court-martialed and shot for this transgression of the rules of war. I reckon: it is hard for any man who offers his services and life to assist to end this war, to be tried for his life when he wipes out a few of these Dutch gentlemen. There will be no more empire building on these terms for me. I shall, come out of this all right. They can't surely crucify me, and I reckon it will be rough if I am cashiered. [10]

On hearing the news that his brother had been sentenced to a life of penal servitude, Ernest Witton began to lobby for the Australian Government to take action. On 26 March 1902 Ernest waited on General Hutton and presented him with a letter from his brother George giving his version of events. [11] The General had already heard Maj. Lenehan's version of events the previous day. [12] The Australian Prime minister, Mr Barton, was around this time, cabling South Africa for more details. The newspapers reported:

> The Premier, Mr. Peacock, received to- day a communication from Mr. John W. Rail, of the National Mutual Life Association of Australasia, who is acting as Victorian Government Agent for military contingents in South Africa. This communication covers a statement written by Lieut. Witton, the officer who was sentenced to penal servitude for life ... Mr. Rail expresses the opinion that Lieut. Witton was the kind of man who would have been amenable to discipline, even under such circumstances as those narrated by him. 'I submit,' says Mr Rail, 'that this is a case that may receive your attention, with a view to the mitigation of the punishment.' The following is Lieut. Witton's statement, as forwarded by Mr. Rail.:-
>
> 'To Mr. Rail, Australian Government Agent, Capetown. – Statement by Lieut. Witton, Bush Veld Carbineers
>
> 'Case. I joined the Bush Veld Carbineers at Pietersburg on the 13th July, 1901. On the 5th of August I was posted to the Spelonken detachment,

which was then under the command of Capt. Hunt. On the 7th, information reached us, at Fort Edward, that Capt. Hunt had been killed at Dunel's Kloof [sic]. Lieut. Morant then being senior, ordered the whole detachment to proceed with him to Reuter's mission station 85 miles east of Fort Edward, to reinforce a small party that had gone there with Capt. Hunt. We reached Reuter's, on the evening of the 8th of August, and obtained full particulars of the Boers, and were also told that Capt. Hunt had been murdered by Boers after his being wounded. We left Reuter's on the morning of the 9th, and in the evening we overtook a party of Boers, 53 in number, at Reitvlei. The laager was immediately attacked. The Boers fled leaving a prisoner of war wounded. The prisoner was then in possession of several articles, the property of the late Capt Hunt, and was wearing khaki. He was taken with us next morning in a Cape cart. When we halted at Mamahiela Kop Lieut. Morant told me that his intentions were to shoot the prisoner. I having only joined Captain Hunt a few, days previously, did not know him sufficiently to remonstrate with him. He had already told me that a proclamation had recently been issued to the effect that all Boers taken in khaki were to be shot. Lieut. Picton joined us again at Mamahiela Kop, and on his immediate arrival Lieut. Morant told him his intentions. A consultation followed and this has since been represented as a court-martial. At the time of this consultation no mention was made of a court-martial. At the consultation Lieuts. Morant and Handcock were in favour of shooting the prisoner. It was stated at the court-martial, which was held in Pietersburg, that the decision, which was arrived at at the consultation was unanimous but this was not so. Lieut. Picton objected; and I took no active part whatever. I was told at the Court of Inquiry, that having only recently joined, and only taken a very subordinate part; I was not responsible. When Lieut. Picton was ordered to command the firing party Sergt.-Major Clark asked me to speak to Lieutenant Morant on behalf of the men. I quite agreed with the men that the prisoner should not be shot, and mentioned it to Lieutenant Morant. He would not listen to anything, and told me that what he was going to do he was perfectly justified in. If the men made any fuss he would shoot the prisoner himself. This is all I know of the Visser case. Sergts.-Major Clarke and Hammett can bear witness to these statements. On the night of the 22nd of August, 1901, Lieutenant Morant received information that a party of eight Boer prisoners were being brought in with a patrol. Early on the following morning he ordered a small patrol and left the fort, accompanied by Lieutenant Handcock, three men, and myself. On the way he made known his intentions. I asked him if he was exceeding his duty, and he gave me to understand that he was justified in acting in this manner, and that I, being a junior subaltern, had only to obey his orders. We came up to

> the patrol with the prisoners, and Lieutenant Morant took charge. When we had come on about two miles he ordered the prisoners off the waggon, and took them about twenty yards off the road. He then ordered them to be shot. I hesitated to fire, and one of the prisoners rushed at me. I then fired to keep him off. They were all shot, and their bodies were buried shortly afterwards. At the court martial, which was held at Pietersburg, on February 3, when this case was heard, Lieutenant Morant took the whole responsibility on himself, and stated that whatever part I had taken was by his orders. At the Court of Inquiry, which was held at Pietersburg, I requested them to write to secure the services of Mr. Rail, the Australian Government representative, to appear for me as the prisoners' friend. At the forthcoming court-martial I was informed that this was not necessary, as it appeared that I had taken a very subordinate part in the charges which were brought against me, and it was not necessary to bring Mr Rail from Capetown. I was led to believe that I could be exonerated from all blame. I have now been sentenced to penal servitude for life, and I beg that you will intercede on my behalf and investigate my case, for I conscientiously believe that I am not guilty, of the charges that have been brought against me. (Signed) George R. Witton, lieutenant, B.J.S., Capetown. March 7, 1902.' [13]

Ernest Witton secured the services of Isaac A. Isaacs in order to attempt to obtain the release of his brother George. Isaacs set about the preparation of an opinion document. [14] Isaacs considered the chances of success very good, though he stated:

> I do not base my view upon any strict legal ground. The Technicalities were, so far as I have opportunity of testing them, satisfied as far as mere legality is concerned.
>
> Formalities were I think, observed. Even as to the evidence of Colonel Hamilton – which at first sight appeared, amid the swift and dramatic events of the time, to have been taken irregularly – was really perfectly in order; for the Court, after the Beyers attack at Pietersburg, journeyed to Pretoria for the purpose of obtaining this officer's testimony, and then returned to complete the trials.
>
> Further I am not in possession of any circumstances which would show any disregard of the Rules of Procedure number 20 (B), in not including as a member of the Court Martial one member at least of the Corps of the officers charged. See Army Act, Section 50 (1), which, with Section 178, gives very large powers of constituting Courts Martial.
>
> Consequently I lay aside, for the purposes of this opinion, all questions of technical legality; and address solely to the substance of the case. [15]

Others with less opportunity of testing the technicalities of the case 114 years later are at odds with Isaacs on the legality of the Courts Martial. In fact, the constitution of the Courts Martial and the omission of an Officer of an Irregular Corps is one of the specific points argued.

Isaacs' main point in relation to the Visser case is Witton's junior position. Witton having only joined the BVC on 13 July 1901 came under Captain Hunt's command no earlier than 5 August and Hunt was killed on 6 August. Witton and Hunt never met. The Visser incident occurred within a week of this and Isaacs' argument was Witton had no choice but to follow Morant's orders. Isaac's also stresses that Witton had objected to Morant about the killing of Visser. [16] Though this is something of a double edged sword, since his objections, though they might count in his favour, also demonstrate that he knew the killing was morally wrong and probably that he knew it was against Military Law. These arguments were exactly the reasons why Lord Kitchener commuted his sentence from death to penal servitude for life. In doing so, Kitchener would have known that ultimately Witton would not serve life.

In relation to the eight Boers case, again Isaacs argued that Witton had little choice but to follow Morant's orders. He goes on to refer to Lieutenant Hannam's statement that Colonel Craddock of the Queensland Mounted Infantry had reprimanded him for bringing in prisoners, and to similar allegations that Brabant's Horse were ordered to take no prisoners. [17] Isaacs makes no distinction between not taking prisoners and taking prisoners and shooting them in cold blood days later, which was what the BVC officers were tried for.

Isaacs also presented an argument based on the woolly concept of condonation. This concept of military law has recently gained credence amongst Morant apologists, though it was not used by Major Thomas during the Courts Martial. Some blame the perceived lack of time to prepare their case on the fact that Thomas did not enter a Plea in Bar of court on the basis of condonation.

Condonation was a term originally used in canon law and is now generally obsolete, meaning the forgiveness by a husband of his wife or by a wife of her husband, of adultery, with an implied condition that the injury would not be repeated and that the other party would be treated with kindness. It could be a bar to divorce. The concept of condonation in military transgressions was given weight by The Duke of Wellington, who said 'The performance of a duty of honour and trust after knowledge of a military offence ought to convey a pardon.' The context of this statement was a memorandum on corporal punishment for minor crimes. Corporal punishment had been abandoned in 1881 and the principle had never been applied to a crime carrying the death penalty. [19] In the Murchison case, which some claim as precedent for condonation of a murder, the defendant's sentence was actually commuted to penal servitude for life on the grounds of mental illness and not condonation. [20] He was not 'released because of gallant service in the siege'.

It has been argued that the concept of condonation is barely touched upon in the Manual of Military Law, and that Thomas and the others would therefore have been ignorant of the concept. [21] Condonation is only briefly touched upon in the Manual of Military Law, being mentioned in 36 (a) and (b) of the Rules of Procedure, but the claim that the defendants and their legal resources were not aware of condonation is untrue. Major R. W. Lenehan acted for the defence in two high-profile courts martial in 1895/6 in Sydney. In the case of Captain Johnson vs Surgeon Lea, condonation was one of the principles used by the defence. [22] Lenehan knew full well what condonation meant in the military legal sense. Why, therefore, did he not suggest it to Thomas?

One answer may be that he knew the argument wouldn't work, as it had not worked in the case of Dr Lea in 1895. Condonation was not simply a case of being let off for having subsequently been temporarily returned to duty. This would not be equitable in law since, if a superior officer cannot legally order a subordinate to conduct an illegal act, which the Manual of Military Law clearly states, why should he be able to condone one after the fact? The application of the principle of condonation changed with time, after the Duke of Wellington expressed his opinion.

A report on military law of 1869 [23] states:

> As regards the doctrine of condonation, perhaps I may be permitted to say that that sometimes occasions great embarrassment. The old doctrine which probably arose from active service in the field, was that a man who was under a charge was put to perform any duty, such performance of duty by permission of a superior authority absolutely condoned his offence. That has been to some degree limited, and in the present edition of the Queen's regulations a considerable change has been made in that respect, at any rate as to private soldiers. It is now held that putting a man to duty shall not absolutely condone the offence, but shall be recorded in the proceedings if the prisoner chooses, and shall be taken into account by the court and by the revising officer; but difficulty still remains with respect to officers, and the question often arises: what amounts to condonation? What kind of service or permitted service really frees the prisoner from liability to trial and punishment?

Six years later T. F. Simmonds in 'The Constitution and Practice of Courts Martial 1875' says:

> 566. The Queens regulations of 1859 laid down that 'the act of placing arms in the hands of a prisoner for the purpose of attending parade or performing any duty, absolves him from trial or punishment for the offence which he has committed.' This rule was modified in 1868, and the regulations now provide that if 'by error' an offender has been permitted to perform any duty, he shall not thereby be absolved from liability to punishment for his offence; but may, if proper authority shall think fit, be summarily punished, or be brought to trial before the court martial, according to the circumstances of the case.
>
> 567. It had, however, previously been held that the principle applied only in cases where an offence has been advisedly overlooked or forgiven by a competent authority. These pleas do not apply where a prisoner has been released under a wrong impression as to the extent of his misconduct, or released without due authority, or without any, by a subordinate ... [24]

By 1902 things had changed further, as noted by Isaacs in Witton's petition:

> It may be argued that the very case is provided for by the King's Regulations, Article 450. The Article, while enacting that an offender is not to be required while in arrest or confinement to perform duty, provides; If by error or in an emergency he has been ordered to perform any duty he is not thereby absolved from liability to be proceeded against for his offence. An offender, when in arrest or confinement, is not to bear arms, except by order of a commanding officer, or in an emergency, or on the line of march. Witton, consequently, could not bear arms except by order of his commanding officer, Colonel Carter. The 'emergency' [referring to the Beyers attack] if the facts relating to the attack and the disposition of the prisoners are correctly narrated, [the emergency] could hardly be so desperate as to render restoration to their liberty and arms necessary to their self preservation. Conceding, however that the commanding officer determined that there was an 'emergency' within the meaning of Article 450 – and enormous discretion must in such a situation be accorded to a commanding officer – and conceding too that the service of the accused was not pleadable as a strict bar to the charges, still, judged by the practice of the illustrious commander whose precedents I have quoted and judge by all those human considerations

> that collectively form our sense of justice, I think this latest service should appeal strongly for clemency towards the young subaltern. [25]

The author of Lt Witton's own petition therefore placed a two-pronged sting in the tail for those currently advocating the concept of condonation for the BVC officers: the commanding officer determined there was an emergency and therefore: 'If ... in an emergency he has been ordered to perform any duty he is not thereby absolved from liability to be proceeded against for his offence'; and 'the service of the accused was not pleadable as a strict bar to the charges'. In simple terms what Isaacs is saying then is that condonation did not apply but Witton's service during the Courts Martial should work in his favour in asking for clemency.

One point is clear; that for condonation to apply the offence must be 'advisedly overlooked' by a 'competent authority', i.e. one in full knowledge of the facts. E. Garth Moore argues that condonation can almost never be a successful plea unless the offence was committed in the presence of the commanding officer or the defendant has made a full confession, or has already been tried and found guilty but is yet to be sentenced. This was reiterated by Lord Goddard CJ, albeit in 1953. 'It is difficult to understand how one can condone an offence until one knows that an offence has been committed.' By this argument, knowledge of a military offence does not therefore occur when the offence is alleged but when it is proved. This appears to be what Isaacs was referring to in August 1902, when he wrote 'Lord Wellington, in a despatch of April 11th 1813, quoted by Clode observes: "No soldier should be put on duty having hanging over him the sentence of a court martial." It is true that in Witton's case there was as yet [referring to his being armed during Beyers raid] no sentence promulgated, but one trial was, it appears, concluded [the Visser Case] and the other was pending, the penalty in both cases was death.' [26]

The complexities of condonation are best expressed in layman's terms by E. Garth Moore:

> The commanding officer, who in effect says, 'I do not know whether you are guilty or not and you must be tried, but meantime carry on,' has not condoned the offence. The commanding officer who says 'I know exactly what you have done and I do not mind, so carry on,' has condoned the offence. So also, perhaps has the commanding officer who says, 'I do not know the truth of this matter and I do not care; it strikes me of little consequence; so carry on.' [27]

In the case of Dr Lea in 1895 R. W. Lenehan and Le Gay Brereton failed with their defence of condonation because when Dr Lea was released from arrest and returned to duty the commanding officer released him without prejudice to the impending court martial. He had not condoned the offence. [28]

So it appears none of the officers who armed Morant, Handcock and Witton during the Beyer raid on Pietersburg, or any of the previous actions which occurred during the investigations, could have condoned the crimes because the Court Martials had not yet been finished and therefore the extent of those crimes was not fully known at that time. The fact of the investigations effectively says 'I do not yet know the truth of this matter, however I do care and I intend to find out.'

Whilst Isaacs was preparing his opinions and working on the petition in Australia, in England, Lieutenant George Witton was initially in the Gosport Military Prison, later transferred to the Sussex Civil Prison at Lewes and thence to Portland Convict Prison. Whilst incarcerated, Witton spent a considerable time in hospital, being treated for enteric fever and laid up between 13 September 1902 and 23 May 1903. [29] Witton's own mortality may have been impressed upon him by this episode, since on 9 April he granted power of attorney to his brother Ernest. [30]

The petition raised in Australia would eventually contain 80,000 signatures but it was not only in Australia where there was growing support for Witton's release. In South Africa, where the politically astute on both sides of the former conflict were looking to the future and starting the slow healing process, prisoners from both sides were being released. It was reported in the British press that 'Generals Botha and De La Rey have been approached in connection with the movement to secure the release of Lieutenant Witton, of the Bushveldt Carbineers, with the result that it has been agreed that both sections will co-operate to obtain signatures to a petition for an amnesty to all persons still undergoing imprisonment for acts committed in the Transvaal and Orange River Colony in connection with the war.' [31]

In Britain too, pressure was mounting to remove some of the remaining barriers to reconciliation. On 8 February 1904, The Board of Visitors at Portland wrote to the Secretary of State 'having regard to the fact that most of the prisoners connected with the war in south Africa have now been released, they hope that the Home Secretary may see fit to give further consideration to [Witton's] case.' [32]

Whilst it appears that there was a general push to free all those still incarcerated following the war of 1899–1902, some British newspapers claimed that Witton gained his release mainly through the efforts of the Hon. J. Logan, a member of the Legislative Assembly of Cape Colony. In June 1904,

Logan seconded a resolution in the Legislative Assembly in Cape Colony calling upon the Home Government to release Lieutenant Witton. Failing to get a satisfactory reply to that request, Logan travelled to England with the object of convincing the Home Office to grant a reprieve. Alice Keppel, the mistress of King Edward VII, also exerted her influence on Witton's behalf. The final decision to release Witton most probably came as a result of the cumulative pressure from all sources and Witton was released on 11 August 1904. [33] 'His Majesty the King has been pleased on recommendation of Army Council to remit unexpired portion of Sentence on Witton'. [34]

On 15 August the Under Secretary of State wrote to the Prison Commission of the Home Office requesting that 'the War Office Authorities ... be approached with a view to their providing a passage back for this prisoner, who is anxious to return to Australia in 10 or 12 day's time'. Witton did not return to Australia until around six weeks had passed and after 3 September he stayed at Cranleigh, Guildford, Surrey, with an auctioneer called Harry Weller. [35] Harry Weller had previously written a letter to the Secretary of State asking for permission to visit Witton. Harry Weller's brother-in-law had married Witton's sister. [36]

On his release George Witton was inevitably interviewed by the press. This interviewer was struck by Witton's easy-going nature. Witton expressed his lack ill will towards the government in plain terms:

> Other people may have what opinion they like as to the justice of my punishment but for myself I have no complaint to make against the Government or anybody else. They saw fit to give me this punishment, and I have suffered it. I am very thankful to be free once more ... Mr. Logan is taking me to Scotland to-night for some grouse shooting, and after that I am going back to Australia to see my mother, sisters, and brothers. Since I have been prison—within the last month—l have lost my father. That has been a great blow to me. When I heard from my brother that father was very ill I petitioned the Home Office to be allowed to see him, but, of course, they could not allow it. Beyond this I have nothing to complain about regarding my treatment at Portland. I asked no privileges, and worked like any other convict. I am afraid I look like one now. [37]

Witton's statement is so straighforward that one cannot help feeling that his comments a week later were influenced by those who had secured his release. Frank Fox wrote 'Witton ... is guilty of nothing but that he was not firm and courageous enough to prevent his superior officer doing wrong. To those who know his character, weak and amiable, the sentence on him seems a savage one.' [38] Witton's later comments:

> The Lieutenant who was recently released from Portland prison, after having been sentenced to penal servitude for life on charge of complicity in the bush-veldt murders in Africa, sails from Liverpool to-day for Australia. Interviewed by Central News representative before leaving London, he said he was sorry to hear that an impression had got abroad that he had declared himself perfectly satisfied with the justice of his sentence. What he wanted to convey was that he was perfectly satisfied with the treatment received from the prison officials at Portland after he had been convicted. As to the charge made against him, he could only say that if he had not acted as he did, and carried out the orders of his superior officer, he would have been found guilty and shot, under martial law, for nothing was done with any criminal intent or malice towards the people Witton was fighting against, and that was why he held that he ought not to have been sentenced as a criminal. [39]

Perhaps if Witton had been a less malleable character Floris Visser might not have been shot. Stressing Witton's junior position, Isaacs forgets that Witton was not a lone voice. Numerous ordinary troopers of the BVC, by the accounts of several witnesses (including Witton himself) and their own testimony, refused to shoot Visser in cold blood. These men perhaps knew enough of Military Law to be confident they could refuse to carry out such orders; and whether they knew or not, they had the courage to refuse. Lt Picton also objected but later carried out his orders. Sergeant Major Clarke had asked Witton to intercede on behalf of the men. So there was some considerable weight of opinion against Morant and Handcock over the killing of Visser. Had Witton and Picton been more forceful, things could gave gone a different way.

Witton sailed for Australia on the White Star Liner SS *Runic* departing Liverpool on 29 September. He arrived at Melbourne Pier on 11 November 1904. [40]

J. F. Thomas had arrived back in Australia in August 1903, about a year before Witton was released. He had immediately written to the press:

> Sir,—I have just arrived in Australia from South Africa, and am proceeding to Sydney. I acted as counsel for the defence for ex-Lieutenant Witton and other officers in connection with the Bushveldt Carbineer court-martial cases, and my attention has been called to the London cable message published in your issue of 3rd inst. intimating that the petition for the release of young Witton has been refused. So far I have refrained from saying anything publicly about these cases, fearing that, by doing so I might prejudice the efforts of Witton's friends on his behalf; but I think

that in view of the determination of the English authorities to carry out the sentence of penal servitude for life it becomes my duty as early as possible to give the public the full facts of these cases. For I can assure you that as far as I can gather from the garbled versions that have appeared in the press the public have no conception of the true facts. Even the official reports published are, I regret to say, in several respects seriously unjust and untrue. To give only one instance—that of the case of the missionary Heese—although the military authorities were engaged for months in working up the case against Lieutenants Morant and Handcock, and employed one of their own hostile troopers to scour the Spelonken district for evidence against them (a trooper who, openly boasted that he would walk 70 miles to be in a firing party to shoot them); although their names were being freely bandied about in connection with the most atrocious lies (similar to those published after their deaths by the 'Morning Leader'); although they were condemned in Germany through the Berlin Mission Society long before the trial; although the preliminary court of inquiry, departing from the most elementary principles of justice and fair dealing, badgered Vet. Lieutenant Handcock (an uneducated black smith) to incriminate himself and Lieutenant Morant (behind the latter's back); although at the last moment the prosecution, fearing that they would fail to prove their allegations against Morant, asked him on two occasions to let them withdraw the charge (which he refused to do saying, 'I will stand my trial'); although the president of the court-martial (a special court demanded by the defence) stopped the evidence for the defence and acquitted the prisoner; although, apart from the court-martial Handcock asked for a special inquiry into the conduct of the preliminary court of inquiry (which application was not granted); yet, in face of all this, the War Office issued to the public the astounding statement that there was a 'strong suspicion' that Handcock, instigated by Morant, shot the missionary, but that the court-martial did not think the evidence sufficiently clear to warrant a conviction. This was tantamount to telling the public that, although acquitted by the court, the prisoners were still guilty, and this after they had been shot.

What I have above stated is absolutely true. I asked for a special inquiry, apart from the court-martial, into the circumstances of the Heese case; And I was stopped during the evidence for the defence because the court wished to hear nothing further. For the War Office, in face of this, to issue the statement they did, apparently to blacken the names of the deceased before the public, seems to me a very strange piece of military justice.

As for the shooting of Boers, there lies at the back of this a rather astonishing story, which if told will considerably open the eyes of the public.

> I may remark that a special application was made for a private inquiry as to how it was that certain other corps had acted on the 'no prisoners' order. This application was also not granted, but Morant and Handcock, to the amazement even of the court-martial, were shot at 24 hours' notice. I have a private letter from a member of the court-martial in which he says that when the news was received in Pietersburg that these officers had been shot 'we were astounded.' Before leaving Pietersburg I was assured by a member of the court that I had nothing to fear, as none of the prisoners would be shot; and there is little doubt but that at any rate the majority of the court were confident that their strong recommendation to mercy would be acted upon. I have gone further than I intended, but I hope as soon as time will permit, to issue a full statement of facts. Yours & c.
> J. F. THOMAS, Counsel for Accused. Melbourne. 4th August. [41]

As to Thomas's attack on the Court of Inquiry it must be remembered he was not there and had to rely on the accounts of the accused, who had to justify why Handcock had confessed and then retracted. Thomas's continual promises to reveal certain facts were beginning to wear a little thin, as the Australain press pointed out:

> The case of Lieutenant Witton, of the Bushveldt Carbineers, is brought up again by Mr. J. F. Thomas ... The petition for mercy for Witton has been disregarded by the Imperial Authorities, and Mr. Thomas writes a long letter to each of the Sydney and Melbourne morning dailies, in which he implies that both Witton and the executed men were the victims of an infamous injustice. He hints that there is more to tell, and there is an inference that the men were sacrificed. But why this mystery? Why the delay? If there is anything to tell, it should be told now: it should have been told when public interest in the fate of the Carbineers was still hot. The people soon forget, and if Mr. Thomas keeps what he knows much longer be will have difficulty in finding a section of the public that remembers Witton. [42]

He claimed 'So far I have refrained from saying anything publicly about these cases, fearing that by doing so I might prejudice the efforts of Witton's friends on his behalf.' If the facts he claimed to have were so unequivocal, how could this be? One reason proposed at the time was that he was still in the Australian Military and therefore to criticise the authorities would be difficult.

On 19 September 1903 Thomas wrote to the Premier of New South Wales that he wished '...to publish certain facts in connection with the case of Lieutenant Witton, but as he is on the Reserve of Officers of the Australian Forces, and as it may be thought that he ought not, as such, to publish any military matters, he wishes in the event of that view being taken to resign altogether from the defence forces.' The authorities agreed that he should indeed resign before 'impugning the decision of the Court Martial'. [43]

On 20 October Thomas wrote to the NSW Premier that it was not his intention to 'impugn' but to 'publish the plain facts of the case'. He enclosed his resignation, which was accepted. [44] In December 1903 the press stated that:

> In regard to the case of Lieutenant Witton ... it is stated that an agitation is to be shortly begun with a view of arousing public interest in the matter. Captain J. F. Thomas, of the New South Wales forces, when In South Africa, acted as counsel for certain officers, and since his return to New South Wales he has taken a keen interest in the case. Yesterday his resignation was announced. On account of his close connection with the local military forces, Captain Thomas could not act in a way that he would desire, but he will now be untrammelled in his action. [45]

With Witton's return to Australia on 11 November 1904, Thomas could say what he wanted. Thomas was now also free of his military ties, 'untrammelled in his action'. There was no reason why he could not reveal what he claimed to know. What did he do? Nothing. He proceeded to say the same old thing over and over; that the Boers deserved what they got, that Morant had not acted on Hunt's alleged orders to take no prisoners until after Hunt was killed, that other units had done the same thing. None of which was much of a defence. There wasn't much impugning going on.

At least Thomas's arguments were consistent, and backed by an unshakeable belief in what he was saying. Major Lenehan's protestations, however, seem much more fuelled by self-interest, with any benefit to Witton or Thomas being largely collateral.

Back in Melbourne on 24 March 1902, Major Lenehan went to General Hutton, the Federal Commandant, with his version of the events in Transvaal. [46] The General was in Melbourne at the time for an inspection of the Victorian element of his command [47] having returned there from Adelaide on the 1st. The Major General, uneasy that the whole story might be calculated to cast the Australian Military in a bad light, advised silence until more detail was received from South Africa.

On the afternoon of 26 March Sir Edmond Barton, the Prime Minister, Mr. Deakin, the Attorney-General, and Sir John Forrest, the Minister of Defence had a long conference with Maj. General Hutton. As a result, Barton announced that he would cable to South Africa for full particulars. Barton said General Hutton would probably obtain a report from Major Lenehan but he did not think the Australian Commandant could demand official reports other than through the Imperial headquarters at the front. [48] General Hutton had already discussed the events in South Africa with Lenehan and Barton's caution may have stemmed from Hutton's reluctance to take Lenehan's version at face value.

Lenehan left Melbourne for Sydney and arrived there on 28 March. [49] Hutton arrived there on 1 April. [50] Amazingly, Lenehan initially tried to deny that he had been charged and tried for anything. The *Evening News* in Sydney published the following on 31 March:

> Referring to the statement that had been going round that he had served three months in prison, Major Lenehan said there was not the least bit of truth in it. 'When I read the statement in Melbourne,' he continued 'I felt like issuing writs for libel, unless an explanation in my regard was made by the papers. Perhaps the papers are not to blame. This absurd story about myself should show Australians how easy it is to libel the living, and to slander the dead while a war is going on. I was never charged; never tried; never sentenced.' He added that the men who were executed were not with him, or immediately under his command, when the events occurred that have given rise to so much discussion. [51]

A number of newspapers duly issued retractions. They would soon learn that it was Lenehan who was putting out false information, not they. This was not the only misinformation presented in the press. The following article appeared in the same issue:

> STATEMENT BY AN OFFICER. LIEUT. MORANT'S STORY. Melbourne, March 30.
>
> A Victorian officer now in Melbourne has made a statement in extenuation of the action which led to the trial and execution of Lieut. Morant last month. He states that he knew Morant before he went to the war, and was therefore greatly surprised when on his arrival in Pretoria, on October 18. He found him with several Australian officers under arrest. He was placed on guard over the accused officers, and while performing that duty Morant made the following statement to him:-
>
> 'We attacked some Boers near a farm at Fort Edward, and Captain Hunt, late of the Tenth Hussars, [52] who was in charge of our men, was wounded. We had to retire and leave him there, but after getting reinforcements we

> again went out to capture the Boers who had wounded our captain. One of the native servants of Captain Hunt then came running up to me, and said, "Captain has his neck broken." This upset me a good deal, and I inquired where he lay. The servant took me to where the body was. There we found another native servant by the mutilated remains, crying like a child. We asked him what was the matter, and he then told us that the Boers had first tied a rope around the captain's neck, and had drawn it tightly against a tree to break it, but finding they could not do so by this means, one of the fellows jumped on his head with his heels. Seeing the captain, my chum, there in that awful state, after we had left him with only a wound in the thigh, it was too much for me. I felt most horribly angry; in fact, I felt savage. Some little time afterwards we captured a Boer wearing Captain Hunt's uniform, and we shot him after holding a court-martial. We held a court-martial on all the Boers we shot. One of them escaped, and managed to get to Pietersburg, where he surrendered, and told the whole story. In the meantime we followed and captured a man named Byrne together with certain Boers, and they were all wearing khaki. We tried them, and shot them also.' [53]

Almost all of this is false. The BVC officers were not arrested until around a week after 18 October when the officer claims to have found them in Pretoria; they were in Pietersburg. Morant did not take part in the attack at Duivels Kloof, He didn't arrive in the area until two days later when Captain Hunt's body had already been buried and he relied entirely on others accounts for the state of Hunt's body. The story about Hunt's servant and the rope must be considered a lie and Floris Visser was not wearing Hunt's uniform, though he had it with him. It is not clear who 'Byrne' is. It is noteworthy that many elements of this story are very similar to that told by the trooper claiming to have been at Duivels Kloof and shown to be false in Chapter 9, which was published a few days later.

And so it was, based on stories such as these, that the myths began – and who should be the origin of those myths but Harry Harbord Morant himself?

Suggesting he had heard more than just Lenehan's version of events, Maj. Gen. Hutton's farewell address to the New South Wales section of the Commonwealth Contingent at the beginning of April 1902 included:

> There is just one unhappy incident in connection with recent stages of the war I should like to allude to, and that is the occurrence of which we have lately read in Australian newspapers by which two officers who went from Australia originally were tried by court-martial and shot, and another officer was sentenced to penal servitude. We here in Australia have

> unfortunately heard only the defence, but I know, though not yet officially, the true version of the tale, and I regret to say it will when published be seen to be a sad one. [54]

Shortly after Hutton's address, stories based on official information discussed in the Australian Parliament were being published making it impossible for Lenhehan to continue denying that he was charged and tried. [55] Lenehan was nevertheless adamant that he had been badly treated, arguing his lenient sentence was an indication of innocence and that he had only been tried because having been under close arrest for three months, those investigating felt they had to charge him with something. His expeditious escort to Cape Town was another indignity he did not deserve. General Hutton granted Lenehan permission to communicate with the Prime Minister. In the light of sensationalist news reports, Lenehan was desperate to restore his reputation and applied for a Court of Inquiry. It has been stated that having considered pleading his case in the newspapers he decided this was a disobedience to General Hutton, which he would have handed the General a prime opportunity to dismiss him from the Military, [56] a curious statement that suggests some pre-existing antipathy between the two. Hutton in answer to the application for a Court of inquiry asked Lenehan to resign. If his resignation was not received within 24 hours he would be dismissed. [57]

It was stated in the Australian House of Representatives and extensively repeated in the Australian press that 'The three convicted lieutenants were serving in the Imperial corps under the regulations of the British army, and as the soldiers of that army they were not in any sense employed as Australians, or a distinctively Australian corps.' [58] But there was still frustration that the Australian Government had not been informed of the whole affair. Sir Edmond Barton was unable on 2 April 1902 to provide answers to questions about the cases and could only state that further information was being sought from the military authorities in South Africa, who had been cabled on 4 April. A reply was received the following day. The lengths that some of Morant's biographers have gone to, to try to incriminate Kitchener in the Morant affair, are demonstrated by their interpretation of the telegraph message from Lord Kitchener to Lord Hopetoun, the Governor General of Australia, of 5 April. More than one author has interpreted the message as a deliberate attempt by Kitchener to mislead the Australian Government. Exactly the same account was sent to the British Government:

> Your Telegram of 4th April, Handcock and Witton were charged with twenty separate murders including one of a German Missionary who had witnessed other murders. Twelve of these murders were proved.

> From evidence appears Morant was originator of these crimes, which Handcock carried out in cold blooded manner. The murders were committed in wildest part of Transvaal known as 'Spelonken': about 80 miles to the north of Pretoria on four separate dates namely 2nd July, 11th August, 23rd August, and 7th September. In one case, when eight Boer prisoners were murdered, it was alleged in defence to have been done in spirit of revenge for ill treatment of one of their officers, Lieutenant Hunt, who was killed in action. No such ill treatment was proved. The prisoners were convicted after a most exhaustive trial, and were defended by counsel. There were in my opinion no extenuating circumstances. Lieutenant Witton was also convicted, but I commuted sentence to penal servitude for life, in consideration of his having been under influence of Morant and Handcock. Proceedings have been sent home. [59]

There are inaccuracies in this, certainly: but what would Kitchener hope to gain from lying to the Australian Government about, say, the distance between Pretoria and Spelonken, or Percy Hunt's rank? And whether Heese had witnessed the murders or not is not of any particular significance in terms of sentencing. In fact, in the Chief of Staff Colonel Hamilton's papers, held by the public records office in Kew, there are three separate versions of this telegram, two being handwritten. One is reproduced below. It does not accuse Morant and Handcock of all 20 murders, nor claim that the German missionary witnessed them. It also becomes clear that 'Pretoria' was a mis-transcription of 'Pietersburg', which is actually about 80 miles from Spelonken. The final draft, which has been taken as proof of Kitchener being mendacious, has probably resulted from the message being written and hastily edited, with the original detail becoming inaccurate in the process. The draft:

> Your Telegram of 4th April. The murders were of Boer prisoners in a spirit of vengeance for alleged ill treatment of one of their officers, Lt Hunt who was shot in action. No such ill treatment proved. Morant was originator of crimes, Hancock carrying out several of the murders in cold blooded manner. There were 20 charges of murder including that of a German missionary of which 12 were proved. Morant had been in Royal Navy and after being discharged from S. Australian Contingent acted as Newspaper correspondent. Hancock and Whitton's antecedents already telegraphed. The crimes were committed in wildest part of the Transvaal known as the Spelonken about 80 miles north of Pietersburg and were committed on four separate dates viz 2 July, 11 Augt, 23 Aug, and 7 Sept. Lenahan

> [sic] reprimanded for neglecting to report knowledge after fact. They were convicted after most exhaustive trial and were defended by counsel. [60]

The only inaccuracies in this version are Percy Hunt's rank and the statement that Morant had been in the Royal Navy, a lie perpetrated by Morant himself. There had been 20 charges brought though not all against Morant and Handcock, and more murders took place but Morant and Handcock were only charged with 13, of which 12 were proved. The murder of Trooper van Buuren and the six Boers had occurred during Handcock's time in Spelonken before Morant had arrived there. Although Handcock was implicated in the killing of van Buuren and the looting of the six Boers' wagon, it was Taylor who was charged with inciting the murder of the six Boers but acquitted. It is also be pertinent that a pencil-written draft of the final, more inaccurate, version was signed 'Hamilton', not 'Kitchener'. [61]

The aggrieved Lenehan set about restoring his reputation. He embarked on a short lecture tour and lobbied the government for reinstatement to the military. Talking at Centenary Hall, York Street, Sydney in late July:'I venture the opinion, which I hope will one day be justified that this charge was brought against me because, having been locked up for a long while, I had to be charged with something.' [62] Lenehan also presented his lecture at Victoria Hall, Newcastle, Maitland Town Hall and Windsor School of Arts, where, perhaps because of the obvious contradiction of his previous claims, the turnout was so poor it didn't pay expenses. [63] This poor turnout at Windsor may have been why he did not lecture at neighbouring Richmond. One world-weary correspondent there wrote: 'The boys are very much disappointed that 'Majaw' Lenehan didn't go to Richmond to lecture, for what they had for his reception won't hatch, and there are no elections on, so the ammunition is wasted, to say nothing of the unnecessary deaths that have been inflicted on sundry and various varieties of cats from the amount of provision collected. The boys were going to change the lecture into a real "Bushveldt Picnic." They say it is a case of Lenehan let down lightly.' [64]

It appears that Major Lenehan extolled the looting capabilities of Australian soldiers, which he claimed rivalled or surpassed even those of the British Tommies. [65] This earned him a scathing attack from the Sydney *Truth*, a scandal sheet, which dubbed him 'Looter Lenehan' and also provided a less than flattering cartoon caricature of him. [66] At Windsor 'A few people attended Major Lenehan's lecture on Tuesday night simply to hear what he had to say about Harry Morant ('The Breaker') who was so well known here. Morant was only incidentally referred to – and the audience was disgusted with the whole show.' [67]

Tedious, disgusting, disappointing or not, it is Major Lenehan's lectures that provide the clearest, if not the only, statements as to basis on which 'Bulala' Taylor escaped justice. 'Captain Taylor had with him fifteen men of the Bushveldt Carbineers. The men with Captain Taylor were not under his [the lecturer's] command. Before Lieutenant Morant joined the fifteen, Captain Taylor's men had killed eight Boer prisoners [presumably he means the six Boers]. For killing prisoners Captain Taylor was tried by court-martial, but acquitted on the ground that he had no military command.'

It was not only the residents of Windsor and Richmond who were disgusted by Major Lenehan's lecture tour. Maj. Gen. Hutton wrote on 7 August 1902: 'I regret to say that this officer has committed the indiscretion of delivering a lecture on the 29th ultimo in Sydney, which considering the position that he holds in regard to his services having been dispensed with by the Commander in Chief in South Africa, can only be characterised as in all respects most reprehensible. I would again urgently request that the order in council submitted on the 13th May for the retirement of this Officer should receive early and favourable consideration by the Minister.' [68]

Hutton wrote to the Secretary of Defence:

> Major Lenehan who has been reprimanded for culpable neglect in connection with serious and peculiarly disgraceful events in the Regiment under his command, and who has since had his services dispensed with in South Africa, is in my opinion unfitted to retain his position on the Active List of the Military Forces of the Commonwealth.
>
> An opportunity has been given to Major Lenehan to voluntarily resign his commission in the New South Wales Artillery which he has declined to avail himself of and I now recommend that he be retired. [69]

And in a submission to the Minister of Defence, Sir John Forrest on 9 March 1903:

> Major Lenehan was to have been tried for his life, as his attitude towards Lieutenant Morant and those concerned in the murders of the prisoners in cold blood was such as to justify the belief that he was Particeps criminis. Sufficient evidence for this was not however forthcoming and he was tried upon the lesser charge.
>
> I have read the statement which you sent me, unsigned and undated but apparently in Major Lenehan's hand writing. It is an Ex parte statement.
>
> Apart from Major Lenehan's conduct as commanding Officer of this unhappy Corps of Bushveldt Carbineers I have the very poorest opinion of this Officer's qualifications as an officer. He served under my command

> while I was in N.S.W 93–96, and also upon active service in South Africa when he commanded a squadron of the N.S.W. Mounted Rifles. I have never heard a good word said for him either in Peace or War. [70]

The exchange between General Hutton and the Minister of Defence continued. The Minister attempted to obtain more information about why Major Lenehan had been so quickly expelled from South Africa under close guard when the charges against him seemed so inconsequential and the outcome of which only been a reprimand. The reply from the War Office on 2 January 1903 was vague and unhelpful:

> ...it was considered by Lord Kitchener most undesirable in view of Major Lenehan's connexion with the events that led not only to his trial but to the trial and execution of other officers of the Bushveldt Carbineers, that he should remain in Transvaal or be continued in military employment after his release.
>
> The Corps which he commanded was consequently dissolved and to ensure him not remaining in the district where the crimes which led to the Courts Martial were notorious, Major Lenehan was removed to Capetown in charge of the Provost Marshal. [71]

Given the paucity of information available to the Minister of Defence his vagueness is understandable. Ostensibly Major Lenenhan had little involvement with the whole tragedy.

In the House of Representatives on 9 September 1902 a remarkable discussion took place. Mr J. C. L. Fitzpatrick the member for Rylstone, who Morant had once shared a house with, [72] and to whom Morant had written from South Africa, asked the Speaker:

> ...in view of the circumstances that Major Lenehan, without being deemed guilty of any fault, or dereliction of duty, has been subjected to punishment of a most iniquitous character, I think it is necessary that some public attention should be called to his case. Major Lenehan has performed splendid service in the interests of the Empire. [73]
>
> ...[There was] nothing in the evidence taken at the trial of those men – Morant, Whitton, and two others – to indicate that Major Lenehan was associated, directly or indirectly, with any of the acts with which they were charged. I have here a very lengthy report of the proceedings at the trial, and in every instance it is shown that Major Lenehan was many miles away from the scene of operations when the alleged atrocities took place. [74]

It was not only 'Fitz' who propounded the erroneous notion that Lenehan was many miles away from the murders 'in every instance'. Mr Sleath the member for Wilcannia stated: 'Major Lenehan was 70 miles away when it leaked out that this sort of thing was going on ... He proceeded to the scene of action and thence to head quarters, where he was arrested before he had time to make a report ... for three months, he was kept in close confinement with an armed guard over him, no charge being made against him at all.' Lenehan had in fact been sent to Spelonken, and arrived on 7 September, the day the van Stadens were murdered. Both Lieutenant Witton [75] and Lenehan himself [76] bear witness to the fact that they had passed each other outside of Fort Edward that 'very day'. Witton wrote: 'I had met him going out as I was on my way to Pietersburg with prisoners'. [77] The Letter of complaint written by the 15 troopers stated 'When the two Boers and a boy were shot Sept 7th, Major Lenehan heard the firing.' At the mess table, in Major Lenehan's presence, Lt Morant elicited from Trooper Botha the statement that he had that day 'shot the Dutch Boy'. [78]

Since arriving back in Australia not only had Lenehan denied ever being arrested, confined and charged he also wrote the following to the Government:

> Thirty days after my arrest, I was brought before a Court of Enquiry, of which Colonel Carter, Wiltshire Regiment, was President. It was then for the first time I learned that the charge against me was 'complicity in some thirteen murders'. I have since ascertained that witnesses, men of my Regiment, had already been examined secretly. Lieutenant Edwards, the Adjutant of the Regiment, was so pressed to give evidence against me; and such endeavours were made to intimidate him that he refused to speak until an Australian representative was present.
>
> Both Lieutenants Morant and Handcock informed me that the court stated to them that if they received orders from me to shoot prisoners nothing could happen to them as I alone was responsible.
>
> They were however too honest to perjure themselves, and save their lives at my expense, and persisted in stating, as they did to the hour of their death, where the orders did come from, viz:- headquarters.
>
> The evidence at the trial proves conclusively that when the shooting of prisoners took place, I was at Petersburg [sic] with the Regiment, more than 70 miles away, and the Detachment was under Lieutenant Morant who received no orders from me. His orders came directly from headquarters Intelligence Staff. [79]

Lenehan was not 70 miles away from the van Staden murders; according to Trooper Botha he was within earshot. Ultimately Lenehen was not charged with complicity in thirteen murders, merely 'failing to report' two. It would be surprising if Lieutenants Edwards, Morant and Handcock were not asked what Lenehan's involvement had been, after all he was the CO of the Bushveldt Carbineers and he had been sent to make inquiries. The idea that pressure was applied to blame Lenehan must be treated with scepticism in view of his involvement in the Spoelstra Case.

Lenehan had been sent specifically to make enquiries into the murders and was not arrested until 21 October. 7 September to 21 October was plenty of time to make a report and the letter of complaint written by the fifteen troopers specifically stated that they believed he was complicit in a cover-up. [80]

> When Major Lenehan was sent to hold an inquiry he endeavoured to bounce the troopers into giving evidence which would exonerate the officers. Particularly he tried to make them swear that the wounded Boer prisoner Visser shot on Aug. 11th was wearing the tunic of the late Capt. Hunt, whereas the witnesses pointed out that the clothes of the Late Capt. Hunt had been continuously worn by Lt Morant who was wearing them at that moment. Lt Morant wore the Late Capt. Hunt's British Warm, riding breeches, tunic and leggings. When the witnesses refused to swear what Major Lenehan required but swore that the prisoner was wearing an old British Warm Major Lenehan ordered the men out of his tent as if they had been dogs saying 'That kind of evidence is no good to us.' [81]

In the Australian Parliament Mr Sleath continued with remarkable ignorance – or dishonesty – since the account of the Courts Martial had been published six months previously:

> At the finish he was tried in his absence, as they were all tried, without having an opportunity to say a word in their own defence. Most of the evidence taken was hearsay evidence, because it was reported in the newspapers that a great deal of evidence had been taken against the men which they were not aware of. As a matter of fact they were not aware that the trial had taken place until their punishment was meted out to them. Those who were ordered to be shot were to be executed within sixteen hours. [82]

This was a ludicrous claim made in the face of newspaper reports of the Courts Martial, which clearly show the BVC officers were present during their trials. This can only have served to frustrate the Minister of Defence who was trying to resolve the spat between Hutton and Lenehan.

The Minister of Defence wrote to Maj. General Hutton; 'As far as can be ascertained, all that is against Major Lenehan is that he was tried by Court Martial for neglect of duty, and was "reprimanded", which appears to be the lightest penalty awarded. It seems rather unjust to punish this officer again by retiring him; and I am inclined not to take any steps in this direction.' [83]

Failing to report would indeed have been a minor neglect of duty during the normal day-to-day operations of his unit. However, Major Lenehan had been sent to Spelonken with specific instructions to investigate alleged war crimes, one of which occurred the day he arrived. The fact that he had failed to report a month later, when the fifteen troopers submitted their letter of complaint to Col Hall and the Provost Marshal, makes this neglect something far more grievous; it is complicity in a cover-up.

So why was Major Lenehan only charged with neglect of duty? It seems highly probable that it was because of his role in prosecuting the Spoelstra Case. The last thing that Lord Kitchener needed was the prosecutor, in a case of 'Evasion of Censorship' against a man who had alleged numerous war crimes had been committed by members of the British Army, to be found guilty of covering up war crimes in his own unit. This probably also accounts for Lenehan's speedy expulsion from South Africa after the Courts Martial. It further makes it highly improbable that pressure was placed on Lieutenants Edwards, Morant and Handcock to place all the blame on Lenehan, as he claimed.

Was the Minister of Defence aware that Lenehan's 'neglect of duty' amounted to complicity and not just tardiness or incompetence? It was not discussed in the House of Representatives or in exchanges with General Hutton, but the *Times*' account of the court cases had been published in numerous Australian newspapers. Maj. General Hutton limited himself to investigations which took place during the Court of Inquiry in his comments:

> It appears from Major Lenehan's own evidence given at his trial that in addition to the offence for which he was tried by Court Martial a Court of Inquiry had been assembled to investigate charges against him of:
>
> Attempted murder, fabricating evidence, complicity in all cases of shooting at the Spelonken, insulting behaviour to a young lady, stealing ivory, and suggestion of cattle lifting.
>
> The fact that charges of such extreme gravity could be entertained and thus investigated speaks for itself.

> I would point out that there is no question of additional punishment to this officer, but it is desirable in the public interest, in view of his conduct in South Africa, that he should be no longer retained in the Military Forces of the Commonwealth and entrusted with the command of a Battery of Field Artillery but should be placed on the Retired List. [84]

The War Office was again asked for information and eventually stated that there was nothing more held against Major Lenehan than that which had been put before the Court Martial.

Hutton then requested that General Finn, the Commander of the Commonwealth Forces of New South Wales, call Lenehan's integrity into question. Hutton asked him to obtain via Lt Col Bridges a statement from Colonel Onslow that 'Lenehan had acted dishonourably in regards to money matters'. What these money matters were is not clear – but General Finn would not play ball. [85]

The Minister's patience finally ran out. He wrote to Hutton on 18 August:

> I desire to express my entire disapproval of the manner in which the General Officer Commanding, by means of a confidential communication to Lieutenant-Colonel Bridges, reflects on the integrity of Major Lenehan on what appears to be unreliable information and for the acceptance of which the General Officer Commanding is responsible. [There has been] unnecessary delay in carrying out my instruction s of 23rd May and so far I do not consider that the General Officer Commanding has afforded any satisfactory explanation. [86]

Hutton responded in a letter of 24 August in which he stressed that it was his responsibility to ensure only fit and proper persons were appointed to the commonwealth forces and that the honour and good name of the commonwealth forces were also his concern. Maj. General Hutton had lost and Lenehan was reinstated.

This prolonged exchange between Major Lenehan and Major Hutton has been outlined by a number of Morant's biographers [87] with the implication that this was a continuation of the perceived victimisation of the BVC officers by the Imperial military. It seems unlikely, however, that the Imperial authorities would want to antagonise Lenehan. He was safely out of South Africa where the Spoelstra case had been such a worrying potential source of trouble for the British goverment. The easiest way to keep him quiet about the whole thing would be to leave him to get on with his business, legal and military. This accounts for the War Office's non-committal responses to the Australian Government's requests.

So why did Maj. General Hutton have it in for Lenehan? Partially, probably, a genuine belief in his argument. But there may have been a personal feud still simmering dating from 1895, when Lenehan and Hutton had previously crossed swords. Hutton was sent to Australia in 1902 by request of the government to organise the new Commonwealth military establishment. [88] Hutton took command of the Commonwealth forces, after federation, in 1902. He had been in Australia previously, between 1893 and 1896 as Commandant of the New South Wales military forces. [89] In 1895 Lenehan was working as a Sydney solicitor and had instructed J. C. Gannon in the defence of a Captain Close in a court martial at the Victoria Barracks in Sydney.

A Captain Morris had laid four accusations against the prisoner. The first charge was that the prisoner had behaved in a scandalous manner, unbecoming the character of an officer and a gentleman in that he had 'seduced' a woman named May Cummins at Wollongong, in November 1893. May Cummins alleged that Captain Close had plied her with drugged champagne, which rendered her unconscious during which time he had sexually assaulted her. Six weeks later she had become ill and her face was disfigured. The second charge was that Captain Close had suggested to May Cummins, who was pregnant, that 'her miscarriage should be procured'. Thirdly, that in May 1894, Captain Close suggested to a Charles Swanston, a surgeon, that he should perform an illegal operation. The other charge was that he had communicated a disease to May Cummins, being well aware that he was diseased at the time.

May Cummins claimed that a miscarriage had been procured at a Mrs Hill's in Albion Street, Sydney. Though having been very ill at the time, May could not state for certain that it had not been the disease which had resulted in the miscarriage. Miss Cummins alleged that Captain Close had promised to marry her but was not allowed to by his mother. May wrote to General Hutton, which ultimately resulted in the court martial. The prosecution called May Cummins' moral standards into question claiming that amongst other things she had already had an illegitimate child.

Testimony by Dr Swanston showed that Close had come to him stating that he had got a girl in trouble and ask him to perform an operation. [90] The result of the court martial was that Captain Close was acquitted of the first two charges but was found guilty of the second two. It was stated that he would probably resign and that it was rumoured he intended to pursue a civil action against his superior officers who had brought the case. [91] In June 1895 Captain Close was permitted to retire from military service and retain his rank as Captain. [92]

Less than a week after Captain Close's retirement was announced, on 10 June Hutton received a letter from Lenehan asking which firm of solicitors would accept service of a writ claiming damages on behalf of Captain Close. This action was to the tune of £5,000, roughly equivalent to £460,000 today. [93] Hutton asked if the Crown Solicitor's office would accept the writ, which they did, meaning the NSW Government would foot the bill if Close won the case. This caused questions to be asked in the NSW parliament and the response from the government was that if Hutton had acted in a private capacity then the Crown Solicitor would withdraw, which would mean Hutton would have to pay. [94]

No further newspaper coverage of the result of this case has been found and it seems likely that it was settled out of court. It seems highly unlikely that Maj. General Hutton had to pay £5,000 – but this episode would not have left Hutton and Lenehan the best of friends. Was this the real source of General Hutton's antipathy towards Major Lenehan? We cannot say for sure.

Whilst in Australia Lenehan was trying the rebuild his military career, those still in South Africa were trying to rebuild much more. Farms, whole towns and probably most difficult of all, trust between the former enemies needed to be rebuilt if any kind of nation was to be reconstructed.

Major Wilfred Nash Bolton, who had been Provost Marshal in Pietersburg in 1901 during the time of the BVC murders, was one of those working on this huge task. He had become Assistant Provost Marshal in Orange River Colony in December [95] of that year, during the enquiry into the Bushveldt Carbineers. He may have hoped that this posting would get him out of having to deal with the whole issue of the BVC. He tried his best not to have to prosecute the Heese case feeling his legal knowledge was not up to the task. He clearly did not enjoy the experience of the whole courts process.

During the court cases, the armoured train from Pietersburg had stopped at Potgietersrus, near the home of Arthur Eastwood. Arthur Eastwood, had first met Morant at a cattle station outside of Sydney, and had later moved to South Africa. During the stopover, Major Bolton was overheard by Eastwood to lament: 'I have a terrible job on hand. I need a stiff whisky. Poor old Tony Morant and Peter Handcock are prisoners on the train. They are to be court martialled and probably shot.' [96]

After cessation of hostilities Major Bolton relinquished his military positions to become resident Magistrate for Pietersburg. In this position his responsibilities included repatriation of families from the concentration camps and POW camps. This was no simple task since the town of Louis Trichardt and some of the surrounding farms had been utterly destroyed.

Furthermore, the list of title register of erven (plots of land) [97] for the Louis Trichardt area had been taken by none other than Alfred Taylor and apparently 'accidentally burnt in a house which was destroyed by fire afterwards'. [98] Bolton visited Louis Trichardt in person on a number of occasions to sort out the mess but hampered by the fact that he had no plan of the area, progress was painfully slow. [99]

During his efforts Bolton found that many previous occupants had returned and were keen to return to or buy land they had previously occupied. As a first step he drafted a list of possible occupiers of erven which were discussed at numerous meetings with the official of the local land department, Mostyn Jones. Bolton and Jones constituted The Zoutpansberg Land Tenure Commission to try and resolve the whole issue. [100] Major Bolton told the Secretary of the Law Department that: 'The delay in issuing title and settling the question of Louis Trichardt erven is causing very general dissatisfaction, it is also causing much distress and want, and if not attended to soon is likely to ruin any chance Louis Trichardt ever had of becoming a township.' [101]

By 1905 Bolton was being helped and advised by an Afrikaaner woman Johanna Brandt, daughter of Revd N. J. van Warmelo and author of a diary published as *Petticoat Commando*. Her family had previously lived in the area. Her lobbying led to destitute people being paid for work on public improvement schemes in the Louis Trichardt area. [102]

Wilfred Bolton was also deeply committed to the task of gaining compensation for the victims of the Bushveldt Carbineers. Bolton became admired in the area for persistence in the process, which continued until as late as 1909. [103] Besides the problems associated with dealing with multiple governmental departments based in London and elsewhere, there was the problem of identifying the victims since, in most cases, the BVC officers had not bothered to do so before deciding that they deserved to be shot. The burial places were not always marked or recorded. Sometimes the relatives had remarried and the spelling of surnames was often inconsistent. The black victims had in many instances come from other districts and were therefore unknown in the area.

Bolton's dogged persistence with the governmental bureaucracies ensured at least some of the families of the victims got some recompense. Of the moneys paid out to the families of victims of the BVC, most came from British Army funds rather than the £3,000,000 which had been allocated as part of the treaty of Vereeniging to aid dispossessed Boer families. One of the earliest and largest grants in relation to BVC victims was £2,500 paid to Mrs Johanna Heese, wife of Revd Daniel Heese, in 1904. This, not unreasonably, is pointed out by some as tacit admission that the murderer was a member of the British Army and not a Boer, as the BVC officers had claimed. [104] Other sums paid out were:

Mrs John Geyser – £1000 and £3 pension per month
Mrs Pieternella Jacoba Vahrmeyer-Viljoen – £200 and further £50 per year
Mrs Aletta Vercuil – £100 and a further £100 for each of her three children
Mrs Carel Smit – £100 and £100 for each of her children
Mrs du Preez – £250
Mr P. J. Westerfhoff of Nykerk Holland father of G. K. Westerhoff – £250
Misses van Staden – £200 each
According to correspondence received by Wilfred Bolton on 5 January 1909 further payments of £100 each were paid by the war office to:
Mrs J. J. van der Merwe
Mrs J. S. Bezuidenhout
Mrs P. J. Booysen
Mrs M. M. Bezuidenhout
Mrs H. C. Vercuil
A further payment of £100 was later paid to Mrs Aletta Vercuil.

After returning from South Africa, J. F. Thomas resumed his Tenterfield Law practice. According to Dr Bennett he later ventured into misappropriating trust funds to construct an opulent dwelling outside of Tenterfield. In 1919 he sold his practice and bought a farm. He valued the property at £2,000, but it was subject to a mortgage of £1,700 to the Rural Bank. Tiring of the land after two years, he sold out for £3,000, nominally, though he received only £500 of the purchase money, [105] which he used to go on a grand rail tour of central Australia.

Curiously, he set himself up as an expert on central Australia, corresponding frequently with Daisy Bates, the self-taught anthropologist who was, fortunately for her, the long-time grass widow of Edwin Henry Murrant. There is anecdotal evidence that Thomas wrote to Charles Henry Mabey, a sculptor who had attended Silesia College where Murrant had worked as tutor. A letter was found on Tenterfield tip from Mabey to Thomas. This suggests that Thomas had realised Harry Harbord Morant was in fact Edwin Henry Murrant, as stated in the press in 1902. [106]

Selling the *Tenterfield Star* he purchased the *Border Record*. This proved to be a financial disaster contributing to his ultimate bankruptcy. By 1920 he had returned to Sydney practising as a solicitor until 1926, [107] selling the family silver to survive whilst fighting litigation concerning his irregular Tenterfield Trust accounts.

His defective knowledge of conveyancing caught up with him in 1926. [108] He was subject to a law suit which could have been settled out of court but he was obdurate in demanding his costs be paid. This was disallowed by the Supreme Court. He racked up more costs in an unsuccessful appeal. He could not pay and was attached for contempt of court. Thomas was committed to Long Bay Gaol in Sydney, which he described as 'Debtors' Prison', complaining of the harsh treatment of the opposing solicitor. Technically he was in gaol for contempt of court. Thomas was released in August 1927 after 20 months' incarceration.

On the Petition of the Minister for Justice he was was bankrupted in August 1928. His misappropriations had previously been publicised and it was ordered that he be struck off the roll of solicitors on 9 March 1928. [109]

After his release he returned to Tenterfield. In September 1929 he wrote a letter to George Witton at his farm. Witton's reply was earth-shattering for Thomas:

> I was surprised to receive your interesting letter of Sept14th. I intended writing before but could not seem to get a start. I have been settled here since 1908 dairy farming, making a living and that is about all, dry spells and drought are too frequent to become prosperous....
>
> I have very little knowledge of any B.V.C. officers. The last I heard of Picton was shortly after my return to Australia. He was then riding racehorses on the Continent. Hannam died about a year ago. Taylor – I have never heard what happened to him.
>
> I saw Lenehan when on my way to Q'land in 1908. He owed me £12 that he borrowed from me at Capetown to see him home – the rotter promised to send it to me but never did although he skited [boasted] he was making £2,000 a year. Baudinet stayed in S.Africa – mining. I still have a sister living in Pretoria. It was she who attended to Morant and Handock's grave.
>
> I took no part whatever in the last war when asked to volunteer. I said, Yes, I'm Fisher's man. He pledged Australia to the last man and last shilling... [110]
>
> Personally I think the attitude you take with regard to Morant and Handcock and the Heese case is not the right one. I am inclined to think that neither of them took you into their confidence over that case. Up to the time of the Court of Inquiry when I was charged with complicity in his death I had no more knowledge of how Heese came by his death than the babe unborn nor did I have at anytime the slightest suspicion that Morant or Handcock was connected with it.

It staggered me at the time but my statement in reply I think cleared me of that count at that inquiry. Subsequently when we were allowed to see each other Morant told me that Handcock had broken down and confessed to everything including shooting Heese.
I saw Handcock shortly afterwards and asked him about the Heese business, he said 'why wasn't you standing beside Morant when he asked me if I was game to follow the missionary and wipe him out.' [111]

I had been with them up to the time Morant returned from interviewing Heese when he drove past the fort. I left them then and went to my tent and did not see them again until they came to dinner about seven o'clock. [112] I believe Morant got Handcock to deny his previous statement in which he had made a clean breast of everything and they got to work to frame up an alibi which you know was successful and the means of their acquittal.

But you must not forget Kitchener held Handcock's 'confession' in which he implicated me as an accessory no doubt unwittingly done while in a high strung nervous state but that accounts for the reason why only Morant, Handcock and myself were punished and the War Office so adamant in my case.

Had there been no Heese case the shooting of prisoners would not have worried them much. But the shooting of Heese was a premeditated and most cold blooded affair. Handcock with his own lips described it all to me.

I consider I am the one and only one that suffered unjustly (apart from yourself).

Morant and Handcock being acquitted my lips were sealed.

I would very much like to peruse the evidence of the Heese trial although I took no part in it or was present. If you have a copy and would care to send it to me I would take particular care of it and return it safely. Personally I do not think there would be much in writing what you term the true story of the Bushveldt Carbineers in face of the fact that the War Office may still hold Handcock's confession. [113]

One might think the publishing of this letter after 1970 would have killed the Morant myth stone dead. Not so. Morant's apologists still find reasons to question Witton's motives in writing it. Some suggest that Witton wrote it to prevent Thomas from publishing what he claimed to know and stirring up the whole hornet's nest again, just when Witton's wife was very sick. If this were the case, why didn't Witton simply ask Thomas not to publish, or to at least postpone publishing, and explain why? Thomas was a compassionate man, at least towards his fellow-Australians. Surely he would have been amenable to this. Mary Louisa Witton died of cancer in Brisbane on 3 March 1931. [114]

The covering letter signed by W. B. Thomas with which this letter is kept at the Mitchell Library:

> Do not know if this is of any interest to Mitchell Library. The letter gives information re Hancock [sic] that is new to most people.
>
> As Mrs Hancock & children are still alive, consider contents of this letter should be observed as confidential. Mrs. H thinks husband innocent. Personally consider the sooner we forget the Morant, Hancock business the better.
>
> If of no interest please destroy the letter.

At the top of the letter is the note, apparently in a different hand: 'N.B. Not to be issued until 1970.'

W. B. Thomas was J. F. Thomas' brother who was administering his affairs after his death. It would appear therefore that the restriction on publication was imposed either by W. B. Thomas or a library curator and not by George Witton himself or by J. F. Thomas, and the opinion that 'the sooner we forget the Morant, Hancock business the better' was not that of either of the latter two. Any inference drawn from this restriction would therefore have little or no bearing on the letter's validity.

Some have used the statements made by Witton himself in his 1907 book to repudiate the contents of this letter. This only undermines *all* of Witton's testimony, on which so much of the Morant myth is based. If he could lie in 1929, why could he not have been lying in 1907 and 1902? There are fewer reasons for him to lie in 1929 than earlier.

Some have argued that Witton did not want Thomas to publish as it might prompt the War Office to publish Handcock's confession, which apparently implicated him. In his book Witton claimed: 'I proved even to the satisfaction of this court that I knew nothing of this case, and the charge was immediately withdrawn'. [115] Since the Court of Inquiry, which he tries to suggest was fiercely partisan, immediately accepted Witton's statement, he couldn't have been that worried about the confession – and in any case the world had moved on. This was eleven years after the the First World War: a Somerset light Infantry Soldier described one action as 'like the whole three years of the South African Campaign rolled in to an hour or so'. A number of the Boer Generals had fought for the British. Was Witton really concerned he might still be implicated in a murder of a man perceived to be a German, which had occurred nearly 30 years before and one for which no one had been found guilty? It seems very unlikely.

How would Witton be implicated by Handcock's confession? Another question might be asked. W. B. Thomas clearly recognised that this letter would be of interest to the Mitchell Library. Why then did he not give all of the papers J. F. Thomas had relating to the Courts Martial to the Mitchell Library? We will probably never have an answer to either of these questions.

There are plenty of reasons why Witton shouldn't have written this letter. It exposes him as disingenuous in his 1907 book, it besmirches the reputation of both Handcock and Morant, and would be a knife through the heart of J. F. Thomas. And yet he wrote it.

So why would he write it so long after the events if it were not true? Witton's line; 'Personally I do not think there would be much in writing what you term the true story of the Bushveldt Carbineers in face of the fact that the War Office may still hold Handcock's confession' would suggest he did not think Thomas knew the 'true story'. And if he did, would Witton not want him to publish it? Wouldn't it back up what he himself had written in 1907?

There is no convincing reason not to believe George Witton's letter of 1929 and the implication is clear: Handcock murdered Revd Heese, at the instigation of Morant. Heese knew too much about what had been going on in Spelonken and was about to go to the authorities in Pietersburg with the story. That Morant feared this can only mean that he knew, or at least feared, that the authorities disapproved of his actions in killing prisoners and might take action against him. When finally allowed to confer with each other, they did exactly as the authorities feared they would if allowed to collude. Probably with the help of Taylor, who had connections with both Mrs Bristowe and Mrs Schiels, they concocted an alibi, Handcock having withdrawn his confession. In the absence of the confession or eyewitnesses the prosecution was left with virtually no evidence in the Heese case and sought to withdraw charges against Morant, which Morant refused to accept.

It was reported in early April 1902, by one returned Australian: 'One young English officer who was arrested was almost broken hearted! He protested his innocence and said, "I shrink to tell you all that has really taken place. If everything comes out it will shock the world, and unless some steps are taken we shall be at war with Germany within a month."' [116] There is little doubt that Lt Picton, the English officer in question, believed that Revd Heese had been shot by a member of the Imperial army and not Boers or bandits.

Were Morant and Handcock 'scapegoats'? Perhaps. They were certainly made an example of. But did Lord Kitchener deliberately target the Bushveldt Carbineers *as Australians*? No, the BVC were not an Australian unit and he almost certainly knew Morant was English. Major Lenehan's involvement in the Spoelstra case would have meant his Bushveldt Carbineers were the last unit in South Africa Kitchener would want to have made an example of for war crimes. But Morant had so brazenly offered himself up, with complaints coming from all sides – including his own troopers – that there was little choice but to bring him and his accomplices to court martial. His pig-headedness in court, showing no remorse, denying J. F. Thomas his best defence of temporary insanity and generally causing the courts as much inconvenience as possible did him no favours. The court had little choice but to find the prisoners guilty of murder but still they recommended mercy. That, once found guilty, Kitchener chose to ignore this recommendation in Morant's and Handcock's cases may well have been influenced by political imperatives. Many Boers had been tried and shot for less. Peace negotiations would be just a matter of time and he needed to be seen as fair. Morant's histrionics in court and implicating Lord Kitchener himself would have angered Kitchener.

Morant probably signed his own death warrant.

13

Some Went Home

THE MILITARY

L/Cpl H Balfour Ogilvy One of the Breaker's mates who enlisted with him from Renmark. Received the DCM in the Boer War. He became a district officer in New Guinea and a major in the Australian Army. He was a great collector of ethnography and donated much of his collection to South Australia museums. Died at Renmark 1945. One of his daughters, Elaine, an army nurse, was murdered as a POW by the Japanese on Banka Island in the Dutch East Indies in 1942.

General Christiaan Beyers Assistant Commandant General. He established a law business in Pretoria and went into politics after the war. He was elected member for Pretoria South in the Union Legislature and became the first Commandant General of the South African Defence Force. Strongly opposed to the invasion of South West Africa in 1914, Beyers resigned his post. He drowned in the Vaal River in December 1914 whilst attempting to escape the pursuing Government forces.

Wilfred Nash Bolton Assistant Provost Martial at Pietersburg and perhaps the best man in the whole episode. After the war Bolton became the resident magistrate at Pietersburg and spent much of his time successfully obtaining government compensation for the victims of Morant's crimes and also the storekeepers looted in Louis Trichardt and Pietersburg. He later became a senior civil servant in Cyprus and by 1920 was the Commissioner of Limassol and a member of the Legislative Council of the Isle of Cyprus. He received the OBE. His first wife died in 1913 and he later remarried. His only child, Nancy, married Herbert Bagshaw, CBE, DSO, a lieutenant colonel in the RAMC in 1917. Bolton died in France of pneumonia in August 1930.

Ramon de Bertodano Despite his name, born in Australia. He was the pompous Intelligence Department officer who claimed much of the credit for having Morant and Handcock arrested and executed. After the war de Bertodano remained in Transvaal on administrative duties for a couple of years. He spent some time searching for the legendary 'Kruger's gold' and also the site of a mica deposit before returning to England in 1905. De Bertodano served in the First World War as a major in the Nottinghamshire Yeomanry and was mentioned in despatches. In 1921 he inherited the Marquisate of Morel from his uncle and became a Spanish citizen. His wife died leaving him with six children, but he married again in 1934 and had two more. In 1933 he collaborated in publishing a book, *The Spanish Republic: A Survey of Two Years Progress*. One of his collaborators was Luis Antonius Bolin who was later Press Chief to Franco. During the Spanish Civil War 1936–39 de Bertodano was an enthusiastic supporter of General Franco and the Nationalists and was their unofficial representative in London. He mixed with some disreputable people at this time and may well have been an informant for the intelligence service. He went to Rhodesia in 1947 leaving his family in England. It is hard to understand why he went off to Rhodesia away from his family and friends. He corresponded with many people involved in the BVC incidents with the apparent desire to write a book. He died in Salisbury (Harare) on 25 February 1955.

Colonel Johan Colenbrander The Commander of the First Kitchener's Fighting Scouts in North Transvaal was born in Natal of Dutch parents in 1856. He was fluent in Zulu and fought in the Zulu War and in Rhodesia. He was competent, ruthless and successful especially in the Boer War and became a Commander of the Bath (CB) (LG 27/04/02). After the war he had a number of unsuccessful business ventures. In 1917 he was involved in a film *The Symbol of Sacrifice* and played Lord Chelmsford. He drowned in the Klip River as he tried to cross on horseback for the film. He is one of the few men known to have killed a lion with his bare hands.

Colonel Francis Hall In command of the whole area between Pienar's River to Pietersburg. He received Cochrane's letter and ordered the arrest of Breaker Morant and his friends. He was posted to India prior to the Courts Martial on a normal preplanned redeployment. Later postings included Brigadier in charge of administration in Malta and with Scottish Command 1908–09. Retired 1909. As a young artillery officer he had served in Afghanistan 1878–80 under Lord Roberts. He fought notably well with the artillery in the early days of the Boer War with three mentions in despatches, became brevet colonel and Commander of the Bath (CB).

Commandant Tom Kelly The Boer Commandant of the Zoutpansberg District who was captured near the Portuguese East African border by a patrol led by Morant on 23 September 1901. Kelly was sent as a prisoner of war to India and ultimately returned to his farm in 1903. His wife died in 1918 and he became a misanthrope before he died there, aged 75, on 27 March 1923.

Lord Kitchener At the battle of Omdurman in1898 General Herbet Kitchener led an army of British, Sudanese and Egyptian men against 52,000 Mahdist warriors. At the cost of just 47 dead, the Dervish force was routed with more than 12,000 killed and 13,000 wounded. Kitchener's fame was assured from that moment and the British would come to control the Sudan. Kitchener became commander-in-chief in India (1902–09). He was promoted to the highest Army rank, Field Marshal, on 10 September 1909. He aspired to be Viceroy of India but was unsuccessful, being made military governor of Egypt (1911–14). He was created Earl Kitchener of Khartoum and of Broome in the County of Kent, on 29 June 1914. In 1914, at the start of the First World War, Lord Kitchener became Secretary of State for War. One of the few to foresee a long war, lasting for at least three years, and to have the authority to act effectively on that perception, he organised the largest volunteer army that Britain had ever seen. He oversaw a significant expansion of materials production to fight Germany on the Western Front. His commanding image appearing on recruiting posters demanding 'Your country needs you!' remains recognised and parodied in popular culture. Despite having warned of the difficulty of provisioning Britain for a long war, he was blamed for the shortage of shells in the spring of 1915 – one of the events leading to the formation of a coalition government – and stripped of his control over munitions and strategy. Kitchener drowned on 5 June 1916 when HMS *Hampshire* sank west of the Orkney Islands, Scotland.

Admiral Sir George Digby Morant The Breaker's putative father retired from the Royal Navy in May 1901. He became actively associated with various undertakings, industrial and other, connected with the Navy, including the Fairfield Shipbuilding Company, of which he was a director. He was also Chairman of the Royal Humane Society for many years. He died at his London home in Redcliffe Square on 13 February 1921. Morant's obituary in *The Times* said that his genial nature and success as a raconteur made him popular among a wide circle of friends. So he had something in common with his alleged son.

Victor Marra Newland Joined the South Australian Mounted Rifles with Morant and served with him in South Africa until Morant went off with Bennet Burleigh. Newland was awarded the Distinguished Conduct

Medal (DCM) and mentioned in Lord Robert's despatch in April 1901. Newland doubled as a correspondent for *The Adelaide Register* and in this role attended the execution of Morant and Handcock. His report of the event is powerful and moving. After the war he went to Kenya and started a safari outfitter's business with a partner and became a member of the local Legislative Council. Newland served in the King's African Rifles in the First World War and returned to Australia as a major with an MC and CBE. He then joined the Adelaide stock exchange and was elected to parliament for the seat of North Adelaide. He died on 14 January 1953 aged 76.

Robert Montague Poore The Provost Martial who investigated the incidents in Northern Transvaal. After the war Poore left South Africa and resumed his military and sporting career in England, playing cricket again for Hampshire until 1906, but never approached his record set in 1899, probably because he broke his arm playing football in Pretoria in 1902. He was the best swordsman in the army and won the best man at arms in the Royal Tournament in 1906 and 1907. He continued his military career in the Seventh Hussars, eventually as commander. He returned to India in 1911 and commanded the Jhansi Brigade as a Brigadier General from 1915 to 1919. Retiring in 1921, Poore returned to England and settled near Wimborne in Dorset building a large house adjacent to a golf course. He continued to play cricket for the MCC and coached boys at the Hampshire ground at Bournemouth. He played golf and became captain of Broadstone Golf Club. He died in July 1937 and was buried under his front lawn, to be joined by wife nineteen years later. Lady Flora was the youngest sister of the 13th Duke of Hamilton and his sister married the 14th Duke, so although he was childless, Poore blood courses through the veins of the Dukes of Hamilton.

Colonel James St Clair The Deputy Judge Advocate in South Africa 1899–1902 was in charge of the legal proceedings. He was born in 1848 and joined the Argyll and Sutherland Highlanders in 1871. He was called to the bar at Lincoln's Inn in 1891. He retired from the army in 1907 and died in 1940.

Major Thomas Souter The Queens Own Cameron Highlander officer who commanded the firing squad in 1902. Souter had started life as a soldier and was commissioned in the field in 1883 after a brave performance at the battle of Tel-el-Kebir in Egypt. He was initially posted to the Black Watch and served with them for several years. He had only just returned to his regiment in 1901 after serving as a staff officer in East Africa when these events occurred. He died in Inverness, aged 47, in 1904 and is buried in Inverness Tomnahurich cemetery.

Captain Alfred Taylor Intelligence Officer and Native Commissioner in the Spelonken during 1901. He is elusive in all the events but was central to them. Taylor was lucky to escape the firing squad and after the war returned to his farm at Plumtree on the South African/ Rhodesian border. It is probable that many of the cattle confiscated from Boer farmers passed through his farm 'Avoca' to his advantage. He served in the First World War as an officer in the South African Native Labour Corps in France. After the war he went on an engineering course in London and then visited Ireland where he was presented with an engraved rifle by the sisters of Lt Lewes Hart Stewart who died of fever in Matabeleland in 1895. Contrary to perceived wisdom, Taylor was neither elected to the Rhodesian Parliament, nor awarded the Distinguished Service Order (DSO) but was respected by both the black and white communities and was still known as 'Bulala' until his death. He died in Bulawayo hospital of pneumonia on 24 October 1941. Taylor was a Rhodesian pioneer who was always at 'the sharp end' and unlike some of the others involved, he knew what he was doing.

Major James Francis Thomas After the executions Thomas remained in South Africa for a time, returning to Australia in 1903. He pressed the government to enquire into the conduct of the Courts Martial, suggesting he proposed 'to publish certain facts'. He offered first to resign his commission and, to his dismay, the offer was immediately accepted. He resumed his law practice in Tenterfield and also the publication of the local newspaper *The Tenterfield Star.* Emotionally scarred by his time in South Africa, he was offended when his attempt to enlist for the First World War was rebuffed. Sadly his whole life went downhill and he started a reckless policy of misappropriating trust funds in order to build a South African style house outside the town. Thomas knew he had performed poorly in the Morant trials, having been outclassed by the prosecution team and committing the most basic error of advocacy in that he identified himself with the cause of his clients. He sold his practice in 1919, and then the *Tenterfield Star.* He made some unwise business decisions and by 1920 was practising as a solicitor in Sydney trying to fend off litigation about his irregular Tenterfield trust accounts. By 1926 Thomas was sued in proceedings that could have been settled, but he was obstinate and eventually sent to prison for contempt of court. After a year he was declared bankrupt and eventually struck off the roll of solicitors.

Thomas, like many of the people involved in the case from Lord Kitchener down, was an enthusiastic freemason. He joined Lodge 55 Tenterfield in 1891 and was senior warden in 1899/1900 at the time he went off to South Africa. Thomas retired from his lodge in 1929.

Thomas returned to Tenterfield a broken man. He never married and went to live in solitude at a small farm called Boonoo outside Tenterfield making a meagre living collecting rents. The Morant case obsessed him and he communicated with George Witton and Banjo Paterson hoping to write a book but declining health and lack of support caused him to abandon the project. He died on his farm on 11 November 1942. He was an interesting man but his attempted defence of the BVC officers in Pietersburg was not his greatest moment.

THE BUSHVELDT CARBINEERS

Lt George Baudinet was born in Tasmania, and joined the BVC on the first day of recruiting having served in the Queensland Mounted Infantry. He stayed in South Africa after the war engaged in mining and died in 1935. He was prominent in attempts to get Witton released and was a member of pressure groups in South Africa to that end.

Trooper Benjamin Beavan who was involved on the fringe of the eight Boers incident returned to Australia and had a barber's shop in Sydney. He enlisted in the Australian Army in January 1916 after a squabble with his wife, under the assumed name of Ernest Whiting. Killed in action in France on 5 September 1916, he is buried in Courcelette Cemetery near Albert.

Trooper John Bonner was a time-expired Victorian recruited to the BVC by Lt George Witton. He joined Steinaecker's Horse in February 1902. He stayed in South Africa after the war and served in the Natal police during the 1906 Zulu rebellion. Bonner gave many years to the militia forces and was awarded the long service medal for the 'Permanent Forces of the Empire beyond the Seas'. He served in the Afrikaner Rebellion in South Africa, August to October 1914, then in German SW Africa, May to July 1915, in the South African Forces. He went to the Western Front in France before returning to Australia. He died in the Benevolent House in Ballarat on 5 August 1950, aged 75. The death certificate listed his occupation as policeman. He was buried in Garvoc cemetery but bushfires in 1983 destroyed the cemetery records and his grave cannot now be located.

Trooper Theunis Botha was an Afrikaner. He was Morant's servant and interpreter and was involved in the shooting of the three Boers and also Visser. Botha testified against the BVC officers and denied that he had requested to be on execution squads. It is said he was shot in front of Pretoria Gaol on his white stallion after the war.

Trooper George Bothwell came from the small Wiltshire village of Horningsham, where his Irish father was the much loved local doctor.

A sailor by trade, he died in Biloxi, MS, USA, on 1 January 1903. His youngest brother was killed in the First World War.

Corporal the Honourable Aubrey Bruce Cooper Cecil from Queensland was the son of a Hampshire County cricketer. He was born at sea on a ship called *Scottish Prince* on the way to Australia. While in England in 1911 he married a widow with seven children and on return to Queensland he was employed as a clerk in Brisbane. He died in 1923.

Trooper James Christie was a New Zealand farmer from the small town of Clutha at the bottom of the South Island. He was a local councillor, school teacher and seemingly a member of every organisation and association in the area. He went bankrupt in 1900. In that year his farm burnt down and he lost four of his children. He went off to the army in South Africa. He wrote a series of articles about his time in the local paper that were ignored by Morant supporters but are remarkably accurate. He was one of the signers of Cochrane's letter to Col Hall. Christie remained in South Africa until at least 1903. In 1909 there was correspondence with the New Zealand military authorities on the issue of his Boer War medal and in the end this was sent from England. Although claiming additional clasps he received the Queen's South Africa medal with clasps Transvaal, South Africa 1901 and South Africa 1902. He was well respected in his community and was on the Clutha County Council. He was the headmaster of the local school. He was another who was an enthusiastic freemason. He died in 1921.

Trooper Muir Churton was born in New Zealand and describing himself as a farmer, had no previous service when he enlisted in the BVC in March 1901. He rode onto the scene immediately after the six Boers were shot in July 1901 and was in the party when Handcock shot Trooper van Buuren. Churton was also present when Visser was shot, but refused to join the firing party. He enlisted in the New Zealand Expeditionary Force as a corporal in 1916 for the First World War and served in France, later serving in the Machine Gun Corps. He went into Germany with the Army of Occupation before returning home. Churton spent his twilight years in the Ranfurley Veterans Home in Auckland and died on 15 March 1977, probably the last survivor of the BVC.

Trooper Robert Cochrane This Norwich-born Australian played a major part in alerting the authorities to the crimes being committed by Morant and the others. He dabbled in left wing politics in his early days in Queensland and became a mine manager, magistrate and journalist in Western Australia. Cochrane went to South Africa in 1900 to devote particular attention to 'metallurgical practice in the Rand' and had several patents to his name for gold extraction. Unable to progress owing to the war, he enlisted in the BVC. After being active in gathering evidence against Morant he was discharged from the BVC in November 1901. He returned to Perth and resumed his career becoming secretary of the Guild of Motor Car Drivers, secretary of the Master Bakers Union of Employers and secretary of the Master Butchers Union of Employers, amongst other positions. Cochrane also stood for election to the state legislature for Geraldton in 1908. His son, Robert Bede Cochrane, was killed in August 1916 in France whilst serving as a driver in the Australian field artillery. He died in Perth in 1933 aged 70.

Trooper Alfred Constancon served as a scout/guide with the BVC and was with Morant when he captured Kelly. In 1908 he was farming at Duivelskloof and seeking help from the Agricultural Department to deal with white ants, which were eating his house. Constancon died at Vereeniging in 1952.

Corporal Charles Foulis was the younger son of a baronet. He served in the First World War and settled in Kenya as the 11th baronet of Colinton. He died in 1936.

Trooper Hameline Glasson was born at Godolphin, Guyong, NSW next door to Willow Cottage, where Breaker Morant had probably lived for a short time. Glasson wrote regularly to his sister and the letters were discovered in 1970 and are now in the Mitchell Library, Sydney. In one of the letters he says 'our officers are a load of rotters ... for my part I would like to see some of them shot but would not be surprised to see it hushed up.' He remained in South Africa after the war and died of typhoid in November 1903 in Natal.

Sergeant Vincent Godfrey British and an early enlistee in the BVC, he became a recruiting officer. He must have liked the country because he returned to Spelonken and married, at the age of 38, the 21-year-old Alice Mary Bristow at Sweetwater House on 24 May 1904 and hopefully lived happily ever after. Major Wilfred Nash Bolton signed the register.

Squadron Sergeant Major Ernest Edwin Hammett A former regular sergeant in the Eleventh Hussars, he seems to have served in the Ninth Hussars in the Boer War for a couple of years. He was arrested along with the officers but released and continued serving in the Pietersburg Light Horse until the end of the war. He went back to Taunton where he had been a land surveyor and an apprentice with the Great Western Railway before joining the army. He wrote an affidavit for Witton from Taunton in 1904.

Lieutenant Charles Henry Goude Hannam had served in the Queensland Mounted Infantry before joining the BVC. He was involved in the attack on a convoy when three children were shot. He was eventually arrested but acquitted and served in the Pietersberg Light Horse (PLH). Hannam returned to Australia and died in Brisbane in 1923. The application for probate describes his occupation as 'gent', an un-Australian way to make a living.

Trooper Jacob Hatfield was a sailor from a seafaring Liverpool family and one of the fifteen who signed the letter of complaint to Col Hall. He went back to sea after the war and became a ship's officer. In the the First World War he was a Royal Navy officer 1915–1919. After the war he was a captain on the Blue Funnel Line. He was an accomplished wood carver and is shown in a magazine *Mersey* in April 1930 with a fine model ship he had made. He was later a freeman of the City of London and Vice President of the Mercantile Marine Service Association. He died working in his greenhouse on the Isle of Man in 1959.

Lieutenant Michael Kelly An old Africa hand, he ran a building supply business in partnership with a Boer named T. W. Beckett with branches in Pietersburg and Louis Trichardt. He was expelled from Pietersburg by the Boers and was one of the originals in the BVC subscribing £100 to the corps insurance fund. Kelly was not involved in the criminal events and resigned his commission in December 1901when he joined the Pietersburg Town Guard as a captain. His stores were looted by the incoming Australian troopers but he re-established the business and died in Pietersburg hospital in February 1906.

Major Robert Lenehan His less than successful tour of command came to an end when he was escorted onto the steamer *Aberdeen* for passage to Australia. Major General Hutton, in charge of Australian Forces, tried to prevent him serving again in the Australian Army. However, the Prime Minister intervened and Lenehan was confirmed as a major in the Australian Artillery in August 1904 and promoted to Lieutenant Colonel in 1913, commanding the Field Artillery brigade on home service duties in the war. His legal practice continued but in 1917 he was cited as co-respondent in a much publicised Sydney divorce case, removed from his military appointment and placed on the retired list. Lenehan died in Sydney on 20 May 1922 of cirrhosis of the liver, aged 56.

Captain Joseph Levy Born in Salford, Manchester in 1851, he was the man behind the raising of the BVC. He subscribed £500 to the insurance fund and became the recruiting officer and paymaster. It is said he really wanted the liquor licence for the stations north to Pietersburg but this was refused. Levy was at Pietersburg when Beyers attacked and helped the town guard. Apparently he died in the asylum at Pretoria on 16 April 1903.

Lieutenant Arthur Waldo Lewis was an American, known as 'Yank', who served until transferring to the Canadian Scouts in November 1901. He returned to the US and in 1904 formed the South African Boer War Exhibition Company, gathering together a group of former commanders from both sides. The company 'exhibited' at the 1904 St Louis World Fair but costs were high (wagonloads of ammunition were expended each day) and Lewis sold out at the end of the year. He later organised the Alaska Yukon Pacific Exposition in Seattle in 1909 and the Panama Pacific Exposition in

San Francisco in 1915. Lewis allegedly served in the Mexican Revolution and is described as a 'capitalist' in a California year book. An enthusiastic freemason, he published a book in 1939 entitled *Song Echoes of a Pilgrim*.

Trooper Harold Harcanute Locke A Victorian from the Moonee Ponds area, he was described as a farmer. He enlisted in the Australian Army in the First World War, served two years and retired as a major. He died on 5 September 1955.

Trooper Ronald Ernest Lord was an experienced Canadian soldier. He appeared before a district court martial in Pretoria with four other discharged BVC soldiers in November 1901 and was later seen working in the streets of Pretoria in convict garb. Lord returned to Prince Edward Island in 1908 and received a 320-acre land grant from the government for those who had served in South Africa under the volunteer bounty act of 1908, The date of his death is unconfirmed but it was probably in 1915. In a bizarre coincidence his first cousin, Lt Eric Skeffington Poole, had the unenviable distinction of being the first British officer executed by firing squad in France in the First World War, on 10 December 1916. He was charged with desertion; he had certainly been suffering from shell shock and possibly brain damage.

Trooper Ronald McInnis A Tasmanian, he kept a diary which formed the basis of a book called *Tasmanians in the Transvaal War*. His views are intemperate and he did not think very much of the BVC officers. He returned to Tasmania to farm and raise a family, and died in 1954.

Lieutenant Stephen Midgley An experienced soldier from Queensland, he was untainted by the sordid events in Northern Transvaal. Mentioned in Despatches and awarded the DSO. He stayed in South Africa after hostilities and served as a lieutenant during the 1906 Zulu rebellion. He operated a mine in what is now Zimbabwe before returning to Australia in poor health due to blackwater fever. Midgley enlisted for the First World War in the Fifth Light Horse and was immediately made up to captain. He served in Gallipoli and on the Western Front and was promoted to Lieutenant Colonel and given command of the 54th Battalion. In 1917 he was examined by a medical board which recommended rest and he returned to Australia in December 1917 with a DSO, CMG and five mentions in despatches. In the Second World War he was in the Volunteer Defence Corps on the Sunshine Coast in Queensland. Midgley died on 25 October 1955. A painting by his sister Ann Midgley, 'The departure of the Queensland contingent to South Africa', hangs in the colonial section of the Australian War Museum in Canberra.

Lieutenant Frederick Neel served as an assistant surgeon in the South African Republic's Malaboch campaign in 1894, despite having no discernible medical qualifications. He came from Jersey in the Channel Isles and owned a farm in the Spelonken district north of Pietersburg. He enlisted in the BVC in February 1901 as a trooper and subscribed £100 towards the establishment of the corps, which probably accelerated his promotion to lieutenant. Neel was not involved with the scandals that beset the unit and resigned to join Kitchener's Fighting Scouts. After the war, he took up farming and wrote letters to the authorities seeking employment as a doctor. He and his wife Louise went to Canada in 1905 and he is found in Vera Cruz, Mexico, in 1908. He enlisted in the Canadian Army in 1915 and served in the 124th infantry regiment and then in 1918 transferred to the Canadian Engineers. He returned to Toronto after the war and is alive in the 1921 census.

Sergeant Dudley Oldham An accountant from Gawler in South Australia, he played a large part in the events in Transvaal and was probably affected by his experiences, particularly the murder of the six Boers. He married and settled in South Africa after the war. He enlisted as a private in the Third Regiment of South African infantry and died of wounds on 20 April 1917 in France. His brother, an Australian army major, was killed at Gallipoli on 25 April 1915.

Lieutenant Henry George Picton was born in Lewisham, now London, in 1878, the son of a coachman. All sorts of nonsense has been written about his early life suggesting that he was descended from General Sir George Picton and had a career in the French Foreign Legion in the Congo. At the outbreak of the war he enlisted in Loch's Horse and, time-expired, he found his way into the Intelligence Department. He enlisted into the BVC as a lieutenant and was described as a 'horsebreaker'. He won a Distinguished Conduct Medal (DCM) at the vicious little battle of Bothaville when the mounted infantry nearly captured General De Wet. After the events in Spelonken he was tried and sentenced to be cashiered, which meant he was returned to England but could never be employed in a government position. On 6 May 1902 the *London Gazette* announced that 'The grant of the DCM to Corporal H G Picton (Loch's Horse) who afterwards became a lieutenant in the BVC awarded in the LG 27 September 1901 is cancelled.' Witton wrote to Thomas that he last heard of Picton working with horses in Europe in 1911. In fact, he made his way to the famed Potocki Stud in Poland and was employed there. He married in Europe in 1927 and had one son, Paul. Picton died in Brighton in 1952.

Captain James Huntley Robertson After leaving the BVC, Robertson's identity was stolen by an Australian petty criminal. A man called Alexander John Herbert Horatio Robertson died in Melbourne in 1967 and is buried in Lilydale cemetery there. In 1965 his daughter, Jessie, wrote a series of letters to the Australian military authorities seeking assistance for her father and giving the stories of his time with the Bushveldt Carbineers. These included working with Handcock and going into Kitchener's office to collect the death warrants of Morant and Handcock. Army Records could find no trace of him and eventually washed their hands of him. He first came to the notice of the authorities when found guilty of passing dud cheques in the first decade of the twentieth century. In fact, he had never served in the army, although he managed to become a member of the Returned Services League in Victoria and cobbled together an extraordinary career, ending up running a guest house. The real Robertson was born in Miraflores, Mexico, in 1873, the son of a Scottish textile mill owner. He is to be found in the 1891 census at a cotton mill in Accrington as an apprentice machine minder. He served for some time in the Royal Scots Greys. In Australia he joined the Second West Australian Mounted Infantry as a corporal. He was shot in the leg in South Africa and eventually joined the BVC. After the events in the Spelonken he was required as a witness at the Courts Martial and ultimately joined Kitchener's Fighting Scouts until the end of the war. Robertson returned to South America, married and then divorced. He married again and, fluent in written and spoken Spanish, worked in Bolivia, Peru, Chile and Argentina from 1908 to 1914. He enlisted into the Royal Flying Corps in 1914 and gave good service. At one time Robertson was the liaison officer between the Portuguese Army and the British High Command. He was awarded the Military Cross (LG 1/1/17). After the war he is to be found in the Scottish *Sunday Post* of 8 June 1919 divorcing his wife. After the war he returned to Mexico. He died there on 24 April 1942. The cause of his death is given as lobar pneumonia and his occupation is shown as soldier. He is buried in the Cementerio Britanico at Jardin Guadalupano, Calz Mexico-Tacuba 1129, Huichapan, 11290 Ciudad de Mexico, D.F., Mexico. His son, Carlos Huntley Robertson, played rugby for Argentina (the Pumas) in the thirties and was also manager of a rugby tour to the UK.

Sergeant William John Setterfield The orderly room sergeant. Before the war his brother and his wife ran the Bandolier Kop hotel, near Fort Edward, but it at the start of the war it closed. They returned in 1902 and William went with them. At a small horse race meeting near the hotel he fell and struck his head and died. He is buried adjacent to the N1 highway in a marked grave. In 2005 a brass BVC badge was found in what was probably the hotel midden and possibly belonged to Setterfield.

Trooper James Skelton was the son of Sir John Skelton, a Scottish lawyer and Vice President of the Local Government Board. He had worked in the intelligence department before joining the BVC. He was one of the fifteen signatories to Cochrane's letter of complaint. Later he was commissioned as a lieutenant in the Pietersburg Light Horse. Skelton seems to have gone to Malaya, possibly as a planter in the Penang area, and died as a civilian internee in Malai Camp, Singapore, on 13 January 1943.

Trooper John Stewart Silke was the son of a 72-year-old transported convict. He worked on horse boats taking remounts to the war and enlisted at Durban with some mates after bringing a boatload of horses from the Adriatic. His importance in the Morant story is that he wrote a diary and was at many of the events including the death of Hunt. He was one of the fifteen soldiers who signed the letter of complaint to Colonel Hall. His diary has been belittled by Morant supporters and was obviously compiled some time after the events described, but letters and newspapers show that it is pretty accurate. In particular, his description of the death of Hunt and the map of that event in the diary have proved to be correct. He returned to Australia and married Eva Mary Hunt. He was secretary of the Loyal Star of Cessnock lodge of the Oddfellows in 1908. He died in April 1960. He was a scallywag in his youth but he knew right from wrong.

Trooper Robert Threlfall A grocer from Sydney, he had served in Sudan with the NSW ambulance unit in 1885. He married in 1898 and his wife, Euphemia, was killed in 1899 when she was thrown from a sulky. He enlisted for the Boer War as a result. He also signed up for the the Great War and was drowned on 24 April 1915 when he was guarding a bridge during a storm, in full uniform, over the Georges River near Sydney and fell in. Not a lucky man.

Trooper Arthur Wyatt Miles Thompson was a West Australian from Coolgardie who described himself as an ironmonger on his enlistment form. He was coerced into killing the eight Boers and was one of the fifteen complainants. He enlisted in the Tenth Australian Light Horse in the First World War declaring his occupation as pearler and agent. He initially served in the 1915 Senussi campaign in Libya in a composite light horse regiment. He then served with his regiment in the later advance to Damascus, was mentioned in despatches in 1917, commissioned in 1918 and awarded the Military Cross (MC) for conspicuous gallantry and devotion to duty in that year (LG 18 July 1918). He was wounded with a gunshot to the head. Thompson returned to Western Australia in 1920, married his cousin and is to be found on the electoral roll of Dumbleyung District 1922–1949 and a trustee of the local hospital board in 1945. He died in 1951.

Lieutenant George Ramsdale Witton A Victorian who served in the Victorian Permanent Artillery prior to the war and enlisted into the Victorian Bushmen. He was nearly invalided back to Australia but met Major Lenehan, who offered him a commission if he could raise a gun section for the BVC. He managed to get time-expired Australian volunteers but the BVC could not get any guns. Witton was unlucky to become involved with Morant and Handcock and admitted killing one of the eight Boers. He was arrested and sentenced to death in the series of Courts

Martial in Pietersburg. His sentence was commuted to life and he was put on a train by Major Poore at 05.34 on 27 February 1902. Sent to England, he was imprisoned in Portland Prison and immediately began petitioning the authorities for his release. Luckily for him, his competent brother Ernest set up a Witton Defence Committee. Ernest obtained a legal opinion from Isaac Isaacs, a prominent Melbourne lawyer. This opinion accompanied a petition signed by 80,000 Australians and was sent to King Edward VII. Meanwhile, support was drummed up in South Africa and James Logan, a member of the Cape Legislative Council, went to London and lobbied members of Parliament in the Carlton Club, including Winston Churchill – himself a former prisoner of the Boers – who asked several questions in the house. The two-pronged campaign was successful and was apparently supported by Mrs Alice Keppel, the King's mistress. Witton was freed on 10 August 1904. Logan collected him at Portland and took him to his Scottish estate for a spot of grouse shooting.

Witton returned home and campaigned to redeem his reputation. Utilising trial notes from Major J. F. Thomas and assistance from Major Lenehan and help from Frank Fox, (Renar) author of *Bushman and Buccaneer,* he wrote his defence, which became *Scapegoats of the Empire*, a masterpiece of spin. By mid-1905 Witton had completed it and sought a publisher. In June 1907 the book was published in Melbourne, almost certainly at Witton's expense. Part of the conspiracy theory built around the Morant story is that the government suppressed and burnt the book. However, many government officials, including Prime Minister Alfred Deakin and Attorney-General Sir Isaac Isaacs, were Witton apologists and they would not have supported any censorship of the book. Witton never claimed it was suppressed and the initial print run was modest. There are copies of the book in libraries in expected quantities and no evidence of government inquisitors torching them. J F. Thomas described the book as 'only a surface description of his trial notes'.

Witton moved to Queensland in 1908 and took up pineapple and dairy farming and married Mary Louisa Humphrey in 1913. He integrated into his local community where there is today a Witton Road in his memory. In 1931 Mary died of cancer and eventually Witton sold up and moved to Victoria in 1940 after a brief second marriage. Ironically, he became a Justice of the Peace in both Queensland and Victoria. Two years later, he suffered a heart attack whilst cranking his car and died aged 68. His ashes are interred in Mary's grave in Brisbane, although there is no headstone for him. Witton lies in a cemetery next to 'Kitchener Road', named after the man who was 'pleased to commute his sentence to penal servitude for life'.

OTHERS

John Hugh Bates Probably born in 1857. The second husband of Daisy Bates and father (probably) of Arnold. He died aged 78 on 13 April 1935 at Mullewa, Western Australia.

Arnold Hamilton Bates The unhappy son and only child of Daisy Bates. His mother totally ignored him and eventually he attended a Christian Brothers School in Perth. He is noted in the *Western Daily Mail,* Perth, as receiving prizes for religion in 1901. Afterwards he was apprenticed to an engineering firm and joined the Australian Flying Corps in the First World War1 as an air mechanic. Daisy Bates tried to make contact with him in 1918 and in 1949, but he refused to acknowledge her. He was living in the Wellington area of New Zealand in 1940 engaged in the manufacture of Bren gun carriers and died there in 1963. It is probable he went to New Zealand because Hugh J. Bates, younger brother of John H. Bates, was living there with his wife.

Frank Fox was an Australian born journalist who by 1901 was working at the *Sydney Bulletin*. After the death of Morant he wrote a book, published in 1902, called *Bushman and Buccaneer: a memoir of 'Breaker Morant'* under the pen name Frank Renar This sold well and, as a result of information from *The Northern Miner,* exposed Morant's true antecedents. He went on to a high-profile journalistic career and moved to England, was knighted in 1926 and died in 1960.

Johanna Heese The widow of the Revd Daniel Heese moved to Pietersburg with her three daughters after the murder of her husband. A son named Carl August Daniel was born in January 1901. She died of cancer in 1908 aged 36.

Leonard Henry Ledeboer A Dutch-born scout and intelligence agent worked closely with Captain Taylor and lived in Louis Trichardt. He was involved in many of the events in Spelonken, particularly the eight Boers case, and is a shadowy figure in the story. He seems to have assisted Bolton, then magistrate at Pietersburg, in his quest to obtain compensation for Morant's victims after the war. He returned to his life as a hunter and also was engaged in recruiting native labour from the local tribes. Ledeboer became a ranger in the newly formed Kruger National Park and died probably in 1959.

William Henry Ogilvie Will Ogilvie was a Scot born in the Borders in 1869 to a farming family and public school educated. Ogilvie was sent to Australia in 1889 to gain sheep farming experience. He started writing for *The Bulletin* in about 1893 under the pen name of 'Glenrowan'. His bush voice was authentic, unlike Paterson who visited station 'big houses' and Lawson who frequented city bars. Ogilvie teamed up with another contributor, Gordon Tidy, 'Mousquetaire', and by 1896 the pair had met up with Morant at

Nelungaloo Station near Parkes and he was involved in the Bogan Gate polo match. After Morant's death he could never come to terms with Morant's complex personality, particularly his drunkenness and his dark side. He returned to Scotland in 1901 and took up farming and later dabbled in right wing politics. He died aged 93 in 1962.

Samuel Foreman Nicker He knew Morant in his early days in Queensland. They broke horses for a living and apparently also worked as blade shearers. They kept up a constant correspondence until the Breaker's death. Nicker (1863–1931) went into cattle farming later in life and the family lived in the Alice Springs area. He died in Adelaide and the funeral arrangements were made by the staff in the mail order department of Foy and Gibson Pty. Victor Foy one of the directors, was Morant's mate and opposing captain in the great polo match at Bogan's Gate. Like many other people in the story he was an enthusiastic freemason.

Andrew Barton 'Banjo' Paterson A Sydney solicitor who wrote for *The Bulletin* under the pen name 'Banjo', the name of his favourite horse. He was a member of the Sydney hunting set and introduced Morant to that world. By the last decade of the nineteenth century his name was a household word in Australia and he wrote *Waltzing Matilda* in 1895. Paterson went out to South Africa as a war correspondent and also reported on the Boxer Rebellion from China. Paterson went on to serve in the Great War, returning to Australia in 1919. He was awarded the CBE in 1939 and appeared on a postage stamp in 1985. He knew all the Breaker's thoughts and wrote several articles about him up to 1939. Paterson died in 1941. One of his best poems is 'Jim Carew', which is widely thought to depict Morant. The second verse reads:

> Gentleman Jim on the cattle camp,
> Sitting his horse with easy grace,
> But the reckless living has left its stamp,
> In the deep drawn lines of that handsome face,
> And the harder look in those eyes of blue,
> Prompt at a quarrel is Jim Carew.

The last line is 'I am or … no I was Jim Carew.' Perhaps that says it all.

Reverend Friedrich Ludwig Reuter It was from his Medingen Mission that Hunt and his men set off to attack the Boers nearby. Hunt still lies in the Mission cemetery and so does Reuter, who died in 1940, alongside his wife who died in 1937.

Reverend Gordon Tidy One-time drinking partner, bush poet and friend of the Breaker. He used the pen name of 'Mousquetaire' and although quite competent as a poet did not reach the standard of Paterson and Ogilvie. He took holy orders and became an Anglican clergyman. At one time was in the diocese of Bathurst and Sydney and in 1931 was rector of Stanton St Quintin in Wiltshire, England. He died in a home for retired clergymen in Tiverton, Devon.

Silas Sono A 17-year-old black boy who came from a small village at the Kreuzburg Mission Station near Fort Klipdam. He witnessed the shooting of Heese and reported the facts the following day. He died in December 1936.

Bibliography and Sources

Blezynski, Nick, *Shoot Straight, you Bastards!* (Sydney: Random House, 2002)

The title gives a clue as to the content. Some good research but the author is fascinated by the idea that the Breaker was the son of a British admiral. This is a novel and should be read as such.

Carnegie, Margaret & Shields, Frank, *In search of Breaker Morant* (Armadale, Victoria: Graphic Books, 1979)

Ahead of its time; broke the back of the myth.

Cutlack, F. M., *Breaker Morant, a Horseman who Made History* (Sydney: Ure Smith, 1962)

Author knew Morant at Paringa as a boy 60 years before.

Davey, Arthur, *Breaker Morant and the Bushveldt Carbineers* (Cape Town: van Riebeck Society, 1987)

Anyone seriously interested in this story should have a copy. An invaluable collection of primary sources.

Denton, Kit, *Closed File* (Adelaide: Rigby Publishers, 1983).

An attempt to tell the real story after the film *Breaker Morant.* Based on an earlier book *The Breaker* (1973), which provided the title for Nick Blezynski's book above.

Leach, Charles, *The Legend of Breaker Morant is Dead and Buried* (Louis Trichardt: Charles Leach, 2012)

A worthy book by a South African enthusiast; excellent local knowledge and a vital book to have if you visit the area. Charles was born in Elim hospital and runs tours around the area.

Meredith, John, *Breaker's Mate, Will Ogilvie in Australia* (Kenthurst, NSW: Kangaroo Press, 1996)

Mainly about Ogilvie, but a chapter on Morant.

Packenham, Thomas, *The Boer War* (London, Wiedenfeld and Nicholson Ltd, 1979)

A wonderful book and a remarkable feat of research.

Reece, Bob, *Daisy Bates, Grand Dame of the Desert* (Canberra: National Library of Australia, 2007)

A concise overview of Mrs Murrant.

Renar, Frank, *Bushman and Buccaneer: Harry Morant – his 'Ventures and Verses.* (Sydney: H. T. Dunn, 1902)

The first book on the subject and written by the assistant editor of the *Sydney Bulletin.*

Robl, Ted (ed.), *Breaker Morant A Backblock Bard* (Pyalong, Victoria: Ted Robl, 2002)

The collected verses of Harry 'Breaker' Morant. The work of an enthusiast, but needs a second edition because of later discoveries.

Witton, George, *Scapegoats of the Empire; The story of the Bushveldt Carbineers* (Melbourne: D. W. Paterson, 1907).

Witton makes a compelling case that he and the other accused were scapegoats. Later evidence, primarily from Witton himself, undermines most of his claims.

Woolmore, Bill, *The Bushveldt Carbineers and the Pietersburg Light Horse* (McCrae, Australia: Slouch Hat Publications, 2002)

Very good summary, fine research and strong on medals awarded.

Sources

Australia

Trove. This resource has opened up research on the subject. It is a rich source of data created and maintained by the National Library of Australia. It is a growing repository of full text digital information with eighteen million pages from more than 1000 Australian newspapers. The main papers relvant to the Breaker story are *The Northern Miner, The Sydney Bulletin* and *The Windsor and Richmond Gazette.* http://trove.nla.gov.au

Mitchell Library Sydney. Contains much Morant material including letters to and from Banjo Patterson.

John Oxley Library, State Library of Queensland, Brisbane. Has much immigration material, particularly on the arrivals of Daisy Bates and Breaker Morant, but under their original names. Also the Almora Diary, written by a fellow passenger of Daisy Bates of the voyage from England to Australia.

United Kingdom

The National Archives. At Kew in London. The document that is not contained here is the transcript of the Courts Martial. There is only one transcript at the Archive of Courts Martial prior to 1914. The rest were destroyed by the Luftwaffe in 1940. However, the following are very useful

WO/100 General class for medal rolls

WO/ 126/100 Attestation papers for BVC (Morant's papers are missing)

WO/127/16 Nominal roll for BVC. Other units are also in this class.

WO/108 General class for Boer War.

WO/108/405 Secret cipher correspondence between Kitchener and London

WO/128 Imperial Yeomanry Attestation papers for Percy Hunt and Francis George Morant.

WO/93/41 Letter book Judge Advocate General South Africa (St Clair).

MH/12 General class workhouse correspondence.

MH/9 General class workhouse staff lists.

WO/32/8033 Board of Enquiry into loss of a convoy at Rhenoster Kop. Major J. F. Thomas in command.

War Office, Manual of Military Law, HSMO, 1899. There are earlier and later editions, but this is the relevant one.

Hampshire County Cricket Club. Archive includes good pictures of Poore and also his cricketing achievements.

Wiltshire County Records. Collected papers of R. M. Poore's father.

National Archives of Scotland. R. M. Poore's Boer War diary. Permission to access kindly given by the Duke of Hamilton.

Somerset County Records Office. Bridgwater workhouse records including Guardian's minutes of meetings.

England Rugby Museum Twickenham. Details of W. N. Bolton's England rugby career and also team photos.

Library and Museum of Freemasonry, London. Records of Edwin Henry Murrant's school career at Royal Masonic Institute for Boys 1873–1880. Also Lord Kitchener's masonic career 1883–1902.

Lodge Virtue and Honor No. 494 Axminster, Devon, England. Details of Edwin Murrant's initiation into Freemasonry 1860. Also Fortescue Lodge, Honiton, Devon and Rural Philanthropic Lodge No 291 Burnham on Sea, Somerset.

The Schulenburg collection. Notes of the South Africa researcher Dr C. A. R. Schulenburg, a copy of which is held by the National Army Museum at Stevenage.

South Africa

Transvaal Archives Pretoria. Contains a large amount of original material from the time of the Military Government including the following:

Military Governor of Pretoria MGP

Provost Martial Pretoria (PMO) Vols 33, 50, 54, 59–60, 70, 76, 81

Secretary for Native Affairs (SNA) Vol 2

Colonial Secretary Pretoria Vol 1092 (BVC) Outrages and Compensation

Orange Free State Archives, Bloemfontein. Commission of Enquiry into the Administration of Kroonstadt District 1901. This severely criticises the activities of Ramon de Bertodano whilst he was in charge of the town

Transvaal Rugby Museum, Ellis Park, Johannesburg. Details of General C. F. Beyers' Transvaal rugby career and photo of 1896 team.

Zimbabwe

The National Archives in Harare, Zimbabwe. Memoir of Marquis del Moral (de Bertodano) and other papers. Papers relating to Captain Alfred Taylor including will and record of service.

Ireland

Order of the Sacred Heart of Jesus, Dublin. This archive contains the registers of the National school at Roscrea when Daisy Bates was a pupil.

Notes

1 The Early Days

[1] Ancestry.co.uk
[2] The Guardian's record books for Honiton are in the Devon Record Office at Exeter and for Bridgwater in the Somerset Record Office at Taunton.
[3] Bridgwater Poor Law Union, Minute Books of the Meetings of the Board D\G\bw/8a/
[4] *Hereford Times,* 27 April 1861
[5] Bridgwater Poor Law Union, Minute Books of the Meetings of the Board D\G\bw/8a/14
[6] Details of E. H. Murrant's induction into freemasonry are contained in the minute book of Lodge Virtue and Honor No 494 Axminster, Devon. After 1861 he probably joined Fortescue Lodge, Honiton and then definitely moved to Rural Philanthropic Lodge No 291 at Burnham on Sea, Somerset, where he remained until his death.
[7] SRO A\DLY/4/1. Records of the Rural Philanthropic Lodge of the Freemasons
[8] D\G\bw/8a/15
[9] *Wells Journal,* 14 February 1863
[10] D\G\bw/8a/16
[11] D\G\bw/8a/15
[12] D\G\bw/8a/17
[13] *Somerset County Gazette,* 6 August 1864
[14] D\G\bw/8a/16
[15] SRO A\DLY/4/1. Records of the Rural Philanthropic Lodge of the Freemasons
[16] *Western Gazette,* 31 April 1864

[17] Belshaw, G., *Bridgwater St Matthews Fair*, (Telford:New Era, 2004)
[18] Hussey, D., in *A Maritime History of Somerset, Volume 1 Trade and Commerce* (Somerset: SANHS)
[19] D\G\bw/8a/17
[20] *Western Gazette,* 19 March 1869.
[21] D\G\bw/8a/25
[22] Minutes of the General Court Committee, GBR 1991 RMIB 1/1/1/8 and 1/1/1/9
[23] Somerset Records Office, A\DLY/3 Lodge of Perpetual Friendship Bridgwater
[24] Minutes of the General Court Committee, GBR 1991 RMIB 1/1/1/8 and 1/1/1/9. Also published in *The Era,* 20 April 1873.
[25] Minutes of the House Committee, GBR 1991 RMIB 1/2/1/4 and 1/2/1/5
[26] Minutes of the General Court Committee, GBR 1991 RMIB 1/1/1/8 and 1/1/1/9. Also published in *The Era,* 20 April 1873.
[27] Minutes of the House Committee, GBR 1991 RMIB 1/2/1/4 and 1/2/1/5
[28] Ibid.
[29] Parks, A. L., Riches, E. A, *The History of the Royal Masonic School for Boys,* Volume 1 1798–1938 (Luton: White Crescent, 1975)
[30] Ibid.
[31] Waterman received the China Medal with clasps Taku and Pekin for his service in China 1860–1864. 67 Foot Medal Roll for China War WO100/41 at the National Archives, Kew. Waterman was the senior NCO, equivalent to Regimental Sergeant Major. Amongst those awarded a VC in the attack on the Taku Forts was Hospital Apprentice Andrew Fitzgibbon, aged 15, the youngest ever winner
[32] This is also reported in *The Freemason,* July 1880, p. 3 on the 'resources' section website of the Museum and Library of Freemasonry.

2 The Teenage Murrant

[1] Bridgwater Poor Law Union, Minute Books of the Meetings of the Board D\G\bw/8a/26
[2] Bridgwater Poor Law Union, Minute Books of the Meetings of the Board D\G\bw/8a/29
[3] Bridgwater Poor Law Union, Minute Books of the Meetings of the Board D\G\bw/8a/30
[4] 1881 UK Census
[5] Diary of Revd Dr Thomas Nichols
[6] Ancestry, Masonic Records
[7] Ancestry, Masonry Membership Records

[8] Barnet Museum File ED05
[9] thebiography.us/en/rivas-groot-jose-maria accessed 25 July 2016
[10] Easby-Smith, J. S., *Georgetown University in the District of Columbia, 1789–1902* (New York: The Lewis Publishing Company, 1907)
[11] 'Mapping the practice and profession of sculpture in Britain and Ireland 1851–1995', Sculpture http://sculpture.gla.ac.uk/view/person.php?id=ann_1277210485
[12] 1881 UK Census
[13] Bridgwater Poor Law Union, Minute Books of the Meetings of the Board D\G\bw/8a/32
[14] Ibid.
[15] Ibid.
[16] *Taunton Courier and Western Advertiser,* 14 December 1881
[17] Bridgwater Poor Law Union, Minute Books of the Meetings of the Board D\G\bw/8a/32
[18] Walton, J., *George Randall – Emigration Officer Extraordinaire: a Biography* (Brisbane: CopyRight Publishing 2007)
[19] *Richmond and Windsor Gazette,* April 5 1902

3 The Morants

[1] The Admiral's denial of paternity was published by many Australian newspapers but this one was from *The Bathurst Free Press and Mining Journal,* Friday 9 May 1902.
[2] Harbord, M. A., *Froth and Bubble. (*London: Arnold, 1915)
[3] Enlistment details for Trooper Francis George Morant, The National Archives WO 108/374

4 Mrs Morant

[1] The first Wimbledon Championships were held in 1877.
[2] Baptism Register Killaloe and Roscrea baptisms held at Roscrea heritage Centre
[3] Archives of Sisters of the Sacred Heart in Dublin. The convent is now closed. The film *Philomena* is about this order and is very critical.
[4] John Oxley reference library, State Library of Queensland, *Almora* shipboard diary
[5] Quoted in an article she gave to a reporter in the *Courier-Mail* (Brisbane), 9 January 1936. Total fantasy.
[6] *Queenslander*, 27 June 1883

[7] The National Archives (TNA) BT 122/72

[8] Named after the gold commissioner W. Charters. The local hills are named from the same derivation as 'tors' in Devon and Cornwall.

[9] Registrar General Queensland A 47836

[10] *The Northern Miner,* 9 and 14 April 1902, comments on the story as a result of information from Helen Veal.

[11] *The Northern Miner* 21, 23 & 25 April 1884.

[12] *The Northern Miner* 14 April 1902 and subsequently

[13] She wrote to the Australian Army in August 1918 and also to the Returned Soldiers League in 1949 seeking information about her son. Both organisations knew his location.

[14] *London Daily News,* 25 March 1887

[15) Kings New Year honours, 1 January 1934. *Newcastle Morning Herald and Miner* (and others), 1 January 1934

5 The Wilderness Years

[1] Queensland State Archives

[2] William Corfield, *Reminiscences of Queensland; 1862–1899,* p. 80

[3] *Sydney Morning Herald,* 25 February 1939. Article by Paterson but no date given to the letter.

[4] Mitchell Library Sydney AM/77/5

[5] Mitchell Library Sydney Doc 1192

[6] *Windsor and Richmond Gazette,* 3 March 1900

[7] Ian W. Shaw, *On Radji Beach.* (Australia: Pan Macmillan, 2010)

[8] *Audrey Tennyson's Vice-Regal Days.* (Canberra: National Library of Australia, 1978)

[9] Gordon Joseph M., *The Chronicles of a Gay Gordon* (London: 1921)

[10] Presented to the court martial

[11] *Renmark Pioneer,* 7 September 1900

[13] *The Chronicles of a Gay Gordon*

[12] Australian Defence department, 'Official records of the Australian military contingents to the war in South Africa.' P L Murray (ed) Melbourne 1911

6 The Bushveldt Carbineers (BVC)

[1] The diary is available in the Scottish National Archive in Edinburgh and may be consulted by arrangement with the Duke of Hamilton.

[2] The National Archive, Kew, WO 126/100

[3] *London Gazette*, 1/1/17 (and also in Edinburgh Gazette)

7 The Old Country

[1] Harbord, M. A., *Froth and Bubble, Edward* (London: Arnold, 1915)
[2] Ancestry Ship Lists
[3] *The Adelaide Observer*, 29 December
[4] Probate Records 1903
[5] *London Gazette*, 1 May 1903
[6] Birth Certificate, Percy Frederick Hunt, 1873, Archives Departementales des Pyrenees-Atlantiques
[7] Records of Bromsgrove School
[8] *Belfast News-Letter*, 27 August 1898
[9] SAMIF records angloboerwar.com accessed 28 July 2016
[10] TNA WO 127/8
[11] Letter to Mrs Eland, 20 August 1901, wife of Sergeant Eland who was later killed with Hunt, from Alfred E Haserick, saying Hunt had been the marriage officer in the military government in Pretoria for some months.
[12] TAB CS 15 01 1742/01
[13] TAB CS 15 01 1742/01
[14] Woolmore, W., *The Bushveldt Carbineers and the Pietersburg Light Horse* (McCrae: Slouch Hat, 2002)
[15] The National Archives (TNA) Copy 1/455
[16] Electoral Rolls
[17] 1939 Register (Ancestry)
[18] Cavalry and Guards Club records provided by Frances Watt, membership secretary.

8 Alfred 'Bulala' Taylor – The Rhodesian Soldier

[1] Zimbabwe Archives
[2] Boggie, J., *First steps in civilizing Rhodesia*, 1940
[3] Transcript in the Taylor file in the Zimbabwe Archives
[4] Zimbabwe Archives
[5] Letter to Ramon de Bertodano from ex-trooper J. R. A. Kelly of Kitchener's Fighting Scouts dated 12 April 1953, Zimbabwe Archives, De Bertodano file
[6] Ibid.

9 Events in Northern Transvaal

[1] Leach, C., *The Legend of Breaker Morant is Dead and Buried* (Louis Trichardt: Charles Leach, 2012)

[2] PRO WO127. Nominal rolls colonial units
[3] Leach, C., *The Legend of Breaker Morant is Dead and Buried*
[4] *The Journal,* 4 June 1901, p. 3
[5] Medal Roll of the Rhodesia Regiment
[6] Bulpin, T. V., *Lost Trails of the Transvaal*, (Cape Town: Books of Africa, 1965)
[7] *London Gazette,* death notice, 5 August 1927.
[8] Knox, J. and Graham, P. Pers Comm
[9] Braun, L. F., 'The Returns of the King: The Case of Mphefu and Western Venda, 1899–1904', *Journal of Southern African Studies,* Vol. 39, No. 2, 271–291, 2013
[10] Ibid.
[11] Bulpin, T. V., *Lost Trails of the Transvaal*
[12] Braun, L. F., 'The Returns of the King: The Case of Mphefu and Western Venda, 1899–1904', *Journal of Southern African Studies,* Vol. 39, No. 2, 271–291, 2013
[13] Ibid.
[14] Ibid
[15] Ibid
[16] Ibid
[17] Leach, C., *The Legend of Breaker Morant is Dead and Buried*
[18] Taylor letter to Col Henderson 1901, in Braun, p 283
[19] *The Bulawayo Chronicle,* 30 October 1901, p. 4
[20] Davey, A., *Breaker Morant and the Bushveldt Carbineers*, (Cape Town: van Riebeck Society, 1987) p. 218
[21] *Die Dorp Louis Trichardt Pieter Hendrik Carel De Vaal Kirsten Drukpers*, 1986
[22] Braun, L. F., 'The Returns of the King: The Case of Mphefu and Western Venda, 1899–1904', *Journal of Southern African Studies,* Vol. 39, No. 2, 271–291, 2013
[23] Taylor letter to Major Cashel in Davey, A., *Breaker Morant and the Bushveldt Carbineers* (Cape Town: van Riebeck Society, 1987) p. 218
[24] *The Bulawayo Chronicle,* 29 May 1901, p. 10
[25] *The Bulawayo Chronicle,* 30 October 1901, p. 4
[26] By 1905 the fish had got larger with Taylor claiming it had been 14 days.
[27] Braun, L. F., 'The Returns of the King: The Case of Mphefu and Western Venda, 1899–1904', *Journal of Southern African Studies,* Vol. 39, No. 2, 271–291, 2013
[28] Leach, C., *The Legend of Breaker Morant is Dead and Buried,* p. 5
[29] Memoir of H. R. Mingard, 8 September 1901 in Davey, p. 45
[30] Leach, C., *The Legend of Breaker Morant is Dead and Buried*

[31] Braun, L. F., 'The Returns of the King: The Case of Mphefu and Western Venda, 1899–1904', *Journal of Southern African Studies,* Vol. 39, No. 2, 271–291, 2013

[32] Leach, C., *The Legend of Breaker Morant is Dead and Buried,* citing De Vaal

[33] Leach, C., *The Legend of Breaker Morant is Dead and Buried*

[34] Davey, A., *Breaker Morant and the Bushveldt Carbineers*

[35] Ibid.

[36] London *Times,* 30 April 1902, p. 10

[37] PRO WO 339/21968

[38] 1891 UK Census

[39] *The West Coast Leader*; 19 January 1918, Lima, Peru

[40] PRO WO 339/21968

[41] Carnegie, M. and Shields, F., *In search of Breaker Morant, Balladist and Bushveldt Carbineer*, (Canberra: National Library of Australia, 1979)

[42] *Odendaal: Noordtransvaal op Kommando*. In Leach, C.

[43] Leach, C., *The Legend of Breaker Morant is Dead and Buried*

[44] Deposition of Trooper George Arthur Heath in Davey, A., *Breaker Morant and the Bushveldt Carbineers*

[45] Tpr J. D. Pacholi, *Bendigo Advertiser,* 14 October 1901

[46] Schulenburg Collection, National Army Museum, Stevenage; Davey, A., *Breaker Morant and the Bushveldt Carbineers*, (Cape Town: van Riebeck Society, 1987) p. 79

[47] Schulenburg Collection

[48] Deposition of Trooper Ernest Browne, 1901 in Davey, A., *Breaker Morant and the Bushveldt Carbineers*

[49] Deposition of Trooper George Arthur Heath, 1901 in Davey, A., *Breaker Morant and the Bushveldt Carbineers*

[50] Leach, C., *The Legend of Breaker Morant is Dead and Buried*

[51] Deposition of Trooper Ernest Browne, 1901 in Davey, A., *Breaker Morant and the Bushveldt Carbineers*

[52] Davey, A., *Breaker Morant and the Bushveldt Carbineers*

[53] Deposition of Trooper Solomon King 1901 in Davey, A., *Breaker Morant and the Bushveldt Carbineers*

[54] Witton, G., *Scapegoats of the Empire*, (Oxford: Benediction Classics, 2007) first published 1907

[55] Christie J. *Clutha Leader,* 11 April 1902, 'From a Soldier's Letter'

[56] *Die lotgevalle van die burgerlike bevolking gedurende die Anglo-Boereoorlog*, 1899–1902, Schulenburg collection

[57] Leach, C., *The Legend of Breaker Morant is Dead and Buried*

[58] Trooper James Christie, 'With the Bushveldt Carbineers', *Clutha Leader*, 22 November 1901

[59] Deposition of Trooper Edward Powell, 1901 in Davey, A., *Breaker Morant and the Bushveldt Carbineers*, p. 96

[60] Deposition of Trooper Muir Churton 1901 in Davey, A., *Breaker Morant and the Bushveldt Carbineers*, p. 98

[61] Carnegie, M. and Shields, F., *In search of Breaker Morant, Balladist and Bushveldt Carbineer* (Canberra: National Library of Australia, 1979) p. 56

[62] *The Times*, April 17, 1902

[63] Witton, G., *Scapegoats of the Empire*

[64] Eland letter to his wife, in Davey, A., *Breaker Morant and the Bushveldt Carbineers*, p. 23

[65] Silke, J., diary, n.d.

[66] Witton, G., *Scapegoats of the Empire*

[67] WO 127 Index to the Nominal Roll of Kitchener's Fighting Scouts

[68] Witton, G., *Scapegoats of the Empire*

[69] *Dundee Evening Telegraph*, 3 April 1902

[70] Eland letter to his wife, 13 July 1901 in Davey, A., *Breaker Morant and the Bushveldt Carbineers*, p. 23

[71] Trooper James Christie, 1901, 'With the Bushveldt Carbineers', *Clutha Leader* 20 December 1901

[72] Ibid.

[73] Trooper McInnes diary, 1905, in *Tasmanians in the Transvaal War,* 1905

[74] Pacholi, J. D., 'Letter From The Front', *Bendigo Advertiser*, 7 January 1902

[75] 'Reports on Military Operations in South Africa and China', July 1901, US Govt

[76] Trooper James Christie, 1901, 'With the Bushveldt Carbineers', *Clutha Leader* 20 December 1901

[77] Silke, J., diary, n.d.

[78] Eland letter to his wife, 18 July 1901 in Davey, A., *Breaker Morant and the Bushveldt Carbineers*

[79] Trooper McInnes diary, 1905 in *Tasmanians in the Transvaal War*, 1905

[80] Eland letter to his wife, dated 18 July 1901 (not sent until later date)

[81] Trooper James Christie, *Clutha Leader*, 20 December 1901

[82] Ibid.

[83] Silke, J., diary, n.d.

[84] Carnegie, M. and Shields, F., *In search of Breaker Morant, Balladist and Bushveldt Carbineer*, (Canberra: National Library of Australia, 1979)

[85] Witton, G., *Scapegoats of the Empire*

[86] A number of sources claim a Sgt Grey was arrested with Morrison. The evidence for this is not clear. Sgt Jim Gray was still at Fort Edward long after this event. Trooper Harold Grey was discharged on 16 October 1901 almost six weeks after Morrison but re-enlisted in the PLH (BVC) on 17 February 1902. Trooper Hyacinth Daly was discharged the same day as Sgt Morrison and his medal roll marked 'undesirable ... no medal'.

[87] Ancestry.co.uk

[88] Davey, A., *Breaker Morant and the Bushveldt Carbineers*

[89] Eland letter to his wife 31 July 1901 in Davey, A., p. 28

[90] Eland letter to his wife 18 July 1901 in Davey, A., p. 26

[91] Eland letter to his wife 31 July 1901 in Davey, A., p. 28

[92] Eland letter to his wife 31 July 1901 in Davey, A., p. 29

[93] Silke, J., diary, n.d.

[94] Silke, J., diary, n.d.

[95] Eland letter to his wife 31 July in Davey, A., *Breaker Morant and the Bushveldt Carbineers*, p. 30

[96] Silke, J., diary, n.d.

[97] Trooper McInnes 'diary', in *Tasmanians in the Transvaal War*, 1905

[98] Schulenburg Collection

[99] Eland letter to his wife 31 July in Davey, A., *Breaker Morant and the Bushveldt Carbineers,* p. 30

[100] Ibid.

[101] Silke, J., diary, n.d.

[102] Christie, J., *Clutha Leader,* 20 December 1901

[103] Silke, J., diary, n.d.; Eland letter to His wife in Davey, A., *Breaker Morant and the Bushveldt Carbineers,* p. 31

[104] Silke, J., diary, n.d.

[105] Ibid.

[106] Christie, J., *Clutha Leader,* 18 April 1902

[107] Silke, J., diary, n.d.

[108] Christie, J., *Clutha Leader*, 18 April 1902

[109] Silke, J., diary, n.d.

[110] Christie, J., *Clutha Leader,* 18 April 1902

[111] Christie, J., *Clutha Leader,* 18 July 1902

[112] Silke, J., diary, n.d.

[113] Christie, J., *Clutha Leader*, 18 April 1902

[114] Silke, J., diary, n.d.

[115] Christie, J., *Clutha Leader,* 18 April 1902

[116] Witton, G., *Scapegoats of the Empire*

[117] Trooper Frank T. Hall, *The Register*, 5 April 1902
[118] Witton, G., *Scapegoats of the Empire*
[119] Ibid.
[120] Christie, J., *Clutha Leader*, 18 July 1902
[121] Silke, J., diary, n.d.
[122] *The Times,* 17 April 1902
[123] Leach, C., *The Legend of Breaker Morant is Dead and Buried*)
[124] 'The Story of an Eye Witness – A Sensational Account', *The Advertiser,* 4 April 1902
[125] 'Captain Hunt's Death – Still Another Account', *The Advertiser,* 4 April 1902
[126] Birth certificate, Percy Frederick Hunt, 1873, Archives Departementales des Pyrenees-Atlantiques
[127] Birth certificate, Lilian Catherine Hunt, 1873, Archives Departementales des Pyrenees-Atlantiques
[128] Veronique Tison, Pers Comm, 2013
[129] Witton, G., *Scapegoats of the Empire*
[130] Cochrane, R. M., Memorandum, CS1092, Letter Book II, PP. 47–62 in Davey, p. 83
[131] Witton. G, letter to his brother Ernest dated 10 March, 1902
[132] James Christie, *Clutha Leader*, 8 April 1902
[133] Botha T. J., Supplementary Deposition, CS1092 Letter Book I, pp. 18–20 in Davey, A., *Breaker Morant and the Bushveldt Carbineers,* p. 102
[134] Witton, G., *Scapegoats of the Empire*
[135] Trooper McInnes 'Diary' in *Tasmanians in the Transvaal War*, 1905
[136] Silke, J., diary, n.d.
[137] Cochrane, R. M., Memorandum to the court of inquiry in Davey, A., *Breaker Morant and the Bushveldt Carbineers*
[138] James Christie, *Clutha Leader*, 8 April 1902
[139] *The Register*, 4 April 1902.
[140] *Edinburgh Evening News*, 12 August 1904
[141] Witton, G., *Scapegoats of the Empire*
[142] James Christie, *Clutha Leader,* 8 April 1902
[143] Cochrane, R. M., Memorandum to the court of inquiry in Davey, A., *Breaker Morant and the Bushveldt Carbineers*
[144] Staton, S. A., CS 1092 Letterbook II, pp. 67–70 in Davey, A., *Breaker Morant and the Bushveldt Carbineers*
[145] Trooper Muir Churton in Davey, A., *Breaker Morant and the Bushveldt Carbineers,* p. 98
[146] Hall, F. T., *The Register*, 5 April 1902
[147] Christie, J., *Clutha Leader*, 8 April 1902

[148] Churton, M., Deposition, CS Letterbook II pp. 87–89 in Davey, A., *Breaker Morant and the Bushveldt Carbineers*, p. 99

[149] Christie, J., *Clutha Leader,* 18 July 1902

[150] Morant, H. H., in Renar., F, *Bushman and Buccaneer: Harry Morant, his 'Ventures and Verses,* 1902

[151] Christie, J., *Clutha Leader* 8 April 1902

[152] Christie, J., *Clutha Leader* 8 April 1902

[153] Van der Westhuizen, Deposition, CS 1092 Letterbook I, pp. 21–24. No 65 in Davey, A., *Breaker Morant and the Bushveldt Carbineers*

[154] Wrench, J. C., Deposition, cs 1092 Letterbook I, pp. 27–31. No 64 in Davey, A., *Breaker Morant and the Bushveldt Carbineers*

[155] South African Military History Society, *Military History Journal*, Vol. 5 No. 4, December 1981

[156] Leach, C., *The Legend of Breaker Morant is Dead and Buried*

[157] Ibid.

[158] Witton, G., *Scapegoats of the Empire*

[159] Leach, C., *The Legend of Breaker Morant is Dead and Buried*

[160] *Williamstown Chronicle,* 7 December 1901

[161] Ibid.

[162] Christie, J., *Clutha Leader,* 25 March 1902

[163] Leach, C., *The Legend of Breaker Morant is Dead and Buried*

[164] Carnegie, M. and Shields, F., *In search of Breaker Morant, Balladist and Bushveldt Carbineer*, (Canberra: National Library of Australia, 1979) pp. 94, 96

[165] Liengme in Leach. C., *The Legend of Breaker Morant is Dead and Buried*

[166] Witton, G., *Scapegoats of the Empire*

[167] Ibid.

[168] Witton. G, letter of 14 September 1929 in Woolmore. W., *The Bushveldt Carbineers and Pietersburg Light Horse*, 2002

[169] Van der Westhuizen Deposition, CS 1092, Letterbook I, pp 21–24 in Davey, A., *Breaker Morant and the Bushveldt Carbineers*

[170] Records of Berlin Mission society in Leach, C., *The Legend of Breaker Morant is Dead and Buried*

[171] Version sent to Col Hall in 1983 Denton, repeated in Davey, A., *Breaker Morant and the Bushveldt Carbineers*

[172] *The Times,* 17April 1902

[173] Ibid.

[174] Brown, E., Deposition No 32 in Leach. C., *The Legend of Breaker Morant is Dead and Buried* [175] Witton, G., *Scapegoats of the Empire*

[176] De Bertodano. R, in Davey, A., *Breaker Morant and the Bushveldt Carbineers*

[177] Pretorius. A., in Leach, C., *The Legend of Breaker Morant is Dead and Buried*

[178] Christie, J., *Clutha Leader*, 11 April 1902

[179] Hatfield, J., statement to Maj. R. M. Poore, 10 October 1901

[180] Ibid.

[181] Ibid.

[182] Witton, G., *Scapegoats of the Empire*

[183] Leach, C., *The Legend of Breaker Morant is Dead and Buried*

[184] Silke, J., diary, n.d.

[185] Christie, J., *Clutha Leader,* 11 April 1902

[186] Glasson, H., 1901 letters

[187] Christie, J., *Clutha Leader,* 11 April 1902

[188] Dr. William Ledingham Christie, New Zealand's first medical graduate. ERLAM HD. *N Z Med J*. 1961 Jan; 60:1–6. (Dr Christie was Trpr James Christie's brother.)

[189] Christie, J., *Clutha Leader,* 29 November 1902

[190] 'Fatal Fire at Toiro', *Clutha Leader,* 6 March 1900

[191] *Otago Witness,* Issue 2654, 25 January 1905, p. 23

[192] Browne, E., Deposition in Davey, A., *Breaker Morant and the Bushveldt Carbineers,* p. 92

[193] Witton, G., *Scapegoats of the Empire*

[194] Wilcox, C., in Leach, C., *The Legend of Breaker Morant is Dead and Buried*

[195] Bolton, W. N. in Davey, A., *Breaker Morant and the Bushveldt Carbineers*

[196] *The Times,* 17 April 1902

[197] Witton, G., *Scapegoats of the Empire*

[198] Ibid.

[199] Ibid.

[200] Ibid.

[201] Ibid.

[202] Ibid.

[203] Christie, J., *Clutha Leader,* 25 April 1902

[204] Lt Morant letter to Maj. Lenehan 25 September 1901, in Renar, F., *Bushman and Buccaneer*, (Sydney, H. T. Dunn, 1902)

[205] Silke, J., diary, n.d.

[206] Silke, J., diary, n.d.

[207] Witton, G., *Scapegoats of the Empire*

[208] Christie, J., *Clutha Leader* April 25 1902

[209] Davey, A., *Breaker Morant and the Bushveldt Carbineers*, p. 74

[210] Charles Leach Pers Comm, originally from Dr Fransjohan Pretorius

[211] Christie, J., *Clutha Leader,* 25 April 1902

[212] Lagden, G. Y., letter to Wheelright, Native Commissioner, Zoutpansberg In Davey, A., *Breaker Morant and the Bushveldt Carbineers*

[213] Lagden, G. Y., letter to Col Henderson In Davey, A., *Breaker Morant and the Bushveldt Carbineers*, p. 67

[214] Henderson, D., letter to Captain Taylor in Davey, A., *Breaker Morant and the Bushveldt Carbineers*, p. 66

[215] Enraght-Mooney, F., 1901. Letter to Sir Godfery Lagden, 11 September 1901 in Davey, A., *Breaker Morant and the Bushveldt Carbineers*

[216] Enraght-Mooney, F., letter to Sir Godfery Lagden, 11 September 1901 in Davey, A., *Breaker Morant and the Bushveldt Carbineers*

[217] Taylor, A., letter to Col Henderson August 3 1901 in Braun, 2013

[218] Enraght Mooney, F., letter to Sir Godfrey Lagden in Davey, A., *Breaker Morant and the Bushveldt Carbineers*, p. 68

[219] Henderson, D., Letter to Sir Godfrey Lagden in Davey, A., *Breaker Morant and the Bushveldt Carbineers*, (Cape Town: van Riebeck Society, 1987) p. 69

[220] Henderson, D., Letter to Sir Godfrey Lagden 27 September 1901 in Davey, A., *Breaker Morant and the Bushveldt Carbineers*, p. 70

[221] Braun, L. F., The Returns of the King: The Case of Mphefu and Western Venda, 1899–1904 *Journal of Southern African Studies*, Vol. 39, No. 2, 271–291, 2013, p. 283

[222] Ibid and Davey, A., *Breaker Morant and the Bushveldt Carbineers*, p. 70

[223] Braun, L. F., The Returns of the King: The Case of Mphefu and Western Venda, 1899–1904 *Journal of Southern African Studies*, Vol. 39, No. 2, 271–291, 2013, p. 285

[224] CAB 37/60, photographic copies of cabinet papers, 1902. No 594 Cipher

[225] Ibid.

[226] CAB 37/60, photographic copies of cabinet papers, 1902, No S789 Cipher

[227] CAB 37/60, photographic copies of cabinet papers, 1902, No 603 Cipher

[228] *The Express and Telegraph*, 4 April 1902

[229] *The West Australian*, 'The Bushveldt Murders. German Missionary A Subject', 10 April 1902

[230] *The World's News*, 24 May 1902

[231] Kay, H. J., in *Music of the Guns: Based on Two Journals of the Boer War*, 1970

[232] CAB 37/60, photographic copies of cabinet papers, 1902, No 636 Cipher

10 The Rise of the Tenterfield Star

[1] Bennett, J., *Law Society Journal* (NSW, Australia) October 2001, 39 (9) LSJ

[2] Ibid.

[3] Ibid.
[4] Court, P., Membership Officer, United Grand Lodge of NSW and ACT, pers comm, 2013
[5] Ibid.
[6] PRO WO 32/8033
[7] Ibid.
[8] Chief of Staff Papers 31st December 1901 he wrote to Sir Ian Hamilton
[9] *Australian Town and Country Journal,* 11 May 1901
[10] H. P. Dangar had proposed Percy Hunt for membership of the prestigious Cavalry Club in London.
[11] WO108/115, Chief of Staff: correspondence and papers
[12] *Goulburn Herald*, 'Letter From South Africa', 8 November 1901, p. 3
[13] *The Age,* 22 March 1902; *The Advertiser*, 29 March 1902
[14] WO108/115, Chief of Staff: correspondence and papers
[15] *The Adelaide Advertiser,* 10 December 1901
[16] Colonel Adye, WO108/115, Chief of Staff: correspondence and papers
[17] *The Age,* 22 March 1902, p. 11
[18] Witton, G., *Scapegoats of the Empire*
[19] Bennett. J., Law Society Journal (NSW, Australia), 39 (9) LSJ 70, 2001

11 Arrest to Execution

[1] Denton. K. *Closed File* (Adelaide: Rigby, 1983)
[2] Bleszynski. N., *Shoot Straight You Bastards* (Random: House Australia, 2002)
[3] *Breaker Morant the Retrial,* TV documentary
[4] Pretorious. A., in Leach. C. *The Legend of Breaker Morant is Dead and Buried,* p. 183
[5] Witton, G., *Scapegoats of the Empire*
[6] Ibid.
[7] Ibid.
[8] Ibid.
[9] PRO WO108/115, Chief of Staff: correspondence and papers
[10] *Manual of Military Law* 1899, Rules of Procedure 124 (b) and (d), p. 666
[11] Davey, A., *Breaker Morant and the Bushveldt Carbineers* and Schulenburg Collection.
[12] Witton, G., *Scapegoats of the Empire*
[13] *The Times,* 17 April 1902
[14] Trove, National Library of Australia
[15] *The Daily News,* 'Mr Cochrane and his League', 12 June 1908
[16] *Kalgoorlie Miner,* 26 June 1900

[17] Ibid.

[18] Ancestry.co.uk

[19] *The Queenslander,* 16 May 1891, p. 950

[20] AustLit http://www.austlit.edu.au/austlit/page/A93916

[21] PRO WO108/115, Chief of Staff: correspondence and papers

[22] Silke, J., diary, n.d.

[23] Witton, G., *Scapegoats of the Empire*

[24] Caligari, B. J., *The Courts Martial of the Buhsveldt Carbineers Officers in Pietersburg, South Africa Jan/Feb, 1902*; also reproduced in Bleszynski. N., *Shoot Straight You Bastards*

[25] Manual of Military Law 1899

[26] Witton, G., *Scapegoats of the Empire*

[27] Manual of Military Law 1899

[28] WO108/115, WO108/115, WO93/41, Chief of Staff: correspondence and papers

[29] Witton, G. 1929

[30] Staton, S. A., In Davey. A, *Breaker Morant and the Bushveldt Carbineers*

[31] PRO WO108/115, Chief of Staff: correspondence and papers

[32] PRO WO93/41, Minute book of out letters from Judge Advocate, Pretoria

[33] Caligari, B. J., *The Courts Martial of the Buhsveldt Carbineers Officers in Pietersburg, South Africa Jan/Feb, 1902*. Also reproduced in Bleszynski. N., *Shoot Straight You Bastards*

[34] Christie. J, *Clutha Leader* 18 July 1902

[35] Hammett E. E. *The Rhodesia Herald* 17 March 1904

[36] PRO WO93/41, Minute book of out letters from Judge Advocate, Pretoria

[37] Hammet and Oldham

[38] PRO WO93/41, Minute book of out letters from Judge Advocate, Pretoria

[39] Ibid.

[40] Ibid.

[41] Caligari, B. J., *The Courts Martial of the Buhsveldt Carbineers Officers in Pietersburg, South Africa Jan/Feb, 1902*. Also reproduced in Bleszynski. N., *Shoot Straight You Bastards*

[42] Ibid.

[43] WO93/41, Minute book of out letters from Judge Advocate, Pretoria

[44] WO108/115, Chief of Staff: correspondence and papers

[45] WO32/8078, Boer War: Staff Diaries July 1901 to January 1902

[46] Davey, A., *Breaker Morant and the Bushveldt Carbineers*, p. 123

[47] WO93/41, Minute book of out letters from Judge Advocate, Pretoria

[48] Manual of Military Law 1899, RP8, p. 579
[49] WO108/115, Chief of Staff: correspondence and papers
[50] Manual of Military Law 1899, RP13, p. 583
[51] Bleszynski. N., *Shoot Straight You Bastards*
[52] Bennett. J., Law Society Journal (NSW, Australia), 39 (9) LSJ 70, 2001
[53] S.T.A. 15/02 (CS58) copy in Davey, A.
[54] Witton, G., *Scapegoats of the Empire*
[55] Bennett. J., *Law Society Journal* (NSW, Australia), 39 (9) LSJ 70, 2001
[56] *Sydney Morning Herald,* ! May 1895
[57] The *Sydney Morning Herald*, Law Report, Supreme Court, 8 December 1893
[58] Carnegie, M. and Shields, F., *In search of Breaker Morant, Balladist and Bushveldt Carbineer*, p. 177
[59] Stead, W. T., *Methods of Barbarism, A Case for Intervention,* July 1901, Trade Union Congress Library
[60] Ibid.
[61] *Nieuwsblad van Friesland*, 31-07-1901, http://www.delpher.nl/
[62] Carnegie, M. and Shields, F., *In search of Breaker Morant Balladist and Bushveldt Carbineer*, p. 177
[63] *Methods of Barbarism, A Case for Intervention,* July 1901, Trade Union Congress Library
[64] Brandt. J., *The Petticoat Commando: Boer Women in Secret Service*, (Rockville: Wildside Press, 2006) p. 121
[65] Murray, P. L., R.A.A., 'Official Records of the Australian Military Contingents to the War in South Africa'
[66] *Illawarra Mercury*, 11 July 1901
[67] PMO 81, MC 21 in Davey, A., *Breaker Morant and the Bushveldt Carbineers*
[68] Ibid.
[69] Ibid.
[70] PMO 15 PM1076
[71] WO93/41, Minute book of out letters from Judge Advocate, Pretoria
[72] Caligari, B. J., *The Courts Martial of the Buhsveldt Carbineers Officers in Pietersburg, South Africa Jan/Feb, 1902*; also reproduced in Bleszynski. N., *Shoot Straight You Bastards*
[73] WO108/115, Chief of Staff: correspondence and papers
[74] Ibid.
[75] Ibid.
[76] WO32/8078
[77] Manual of Military Law 1899, p. 583, Rules of Procedure 14
[78] Witton, G., *Scapegoats of the Empire*

[79] Ibid.

[80] Ibid.

[81] Davey, A., *Breaker Morant and the Bushveldt Carbineers*,

[82] *The Times History of the War in South Africa 1899–1900*, Vol. II

[83] Ibid.

[84] *The Times*, 23 November 1901

[85] Ibid.

[86] British Library IOR/L/MIL/7/10143 M 8864 1901

[87] Ibid.

[88] Caligari, B. J., *The Courts Martial of the Buhsveldt Carbineers Officers in Pietersburg, South Africa Jan/Feb, 1902*; also reproduced in Bleszynski. N., *Shoot Straight You Bastards*

[89] Ibid.

[90] *The London Gazette,* 24 February 1903, p. 1219

[91] *Sheffield Evening Telegraph,* 4 April 1902

[92] *The Argus,* 27 March 1902

[93] *Evening Journal,* Adelaide, 27 March 1902

[94] *Sheffield Evening Telegraph*, 4 April 1902

[95] *The Express and Telegraph*, 2 April 1902 p 2

[96] Ibid.

[97] *Windsor and Richmond Gazette,* 29 March 1902

[98] *Evening Star,* 25 October 1893

[99] *Clutha Leader,* 8 April 1902

[100] *Clutha Leader,* 11 October–24 December

[101] Glasson. H., letters, Mitchell Library Manuscript, MLMSS 3858, transcribed by Frank Shields

[102] Renar, F., *Bushman and Buccaneer*

[103] Jarvis, Major C. S., *Half a life* (London: John Murray, 1943) p. 131

[104] Assistant Provost Martial Orange River Colony

[105] W. N. Bolton, letter, TAB GOV 209CON 5/05, 1905

[106] Christie. J., *Clutha Leader,* 18 July 1902

[107] Witton, G., *Scapegoats of the Empire*,

[108] Denton, K., *Closed File* (Adelaide: Rigby, 1983) p. 104

[109] Davey, A., *Breaker Morant and the Bushveldt Carbineers*

[110] *The Argus,* 27 March 1902

[111] Jarvis, Major C. S., *Half a life* (London: John Murray, 1943) p. 131

[112] Woolmore, W., *The Bushveldt Carbineers and the Pietersburg Light Horse*

[113] *Sydney Morning Herald*, 25 February 1939

[114] Witton, G., *Scapegoats of the Empire*

[115] *Examiner*, 7 April 1902

[116] Caligari, B. J., *The Courts Martial of the Buhsveldt Carbineers Officers in Pietersburg, South Africa Jan/Feb, 1902*; also reproduced in Bleszynski. N., *Shoot Straight You Bastards*
[117] Manual of Military Law 1899, p. 22
[118] Ibid.
[119] *Morning Bulletin,* 6 June 1902
[120] *Lancashire Evening Post,* 29 August 1917
[121] *Clutha Leader,* 28 August 1902
[122] Renar, F., *Bushman and Buccaneer*
[123] Woolmore. W., *The Bushveldt Carbineers and The Pietersburg Light Horse*
[124] Witton, G., *Scapegoats of the Empire*
[125] 24th January 1901
[126] Woolmore. W., *The Bushveldt Carbineers and The Pietersburg Light Horse*
[127] *The Times* April 17, 1902
[128] Witton, G., *Scapegoats of the Empire*
[129] Poore. R. M., *Diary*. Scottish National Archive, Edinburgh. 1901
[130] Poore. R. M., *Diary*. Scottish National Archive, Edinburgh. 1901
[131] Witton, G., *Scapegoats of the Empire*
[132] *The Times* 17 April 1902
[133] *Bendigo Advertiser,* 14 October 190.
[134] *The North Western Advocate and the Emu Bay Times,* 25 October 1901
[135] Witton, G., *Scapegoats of the Empire*
[136] Stirling. J. F., *The Colonials in South Africa, Their Record,* 1907
[137] Strathcona's Horse Regimental Diary
[138] Christie, J., *Clutha Leader,* 17 April
[149] *The Register* 15 April 1902
[140] *The Argus,* 28 July 1904
[141] *The Argus*, 31 March 1902
[142] Letter of complaint CS1092, letterbook II pp. 37–46 in Davey, A., *Breaker Morant and the Bushveldt Carbineers*, p. 81
[143] Memorandum, CS1082, letterbook II PP 47–62 in Davey, A., *Breaker Morant and the Bushveldt Carbineers,* p. 86
[144] Bleszynski. N., *Shoot Straight You Bastards*
[145] *The Times*, 17 April 1902
[146] Hansard
[147] *Evening News,* 30 July 1902
[148] WO93/41, Minute book of out letters from Judge Advocate, Pretoria
[149] Conan Doyle, A., *The War In South Africa: Its Cause And Conduct* (London: Newnes, 1902)

[150] *The World's News*, 24 May 1902

[151] Kitchene'rs despatches relating to the Northern Transvaal, issued 8 January, 8 February, 8 March 1902

[152] 'OPINION of the HON. ISAAC A. ISAACs, K.C., M.P., re the case of Lieutenant Witton', dated 28 August 1902

[153] Ibid.

[154] Witton, G., *Scapegoats of the Empire*

[155] Manual of Military Law 1899, p. 386

[156] *The Advertiser,* 1 April 1902

[157] PMO 81, MC 21 in Davey, A., *Breaker Morant and the Bushveldt Carbineers*, p. 122

[158] Witton. G., letter to J. F. Thomas, 1929

[159] Bolton, W. N., letter to H. R. M. Bourne in Davey, A., *Breaker Morant and the Bushveldt Carbineers*, p. 19

[160] PMO 81, MC 21 in Davey, A., *Breaker Morant and the Bushveldt Carbineers*, p. 122

[161] Ibid.

[162] Bleszynski. N., *Shoot Straight You Bastards*, p. 208

[163] *The Age*, 5 August 1903

[164] Witton, G., *Scapegoats of the Empire*

165]The *Times* 17 April 1902

[166] Eland letter to his wife in Davey, A., *Breaker Morant and the Bushveldt Carbineers*; Silke, J., Diary, n.d.

[167] Witton, G., *Scapegoats of the Empire*

[168] Leach, C., *The Legend of Breaker Morant is Dead and Buried*

[169] http://www.lieutpjhandcock.com/2014/04/wittons-letter-to-thomas-21-october-1929.html

[170] WO93/41, Minute book of out letters from Judge Advocate, Pretoria

[171] WO93/41, Minute book of out letters from Judge Advocate, Pretoria

[172] Manual of Military Law 1899, p. 523

[173] Caligari, B. J., *The Courts Martial of the Buhsveldt Carbineers Officers in Pietersburg, South Africa Jan/Feb, 1902*; also reproduced in Bleszynski. N., *Shoot Straight You Bastards*

[174] Parritt, B. A. H., *The Intelligencers, British Military Intelligence from the Middle Ages to 1929* (Barnsley: Pen and Sword, 2011)

[175] Ibid.

[176] Clode. C. M., *The Administration of Justice under Military and Martial Law.* 1784

[177] *Sydney Morning Herald*, 25 February 1939

[178] WO93/41, Minute book of out letters from Judge Advocate, Pretoria

[179] Lenehan, R. W., *Newcastle Morning Herald and Miners' Advocate,* 15 September 1902

[180] WO93/41, Minute book of out letters from Judge Advocate, Pretoria

[181] WO 339/21968; and 1891 UK census

[182] Birth certificate, Percy Frederick Hunt, 1873, Archives Departementales des Pyrenees-Atlantiques

[183] Leach, C., *The Legend of Breaker Morant is Dead and Buried*

[184] Silke, J., Diary, n.d.; Christie. J., *Clutha Leader*, 8 April

[185] WO93/41, Minute book of out letters from Judge Advocate, Pretoria; also in Davey, p. 139

[186] WO93/41 Minute book of out letters from Judge Advocate, Pretoria

[187] Manual of Military Law 1899

[188] Ibid.

[189] WO108/115, Chief of Staff: correspondence and papers

[190] Witton, G., *Scapegoats of the Empire*

[191] Caligari, B. J., *The Courts Martial of the Buhsveldt Carbineers Officers in Pietersburg, South Africa Jan/Feb, 1902*; also reproduced in Bleszynski. N., *Shoot Straight You Bastards*

[192] Ibid.

[193] WO93/41, Minute book of out letters from Judge Advocate, Pretoria

[194] WO32/8735

[195] Ibid.

[196] Ibid.

[197] Caligari, B. J., *The Courts Martial of the Buhsveldt Carbineers Officers in Pietersburg, South Africa Jan/Feb, 1902*; also reproduced in Bleszynski. N., *Shoot Straight You Bastards*

[198] Manual of Military Law 1899. pp. 738–739

[199] Manual of Military Law 1899, p. 390

[200] Manual of Military Law 1899, p. 618

[201] Davey, A., *Breaker Morant and the Bushveldt Carbineers*

[202] Witton, G., *Scapegoats of the Empire*

[203] Ibid.

[204] Attestation Paper for Peter Joseph Handcock, PRO WO / 126/100

[205] *The Argus,*16 April 1902

[206] https://www.parliament.nsw.gov.au/prod/parlment/hanstrans.nsf/V3ByKey/LA19011003/$file/LA19011003. viewed 15 November 2015

[207] *National Advocate,* 4 October 1901

[208] Photocopy of the Will of Harry Harbord Morant provided by Charles Leach.

[209] Thomas. J. F. letter to Maj. R. W. Lenehan, 27 February 1902 in Witton, G., *Scapegoats of the Empire*

[210] Ibid.

[211] *The Argus*,'How Morant And Handcock Died, Letter From Their Warder Adelaide', 3 April 1902

[212] WO108/115, Chief of Staff: correspondence and papers; Car negie, M. and Shields, F., *In search of Breaker Morant, Balladist and Bushveldt Carbineer*, p. 136

12 Aftermath

[1] *The Advertiser*, 10 March 1902

[2] *The Advertiser*, 27 March 1902

[3] *Windsor and Richmond Gazzette,* 31 May 1902

[4] Carnegie, M. and Shields, F., *In search of Breaker Morant, Balladist and Bushveldt Carbineer*, p. 152

[5] *Windsor and Richmond Gazette,* 5 April 1902

[6] *Windsor and Richmond* Gazette, 5 March 1904

[7] Bennett. J., *Law Society Journal* (NSW, Australia), 39 (9) LSJ 70, 2001

[8] *Evening News,* 1 April 1902

[9] *Evening Journal,* 27 March 1902

[10] *The Evening Star,* 29 March 1902

[11] *Barrier Miner,* 27 March 1902

[12] *Benalla Standard,* 28 March 1902

[13] *The West Australian,* 4 April 1902

[14] 'OPINION of the HON. ISAAC A. ISAACs, K.C., M.P., re the case of Lieutenant Witton', dated 28 August 1902

[15] Ibid.

[16] Ibid.

[17] Ibid

[18] Caligari, B. J., *The Courts Martial of the Buhsveldt Carbineers Officers in Pietersburg, South Africa Jan/Feb, 1902*; also reproduced in Bleszynski. N., *Shoot Straight You Bastards*

[19] Opinion of Peter Latta, Legal Researcher and Lawyer for Zoutpansberg Skirmishes

[20] *Queensland Times,* 23 November 1917

[21] Caligari, B. J., *The Courts Martial of the Buhsveldt Carbineers Officers in Pietersburg, South Africa Jan/Feb, 1902*; also reproduced in Bleszynski. N., *Shoot Straight You Bastards*

[21] *The Sydney Morning Herald,* 3 May 1895

[22] 'Reports form Commissioners, Twenty Two Volumes, Session 10 December 1868–11 August 1869. Second report of the commissioners appointed to inquire into the Constitution and practice of Courts-Martial in the Army and the present system of punishment for military offences together with the Minutes of Evidence and Appendix', 1869

[23] Simmonds, T. F., *The Constitution and Practice of Courts Martial with a summary of the Law of Evidence as connected therewith*, 1875

[24] 'OPINION of the HON. ISAAC A. ISAACs, K.C., M.P., re the case of Lieutenant Witton', dated 28 August 1902

[25] Ibid.

[26] Moore, E. Garth, 'Military Law—Condonation—Court-Martial—Power to Dissolve—Common Law of the Army' *The Cambridge Law Journal*, Vol 12, Issue 01, April 1954, pp 30–32

[27] *Sydney Morning Herald,* 7 October 1895

[28] PRO HO 144/580/A63460

[29] Ibid.

[30] *Derry Journal*, 26 August 1903

[31] PRO HO 144/580/A63460

[32] Ibid.

[33] Ibid.

[34] Ibid.

[35] Ibid.

[36] *Gloucester Citizen*, 12 August 1904

[37] *Advertiser,* 2 July 1902

[38] *Shields Daily Gazette*, 29 September 1904

[39] *The Age,* 12 November 1904, p. 11

[40] *The Age,* 5 August 1903

[41] *Petersburg Times* 18 August 1903

[42] Precis in Kit Denton papers, State Library of New South Wales

[43] Ibid.

[44] *The Sydney Morning Herald,* 8 December 1903

[45] *The Argus,* 26 March 1902

[46] *The Argus,* 3 March 1902

[47] *The Advertiser,* 27 March 1902

[48] *Evening News,* 31 March 1902

[49] *The Advertiser,* 1 April 1902

[50] *Evening News* 31 March 1902

[51] Percy Hunt was actually in the 13th Hussars.

[52] *The West Australian,* 31 March 1902

[53] *The Argus,* 3 April 1902

[54] *Queensland Times, Ipswich Herald and General Advertiser,* 3 April 1902
[55] Carnegie, M. and Shields, F., *In search of Breaker Morant, Balladist and Bushveldt Carbineer*, p. 154; and Kit Denton papers
[56] Ibid.
[57] *Daily Telegraph,* 3 April 1902
[58] Woolmore, W., *The Bushveldt Carbineers and the Pietersburg Light Horse*, p. 146
[59] PRO WO108/115, Chief of Staff: correspondence and papers
[60] Ibid.
[61] *Evening News,* 30 July 1902
[62] *Hawkesbury Herald,* 8 August 1902
[63] *Windsor and Richmond Gazette,* 23 August 1902
[64] *Hawkesbury Herald,* 8 August 1902
[65] *Truth,* 3 August 1902
[66] *Windsor and Richmond Gazette,* 16 August 1902
[67] Hutton E. T. H., letter to Secretary of Defence, Mitchell Library; Denton papers, State Library of New South Wales
[68] Department of the Army, General Correspondence Files. Control Registry Systems, 1902–1905 Australian Archives. Accession MP78 AWM File 207/1/20; Carnegie, M. and Shields, F., *In search of Breaker Morant Balladist and Bushveldt Carbineer*
[69] Kit Denton papers, State Library of New South Wales; Carnegie, M. and Shields, F., *In search of Breaker Morant, Balladist and Bushveldt Carbineer*
[70] Carnegie, M. and Shields, F., *In search of Breaker Morant, Balladist and Bushveldt Carbineer*, p. 157
[71] Kit Denton papers, State Library of New South Wales
[72] *Windsor and Richmond Gazette*
[73] Hansard (Australia), 9 September 1902
[74] Ibid.
[75] Witton, G., *Scapegoats of the Empire*
[75] *Albury Banner and Wodonga Express,* 4 April 1902
[76] Witton, G., *Scapegoats of the Empire*
[77] Davey, A., *Breaker Morant and the Bushveldt Carbineers*, p. 86
[78] Carnegie, M. and Shields, F., *In search of Breaker Morant, Balladist and Bushveldt Carbineer*, p. 124
[79] Davey, A., *Breaker Morant and the Bushveldt Carbineers*,
[80] Ibid.
[82] Hansard (Australia) 9 September 1902
[83] Carnegie, M. and Shields, F., *In search of Breaker Morant Balladist and Bushveldt Carbineer*, p. 159

[84] Ibid. pp. 159–161

[85] Ibid. p. 161

[86] Carnegie, M. and Shields, F., *In search of Breaker Morant, Balladist and Bushveldt Carbineer*; Woolmore. W., 2002

[87] Carnegie, M. and Shields, F., *In search of Breaker Morant Balladist and Bushveldt Carbineer*; Woolmore. W., 2002, p. 153n

[88] *The Sydney Mail and New South Wales Advertiser*, 11 March 1893

[89] *The Argus*, 27 February 1895

[90] *The Richmond River Herald and Northern Districts Advertiser*, 12 April 1902

[91] *Evening News*, 4 June 1895

[92] *Adelaide Observer*, 15 June 1895

[93] *Armidale Express and New England Advertiser*, 18 June 1895

[94] W. N. Bolton, TAB GOV 209CON 5/05, VAB CO LEER vol 51 01 4597/01, 1905

[95] Wongtchowski. B,. Between Woodbush and Wolkberg.– Googoo Thompson's Story, 2003

[96] Erven were a measurement of land holdings used by the ZAR before the war.

[97] W. N. Bolton, Pietersburg, Secretary to the Law Department, TA LD175. No. 6088/02

[98] Pretoria, 12 June 1902 in Templehoff., J. W. N., *The Townspeople of Louis Trichardt,* 1999

[99] Templehoff, J. W. N., *The Townspeople of Louis Trichardt,* 1999

[100] Ibid.

[101] Ibid.

[102] Ibid.

[103] Leach, C., *The Legend of Breaker Morant is Dead and Buried*

[104] Ibid.

[105] *Truth*, 10 March 1929

[106] *Northern Miner*, 14 April 1902

[107] *Glen Innes Examiner*, 10 March 1928

[108] Bennett. J., Law Society Journal (NSW, Australia), 39 (9) LSJ 70, 2001

[109] Ibid.

[110] Carnegie, M. and Shields, F., *In search of Breaker Morant, Balladist and Bushveldt Carbineer*, p. 168

[111] Carnegie, M. and Shields, F., *In search of Breaker Morant, Balladist and Bushveldt Carbineer*, p. 149 and http://www.lieutpjhandcock.com/2014/04/wittons-letter-to-thomas-21-october-1929.html

[112] Carnegie, M. and Shields, F., *In search of Breaker Morant, Balladist and Bushveldt Carbineer*, p. 149

[113] http://www.lieutpjhandcock.com/2014/04/wittons-letter-to-thomas-21-october-1929.html. Accessed 20 June 2016

[114] *Maryborough Chronicle, Wide Bay and Burnett Advertiser*, 9 March 1931

[115] Witton, G., *Scapegoats of the Empire*

[116] *Coolgardie Miner*, 5 April 1902

Index